Days of IRON

*The story of
West Ham United
in the Fifties*

Front cover shows; West Ham United team pictured in 1957-58, the season the Hammers stormed back to the top-flight and scored over 100 goals on the way.

Days of IRON

The story of West Ham United in the Fifties

Brian Belton

This edition published in Great Britain in 2013 by DB Publishing, an imprint of JMD Media.

Copyright © Brian Belton 2013

All Rights Reserved. No part of this publication may be reproduced, stored in a retrieval system, or transmitted in any form, or by any means, electronic, mechanical, photocopying, recording or otherwise without the prior permission in writing of the copyright holders, nor be otherwise circulated in any form or binding or cover other than in which it is published and without a similar condition being imposed on the subsequent publisher.

ISBN 9781780912080

Printed and bound by Copytech (UK) Limited, Peterborough.

Contents

Foreword – Frank O'Farrell — 7

Introduction — 9

1949-50 – For the Hammers are our team! — 13

1950-51 – Football is just a reflection of life — 43

We were called 'Fenton's Furies' — 63

1951-52 – Togetherness is what I remember... — 79

1952-53 – Be amazed... this was Dick Walker — 101

I played cricket for Ireland — 123

1953-54 – Andy Malcolm, he was never really beaten — 129

1954-55 – 'Harry Hooper told me to get a bicycle' — 143

Allison was a god in his own right — 151

1955-56 – West Ham is a way of life — 179

1956-57 – It went from one end to the other — 189

1957-58 – I remember in the promotion year...the fans chanted; 'We want six!' — 203

1958-59 – John Dick was an honest playing footballer — 219

1959-60 – You were carried by the majority, you weren't just carried by yourself — 233

I could never lose my gratitude for Ted — 259

'I think I'll have a bit of that jam pie and custard' – The tale of the Fifties — 277

Extra time — 291

Chronology of West Ham in the Fifties — 327

Bibliography — 329

Glossary of players — 330

Days of Iron – The story of West Ham United in the Fifties

Foreword – Frank O'Farrell

I came to West Ham United from the Irish city of Cork in January 1948. This move had a significant influence on the direction of my life. As soon as I arrived in East London everything changed for me. First of all it put an end to my ambition to be an engine-driver - I had worked on the Irish Railways for four years as a cleaner and fireman. That experience, in some respects, prepared me for the ups and downs of professional football, as a player and manager. Working on an engine when it was making plenty of steam and completing a journey on time, brought a great sense of satisfaction and happiness. That engine could prove a most temperamental beast, which did not always respond in the way the driver and fireman desired, despite their superhuman efforts.

West Ham was my first experience of full-time professional football. I look back on my career at Upton Park with a great deal of gratitude. The club, through the influence of the Cearns and Pratt families, and the managers during my time with the Hammers, Charlie Paynter and Ted Fenton, instilled good, solid attitudes in the players. We carried these with us throughout our careers. There was a 'West Ham way' of doing things - this was about being treated fairly, and promoting an understanding that on the pitch we were expected to uphold the values that West Ham fostered and remember that the club's reputation was important. Behaviour, on and off the field of play, that brought the good name of West Ham United into disrepute was frowned on.

We were close to the supporters during the match, but most of us also lived in the area surrounding the Boleyn Ground. As such, we came in to contact with the wider community a great deal. We met fans in local shops and on public transport (which was the way we got around in those days) and this helped us to develop the values held dear by the club. The East Enders had come through a traumatic four years of war. The massive bombing of the area meant that few of them had escaped the loss of family members, neighbours and friends, so losing a football match, although disappointing, was not a tragedy to them.

The world has moved on since those far off days and football, like life itself, has become more competitive and cut throat. Now, West Ham United has to compete in this environment, but I hope that the values and the example the club has held on to down the years will not be lost completely in the quest for transient success. I also hope the 'West Ham way', the way that had a good influence on my life, will prevail. A line from a song written about another town in Ireland could apply equally to the people of Newham (the London borough that is the home to the Irons) - *I learned about life and I found me a wife in the town I loved so well.*

Frank O'Farrell

This book is dedicated to the disreputable, the rebellious and the radical; those who save us from the banality of conformity and resist the platitudes of lickspittles, who salivate for the adoration of fools; the inventive and adventurous spirit of Malcolm Allison

Introduction

For me, the Fifties were in black and white. Something Brian Inglis looked at on the television in programmes like *All Our Yesterdays* and *Just Twenty-five Years Ago*. I started going to Upton Park long after those days, my era was the Sixties and Seventies. The championship, the exploits of Vic Keeble and John Dick, the dreadnought qualities of Andy Malcolm and Ernie Gregory, were part of a mythology, the stuff of legend. As such, my odyssey, that involved 50 former players, from over 50 years ago, causing me to travel around 50 hundred (5,000) miles by road alone, was a journey into the a world of the collective imagination of a generation of supporters. However, it became something else as I went on. I discovered the 'Fifties'. A different place, caught in the middle of a century, populated by a group of people who were kind, generous and trusting. These folk spent time with me, invited me into their homes, gave me food and drink and in one case, as the night closed in and the weather worsened, asked if it would be better for me to stay the night with his family.

As such, these men coloured those days, their days, for me. Each story is lifted from the palette of existence, the many hues of lives lived. My project became an archaeological expedition into relationships, an anthropological search for the roots of identity. I came away with massive respect and admiration for the men I'd met, their families and loved ones. The message that comes out of it all is that respect begets respect - you can't have it, without giving it. Maybe there's something there for the modern player and many of us who demand respect without sometimes offering much to admire in the way of values, principles, achievement, ethics or personality.

During the time I was writing this book, I heard a lot about West Ham players. A great deal of it was mundane, some of it was extremely personal and had to remain confidential. This is both flattering and frustrating. I now feel I know more than anyone about West Ham in the Fifties and can't tell a soul about quite a lot of it. There were players who had to get married for fear of the scandal of the times. And there was the strict Catholic whose wife thought he was having an affair. Another wife got her to turn up the gas in the mornings without him knowing so that when he lit it, a flame would burst from the jet, feet high. The regularity of this provoked fear. He took it as an omen and returned to the fold of fidelity. Another wife, who again thought her footballer husband was playing away, arranged with another wife to use her house to disappear for hours on end. Not knowing where his wife had gone, the possible stray remained at home more. At least two wives have talked about writing an exposé of the club in the Fifties. I have met, in the wife of one player, the Dame Edna Everage of the football world. Another spouse, tumbler of whisky in hand, espoused bawdy tales and stoically championed her loved one's cause. She knew her man and her football. If ever I have to go to war, I want her with me.

I spoke to one ex-player when he was alone and sadly drunk and one or two who didn't want to be named. Some of the players included also made comments they did not want ascribed to them, others told me things they did not want published. I have, of course, honored all their wishes

The overwhelming majority of the former players gave wonderful and moving examples of the humanity and warmth people can offer each other. However, on a couple of occasions this was not the case. I've been ignored by a man who was recently part of the England set-up, who was too big to talk to me, refusing even a ten-minute telephone interview. Another, who played for West Ham for a matter of months in the mid-Fifties, although now retired, had no time for a fan.

There have been funny moments too. I got to one former player's home, after making an appointment. I stood ringing the door bell for a good while. I had made a 500-mile round trip especially to see him. Just as I was about to give up, his wife opened the door. It had slipped his mind that I was coming and he was sitting in his front room in his underpants when I had arrived. Having thought his caller (me) might be selling something, he had hid out of sight. We had a laugh about it though, and it was good to see that this man, of towering distinction in the game, could still be amused at himself. That humility is rare and something that makes you like people.

With the return of peace to war-torn Britain, life was slowly returning to something resembling normality in 1950. From 1945 Clement Attlee's Labour government took control of the country, struggling with the economic and social consequences of half a decade of war. Organised sport had a crucial role in the rebuilding of society. It had been understood during the war that football was a useful tool; it kept people fit and entertained large sections of the population at very little cost to the individual.

Social attitudes immediately after World War Two differed from those of 1918. After the appalling toll of the trenches, Britain, in a search for security, looked to re-establish pre-war values. This was not the case in 1945; the horror of the Holocaust and

Introduction

the use of the Atomic Bomb on civilians caused most people's minds to be focused on the future. There was some hope that a new world could emerge from the carnage and ruins of Europe. This was partly the reason why Winston Churchill lost the postwar election which cleared the way for the flowering of the Welfare State.

It was out of this strange blend of austerity and hope that the modern West Ham United was wrought. The team that took the field in the autumn of 1949 were a blend of old hands who had either fought or rusted in the forces, and young men emerging from the bombed streets of East London and the other great cities of Britain. These men were the material and substance of West Ham's hard days in the Fifties, those, *Days of Iron.* This is their story.

Days of Iron – The story of West Ham United in the Fifties

1949-50 – For the Hammers are our team!

Just before the start of the 1949-50 season, London's industrial dockland was the backdrop to the Boleyn Ground. This area supplied West Ham United with the hardcore of its support. The dockers were just concluding a dispute that resulted in 13,000 of their number withdrawing their labour for over three weeks. From the dispute's inception, the Labour Prime Minister, Clement Attlee, had condemned the action which left half the ships in the Port of London stranded. But at least some things were turning from sour to sweet. The rationing of chocolates and confectionery was finally ended, so children could go to the sweet shop and buy as many of their favourite sweets as they could afford.

It was in this context that the annals of West Ham United in the Fifties opened. However, like all organisations, football clubs are the products of their environment. Their ethos and how they function are generated by two related groups of people; the players and the supporters.

If the history of the Hammers could be personified in any single person, it would be Ernie Gregory. Even in the autumn of his life Ernie was an imposing figure. Although the dark hair had turned grey, when I met with him for the first time he was instantly recognisable as the tall, muscular custodian of the posts, the strong, last line of West Ham's Fifties defence. I met Ernie several times over a number of years at his home on the East London/Essex borders. He was West Ham's number one at the start of that first season of the second half of the 20th century and was to keep his place for most of the 1950s, eventually becoming the club's longest serving member of staff, and the finest 'keeper ever to guard nets for the Irons.

Ernie Gregory was very much a local boy. He was spotted by the Irons' manager of the time, Charlie Paynter, playing for West Ham Boys. Having beaten mighty Sunderland in the semi-final of the English Trophy, Ernie's side was up against Preston in the Final. After the game, which finished in a 1-1 draw (the teams shared the trophy) the 15-year-old 'keeper was approached by a number of top clubs, including Sunderland and Arsenal, but, in his own words; "There was only one team for me - they were my local side."

It was not long after this that Ernie would meet Yvonne, a Stratford girl. They married in 1942, the start of what was to prove a 50-year plus partnership. Looking back on his early days at the club, Ernie recalled that Jackie Morton was his hero. Morton played for England alongside Len Goulden, two West Ham players in the same international side, against Czechoslovakia in 1937. But it was his manager, Charlie Paynter, who was, for Ernie, number one. "He was always so smart, a real Beau Brumel, and he knew it; disciplinarian, but a wonderful man. He was great at motivating people, and was good at getting youngsters into the club. In the end we had too many youngsters."

It was Paynter, under Reg Pratt, the chairman, with Wally St Pier, the chief scout, who started West Ham's long commitment to the development of young players. For Ernie; "West Ham had a fantastic youth movement, they were really the first to do this, although Chelsea and Spurs came a bit later."

Paynter's strength was what was known in the Fifties as 'man management'. He was able to get involved with the players, but still hold on to their respect and remain in command. Ernie recalled that occasionally, in the cause of entertainment, the night before away games centre-half and skipper Dick Walker used to do a bit of tap dancing and Charlie would get up and have a go with him. Then he'd look at his watch and say; "Right lads!" and everyone would troop off to bed. Paynter also made sure none of his troops went AWOL. Trainer, Billy Moore was sent to the door of each bedroom and would knock and ask; "All right lads?" Everyone had to answer. Billy carried out a similar round the next morning.

Jim Barrett senior was a trainer at Upton Park in the Fifties, but he was the captain and centre-half before Walker took over. During Ernie's early days playing for the senior side Jim was one of the young goalkeeper's mentors on the field; "It was good to play behind him, he would talk to me all the time."

For all Barrett's determination and professionalism, Ernie was also impressed by his famous sense of humour; "Big Jim was a comedian, always laughing and joking."

As word of his skill and athleticism spread, Ernie Gregory had a number of offers to join other clubs. However, apart from Reg Pratt telling Arsenal that 'they didn't have enough money to sign the West Ham goalie', Ernie never wanted to be anywhere else; "I was on the maximum wage so I wouldn't have been any better off and West Ham were good to me."

The supporters also had a role in keeping Ernie at the Boleyn Ground; "They were fantastic. It was them that kept you at West Ham. Marvellous people! We weren't the best of sides - an ordinary Second Division club really - but people still came to watch us, even when they moved out of the East End. It was great running out to *The Post Horn Gallop* and with all the swaying and singing of *Bubbles*"

1949-50 – For the Hammers are our team!

Chanting didn't really catch on until the Sixties, when the pop scene started. There was the occasional 'Come on you Irons', but mostly it was just *Bubbles*. It would start in the Chicken Run - swaying continually. It was taken up all round the ground and everybody finished together, rather than in patches as happens today. Relatively, the contemporary Upton Park crowd seem to rush to get to the end of the song. Their predecessors would also sing a verse not heard now;

I will always follow,
West Ham wherever they play,
In League or Cup,
We will back them up,
And give them a hearty cheer
From Upton Park to Wembley (Next year)
We will always be,
So play up, play up West Ham
For the Hammers are our team!

The crowd, crushing on to the terraces, was a weapon in itself. Festooned in claret and blue silk rosettes, home knitted scarves and hats, many furiously shaking huge wooden rattles, they would holler the Upton Park war cries; "Up the Hammers!" and "Goo-on-U-I-ons!" They were a cascade of people, sweeping down to the touchline, into the very faces of the opposition. This Cockney hoard could give out a chorus of *Bubbles* that, with the whole crowd swaying in time, would shake the very foundations of the Boleyn Ground. The anthem of all the Hammers could be clearly heard from the River - whose tugs and barges would hoot in reply - to Wanstead Flats, on the fringes of the Royal Epping Forest, where deer started on the opening notes. As spring came to the backyards and gardens beyond East Ham Town Hall, the theme would drift to the ears of sleepy babies in their prams, who were lullabied by the steady tune, while girls walking home across the Hackney Marshes from the afternoon shift at Lesney's Matchbox Toys factory, sang along. The realm of the Irons would know we were at home, and that Ernie was protecting our hopes, saving our dreams.

Ernie Gregory remembered how West Ham players were keen to try out new ways of doing things. This was the start of a tradition at Upton Park, attracting and encouraging professionals with a penchant for innovation; "Some players experimented playing without shin-pads. The outfield players cut down the shorts and shirts. We were the first team to look like a continental side. We wore the white kit, with the claret rings." This was the result of thinking about efficient heat loss, and Ernie took the idea into the goalkeeper's province; "I refused to wear the roll-neck jumpers all the 'keepers wore then. I got Yvonne to cut my jerseys down. I wanted to play in black, like the goalkeepers abroad, as this meant you blended into the background more, so the opposition players, at a quick glance, could misjudge where the 'keeper was. But they said we had to stick to our blue or green tops so as not to clash with the referees."

Ernie, unlike many players of the time, took an interest in coaching while he was still involved in playing football. Close to his 80th year he told me; "I still have my coaching badge. It's like new - still in the envelope it came in." He recalled that it was England manager Walter Winterbottom who told him, pointing to his own badge; "If you want to stay in football when you're finished playing, you've got to have one of these."

As a youngster Ernie didn't have an easy life. He was one of four children (he had two brothers and a sister) and his father had sustained wounds during World War One, dying from the effects a decade later. Ernie attended St Paul's School in Stratford, where his sports teacher, Sid Dench, was secretary of West Ham Schoolboys. St Paul's was destroyed by a bomb during World War Two; all the trophies that Ernie had helped the school to win were destroyed.

Ernie never played in goal for his school – as a lad he was a defender. He only went in goal because his brother, Bob, broke a leg playing football and the older Gregory lad was the most obvious replacement, although it wasn't his preferred role; "I went in goal, but I never liked it. I was much happier playing out." However, he fitted in well enough to be chosen for West Ham Schoolboys, Essex and London.

Ernie was playing for the district side when Charlie Paynter noticed him. The West Ham boss put his arm around the young man's shoulder, asking; "How would you like to stay with Uncle Charlie? Not the kind of opening line that would go down well today perhaps, but it was his way of inviting the talented young 'keeper to join the Upton Park ground-staff. "Come and see my Ma," replied Gregory. The day Paynter arrived outside the Gregory house to sign Ernie on amateur forms, he drove a green Hillman. The local kids clustered around in awe. A car was a possession that aroused a deal of admiration in the East End in the mid-Thirties. As Ernie told me "there weren't many about". When Mrs Gregory agreed to Ernie joining the Irons, Paynter told her;

1949-50 – For the Hammers are our team!

"He's got to wear a collar and tie." "I wanted to be a footballer," recalled Ernie, "and I thought Charlie *was* West Ham."

Ernie got £1 a week to start. "Give your Ma 15 shillings," Paynter instructed him, "and keep five bob for yourself." The boy goalie did what he was told and started his football apprenticeship by weeding the Boleyn Ground and sweeping the dressing-rooms. When he signed professional in 1939 he was rewarded with a £10 signing-on fee. Paynter told him; "Treat your mother. Put the rest in the Post Office." Again, Ernie obeyed. He said of Paynter; "His word was law to me. He was the smartest manager in the game."

Dave Bailey, a former West Ham goalkeeper who had become a painter on the Upton Park staff, was one of the first big influences on Ernie. Dave went with Gregory to the training area at the front of the ground every day at lunchtime and worked with him on low shots. "I was okay in the air," Ernie recollected; "but I was not so hot down below at the time because of my height." This practice improved the young goalkeeper's game until the point when he was as good on the ground as he was in the air. He also received help from Herman Conway, the man who acted as cover for the one of the great West Ham 'keepers, Ted Hufton.

A career at Upton Park was no picnic however; "I had to take my boots home with me. You made your own studs. We weren't allowed to use rubber, just leather." These boots were of the Dreadnought class, having more in common with armour than footwear. Ankle-high and with steel toe caps, dubbing had to be constantly applied to make them wearable. Ernie recalled that players were each given two crepe bandages to bind their ankles, this as much to protect players from their boots as from assault by the opposition. Footballers, like boxers, were good with bandages. As such, before a ball was kicked, players had laboured hard and long to prepare themselves and their kit for combat.

Like many professionals, Ernie was obliged to work when the season was over, when, as well as losing bonus payments, a footballer's basic wage dropped dramatically. He made the point that he had to work on the ground for two weeks in the summer to make some money to help towards a holiday.

While the footballer's wage was better than most people in the East London area could expect, it was the post-war era. The dock districts had been decimated by Hitler's Luftwaffe, leaving that district in particular, with a massive housing shortage. As such, finding a place to live within commuting distance to Upton Park was difficult.

According to Ernie; "Those were hard days in the East End. I heard one player tell a mate that he'd found three rooms above a grocers and being over the moon about it.

"There were plenty of good times at the club though. We were all good mates. We all went to Southend on Wednesdays. We'd catch the coach at Upton Park, pick up the directors and when we got to the sea we'd run the pier and back. After that we'd go to the salt baths. Then we'd go to Garons for a feed and finish off at a big hotel for a knockout snooker or billiards tournament. Charlie Bicknall asked Joe Payne, when Joe first came to West Ham, if he was any good with a cue. Joe said he wasn't bad. He ended up beating Charlie hands down."

The coming of war meant that Ernie was obliged to wait a long time to get into the first team, but despite this he played 406 games for the club. His debut was the 4-1 defeat of Plymouth at Upton Park in December 1946. According to Ernie; "We should have been a lot better than we were. West Ham could have been a great side. We had the crowds and, before the war, we had some great players. A lad called John Bickles could have been one of the best, but after he went on a FA training course he wouldn't head a ball. Len Goulden could jump as high as any big bloke, although he was only about 5ft 6in himself. Len could score goals, but he was a creator too. He was the best player I've seen at Upton Park. He had a wonderful football brain. There was Joe Cockcroft, Jackie Wood -I never saw anyone move faster - Archie Macaulay and Ron Cater, all good, good players."

When asked about his own strengths, Ernie looked at me seriously, paused briefly, and, with gentle but firm conviction, said simply; "I didn't like to lose." However, all the former players I spoke to were at one with Bill Lansdowne who said; "Ernie Gregory was a great player."

Words of wisdom were often Ernie's gift to younger players. Many found that these insights would guide them throughout their lives. George Petchey, a young player in the Fifties, told me; "Ernie always said that the most important thing was the distribution and the passing and that was right, then and now. It's no good if you can't pass it - go and get a job!"

George Wright said of Ernie; "He looked after me like a father." Marcella, George's wife, would often visit Upton Park with their son; "I used to take Gary down to the club when he was little. I remember Ernie's great big hands looking even bigger when Gary was holding on to his hand." George went on; "When you played in front of Ernie Gregory, you had to listen; he told you what to do for your own good. If you took notice he would have all the time in the world for you. If not, he had no time for you."

Despite the efforts of the former Charlton Athletic player Bill Robinson, who scored 23 League goals, the Irons did not do well in the 1949-50 season. The champions, from White Hart Lane, finished 19 places above them. West Ham had been on the end of 4-1 beating when they visited Spurs in March. They had lost to the North Londoners by the only goal of the game at Upton Park earlier in the season.

Match programmes in those days were two old pence for four pages. A seat in the stand was five shillings (25p). After the game you could get a good seat at the cinema for less. *Take Me Out to the Ball Game* with Frank Sinatra, Gene Kelly and Esther Williams and *The Sands of Iwo Jima* staring John Wayne were pulling them in at the 'flicks'.

It was now 11 peacetime seasons since West Ham had played in the top flight. Including the war period, the Hammers had not played in Division One for 19 years. As the new decade of the Fifties dawned, only a handful of people with the club could even remember those days. One was Eddie Chapman, but he was also one of the few who could recall the years when the modern game started to take shape at Upton Park. As he said himself; "Ernie has more to say about the playing side, but as far as the business side goes, I'm the only one who was there." Laughing, he pointed out; " No one can say I'm not right."

Most players of the Fifties, when asked about Eddie Chapman, would respond a bit like Malcolm Pyke; "Eddie Chapman was a blinding man. I liked Eddie a lot. When I first signed he was playing full-back in the 'A' team, in the old Eastern Counties League."

John Bond remembered; "Eddie Chapman always gave you the impression that he was looking after the club's interests." For others he was something of a background figure. Bill Lansdowne saw him as a mouthpiece for the board." Eddie Chapman had a job and got on with it. He was an ordinary man doing an ordinary job." However, Malcolm Allison commented; "I didn't like Eddie Chapman because he went along with Ted about teams and money. He was probably very strong."

Such was Eddie Chapman's modesty, however, not everyone would know that there was always much more to the man than this. Through his exploits on the field as a boy, Eddie drew considerable attention from professional clubs. It was just one year after Ernie Gregory had joined the club, Eddie was making his way on to the field at the start of a game; "I was half trotting when behind me I heard someone shout; 'Eddie,

Eddie!' I stopped and turned round and there were a couple of gentlemen. One had a big waxed moustache and a gold chain, that was Bert Davies, the vice chairman of West Ham, and with him was the chief representative Sid Gibson. Mr Gibson said to me; I have a question for you. Would you like to sign for West Ham?' Just like that. I said; 'Oh yeah!' I'd scored 128 goals that year. I told him; 'I'll have to ask me dad. He's over there actually.'" Eddie chuckled as he recalled this statement. He went on; "My dad never missed a game and I played all over the place, including for Essex and London. The game ended in a 6-1 win for my side, I got four. My father was in shipping with the New Zealand Shipping Company. He must have had more time off than anybody else in the firm, going to watch me playing football and cricket."

After the game Eddie's dad talked to the men from Upton Park. Eddie explained; "Dad said; 'Well look, the only way I'll let my son go to West Ham is if you'll have him in the office so he can learn the administration.' This was agreed. So, I signed amateur forms." Eddie looked thoughtful; "In some respects my dad did me a favour, because I was able to carry on after playing. On the other hand, my playing became secondary. I didn't like that because I really thought I'd have made something at West Ham. I suppose I did. I made the first team and what not, but I was very grateful to him really. I was there 49 years."

Now on West Ham's books, Eddie began to ready himself for becoming a professional player; "I guested for Romford immediately after I finished school. My schoolteacher, John Waskar, taught me an awful lot. I learned more from him than I did from anybody at West Ham. He was a born coach. He really taught me the tricks of the trade; I was very, very fond of him. He asked me to play for his team, Cranbrook Wesleyan, a church side. I started off the next season playing for them. My brother - I had just the one brother - played in the same league, the Ilford and District, with St Albans, another church team. He asked me if I could come over and play for his side, so I started the following season playing for them. Then Romford wanted me. So I guested for them for some time, it was a sort of a nursery for West Ham. West Ham didn't start their youth team until after the war. Ernie Gregory played for Leytonstone, who did the same sort of thing for West Ham. I also played a few matches for Ilford 'A' and some games for Leyton. So I mixed myself up a bit."

Eddie exemplified the loyalty and thoughtfulness, so indicative of West Ham players of his time when he told me; "John, my teacher, died about six years ago. We corresponded, by the way of Christmas cards, ever since I left school. I have about half-a-dozen friends who I went to school with who do the same thing. I phoned John up one night, and said; 'John, I just thought I'd like to thank you for everything you've done for me.' I said I was so grateful. He said; 'Thank you very much.' I know teachers, my son's a teacher. John valued that bit of remembrance from one of his pupils. Do you know, within three months he died. I was so pleased I phoned. He was a tremendous chap, he taught me a lot. When I was young and at school I idolised the man. When I left school, I remembered the things he taught me. Now and again he would come and watch me. He was a big influence on me. Without him I wonder if I would have developed as I did as a footballer. The game is in you, but he taught me the little things which you need to know to be that little bit better."

West Ham was not the only club to appreciate Eddie's talents as a boy; "I was approached by Fulham. [Eddie had press cuttings going back to 1937; his dad harvested them from the local newspapers and pasted his lad's career record in a scrap book] I was offered another 13 shillings (65p) but decided to stay with West Ham. I started on 25 bob at Upton Park (£1 25p). Nobby Strange was on the ground-staff at the time. He used to play for Loxford Boys." Nobby was, like Eddie, something of a schoolboy phenomenon. According to Ernie Gregory; "He could have been a great player, but Nobby was killed during the war." A German torpedo robbed him of his life and deprived the Hammers of a star.

Eddie told me; "After a while we were all called up to the secretary's office, and the chairman told us; 'I've got you all here to tell you you're all going to have a rise, 2s 6d [12 ½ p] a week.' So we all got another half a crown a week and went out as happy as sandboys. We thought we were wealthy! More than once I used to take my friend, Alf, to the pictures. He was getting 12s 6d (62 ½ p) a week learning to be a printer. I bought my wife Edith, my girlfriend then, a watch for 25 bob, which was a lot of money. When I joined the Army Edith went to West Ham in the office. She did the office work I'd been doing." By the time of Eddie's death the couple had been married for the best part of 60 years.

The story of how Edith Wilson and Eddie got together would make a decent romantic novel in itself; "War had just started, and all the youngsters I knew got together and had a party. Edith was there. Another party followed this, and it started from then. The very first time we met I was 13 and she was 11. We were both on a Sunday School outing, two different churches went. The plan was to meet up at Southend. I was with one church and Edith was with the other. I remember sticking my neck out the window and I got a bit of dirt in my eye from the engine -trains then were all steam driven of course. Edith, who was from Ilford, was in the next carriage. I was trying to reach her hand and got an eyeful of coal for my trouble. I was only 19 when I got married."

In Eddie's early years at Upton Park, Charlie Paynter was in charge of the side; "Charlie Paynter was my second dad. He looked after me something wonderful." Right from the start, Eddie was at the nerve centre of operations at the Boleyn Ground; "Alan Searles, who was secretary at the time, used to get behind one of these big roll top desks. On Monday mornings I used to see him with his old pen; he'd have a bottle of ink eradicator at his arm. He'd be working away there with his little razor blade." Eddie laughed; "I use to go home and say to my mum; 'Mr Searles don't half make a lot of mistakes.' All the time he was cooking the books. It came to a couple of thousand. The club just let him go. He was pro-Nazi. Once he told me to take a package up to London Bridge, to a church. It was odd. I went round the back door and just handed the parcel in and came straight back. He used to have a whacking big map of the world on his office wall. Just before the war started he told me; 'When the Germans get over here Ed, I shall get a good job and I shall see to it that you do too.' I never forget those words. I came home and I told my mum and dad and they went potty. I read a great deal about the war. My wife has told me that if ever there's another war with Germany, they'd intern me. I've got a load of books about the war, and a copy of *Mien Kampf*', I must admit, having been brought up in a close relationship with my grandfather who had play a role in liberating Europe from Nazi rule, and having regular contact with a Gypsy uncle who had been among the first Allied soldiers to reach the Concentration camps, this odd interest in Fascist power was not a little disconcerting.

Eddie Chapman was appointed assistant secretary to Alan Searle and became a competent typist and bookkeeper. He was assistant secretary from 1937 to 1956, remaining all that time on the playing staff as well. Like most ex-Hammers of the Fifties, he had good memories about the Upton Park fans; "West Ham supporters have always been wonderful. I don't think there's any better. And I'm not saying that just because I've been at West Ham. But there was one bloke, just before the war, who was having a go. I wasn't having a very good game. It was the Reserves and I went over to take a throw-in. He shouted; 'You wanna put your alarm clock on a bit earlier in the morning, Chapman!' I threw the ball at his head - it hit him right on the bonce! I got away with it, nothing happened at all. I wasn't reported. I never did it again.

1949-50 – For the Hammers are our team!

"You do hear the isolated shouts from individuals. You do hear them, especially if you're out on the touchline. In those days they did pick on individual people. I don't think you get so much of the personal stuff now, but one player they did pick on was poor old Harry Redknapp. When I left one of the matches when I was secretary, I was just getting in my car in the car park. Harry comes out and he had tears in his eyes. I said; 'What's the matter Harry?' He said; 'I can't stand it any longer - over in that Chicken Run, they're giving me hell.' 'Never mind Harry,' I said; 'you'll just have to put up with it, won't yer boy?' He didn't like playing over that other side. They used to tell Michael Grice that he'd forgotten his handbag. He had a bit of an odd run. It can effect you. You can't always be on top.

"There wasn't a big social life at West Ham in the Fifties. I used to room with Terry Woodgate and I was very fond of Eric Parsons." However, the life of a professional footballer before the war cannot be compared to the experience of players of the present day. When he was playing for the club, Eddie would commute to Upton Park by public transport from his home in Ilford; "We did our training round the back of the ground. Pre-war, after Tuesday, we weren't allowed to kick a football. I remember Billy Moore, who used to play for us, he was the trainer. He'd bring out the ball on a Tuesday and if he saw you with a ball on a Wednesday, he'd whip it away quick. You never touched a football from the Tuesday to the Saturday. I mean, the game's all about football. That changed of course after the war. They were worried about injury, but you never know when you're going to get an injury whatever you're doing.

"Following the war I was more involved in the admin side, so my biggest memories about West Ham are wartime ones. I was just 16 - just a bit younger than Joey Cole who broke into the West Ham first team in 1999 - playing with the likes of Eric Parsons. I was called up in 1942 and went to the Isle of Wight for six weeks training. I couldn't even pump-up a bike tyre at the time. After the test they gave you, to see which part of the service you were best suited for, I came out as a Royal Engineer, although I'd wanted to be in the Royal Artillery. I went to Chatham and became a field works instructor in a few months. I was teaching after that. I was determined to try to get on a bit in the services. After a while I saw the sergeant-major and asked to go on a PT course. I done a three-week course in Aldershot. I came out and got my cross-swords, then I carried on at Chatham. After a couple of years I was posted to Longmoor Camp, in the Portsmouth area. It was sport all the time. I virtually slept in the gymnasium.

"I was stationed at Chatham. Gillingham Football Club wasn't too far away, so I played for them. Football League regulations had it that you couldn't earn more than 30 shillings [£1-50] a game, but Gillingham were in the Kent League at that time and I got a fiver a match from them. So sometimes I used to say to Charlie Paynter, 'Can't make it this week Charlie, playing for Gillingham.'

"After the war, West Ham signed George Dick from Blackpool and that limited my chances. I don't think W. J. Cearns, the chairman, was too keen on me. It was before my last match that Charlie said to me; 'Give 'em your stuff today, Ed.' If I hadn't, I think W. J. would have got rid of me. After that I had a lot of Combination games."

In the late Forties, Eddie developed a special relationship with Frank Cearns and Reg Pratt, a relationship which saw him, in 1950, unusually for a player, negotiate his salary directly with the chairman, overriding the normal initial discussions with the manager. His wages, taking into consideration his wide range of duties, were increased to £10 a week, backdated to the start of the season. Although not playing a single first- team game in the Fifties, Eddie collected a £300 benefit payment in 1955. In this time he had sat in for secretary Cearns at board meetings and had been given most of the responsibility for overseeing the facilities at Upton Park and administering the staff wages. When Frank Cearns retired in 1956, Eddie Chapman took over.

Even though his footballing talents might not have blossomed as he would have liked, Eddie brought innovation and inventiveness to his role at Upton Park; "We were one of the last to have advertising all round the ground. In the West Stand, if you stood in front, you could just about see above the wall. There was no room to put in advertising boards. I was looking at it about ten minutes before a board meeting where we were due to talk about advertising boards around the ground. It suddenly struck me that we never got 8,000 full capacity in that stand. It was usually around six. I suggested that we pushed the whole lot back, so, as you went back, the wall could be higher. We lost two or three rows in front, but that's how advertising boards first came to Upton Park."

When listening to Eddie Chapman, you can't help but wonder why West Ham didn't use him more as a player; "I was speedy and an opportunist, anything loose around the goal I'd pounce on it. I read the game well. I thoroughly enjoyed playing. I never even thought about the result. I was so interested in the game itself. It never occurred to me that 'if we win this I'll get a couple of quid extra.'"

The press cuttings his father so lovingly preserved are testament to Eddie's qualities. His record was impressive, including achievements like that of 19 December 1936, when Ilford Boys beat Stepney 20-0. Eddie got four that morning and went to Willesden in the afternoon and played for London. His side won 3-1. The chronicle also told of how Ernie, playing for Ilford, had put 13 goals past an Acton defence. The story also included his nine goals playing for the Army against the RAF; "The very next week I scored seven. In the papers it said I got seven in each game. I was annoyed at that. I remember saying; 'I got nine! I got nine!'" In one season he netted 109 times for Loxford and over 20 for Ilford. All this didn't go without recognition, Eddie pointed out; "I had a trial for England, playing for the South of England."

In the third match of the Division Two campaign of 1949-50, West Ham was at home to Barnsley, and Ken Bainbridge was adjudged to have scored after only nine seconds of the game. The description of the goal reads that Bill Robinson sidefooted to Gerry Gazzard, Gerry passed it to Ken and he took it forward a few yards and shot into the net. However, Ken remembers it slightly differently and a bit faster; "I suppose it was the best goal I scored - it took four seconds. From the kick-off, the ball was passed out to me as I ran towards the penalty area. I just kicked it as I ran and the ball went into the near corner of the goal." The Barnsley side that day included Danny Blanchflower. Ken said; "I don't think I will ever forget that goal. I thought about it in later years and had to check my books to make sure I did it in such a short time - happy memories."

****

The biggest win of the season came in the FA Cup when Ipswich was beaten 5-1 at Upton Park in the third round. The fourth-round tie saw the Irons defeated 2-1 at the Boleyn Ground by Everton, then a poorly-placed First Division side, but the Toffees kept their 100 per cent Cup-tie record over the Londoners intact.

After winning at Griffin Park in November, the Irons won only two further points away from home. Their home record was not much better. The visit to Chesterfield in February was marred by a series of mishaps. A freight train collision blocked the line at Leagrave. A convoy of cars had to take the team to Leicester to catch another connection to Chesterfield. The players changed into their kit on the train and finally arrived at the ground at 4.25pm. It was snowing by this time and a sparse crowd of only

3,036 were still in attendance. Not surprisingly, the events of the day had dampened the enthusiasm of the West Ham side and a 1-0 defeat followed.

The excitement generated by football in those grim years after the war is hard to imagine from a 21st Century perspective. British society as a whole faced unexpected difficulties. By 1950 rationing was even more severe than in 1945. The man who best reflected the times was the vegetarian Chancellor of the Exchequer, Stafford Cripps, who at one stage raised the basic rate of income tax to an excruciating 9s 6d (about 48p) in the pound. Cripps was once caricatured as living off watercress, grown on Downing Street blotting paper. Whole sections of the population - including the Redknapp family in the East End - lived in prefabs. These were production line, factory-built (prefabricated) houses; essentially boxes with flat roofs made often with amble quantities of asbestos. German industry was being rebuilt from the ground up through American finance, while Britain was obliged to contribute to the expensive occupation of the former Nazi state. A lot of people looked at this and wondered if victory in war had brought any long-term advantages.

In March 1950, W. J. Cearns died. Known to be a hard, but fair man, he had steered the Hammers through the difficult years of the war, and before that period had led the club into the frustrating Second Division campaigns of the Thirties. Reg Pratt, a board member since 1941, took the chair. In August, 72-year-old Charlie Paynter retired as manager. He had served West Ham for half a century and had been trainer, secretary and manager, as far back as the early days at the Memorial Ground, Canning Town.

It was no surprise that Paynter retired. He had announced his intentions some time before and it was on his suggestion that Ted Fenton had been appointed assistant manager with the aim of him taking over when Paynter stood down. However, as Eddie Chapman told me Paynter was seen as "...the old guard...the board wanted a more modern manager, someone who could bring in new ideas about fitness and training".

Paynter had been around West Ham for over 50 years, and for almost 20 he was manager. This exemplifies the loyalty that West Ham has traditionally extended toward its managers, although for Malcolm Allison "...in those days a manager's job was more or less for life unless they messed up big time...there was no real pressure on them to produce results, they were more like wardens; go-betweens that just passed down the orders of the board...few of them had any obvious skills or know-how ".

For all this, Eddie Chapman was able to tell me about many examples of the comradery that existed between players at Upton Park and the support they gave to each other; "Dick Walker was a wonderful character. Working in the office, I knew all the lads' handwriting, so I know it was him who put the note up on the dressing-room door before my first Second Division game. It read; 'All the best wishes to you tonight - some of the lads thought you should have had this chance years ago.' It's such a shame that Dick went funny in the head towards the end. Ernie Gregory told me that he bumped into him at Chadwell Heath [West Ham's training ground] and his hair had grown over his shoulders. He was walking along the gutter. He had been such an immaculate feller. When he done a bit of scouting for Tottenham, he had a rolled up umbrella and was so smart."

Eddie was good enough to show me the long-service award - a little rectangular shield -which he was given by the Club, and a small plaque commemorating West Ham's first appearance in the FA Charity Shield. He also let me see a glass football, about eight inches across, presented to him by the Football League Club Secretaries' Association when he retired, and a silver cup, about nine inches high. Ron Greenwood had the only other one like it. These had been presented to the two men within half-an-hour after the West Ham's 1964 Cup Final win. Each was engraved with a record of the team's progress to the Final, including the Wembley result. These seemed modest recognitions of what was exceptional service to the hierarchy of the Boleyn Ground, not entirely adequate in terms of marking how much Eddie had given to the West Ham cause and insufficient recognition of his contribution to the game.

But in 1950, it was unlikely that Eddie Chapman was thinking about completing half a century at Upton Park, or that anyone other than the most starry-eyed of West Ham supporters considered the Hammers capable of winning much more than the occasional few games.

****

Eight months after scoring his lightning goal against Barnsley, Ken Bainbridge played his last game in a West Ham shirt. A month later he was a Reading player and enjoyed a 'second career' at Elm Park. He recalled; "I didn't mind the move to Reading in exchange with Vic Niblett. As the years were catching up on me, I thought a change could do me good, which it did. Elm Park was a nice ground and the Reading people were not so rowdy as the London supporters. Don't get me wrong, the London fans were honest, very good supporters. I was fairly quick. I remember someone in the Chicken Run that always came out with the crack; 'Ken, you can beat the full-back in your sleep.' The spectators in those days were more a part of the team than they are today."

Ken made a point about the way football was understood at clubs as the Fifties dawned. "Training facilities were the same wherever you played; the idea of training was to keep you agile and alert. Clubs didn't appreciate that players could be made better through training and the cultivation of their skills."

Ken came to prominence with Leyton during the war. He recalled; "As a young player my biggest influence was Stanley Matthews, but at West Ham I think it was Archie Macaulay. My family were very encouraging, too, especially my dad and mum. My dad worked for himself doing gardening jobs, laying lawns etc." But things were hard for the young footballer - one of five children - and his family; "My mother was killed in a motor cycle accident in 1936, I was only 14.

"In the early part of the war I worked in the Murex Factory at Rainham Essex, which meant I was exempt from the forces. It was a chemical factory, though, and it worried me. I played for a Sunday morning team, where I was spotted by a West Ham scout. He offered me a chance to go training at West Ham and play for Leyton, the amateur club. I had been approached by a scout from Tottenham Hotspur previously, but I preferred West Ham. I had been with Leyton for two seasons when I was again approached by a Spurs scout. I was on West Ham's books as in amateur and when I mentioned to West Ham that I had been approached by a Spurs scout they signed me on pro forms. I was no longer exempt from service, so, shortly after signing for West Ham, I was called up for the Army. I joined the Middlesex Regiment. I was with them for a while and then transferred into the APTC [Army Physical Training Corps] at Aldershot.

"While I was stationed at Blacon Camp near Chester, I guested for Chester FC. During the war you only got paid when you played. The pay when I first started was ten pound a week. "The social life at West Ham was very limited in those days. Your first consideration was football. Living in the area, you were so well known you had to behave yourself...there was always someone trying to make a name for themselves by reporting you to the club if you were stepping out of line. I suppose Terry Woodgate was the player I was closest to. We lived next door to each other, in Westbury Road, Forest Gate, which was a 15-minute walk from the ground. But all the players at the club were very sociable. West Ham was a very happy club to play for, and Mr Paynter was a very jovial person off the field. When you were on the field he was very serious, but he was a good manager.

"Unlike most players I didn't have to work part-time at all as the wages, plus bonuses for a win, were good. I was happy with my wages. But when Ted Fenton took over, I left West Ham to go to Reading FC where I had a very happy five years. If I had stayed at West Ham when Ted Fenton took over, I don't think I'd have got in the team. Mr Paynter was easy going as long as you did your job. Ted was more of the modern manager, but both were good managers. But I'm not sure Ted knew what he wanted. It was a time of transition for the Club I think. The board were the people who called the tune, but you only knew about that from the manager; that's as far as players got. A player was like a shop-floor worker and was expected to do as you were told, which is fair enough since you got your wages for doing something that was mostly fun. But you sometimes wondered how they [the board] would have made money without the players. I mean no one turned up at the ground to see the board did they! That's why the players get paid so well today - the game is really about players and supporters; everything, everyone else in football, relies totally on what the supporters and players do."

Ken played 17 wartime games for West Ham, scoring six goals in two seasons. These were big games, playing with top professionals, attracting a lot of fans, and West Ham did well in the two seasons in which he turned out for the club - runners-up in 1945 and seventh in 1946.

"After a while in the Army you were allowed leave to play for your club. It was very difficult to fit your training in but I was in the APTC so you were training every day with the physical work. I think the only difference from being full-time with a club was being able to fit in your training - your duties always came first."

In peacetime Ken scored on 17 occasions for West Ham. The first came at Upton Park in October 1946, in a 2-2 draw with Tottenham. He was a fast winger, a bit of a handful for defenders, and not afraid to have a crack at goal.

"As a player I had two great feet. I was reasonably fast and game. I always enjoyed playing Laurie Scott, the right-back for Arsenal. He was fast and we used to have some great battles -happy memories. You played as a team not as individuals. I admired Archie Macaulay. He was a brilliant inside-forward."

In all Ken Bainbridge played 84 games for West Ham, his debut, in September 1946, when he was still in the Army, was a 3-1 win at Upton Park against Millwall.

Another player making his first-team bow that day was Derek Parker, who, mostly playing from the basis of a defensive mid-field role, scored nine goals in 207 games for the Irons. Two of these came in 1949-50, the winner against Bradford and one in the 4-0 victory over Bury, both games at Upton Park. He came to the club as an inside-forward, but later took on the role of half-back. "I was picked up by the West Ham scouts when playing for Grays. Portsmouth was also interested. It was dramatic really. Charlie Paynter came down to where I was working in 1944, when the war was on, and he wanted to sign me as an amateur. I said; 'I'd like to be a professional,' and he said; 'Well, if that's what you want... I was about 20 and started on about a couple of pound and my expenses. I was able to finish my apprenticeship at 21. I was a shipwright's apprentice, building boats. When war broke out, it was a reserved occupation.

"I went to the local village school, Row Edge, just outside of Colchester. I left at 14. As a footballer I was drawn to the better ball players as opposed to the harder players. I was small in stature.

"I was a right-winger when I went to West Ham. We had trial games before the season started. I remember, so distinctly, playing in midfield, right-half, against Archie Macaulay, the great Scottish player. He was one of the stars. I had such a good game; I played so well against him, I just stayed there. There's not a better feeling to play at home and you're on top and you're winning. I had speed, I could read the game and I was quite an attacking player, as my full-backs were always telling me.

"Dick Walker was a great influence on everyone. People like Eric Parsons were internationals at Upton Park just after the war. Of course, I was at the club when Lenny Goulden was still around.

"We were part of the local community at the time. You'd get on the same train as the fans, who were a good bunch - still are - and always right on top of you, being so close to the pitch. They were always fair for me, but being tucked in midfield wasn't like being a winger, you could get away with murder. Everybody knew us when we got on the bus down to the Denmark Arms - we got a free meal there on Fridays, rationing was still on. Dickey Walker was in his element."

Like most players, Derek was loath to leave the Boleyn Ground; "I never wanted to move. West Ham was friendly. I played against some terrific players. There were some good inside-forwards around; Peter Doherty, Jimmy Hagan, Raich Carter. The players were close at West Ham. Frank O'Farrell was my roommate. He's a very Christian living man. He would often be by the bed saying his prayers at night - it needs courage to be like that. When I lost my wife he sent me a lovely book relating to death and mourning. He's got a daughter who lives about five miles from my home. I like Frank. I was also close to Malcolm Musgrove. Most of the players lived in the same area. I lived in Forest Gate before I got married, and in East Ham after.

"Benny Fenton at Colchester came in for me. He'd play at West Ham. It was a rung lower, but I was getting to the stage where I needed to move on. Colchester was my hometown, it was an opportunity to come back home for four years. I hated the thought of leaving, but my performance was levelling off. Colchester were a small club, the training was different. It would have been a nice experience to have been part of the championship side." It would, though, have been difficult for Derek to have got into the Hammers side, as he pointed out; "Andy Malcolm followed me." Malcolm was the quiet, tough man, born just down the road from the Boleyn Ground. He was to become one of the finest wing-halves to wear the Hammers shirt.

In 1951 Derek was chosen to tour Australia with a FA team; "I stopped over in New York for 48 hours on the way to Australia. We flew - hardly anybody flew about in those days. It was a propeller-driven aircraft. We went down to San Francisco for a few hours, then the Islands, Honolulu and all the rest of them. We were getting paid so much a day spending money - and we had all our wages waiting for us when we got back. It wasn't a huge amount, but in those times it was worthwhile. It was a wonderful experience; all the boys had a good time. We played a game in the States and I got friendly with a girl there; we've written cards and letters every Christmas ever since. This was no hidden thing when I got married. I've never seen her since.

"The tour wasn't a full international situation but I got a cap for the FA match against Australia. I played alongside some really good players - Jimmy Hagan, Frankie Broome, Sam Bartram. I was also picked to play for the London Combination select a few times, so I suppose I was on the fringe of international honours."

Of his team mates Derek said "I picture them as I knew them. I haven't seen most of them for over 30 years. The only times you see them are at funerals." Derek recalled; "Kenny Tucker was quite a character." Tucker, who was something of a wag, owned a tobacconist's and sweet-shop and was never short of money, as Ken Brown recalled; "Ken Tucker used to give you a wad of notes, about two hundred quid, and say; 'Look after that'. Tommy Dixon told me how Tucker was 'the ace in the hole'; "He would always be pulling out a role of money. Tommy Mahony once rolled a fiver round a wad of toilet roll and give it to Ken. Ken was amazed. He asked; 'Where did you get that from?'" Harry Hooper remembered; "Ken used to drive down from East Ham in a big American car. If there were any photos, he had to be in them. He'd jump in front. Once we thought we'd got one without him in it, but he said; 'Do you see that hand? That's me!'"

Ken Tucker was renowned for his ability to back-heel the ball, as Albert Foan confirmed; "Ken Tucker could run like the clappers. He could back-heal a ball 30 yards as did Tommy Dixon. Ken would rather back heel the ball in the net than kick it in." Eddie Chapman recalled; "We used to say to Ken; 'Can you back-heel a packet of fags on the shelf?'"

Ken Tucker turned out on 93 occasions for the Hammers, but only twice in the season that took West Ham into the second half of the 20th Century. He netted 31 times from the wing during his career at Upton Park. However, his record in the reserves - 191 games and 73 goals - begs the question as to why he was not included in the first team more often. Fast and powerful, when he did get a regular spot in the Second Division in 1955-56, he scored 15 goals in 37 matches, an impressive tally from a winger.

Tucker's experience at West Ham was coloured by him having his own business; "My mum gave me her tobacconist and sweetshop business as a wedding present when I got married in 1947." Before this he had worked as a charge-hand at the Riverside Film Studios where his uncle was a prop-master. "I was in the Navy, when I was asked by some friends to turn out in a Cup game. I had to come home on the train from Portsmouth, and didn't arrive at the match until just before half-time. The team was losing 1-0; there were no substitutes in those days, but they had decided to take the chance and start with ten men. We ended up winning 10-1; I scored eight goals in the second half. Soon after I got a letter from Charlie Paynter, who thought I was a centre-half. I went to see him and he asked me to play for Finchley in a game with West Ham reserves on the Saturday. When I turned up at the Hare and Hounds ground, I found I was up against the English amateurs' centre-half. It was a bit hard, but I could play anywhere. Although we lost 3-0, the Finchley manager asked me to turn out for them until the end of the season. At that, Charlie Paynter butted in saying; 'He's my player!' He signed me as a pro pretty quick, but it was agreed that I would turn out for Finchley until the end of the season.

"West Ham were my team. I'd always wanted to play for them. Of course, the war broke out the last year I was at school and that held me back a bit as far as the football was concerned. As a boy I was a great admirer of Jackie Morton and Lenny Goulden.

"My brother played a few times for West Ham. I think he played for England Schools, and he certainly boxed for England as an amateur. He played alongside Ben Fenton at Clapham.

"On my debut I scored with my first touch of the ball - I remember Dick Walker shouting at me to 'take the full-back on'. That was against Chesterfield at Upton Park in 1947." Ken hit as hat-trick that day but didn't score again for another four years, although he did have only 14 outings in that time.

When I asked Ken about West Ham being a family club he took the opportunity for a gentle joke; "Reg Pratt once asked me if he was related to me, but I didn't have a clue if he was, but I said, 'If I am maybe you can let me have a few shares'. I don't think he'd ever been spokend too like that by a player. Him and the Cearns family were like royalty at West Ham. But of course, I wasn't like most of the players, I didn't care that much what they thought of me." The fans were always great. We played against Arsenal in the London Cup once and the game drew a 30,000 crowd. The supporters would take the mick every now and then, but I took it in the spirit it was intended. Sometimes they would throw sweets at me because they knew I ran a sweet shop. Occasionally I'd pick a fruit one up, unwrap it and pop it in my mouth, just to make 'em laugh. I remember one bloke who, every time it got a bit quiet, would shout out; 'YOU SILLY TUCKER!' It never offended me, it made me laugh.

"Malcolm Allison, myself and a few others would go out together to West End clubs. I suppose we were seen as the non-conformists. Malcolm was understood to be a bit of a rebel, but he only wanted the best for himself and other players. Of course, most of the lads were hard up, but I wasn't, so I could help them out a bit. I had just got another shop on the other side of the Barking Road [At the time, this was the main thoroughfare connecting Essex to the Commercial Road, the docks and the City of London]. I had a shop at 116 and one at 225. That meant I covered both sides of the road, so I always had a bit more money. Noel Cantwell used to lodge just round the corner in Compton Road. Noel was my best pal at Upton Park. He was a young lad and I took him under my wing a bit. I knew from the start he was a very bright feller. I treated the game like a hobby really, but him and Malcolm, well to them it was one of the most important things in their lives. I wasn't that interested in talking about it outside training and games, but they'd be happy to discuss nothing else. I think it's not too far fetched to say they invented the way West Ham played in the late 1950s."

Ken moved to Notts County in March 1957; "I scored against West Ham when I moved to Notts County. I took a penalty, the only goal of the game. I used to go back to London after games, so I went back on the same train as the West Ham team. Fenton was none too pleased with me. As I was a regular the stewards used to save me the same seat for every trip. Fenton came up to me and told me that my seat 'had been reserved for our wives'. I told him that they'd have to sit somewhere else. He often tried to pull rank on players, but few of the better ones took much notice of him. Most often we worked out the way we'd play; Malcolm was the one who organized everything on the field and most of the training. I don't think Fenton was a man-manager; he was just the mouthpiece of the board, although to be fair he understood enough to know the players were best placed when it came to the way we played.

"Eddie Chapman was a nice bloke, always helpful. When the FA put up the wages from £12 to £14, West Ham only offered us £13. I told them I wouldn't sign. Ted said to me that Dick, Noel and Allison had all signed and asked; 'What makes you think you'll get £14 when they have settled for £13?' I told him that I'd retire. Well, I didn't get any pay that summer, but come the pre-season training I got a call from Eddie asking me to come and sign. I told him I had retired, but he told me that they were going to give me the £14. Afterwards Ted asked me why I had made 'all that fuss over £1'. I told him that he had made the fuss, not me. He complained that he had been obliged to give it to all the first teamers. 'That's your problem,' I said. They shouldn't have got it. They didn't have the guts to ask for it so they shouldn't have got it. Any way, I found out later that they'd never been any question that Noel and Malcolm wouldn't get £14; I suppose I pretty much had guessed that straight away."

By May 1950, Ken Tucker had played only eight first-team games for West Ham and really was at the start of his career at Upton Park. He had just two games that term. Ron Cater had played only two games more that season, but for him it was to be his final phase with the club, having turned out 70 times in Hammers colours. He'd spent half his life at Upton Park. "I went to West Ham from school at the age of 14, on the ground staff. It was about the same time as Bill Lewis and Ernie Gregory. I was from West London, but my headmaster, Mr Struton, put me in touch with West Ham. I also played for East Ham and London Schoolboys where I was picked to play my first game for England Schoolboys at Hampden Park. I went to Napier Road School, in Fulham. Mr Black, my sports teacher, helped me a lot. He took me to Ireland when I played against them with England Schoolboys. West Ham was the only club I wanted to play for. When I was a child my father took me to Upton Park every week. My mum and dad were a big influence in my life and loved watching me and my two brothers play. My wage-packet was thin at 14 - £1 a week. I was approached by Chelsea and Luton, at about the same time, but my heart was with West Ham, I wasn't interested in any other clubs."

Fifteen other West Ham professionals were in the same army squad when Ron was drafted into the side; "We, the West Ham lads, were also in the Army with the Stoke City players and I know we all enjoyed playing for the British Army together. We played in Germany against the British Army on the Rhine, who had such players as the great Tom Lawton, Billy Wright and so many of the old time greats."

Ron did his National Service while registered at Upton Park, serving in the Essex Regiment and the Royal Artillery. "As we were in the Army, I played for West Ham when I was on leave. But I was stationed in the North of England so I played as a guest player for Preston, Blackburn Rovers and Doncaster Rovers, who all wanted me to sign pro for them.

"Mr Paynter had a lot of influence on me, he was a grand gentleman. The trainer at West Ham, Billy Moore, and all the players, such as Joe Cockcroft and Len Goulden, made me feel as if I belonged and had a great effect on me. They gave me lots of encouragement as did Mr Paynter and the directors."

It was in the League South that Ron made his initial appearance for the Hammers, against Coventry. West Ham won 5-2. His first Division Two match was at the start of the 1946-47 season when West Ham lost 3-1 at Plymouth. "All the matches I played were great games and it was an honour to play with those lovely mates of mine. Terry Woodgate was one of the fastest men I've seen, he was a character to be sure.

"The fans were all good. They went to watch a good game and were never any trouble. It was lovely to hear them singing the old *I'm Forever Blowing Bubbles*. My great friends who we used to meet up with, along with their wives, were Ernie Gregory, Terry Woodgate, Jackie Woods, Dickey Dunn, Arthur Banner and Dickey Walker. We had some great times and laughs. Eddie Chapman was also a nice chap. I would never say otherwise, of course. He was in the office mostly, although he was with us when we toured Switzerland, which was wonderful.

"I lived at Bristol Road, Forest Gate. West Ham was great to play for; it was a very friendly club. We all got so much joy from playing with such smashing lads and I can't recall any difficulties. After all, we were paid the same wage and played football for the love of it.

"There were so many good players who were my friends. Of course, Ernie Gregory was such a good goalkeeper; he should have played many times for England. Also, not forgetting my friends the Irish boys, Tom Moroney, Danny McGowan, and Frank O'Farrell; all wonderful players. I also remember Archie Macaulay, Jack Woods, Dickey Dunn, Ernie Devlin. I have so many wonderful memories of them all, and of course the great Dickey Walker - such a character."

Ron moved to Leyton Orient in 1950 - "I was sorry to leave West Ham. I found that Orient trained less; it was, different from West Ham. But I enjoyed my time there. My vivid memory of West Ham was the comradeship between the players, the directors and the manager."

Another player moving away from Upton Park in 1950 was Eric Parsons, but as Ron Cater was settling into life in Division Three South, Eric was on his way to Division One. I met Eric and his wife, Joan, at their home on the South Coast. It was a late winter Sunday, just after midday. The sun was bright, but the sea, just a couple of minutes from the Parsons' home, was choppy in the high winds. Eric was quite an enthusiastic gardener, but after moving - Eric and Joan, when they invited me into their home, were living in a very attractive apartment - he missed this aspect of his life.

Eric Parsons played 40 times for the Irons in 1949-50, scoring nine goals. In all Eric played 151 games for West Ham, making his debut at Filbert Street in a 4-0 defeat in January 1947. He moved to Chelsea for £23,000 in November 1950 (quite a fee at that time) and was a member of their 1955 First Division Championship side, in the same team as Ron Greenwood.

"I was one of the fastest wingers around," Eric recalled. "I had speed and stamina." His pace and style were certainly direct - it was said locally that he could catch pigeons or chase greyhounds. He signed from Worthing Boys, following a game against West Ham Boys at Upton Park.

"We got beaten in the last blessed kick of the game in the English Schools Shield. I was approached and I told them to see my teacher. My teacher asked me; 'Has anyone seen you?' I said; 'Yes, they said they'd seen you.' They told me that they'd seen my teacher. So it ended up with me going down to the boiler room and signing amateur forms for West Ham, virtually as I came off the pitch. Sid Gibson signed me – he was leading scout at that time. He died before I went back. I had played for Sussex Boys and a schoolboy international trial, North versus South, which was at Shrewsbury. I didn't play very well. I was out of position. As a schoolboy I used to play centre-half, attacking centre-half. I used to get a few goals. I played that day at wing-half. I was running between the inside-forward and the wing-half, and I never really got anyone to mark.

"Dad worked for Worthing Corporation. Mum did the ironing and Dad did the stealing -they worked in the iron and steel works," Eric laughed. "That's an old one! I went to school at Sussex Road, in Worthing. I had some good teachers for football, which is what is required now - they don't get enough of it. Johnny Spawn, Bill Stone and Pop Kennard, they were all keen on football. They came up when we played West Ham Boys. During the war, Sussex played one or two Red Cross games at Worthing, and I was very impressed by Jimmy Hagan - he had control and speed and was a very good ball player too.

"It all started when I used to run to school and see what time I could do it in. I always wanted to try and beat that time. I used to run for two miles. I was about ten. I loved it, I thrived on running; I didn't seem to get out of breath.

"On the ground staff at West Ham you got about £3 a week. I had to pay for my digs out of that and I sent some money home to my mum. I lived in Henniker Gardens, that was before I moved to Montpellier Road. I moved just before the war, then I came home, so I lived in Worthing and travelled to play and train at West Ham. I'd finish my training at 12 or 1 o'clock and I went back to Worthing. I used to go down to the Denmark. They used to give us a meal. It was the rationing period. We'd get on the trolley bus, down to the East Ham Town Hall, and get our vitamins. We were all mates at Upton Park, there was no ill feeling. Tommy Moroney was playing at the time, he was a good wing-half. Len Goulden, who was a fine player, was a big influence, as was Bob John, who came from Arsenal. But they changed the side around a good bit and they never had a good centre-forward. There were no actual tactics. We, the players, more or less made it up as we went along. You knew certain teams and particular players, you had an idea how you might compete against them, but the manager never said 'do this or that'. There was the sort of pep talk most often, but if you got to half-time no one was shouting or hollering; we didn't start accusing people of things. Ernie Gregory might have a little moan about something, but that never came without some advice.

"That said, Charlie Paynter helped me at West Ham and he did dress me down on one occasion when I went to Chesterfield. I had a roll-neck jumper on. He didn't like that. One of the England selectors was on Chesterfield's board. He wanted you in a collar and tie."

Eric scored 35 goals in claret and blue, his first in a 4-3 defeat at Nottingham Forest in April 1947. "That year was a bad one for snow. So they had some games in May. I played more games for West Ham at inside-forward than I did at outside-right. I played in the England 'B' side when I was at West Ham, against Holland and Finland. Of course, Tom Finney and Stanley Matthews were around at the time, so there wasn't much chance to get into the England side. I got an 'Oscar' [the trophy looked a bit like the film award] in Finland, as the best player on the pitch. We won about 4-0.

"The fans were always humorous. I'll always remember that - the usual Cockney stuff. They were good supporters at Upton Park." Eric was known as 'Rabbit' because he was small, fast, and quick off the mark.

"It was the way I used to play. I might have run a bit like a rabbit! That came from Upton Park, and went on to Chelsea. They also called me 'Quicksilver'. The crowd was right on top of you at Upton Park, not like at Chelsea with its dog-track [at one time Stamford Bridge hosted both Greyhound and Speedway racing]. West Ham had a small pitch. You had to use your ingenuity. A think that's part of the reason so many good players came out of Upton Park.

"I enjoyed football and being at West Ham. We used to train very hard. I was dedicated. I loved it and thrived on it. I spent half my life doing something I loved and getting paid for it. I had some good games at Upton Park. If you had a good game, Charlie Paynter would say; 'You go round to Morrie Finkleson and get a tie.' it was just round by the Odeon, in the Barking Road.

"I liked West Ham. I really didn't want to leave. I think I was entitled to a benefit. In those days players were given benefits, a sum of money for continuous service. I signed pro for West Ham in 1943 and my first game was at Southampton. That's why I was in dispute with West Ham. Because I was abroad with the forces from 1945 till 1947, they told me that I wasn't due my benefit. I was in Germany! The boys who were at home had the benefit! I'd have loved to have been at home playing for West Ham, earning money, but I was in Germany. I didn't like that. I had a wife and a kid, and a mortgage. But the board were sometimes like that; any thing to save a few quid, although that cost them dearly more often than not. So, I asked for a move. Wolverhampton were after me at the time, but I happened to knock at Chelsea. I never got the £750 benefit until I moved."

1949-50 – For the Hammers are our team!

Eric played every game for Chelsea in their 1955 League championship season. "There was a lot more social life. They took us to France when we won the championship. You travelled first-class stayed in first-class hotels. You'd have never have got that out of the West Ham board! But there wasn't so much drive at Chelsea in terms of training - Billy Moore at West Ham pushed you. Albert Tenant was at Chelsea, well he'd use a tape recorder during matches, picking out problems and strengths. I'm not sure that worked. I think he might have liked the sound of his own voice! But looking back I suppose it was innovative."

As Eric was finishing his career at Upton Park, Gerry Gazzard, like Ken Tucker, was establishing a regular first-team spot. He made his initial appearance in the first team in the first game of the 1949-50 season; a 2-2 draw at Luton.

"My first game for West Ham led me to query my signing into League football. I remember getting many tips from well wishers. I recall being called to the manager's office, expecting no praise but much criticism of my performance. However, the manager at that time was excellent and I was given time to settle in and a chance to get used to the difference between amateur and League football."

Gerry played 40 times in League and Cup that season, scoring a handful of goals. "I attended East Dean Grammar School, Cinderford. My brother served in the RAF as a pilot. I moved to Cornwall after my National Service, I was in the Navy, stationed at Truro on landing craft ships until my discharge. My parents and my brother stayed in Gloucestershire. My father worked in the coalmines in the North, he moved to Gloucester after the war and got employment in the service works. On my release from the Navy I continued to live in Truro in Cornwall, moving to Penzance later." Hence the West Ham crowd knew Gerry as 'the Pirate of Penzance'.

In the West Country the young Gazzard joined the local football club. "I met my future wife in Penzance. No other Football League club were interested in signing me, until a scout from Burnley approached me with a possibility of having a trial game. But Burnley was so far away from the Penzance area, so I decided I would go to West Ham when I received an invitation to play for them."

Gerry's first Hammers goal was scored against Barnsley in a 3-1 win. "I recall scoring my first goal, but little about getting the final touch. I recollect it giving me a real boost." In all Gerry scored five goals in the 40 games he played in that first season. He scored 32 during his time at the Club. "I will always remember the best goal - it was a header from a long cross and I wasn't the best header of a ball."

"I played alongside some good players at West Ham. I recall the names of Ernie Gregory, Dick Walker, Jim Barrett and Harry Hooper and many more. Eddie Chapman was secretary. He was a very good player too, when given the opportunity. He was very helpful. I wouldn't normally select a best player. I remember being given encouragement from so many, but I especially recall Dick Walker. In my early days his advice stood me in good stead for later games. I lived out at Barkingside and this made it more difficult to join in the social side of the Club. But there was always a family feeling among the players, the senior staff helping to bring harmony among the professionals. Pay was debatable. I was paid between £12-13 plus £2 bonus for a win and £1 for a draw.

"The Second Division was workmanlike in many ways, but allied with good players who were capable of reaching high standards, we were able to produce some good football. The West Ham fans were marvellous to me, particularly in the early days. They were very helpful when things were going badly and I knew they were genuine. They have a wonderful manner and were always encouraging."

After cartilage problems, Gerry lost his place to John Dick and moved to Brentford in 1954. He was a fine player, picked out by many of his contemporaries as one of the best performers at Upton Park during the early and mid-Fifties.

The final player to break into the West Ham first team in the 1949-50 season was Jim Barrett junior. Jim W. Barrett was just over 19 when he took the field at Ewood Park late in April 1950. It wasn't a good day for the Hammers, who made their way back to London with a 2-0 defeat to think about.

Jim was the son of Jim G. Barrett, a Hammers stalwart between 1925 and 1938, the veteran of 467 games. He became known as 'Big Jim' after his boy made the side. There was some irony here, both father and son could never be accused of having a height advantage. Big Jim had been one of the most popular West Ham players of the Thirties.

Jim Barrett junior was very much a local creation. In five years he made 87 first-team appearances but had to wait until October of his first full season for the first of his 25 goals for the Irons. He grabbed the winner in a 2-1 victory at Chesterfield's Recreation Ground, Terry Abodgate had opened the scoring for West Ham.

I travelled to Jim's home, near the Essex-Cambridgeshire border, on a cold and grey winter afternoon. After welcoming me into his cosy house, he told me; "I was born in Howard's Road, the local maternity hospital in Plaistow. I was one of three children and have two sisters. I went to Upton Cross School, although I was evacuated to Wantage, in Berkshire, on my own. The family went to live in Vange, near Basildon, after the war. I grew up with the big names. I went every game at West Ham. I liked Jimmy Logic, at the Arsenal, but there were also Matthews, Mannion, Mortensen and Raich Carter. I was brought up with West Ham. I joined them through ny dad."

Big Jim' was still playing a bit at the time his son came to Upton Park, but his main role by the mid-Forties involved training the players. Jim junior recalled; "I was 14 when I started during the war. A doodlebug landed on the pitch on my first day. Charlie Paynter sent me home.

"I started on £2 10s [£2.50]. You got £6 in the summer, £8 in the reserves and £12 if you got in the first team. In those days the clubs had all the money and the players were skint. The 'A' team were all professionals. We had a series of friendlies after the war. We went to Carshalton in Surrey. We were taken to the wrong ground, but by the time we sorted it out and got back to the coach we found that the driver had gone to the pictures. We all had to get the bus. We got to the ground, but we only had time to play about 15 minutes each way. For a time I played with dad in the 'A' team. Dad was the shortest feller on the park.

"West Ham was a family club. We had a billiard room and there were always parties for the kids at Christmas. We also got a turkey at Christmas. The married blokes got the bigger birds. I met Kathleen, my wife, in Basildon. When I got married we lived in Plaistow, near to Fred Kearns, Albert Foan, Jimmy Andrews, Terry Woodgate. John Gregory lived in Wigston Road [his son was managing Aston Villa in the late 1990s]. We got nearly three months off, of course. Dad worked at Stratford market, so I got some work down there. It kept you fit.

"The club offices were not in the ground at that time, they were in the Boleyn Castle [something of a folly situated just outside Upton Park stadium]. We had a professional staff of around 50. The reserve matches used to attract as many as 10,000-12,000. Everyone at the club was easy to play with. Tommy Moroney and Dick Walker were good on the park and in the dressing-room. But it was always hard to go to Anfield. The crowd made you feel as if you were one down before you started."

Jim went to Nottingham Forest at Christmas 1954. "I went to Forest for £9,000, which was a substantial fee in those days. I really hit it off at Nottingham Forest. Billy Walker, the manager, asked me what I was doing playing wing-half. He told me to come through and score goals." Jim became top scorer for Forest in 1956-57, doing his bit in their successful promotion campaign of that season. He also won an England 'B' cap while he was at the City Ground.

Nineteen-fifty was a World Cup year, the first since 1938. England qualified for the World Cup Finals in Brazil by regaining the Home International championship from Scotland. Scotland could have competed as runners-up but decided, before the domestic championship started, that they would only enter the tournament as champions of Britain. The England team that went to South America looked strong, including Alf Ramsey, Tom Finney, Wilf Mannion, Stan Mortensen, Jackie Milburn, Stanley Matthews, Billy Wright, Bill Nicholson and Bert Williams. From this distance it is hard to see how this team of legends didn't walk the tournament, and things did look good following an opening 2-0 victory over Chile. However, England couldn't get over the embarrassment of being beaten 1-0 by the part-timers of the USA in the next group match. They lost their final game against the Spanish, again by the only goal of the game.

In the top flight, Portsmouth and Wolves finished level on 53 points, but Pompey took the title with a better goal-average. Arsenal, with the Compton brothers and Joe Mercer, met Liverpool in the FA Cup Final. The Gunners took the trophy with a 2-0 victory. Reg Lewis scored both goals.

Outside football, at the end of May 1950, the future was beginning to take shape. Yugoslavia and Albania severed relations. Who would have been able to say what this would lead to almost 50 years later? Sheffield Wednesday went into Division One with Spurs. Wednesday, with a goal-average of 1.395, edged out their neighbours, United, whose average was 1.387 and Southampton (1.333).

West Ham finished the 1949-50 season only four points clear of relegation, two points ahead of QPR. Plymouth and Bradford Park Avenue went out of Division Two. The Hammers were not yet on the rise, but another, more sinister, team was developing in the East End. In 1950, a 16-year-old Hackney boy called Harvey was found badly beaten up by fists, boots and bicycle chains. There were witnesses, but when the Kray twins, who were about the same age as Harvey, were put on trial at the Old Bailey - their debut at that venue - the case was dismissed for lack of evidence.

1950-51 – Football is just a reflection of life

By the start of the new season, Britain was involved, through the United Nations, in a war in South East Asia. At the end of World War Two, Korea had been arbitrarily divided at the 38th parallel, with a Soviet-supported regime in the north and an American-supported state in the south. Although they had originally wanted a united democratic republic, both sides remained bitterly opposed. As the USA and the Soviet Union removed their occupying forces, both South and North declared themselves to be independent republics.

On 25 June 1950, North Korea invaded South Korea, which was still unofficially under the auspices of the United Nations, and strongly influenced by the USA. The UN called for an immediate withdrawal of North Korean forces. This call was ignored and the USA moved to support its client state of South Korea with General Douglas MacArthur as Commander-in-Chief of the UN forces. North Korean forces soon occupied most of the peninsula and the United Nations forces - nearly all American - were cooped up at Pusan in the south east.

An own-goal after only 30 seconds, by Hull City full-back Vigo Jensen, gave West Ham their opening goal of 1950-51. In the visiting side that day were Raich Carter and the future Leeds United and England manager, Don Revie. This was the first game of the season and although the Hammers ended it with only a point, the Upton Park crowd saw a thrilling game as north and south shared six goals. Gerry Gazzard and Bill Robinson completed the scoring for the home side.

Ted Fenton was beginning to sow the seeds of the Upton Park youth policy; this was probably to be his greatest and most lasting contribution to the Club. However, West Ham still had to seek talent in the transfer market. Albert Foan made his debut in the Hull City match.

I met Albert and his wife, Margaret, at their home in the Norwich area. Albert told me; "My dad was in the Navy and then became a riveter on the barges, working on the Thames. My mum died within six months of me going in the forces." Mr and Mrs Foan had three children; Albert, a brother who lost a leg when he was ten, and a sister. "As a boy, I went to Albion Street School, Rotherhithe. It's still there. Mr Howe was the sports teacher."

Young Albert was not enamored of the clubs in his South or East London home territory. "I followed Arsenal as a kid, and was always impressed by Alex James." Albert played for London Boys, but before any professional clubs took the opportunity to sign him, like so many young men of his generation, he went into the military. He explained that this was what took him, a South-East London boy, to Norwich City Football Club; "I played for the Army in Germany and a friend who was from Lowestoft wrote to Cyril Spears, who managed Norwich at that time. I joined Norwich as soon as I came out of the forces."

The Canaries were in the Division Three South during the immediate post war period. Albert recalled "When I got to Norwich, I was warned that this place grows on you. Wherever you go, you'll be back. That was right.

"Ted Fenton spotted me after a time and I started with West Ham on £8 a week." Albert was now approaching 27, but soon settled into life back in the East End. "While I was at Upton Park, I lived in Cumberland Road. Sometimes I'd thumb a lift to the ground. Once I got a ride in a hearse!

"I didn't really get involved in the social life at the Club. Dick Walker was some character. And I was friendly with Malcolm Allison and Jimmy Andrews.

"I could play on the wing or at inside-forward and I could beat people. I took people on. When you're small, you learn to take care of yourself and I nearly always came up with something. We had to contend with some terrible pitches; you could stand on your spot at the start of a game at Upton Park and feel yourself sinking into the ground, but West Ham always seemed to play better in the wet."

Although he was with the Irons until 1956, Albert had only a couple of extended runs in the first team, but he played 60 times in Division Two, scoring nine goals, the first being one of two in a home match against Lincoln, late in 1952. The lack of first-team opportunities meant lower earnings and out of season Albert looked to supplement his income. "I always used to look for a summer job. One year I worked in a barrel factory, near Maryland Point [not far from the 2012 Olympic Park] moving the things around.

"At times I thought that I didn't have much of a chance at the Club, and that I should leave, but it was like a family. They treated players well - no one was hoofed out if they were struggling. I also remember the Chicken Run letting thousands of balloons up in the air as they sang *Bubbles* one day." For a second I could see that rising mist of dreams and affection, the bright winter sun shining through the translucent cloud, bathing the green of the Boleyn Ground in a claret and blue haze.

The then manager-elect Ted Fenton was beginning to get his feet under the table and one of the first things he wanted to address was the club's publicity policy. He thought that West Ham might have taken supporters for granted. He later declared that he "…wanted them [the Club] to do more public relations."

"He was a natural for the job," Trevor Smith, the discerning football correspondent of the *Ilford Recorder,* said of the new manager. "You had to notice Ted Fenton because he was always grabbing publicity." Fenton signed players on television, started rumours about possible signings, and created what are now known as 'sound-bites' to promote what was happening at Upton Park. He might have changed his stories from week to week, but that just created more excitement. People began to think that something novel and interesting was going on at Boleyn Ground. It could only boost attendances, and the publicity was not without its attractions to players that were needed to make West Ham a winning side.

Fenton still needed to substantiate his own publicity. He had to provide entertaining, winning football. Since the turn of the century East London had prided itself on the production of talented footballers, but West Ham didn't have the greatest of records when it came to attracting the best of local players. Fenton decided to develop the scouting system. Ted and Wally St Pier, an ex-player, begun to attend a huge number of matches in the East End, fostering a small regiment of voluntary scouts, the forerunner and exemplar of which was the locally famous Reg Revins.

Fenton and St Pier ingratiated themselves with schoolmasters, football officials and parents. They emphasised that things had changed at the Club and that West Ham was really interested in local talent. This was the foundation of what West Ham would become over the next 20 years and established the Clubs 'Academy' tradition. However the policy arose mainly out of necessity. Fenton, looking back on what he did said; "The only way to build the Club was youth. There were lots of good players around, but I had no money to buy the key players we needed. There were always the problems of running a club on a shoe-string."

St Pier and Fenton used local pride as a selling point for young players, but they also pointed to what Fenton described as 'the lowly status of the Club' as a way to show boys and their parents that they could advance in a hurry. This cunning use of terminology, actually deriding the Club, and by association himself, did work on a good number of people. However, the underlying statement; 'We're crap, so even you could get a place in the first team,' had the potential to turn off the more confident or determined players that are needed to push a club towards its potential. In effect, Fenton was unconsciously reinforcing the psychological culture of the Club he was brought up with and that still exists today. West Ham is second best; a nursery club in all but name for the likes of Arsenal, Liverpool or Manchester United. What success West Ham has had has been built on players and supporters refusing to take on the lack of ambition that the management of the club has always called 'realism' or 'pragmatic'. People forget that in 1974, Manchester United was relegated for the third time in the 20th century. They went down in 1931, the year before West Ham. No club has more right to success than any other. West Ham is not inherently inferior. If the analysis, so often reiterated by employees of the Club, about West Ham's prospects, were applied to an individual, it would be seen as an example of the worst kind of prejudice and discrimination. The trick of the clever bigot is to convince others that their (the bigot's) perception of the world is correct. As such, the armour of the West Ham, or the Southampton, or the St Albans or the Old Biggies and Wickersthwaite Contemptibles supporters, is not to believe everything that everyone tells them. What a board or a manager thinks is just that; what they think (or say they think). At best it is *a* truth. It isn't *the* truth.

Understanding that it would take years before his youth policy would begin to pay off, Fenton, in the mean time, had to bring mature talent into the club. The season was ten games old when Tommy Southren made his first-team debut at the end of September 1950, against Sheffield United at Upton Park. It wasn't the best start for the Sunderland-born outside-right, although Bill Robinson scored a hat-trick, including two penalties. Three times West Ham was in the lead but the game ended with the Blades coming out 5-3 winners. Tommy recollected; "Ernie Devlin got two, but in the wrong net, he slid them in." A Furniss penalty finally broke the Hammers that day.

Just a few days before Southren's debut, the United Nations had recaptured the South Korean capital, Seoul, which had fallen to the North Koreans just three months earlier. This came as part of a powerful counter-attack by United Nations forces, aided by a bold amphibious landing at Inchon on 14 September. By the end of September, the North Koreans were back at the 38th parallel.

I met with Tommy Southren and his wife, Elsie, at their home in Welwyn. Tulips were just beginning to bloom, and seemed to be everywhere in that pretty, green, almost landscaped area of South East England. Tommy met Elsie in 1953 at a dance at the Cherry Tree, in the Sugar Market in Welwyn. Elsie was a local girl, but her mum was from Newcastle. Tommy still spoke in a broad North Eastern accent, which raised the question of how he came to begin his career in Hertfordshire.

"I started with Pear Tree Boys' Club. It was a good club. A scout wrote to Paynter and asked me if I'd like to play for West Ham. I said; 'I wouldn't mind.' Secretly I was thinking 'yes!' When I signed for West Ham, Charlie Paynter filled in all the forms - that was him finished. I didn't see much of him after that. I went straight into the 'A' team. That's the way it was. I'm not sure what the manager's did then!"

Tommy hadn't gone unnoticed before this point; "George Allison approached me to play for Arsenal when I was still at school, I wasn't 14. They had something to do with a Ministry of Information film that was being made in the area. I didn't think I was good enough."

The Southren family moved to Welwyn in 1939. There were five children in the family, although three more siblings died at birth and another passed away at nine months. Tom also lost a younger brother and sister. He had two surviving sisters. Tommy's dad worked at De Haveland's, the aircraft company. As was the way in that time, Tom's uncle, his dad's bother, who worked in the company before Tommy's family moved south, had put in a good word for Mr Southren senior. Tom's dad had been in pit work in the North East, but had to give that up after contracting double pneumonia. Tommy said; "Dad was the biggest influence on my football, he enjoyed the game. He played a bit and went every week [while the family still lived in the North East] to see Sunderland."

Young Tommy attended Hanside School. "They didn't really bother with football, although I remember playing St Ignatias, that was a Spurs school." The Navy took Tommy into its ranks before he could establish himself at Upton Park. "I was stationed at Leigh-on-Solent, but played only two games while I was in the Navy as I was sent out to Australia and Hong Kong." But Tommy was still on people's minds at Highbury. "Tom Whittaker, the Arsenal physiotherapist, came back when I was in the Navy." But Tommy was still of the same mind, doubting his own ability. "West Ham was a friendly club - you didn't talk about anyone you didn't like. I had to come home to Welwyn every day and I took the summer off. Eleven weeks, that was nice, but this meant that I didn't get too involved with many other players at the Club, although I was good mates with Jim Barrett junior."

Jimmy Andrews talked affectionately about Tommy Southren; "I always remember Tom especially. He wanted a rise but he was a very shy lad, and we were always egging him on. He went to see the manager eventually. He knocked on the door and a voice said; 'Come in.' He went in and looked around and there was no manager there, just an empty desk. So Tom said; I've come to ask for a rise, boss. 'Oh yes Tom.' It was Fenton's voice, but Tom was still looking around. 'Yes,' said Tom, 'I think I should get more money. Some of the other lads are on more.' The reply came; 'Have you thought about it Tom?' Tom is still looking around. Then the door quietly swung closed - and the manager was behind the door, standing on his head! Sometimes West Ham was like a comedy film."

Tommy continued; "The crowd at Upton Park were brilliant. Happy, no fights. Elsie used to go up with my dad every other Saturday. They always had a drink in the Boleyn. She had her pineapple juice and pie. They sat in the West Stand. "Away from home, Ipswich was the best ground. I played at Spurs when the mud was over your ankles in the bottom corner. Luton had a tilt."

It is hard to see the attraction of encounters played on such surfaces. Talking to supporters of the time it seems there was something gladiatorial about it. Strength and endurance were valued above showboating, that was viewed as suspicious, being slightly effeminate. As Tommy said; "They don't play football now." Looking back at those he played alongside, he concluded; "Ernie Gregory was a great player. Dick Walker would run at 'em. I was a run-of-the-mill player." This was probably a somewhat modest assessment. Tommy was chosen to play for the London FA team that beat Berlin 'easy', according to Tommy. "I had a little drink of champagne after that. I keeled over - it was vicious." This honour came in the same season, 1953-54, that, as a consistent member of the reserve team, he won Combination League and Cup medals. It is also unlikely that a mediocre player would have attracted the attentions of First Division Aston Villa, as Tommy Southren did when he swapped claret and blue for blue and claret, moving to Villa Park at Christmas 1953. He spent four years with the Villains, turning out for 63 League games, netting half-a-dozen times, but unfortunately he wasn't selected for the 1957 FA Cup winning side.

Tommy looked back on how the move to Villa came about; "Ted asked me if I wanted to go to Villa. I told him; 'As quick as you can.' He didn't treat me too well. He had his favorites, although he didn't have the players respect on the whole. Our talk about my moving to Villa happened at a Saturday night dance. I signed in the back of a cab. Eric Houghton, the Villa manager, was on his way to Euston to catch the train back to Birmingham. Ted Fenton had to take us to London in his car. When you had been five years with West Ham you got £750 when you were transferred. When I was about to sign for Villa, Ted told me not to worry, I'd get my £600. I told him it should be £750. He said; 'Oh, all right.' Not a lot of conviction there. Fenton brought in Harry Hooper to replace me."

As he told me all this there was some disappointment in Tom's voice and there is little doubt that neither West Ham nor Villa got the best from him. It appears that there was something 'Brazilian' in his play, a feel for the game that would have blossomed in a later generation. As I thanked him and Elsie for their kindness in seeing me, Tom said; "Playing for West Ham was great!"

It goes without saying that without players there is no game. It is the skill of the professional player that raises the game above the level of what the supporters can do. As a player slogan from the baseball strike in the USA of 1982 reminds; "We are the game." For most of the Fifties, at the start of every season, between four and seven players chose not to sign when terms were first offered them. On about half of those occasions the terms were increased, usually in the range of 10s (50p) per week. These players were, in the main, first-team members. This negotiation became a ritual for some professionals, a kind of a gesture. The men who rejected terms usually repeated the practice over a period of years. Among others, the players who had come to West Ham from the Republic of Ireland - Danny McGowan, Tommy Moroney and Frank O'Farrell - refused each year to accept the initial terms that were offered to them. O'Farrell summed up the start of a new awareness on the part of the players when he recollected; "When it came to the manager and the board, I'd learned how to take care of myself."

Frank O'Farrell had replaced Tommy Moroney in the Cork United side when Moroney left Ireland for Upton Park. O'Farrell came to the Boleyn Ground in January 1948. He worked under Charlie Paynter at first, but came into the side when Fenton took over. His first memories of the Club included the funeral of W. J. Cearns, "which was a grand and solemn affair". He also recalled Billy Moore, the trainer at the time, with some affection. He reminisced; "Many players had been in the forces and were coming back to the club - Jackie Wood for example. He had been an outstanding outside-left for West Ham before the war. Jackie had been a dispatch rider. He had been wounded and had a plate in his head." Ken Wright had been a pilot and had been awarded the Distinguished Flying Cross. However, according to Frank, "Most of the players didn't get further than Wanstead Flats in the war."

In Korea, General MacArthur did not stop when he reached the 38th Parallel. On 1 October, South Korean troops crossed into the North. No objections came from the United Nations. Within three weeks MacArthur had driven the North Korean forces almost back to the Manchurian border and had reached the River Yalu at several points. It was at this stage in the conflict that Chinese volunteers were beginning to appear in the ranks of prisoners. However, it was at the River Yalu that the North Koreans began their own counter-attack.

After completing his half century of reserve games, Frank O'Farrell got into the first team on a regular basis, making his debut at Notts County on 25 November 1950, replacing his fellow countryman Tommy Moroney, the man whose boots he had filled when Moroney left for East London. Terry Woodgate scored for the Hammers, but County won the day with a convincing 4-1 victory. Frank played 20 games in the 1950-51 season.

There was no sense among the players that they were making a general statement by not accepting terms. It seemed to be a personal matter. They thought that they deserved more. One exception to this was Malcolm Allison. His yearly objection to the wage he was offered was part of his usual policy of generally challenging the management of the club. It is difficult to say how much Allison objected to authority in general, but he did genuinely find a great deal of the management practice at West Ham was wrong or just stupid.

Frank O'Farrell, was, and still is, a thoughtful, intelligent man. He discusses many things in terms of principles. Interestingly, he never gained the reputation as a troublemaker, the allegation sometimes levelled at Allison. Yet he was at least as forthright about his position. Maybe he had learned other tactics from his experience of coming to London from a very different culture.

"When I first came to London I stayed in digs with two other players from Cork United, Tommy Moroney and Danny McGowan, then I got digs on my own in Nigel Road, Forest Gate. The Club looked for family lodgings. It kept the players happy and out of trouble and made it easier to recruit new Irish players."

When he first came to the East End, Frank thought the Cockneys were speaking a different tongue altogether, and the host community seemed to have as much trouble with the pace and brogue of his speech, he recalled.

"I had to learn a different language. It was hard work to understand the Cockney accent and everyone else had to work on my Irish accent. I had to talk more slowly. But

I found East London a friendly place. The Club was friendly too; it had good standards. There was respect for older people, W. J. Cearns and Charlie Paynter for example."

Frank recalled that Paynter's office was at the top of the stairs."This was a good idea, if you were a bit knackered after training you were out of breath and sweating by the time you got to him. Not the best state to be in for negotiation. We always called him 'Mr Paynter'. One day I went up to see the manager about getting a chance in the first team. I was quiet, but I would speak up for myself. Players were not always as honest with one another about each other's progress as the manager would be. The players supported one another, had sympathy for each other. They would say, to encourage you, that you were playing well enough to get a game, when perhaps this wasn't always the case. The manager told me that I didn't have enough experience. I asked how you could get experience if you never got in the team. I said that the Battle of Britain pilots hadn't had the experience. He took my point but I still didn't get a game. But he had listened to me and although he didn't agree with me, I respected the manager's point of view."

West Ham realised that Frank, at the age of 20, needed a home situation that understood the needs of his culture and religion. Frank remembered the support provided by the Club Secretary, Frank Cearns, who had converted to Catholicism, and this helped the Irish lads. "He'd make sure we knew the times for Mass and so on." Religion was more important to some of the Irish players than their nationality. They met other Catholics at social functions as well as at church. O'Farrell joined the Catholic Action Group and assisted in making its census of the local Catholic population. During one interview he realised how closely some people paid attention to West Ham. One woman told him that she would start coming to Mass if he made the first team."She kept her promise and also started bringing her husband who wasn't even a Catholic."

O'Farrell didn't view the almost annual rejection of his wage as a kind of symbolic rebellion against the Club. He felt he deserved more money. He was making a statement to the manager and the chairman about his own worth and saying that they should not take him for granted. West Ham players of the Fifties, the same men who demonstrated such great independence from management in their attitude towards football, did not feel they were being abused by the wage system under which they worked. Most of them reported that they were at least satisfied with their wage. Dick Walker probably summed up not only the position of West Ham players but most professional footballers at the time. "We didn't think a lot about money…but we were doing a lot better than most of the people we knew."

As Frank recalled; "There were over 40 players in the first-team squad. I had to wait two years for my chance. With squads of that size, you had to be a very exceptional player, and a bit lucky, in terms of steering clear of injury, to get into the first team. The maximum wage kept us near to the public. I had negotiated £9 all year but most players got less in the summer, £7 to £8. Nevertheless, I had to get part-time jobs, which kept you close to the supporters. Of course, you'd also see them going to and from the ground and we would talk to them when shopping and so on."

Ted Fenton gave Frank his first chance in September 1950, against FA Cup holders Arsenal in Charlie Paynter's benefit match. Many important dignitaries from the Football Association and the Football League attended. The evening was a festive occasion with many old players present, including those who had played in the 1923 Cup Final. It was a well contested match, attended by 18,000 fans who saw the Hammers win 3-1. Frank recalled; "I had my tea at my digs and went off to watch the game. When I got there I was told I was playing. I was about fourth choice and was only in because of injuries to other players. I was up against Reg Lewis and had a good game. "Charlie Paynter always wore a tie stud. He was a very dapper man. Sometimes the players would rub themselves down with oil on cold days. If it got on their shorts, then he would tell them to change. He got people looking right. He didn't like to see players going out to play in kit that was wrinkled or creased."

It wasn't just Charlie Paynter who subjected the players to some meticulous scrutiny. Frank remembered; "The crowd was close to the team, not only in terms of the pitch, and would give you some stick at times. Once I was caught in possession and someone shouted out; 'Finishing your Murray Mint, Frank?' This was a reference to the old advertisement; 'Murray Mints, Murray Mints, Too good to hurry mints.'"

Frank remembered a particularly poignant demonstration by the supporters standing on the terraces of the North Bank. "During one game everyone in the North Bank sat down. It was a kind of protest. It was a sunny day and we were involved in a pretty dire match that had failed to produce a goal."

One supporter who has stuck in Frank's mind was 'Mr Smith'. "He would habitually take his position in the Chicken Run. He always stood on the halfway line. When opponents attacked he would shout; 'Shut the gate, shut the gate' in his broad Cockney accent."

1950-51 – Football is just a reflection of life

Although Frank had his challenges at Upton Park, he reflects on his time at West Ham with affection. His experience of Charlie Paynter, his relationship with the fans, the wider community and his fellow players helped him discern a particular ethos that enveloped the Club. It affected the way the team played and how the side was supported. It informed his opinion that 'football is just a reflection of life'. West Ham were what West Ham were; of a time and a place, created by people of a particular, and in many ways peculiar, type, living in the same social environment as the Club. Even if you have no interest in the game, if you live within a ten-mile radius of Upton Park, you can't help knowing about the Club and be affected by its quintessence. West Ham, the football club, grew out of its locality. At the same time it helped to define the character of the area, being the most powerful and material aspect of its identity. Likewise, the East End gave the football club its unique persona.

So, Frank O'Farrell was right when he said that football is just a reflection of life. But football also plays a part in shaping the life of a community and the whole of a society wherein football is a ubiquitous presence. This shows that the relationship between West Ham and its players was based on more than wages. The wage demonstrated how highly the board rated a player, but there were other rewards including benefits - a system of payment based on service - which could be offered to a player and not go against FA or League regulations. There was also a system for assisting with travel expenses and the Club took on responsibility for housing players; the latter also became a form of player reward. By 1950, West Ham owned 18 properties. As soon as a player vacated a flat or a house, there were requests to move into it. Rent in most cases was below £1 10s (£1.50) a week. The houses cost between £500 and £1,600 and individual players negotiated rent and terms. Occasionally the Club helped with furnishing, decoration and maintenance. This extended the paternalism of the board, who had a tradition of exercising disciplinary control over the off-field activities of the players. They were particularly concerned with the temptation of drink. A system of fines for drinking and other misconduct was introduced with the founding of the club. This must have excused Syd King, who was known to appreciate a generous suck at the sauce bottle.

A disputed goal ended West Ham's Cup hopes at Stoke after a third-round home win over Cardiff City. This was about the time when Fenton brought Malcolm Allison to Upton Park from Charlton for £7,000; Fenton's first buy, independent of Charlie Paynter. From the start Allison brought a phenomenal appetite for a remarkable understanding of the game. He was willing to push people and was the antithesis of what had come to be recognised as the traditional West Ham player. Some of his colleagues felt he showed little patience or regard for them - and he certainly did not take the making of mistakes lightly. However, he raised the skill level of the players around him. He was impatient with the club and appeared to be unconcerned about the reaction that he got from those he had no time for. He disregarded some fellow professionals, did his best to ignore the manager and all but dismissed members of the board, considering them little more than an annoyance.

For all this, the fans admired Allison's ability to motivate and inspire the team, although they may not have always appreciated his methods. His influence could be seen in many other players. There is not doubt that Allison's arrival at Upton Park was to have long-term effects, the vibrations of which could still be felt in West Ham's successful sides right up to the mid-1960s. Ron Greenwood, the man who presided over those golden years, confirmed this. Greenwood, no admirer of Allison's approach, recognised the effects of the older school of Malcolm Allison, Noel Cantwell and company.

However, there were other players feeding into the body of knowledge being developed at Upton Park. For example, a number of players were gaining representative honours. Frank O'Farrell, having come to the notice of his national side after playing for the Football Combination against the Brussels League, gained the first of his nine Republic of Ireland caps in 1952; he played seven international games while with West Ham. His full international debut was made against a talented Austrian side. He recalled; "I brought back a lot from playing for Ireland. That and playing against clubs like Inter Milan which opened up our vision. We played sides from all over the world, mainly because we had to use the floodlights."

Under Fenton, with the influence of Allison, the Hammers were becoming the adventurous, groundbreakers of football. Frank looked back to the first time he played against his old club after moving to Preston; "The Preston players were amazed to see West Ham coming out in beige track suits. They warmed up! I didn't always see eye to eye with him, but Ted was a bit of an innovator. He could learn and his time as a PE instructor in the forces had given him much more dimension than the previous generation of managers; he was similar to the likes of Matt Busby in this respect."

Frank explained his departure from Upton Park; "I didn't ask to leave West Ham, but Preston wanted a left-half and Ted needed a centre-forward." Despite the annual pay negotiations Frank had with the club, he was happy at West Ham. "West Ham was a community club", he recalled; "the conditions of employment kept us close to the public. Not like now. Most of the players lived locally; the single lads in digs. We would often go to the cinema together. The Granada was a good deal at East Ham; two films and a stage show for 1s 9d [about 8p]. We didn't have cars. For the most part we'd walk to the ground, although we got free rides on the trolley bus if the conductor recognised us. Because of the rationing, the club gave a free lunch to the players at the Denmark Arms, a few minutes walk from the Granada. I would bring my landlady back butter and chocolate from Ireland - there was no rationing there. I would also bring back clothes. I brought back a nice sports jacket once and flogged it. I used to go round to Jim Barrett junior's house to watch television. He married young. There were very few televisions about then."

While television was yet to become the mass provider of news and current affairs it was later to be, the radio and newspapers kept people appraised about events in Korea. In November, United Nations forces had been obliged to undertake a concerted retreat. MacArthur replied with another big push, this time to conclude the war once and for all. But at the end of the month, Chinese forces crossed the Yalu River in large numbers and had soon driven the UN troops back to the 38th parallel. On 28 December, the Chinese were in the South.

The Korean War had now polarised itself along East-West lines, with two great ideologies that produced the Cold War facing each other. To the north were the Communist forces of China and North Korea with large numbers of Soviet advisors. To the south were the forces of the West, mainly American and South Korean, but with contingents from Britain, the Commonwealth and other Western States.

Chinese expansionism also affected other states at this time. On 24 October, China announced the movement of its forces into Tibet, penetrating as far as Lhasa, the Tibetan Holy City. On 13 November, Tibet appealed to the United Nations for aid against Chinese aggression. However, the Chinese had moved at an opportune moment with the UN so taken up with happenings in Korea.

On Christmas Day, a Terry Woodgate hat-trick gave the Hammers a 3-1 win at Upton Park against Leeds. It was also a happy Christmas Day for Sugar Ray Robinson. He beat the German, Hans Stretz in the fifth round. This was his fifth win in a triumphant European tour. He was to win the world middleweight championship two months later. As Robinson and West Ham were celebrating, Scottish Nationalist activists were heaving the Stone of Scone out of Westminster Abbey, where it had been under the Coronation Chair for 690 years. One wonders if Alex Salmond would be up to that.

It was early summer when I made my way to see Harry Kinsell. He lived in a suburban district of the Black Country, very close to where he was born. "Dad was a miner. There was an open coal mine at Cannock. My mum and dad lived here, about 200 yards away."

Harry, a fast, intelligent defender in the days when full-backs were not supposed to be found too far away from their goalkeeper, came to the Boleyn Ground from Reading for £5,250. He told me; "Harry Hooper senior came to watch me play. I had played against Eric Parsons and blotted him out of the game. Charlie Paynter told me that was the best defensive game he'd seen. I came to West Ham because Reading were almost bankrupt and had to sell a player."

When he got to Upton Park, Harry had to find work outside of football. "You had to. Out of season you only got £6 a week. I did some work for Salter's, as a driver. They sold prams and things for small children and babies. A lot of players worked at Seaman's, the electronics firm, just through the foot tunnel at Woolwich."

Harry was brought into the West Ham side early in 1951 as left-back replacement for Jack Yeomanson. Harry had started his football career with West Brom, his local club, helping them to promotion to Division One in 1949, playing outside-left. He moved from The Hawthorns for a record £8,000 transfer to Bolton when Len Millard won his place with the Baggies.

Looking back at his time with the Trotters Harry told me; "At Bolton, we'd go for a road run and stop for a pint on the way," he chuckled. During the war he had also played for Grimsby, Middlesbrough and Blackpool, winning a Football League championship medal and appearing in the North Cup Final which the Seasiders lost at Villa Park.

In his 30th year, when he came to the Boleyn Ground, Harry had played in three Victory internationals during 1946, games which celebrated the end of World War Two. He appeared in a 4-1 win over Switzerland, a 1-0 win over Ireland, and in a 1-0 defeat by Wales, in the first international match played at The Hawthorns. Harry showed me the very grand certificate he was awarded for one of these matches - the teams were not given caps. He played alongside Tommy Lawton and Raich Carter. "Carter and Peter Doherty, when they were both with Derby, were the best players I ever saw."

1950-51 – Football is just a reflection of life

In some books it is claimed that Harry Kinsell was sent off in one of these internationals. He asked me to clear this up; he was never, in his entire career, at any level, sent off. He explained; "We used to play Coventry in the local derbies at West Brom. George Lowrie, who was playing for Wales, was a Coventry player. He kicked me and I told him; "Next time Georgie, I'll give it yer!" Harry held up his fist.

But he was never known as an overly physical player at Upton Park. He recalled; "There wasn't much difference between Reading and West Ham, although West Ham did have the training ground at Chigwell. We'd go there Tuesdays and Wednesdays. Steve Forde helped me settle in at West Ham. We were both full-backs. I lived in the street behind Steve, Central Gardens, and we used to walk to work together. The players' haunt was Cassatarri's [a café, a few seconds walk from the south end of the Boleyn Ground]. You knew the fans from Cassatarri's - they were always fair to me. They'd be queueing out of the gates for autographs."

Harry, who often skippered the Irons, played 105 games for the first team in his five years with the Hammers. His debut was at Boleyn Ground, at the end of January, in a 3-2 defeat at the hands of Blackburn. "I thought; 'That's a bloody good start.'" He scored twice for the first team. They were both Upton Park goals. The first came in 2-1 defeat at the hands of Birmingham in April 1951. Gil Merrick, an England international 'keeper, was between the sticks for the Blues. Harry netted again against Everton in a 3-3 draw in November of the same year. "I gave Jimmy Andrews the ball down the wing. He put it back to me and I hit it and it went into the net."

For Harry Kinsell, West Ham were a friendly, happy club. "That's the reason I stayed. In that respect it was like West Brom. There were a lot of local lads. I was close to Frank O'Farrell, Steve Ford, Bert Hawkins and Doug Bing was a very nice man. Charlie Paynter was a nice man. George Wright took me under his wing when I first came to the Club. There was always an end-of-season dinner-dance. Some of the lads really liked a bet. I went with them to the dogs a few times, but I'd have a couple of bets and then stop. The likes of Jackie Dick, Noel Cantwell and Malcolm Allison though, they'd bet on two flies going up the wall."

I asked Harry who he regarded as the outstanding player at Upton Park in his era. Without hesitation he replied; "I was!" We both laughed. Then he told me; "Ernie Gregory was a good 'keeper, Tommy Southren could play, as could Frank O'Farrell and Tommy Moroney…you had to play in deep mud, in steel toe cap boots, with a wet, heavy ball." I think Harry was saying something about today's game here. The best of so many players was never seen because of the very poor state of grounds in those days. It was a tremendous waste in many ways. Harry went on; "The most memorable moment was scoring that last goal, and I enjoyed the trips to Brighton prior to cup games. I had some good years there."

It was around the time that Harry Kinsell took his first kick in defence of Ernie Gregory's goal that the seesaw war in Korea went against the United Nations. As the world moved into 1951, the Chinese mounted a major offensive and the UN American forces were again forced to retreat. The Communists soon broke through and four days after the offensive they had captured Seoul.

General MacArthur was growing impatient with the progress of the war but President Truman was aware of the symbolic importance of this East-West conflict and made it clear that the Americans would fight on. And not everything was going according to plan for the Chinese; their lines of communication were stretched and the American Air Force was mounting massive bombing attacks. The Chinese were being pushed back towards the 38th parallel and the UN forces once more prepared to fight for Seoul.

Before the first month of the year was over, the United Nations forces were able to stem the joint Chinese/North Korean Army sweeping down from the North and hold them near the 38th parallel.

Tom Jenkinson, a local Labour councillor and last mayor of West Ham (before it merged with East Ham to become Newham) became chairman of the West Ham United Supporters' Club in 1951. In 1923, the year of West Ham's first Wembley appearance, Tom's parents moved to Poplar Workhouse - "A place more like a warehouse than anything else...where kids like me used to wait for crusts of bread and scraps." It had taken the West Ham board many years to recognise the Supporters' Club, but the Fifties were to see the start of a new relationship. In many ways the board, with Reg Pratt at the helm, were about as far socially from the Supporters' Club, led by Jenkinson, as one could imagine, but the relationship worked, and throughout the decade the Supporters' Club raised a tremendous amount of finance for the Football Club.

It was shortly after Christmas, just getting dark, when I arrived at the home of Harry and Meg Hooper. They were in the middle of redecorating. This didn't stop them making me comfortable. Harry was still a compact man. His was one of the first interviews I carried out for this book, so I was a little nervous anyway, but Harry is

1950-51 – Football is just a reflection of life

a legend at Upton Park, a true hero of the fans, many of whom thought that he was never adequately replaced when he left to go to Wolves. He looked fit and sturdy, but spoke in a soft North-Eastern accent, responding thoughtfully to my questions.

Harry comes from something of a footballing dynasty. Harry senior, a defender, played professional football for 15 years with the same club. "Dad captained Sheffield United in the 1936 Cup Final, when they lost 1-0 to Arsenal. My mum and dad lived with my grandparents for a time. Mum worked in their shop, that's where I was born. My brother came along nine years later."

Harry senior spent three years with Hartlepools United after his days at Bramall Lane. "I went to school in Durham, Nevilles Cross. Mr Trotter encouraged me. I played in goal as a boy. As a young player I'd play anywhere from goalie to centre-forward. I once played against Harry Cripps [one time hard-man Hammer and all-time Millwall legend]. Everyone told me to watch out but he was fine. I was a great admirer of Stanley Matthews and Johnny Spuhler at Sunderland. I would go to Newcastle and Sunderland on alternate weeks, but Sunderland was my team."

Harry began playing for Hylton Colliery in the Durham League and as an amateur for Sunderland. "But Dad wouldn't let Hylton Colliery sign me for Sunderland. He thought that young players weren't given much of a chance at Roker. I played for Durham youth in the semi-final of the county championship. We were up against Essex at Fulham. We lost 2-1 and Ally Noakes scored with a blinding left-foot shot. After that Chelsea and Middlesbrough came after me." However, Harry's dad was appointed trainer at Upton Park in November 1950, so naturally the young winger chose to join the Hammers. Harry senior took charge of the Combination team at the Boleyn Ground, steering them to a League and Cup double in 1954. He went on to manage Halifax after working at West Ham.

In 1951, shortly after coming to Upton Park, Harry junior started his National Service. "When I got called up I was stationed at Crookham in Surrey. I was picked to play for the Army before I went in. Colonel Prince was in charge. I was in the Medical Corps. I didn't have much to do with medicine though. After a while I was transferred to Woolwich." This allowed Harry to continue to develop his career at Upton Park. "In my first game for West Ham [it was Barnsley's 1951 visit Upton Park] I laid on the cross for Bill Robinson's first goal." Bill scored two that early February day; Gerry Gazzard matched him to give the Irons an 4-2 win. According to Harry; "We always played good football at West Ham - always!"

Harry played 130 games for West Ham, netting 44 times. He opened his account in front of nearly 26,000 roaring Cockneys, on 23rd March 1950, scoring the Irons' goal in the 1-1 draw with Swansea Town. Whilst at West Ham, he played six times for the England 'B' side, twice for England Under-23s and twice for the Football League. The first game, in 1954, was against the Irish League. In the second match, the following year, Harry faced the defenders from the Scottish League. He got into the senior England squad, but never played a full international. "I played with Matthews and Finney with the England squad", he recalled. He put his finger on the reason why England were usually so strong at home, but never made much of an impact in tournaments like the World Cup. "Foreigners were better ball players, they had better pitches."

For Harry, West Ham fans were fair and gave credit to away teams. "I remember when we played a German team they sang; 'Hands, knees and bumps-a-daisy!' When they thought I didn't have enough to do, they'd shout out things like; 'Go make the tea, Harry!'" Meg is from East London. The couple married in 1955, while Harry was with West Ham. She had been a teacher before her retirement. She remembered; "I went to the matches with my dad. We never missed a game in the Chicken Run."

According to Harry, West Ham was a friendly club "I couldn't say anything against them. I was friendly with Andy Malcolm. There were about 70 players on the staff. Tommy Southren was on the wing when I joined. I was 17 when Parsons and Southren were injured. Terry Woodgate, like me, could play on either wing. Dick Walker was a good captain, he would help bring the youngsters on."

Like many of the players, Harry was given a Club house, in close proximity to his colleagues. There was a community of football families nestling around the Boleyn Ground. This built team, family and community spirit. "I lived quite close to the ground, in Thorne Road, before I got married and afterwards we lived in Wanstead. West Ham played for each other, they played as a team."

Harry touched on the appeal of the game in the early Fifties. "We played Huddersfield in the Cup. It was thick mud - Upton Park had a horrible pitch - but it was an exciting match." This was in 1954 and Harry got two in West Ham's 4-0 victory. His mind moved on to 1956, his last season with the Hammers. "We played Spurs in fifth round. John Dick got three. I think we would have won the Cup that year if we had held on; we were 3-1 up in the first half. Billy Dare was sent off. They scored from the penalty. We drew 3-3 and lost the replay 2-1.

"I enjoyed playing in the First Division when I went to Wolves, but I didn't want to leave West Ham." The feeling was mutual as far as the fans were concerned. A supporter of the time remembered; "When West Ham sold Hooper it confirmed most people's feelings. The supporters seemed to have no expectations of the team. When Hooper went to Wolves, Dad swore indoors, which was rare. West Ham was seen, even by the supporters, as a middle-of-the-table Second Division club. Many people saw the Club as being about the money."

As this attitude indicates, those who watched the team week in, week out, felt let down by the sale of Hooper. Harry recalled the initial stages of negotiations about his move. "I was to meet Stan Cullis at Paddington. I felt a hand on my shoulder and it was Jimmy Anderson, the Spurs manager. He asked me to come to Spurs instead. Wolves were doing better at the time, next to top, Spurs were near the bottom, in danger of going down. So I went to Wolves. It was the worst thing I did. I was top goalscorer in my first season, from the wing." Meg said; "When Harry was at Wolves, the papers said I wanted the bright lights!" Meg certainly didn't seem like the type to be in search of bright lights, and if she was, despite Wanderers being probably the most famous British club of the era, she would have been unlikely to find many in mid-Fifties Wolverhampton. In fact it was West Ham who got the bright lights. Part of the £25,000 transfer fee the club got from the sale of Harry Hooper in March 1956, a record for a wing-forward, was spent on erecting new floodlights at Upton Park.

Harry was certainly a real favourite with the Irons' supporters. He was fast and could hit and cross a ball. "I was a winger who scored with either foot." It was obvious that Harry still watched the Hammers closely. As I said my goodbyes, he made the point that it was ridiculous to play a natural winger like Australian Stan Lazaridis so deep. At the time, the Hammers manager Harry Redknapp was using 'Stan the Man' as a wingback. Hooper had a point, Lazaridis tackled with all the venom of Po from the Telly-Tubbies. In fact he was.. .no, lets not go there.

I left Harry and Meg not quite believing that I'd had tea with the flying flanker of Upton Park. The man who had sent in more crosses than Buffy the Vampire Slayer. Wide-man Harry, King of the Wing...Super Hooper!

Although UN troops recaptured Seoul on 14th March, the conflict in Korea had settled down to an uneasy stalemate. This was abruptly broken when MacArthur threatened to invade China. As he was already on record as having wanted to use the atomic bomb against his opponent, this threat gave the war an alarming new dimension.

It infuriated Truman who wanted to contain the conflict and had been increasingly annoyed by MacArthur's political statements. In April, he sacked the Commander-in-Chief. This caused an enormous outcry in America but at least focused the minds of both sides on the dangers of the situation. Soon the combatants began to look for ways to end the war.

West Ham finished the 1950-51 season with a dull goalless draw against Cardiff at Upton Park. Just over three weeks after the Hammers finished in an unexciting 13th place in Division Two, the Festival of Britain Pleasure Gardens opened in Battersea Park. This went some way to temporarily lifting the post-war gloom still prevalent in Britain, well in London at least. The Festival was opened by the King and Queen at the beginning of May and was an immediate success and not only with Londoners. People from all over the country (and the world) flocked to it in their tens of thousands. The Festival's architectural style was very influential and changed public tastes permanently. Skylon was the name suggested by poet Margaret Sheppard Fidler for the vertical feature of the South Bank. Symbolising the spirit of new hope, it illuminated from within at night and appeared to hang in the sky with no visible means of support; a bit like Bill Robinson when meeting a Harry Hooper cross...

We were called 'Fenton's Furies'

Ted Fenton was the manager of West Ham throughout the Fifties. He is the man who history will credit with building the championship side and the manager who laid the foundations for modern football at Upton Park. As Derek Parker reflected; "I don't know if he ever got full credit but he was the manager who got them promotion."

The methods and systems that were first experimented with at Upton Park in the mid/late Fifties would be enhanced by Ron Greenwood, along with players brought up in the innovative environment of West Ham in the Fifties - the likes of Bobby Moore and John Bond. West Ham's seminal European Cup-winners' Cup campaign of 1964-65 was a product of the same. This was only the second-ever English victory in a European competition and the first (and last) by an all-English team (only English players were involved in the West Ham side in every round). What might be called, the 'West Ham' culture, influenced the reincarnation of the English game in 1966 and, by association, was the seed of the early European Cup successes of Manchester United and Liverpool.

This analysis makes Fenton to English soccer what Babbage, the man who developed the first computer, is to information technology. However, while the Boleyn Ground is arguably the cradle of English football in the second half of the 20th Century, seeing Ted Fenton as midwife to the same may be too straightforward. Indeed, it is not even clear how much of an impact he had on the development of even the Second Division Championship side. The analysis of his role reveals a great deal about West Ham in the Fifties, but also demonstrates how the Club was cultivated in the Sixties and Seventies.

Born close to West Ham's Upton Park home, Ted Fenton had been a prolific scorer for the Odessa Road School side. When called up by West Ham Boys he continued to hit the back of the net. He was denied an England Schoolboy cap when, having been selected for the team, the match, against Scotland, was called off due to an outbreak of smallpox. However, in 1929 he played in his country's forward line at this level, facing the Scots at Ibrox Park.

Fenton came to the Boleyn Ground as a youngster. He had left school at 14 and was pushing a cart for a living when he got the chance to play for West Ham. He was, he said 'amazed' to be offered a contract. When he got ten shillings (50p) for turning out in a practice match with the Irons he remembered thinking; "I would have paid them to let me play." He had dreamed of being in the West Ham team, but had not thought of football as a profession. As such, when travelling to matches, Ted got a tremendous thrill from showing off the shiny leather bag with 'West Ham United' emblazoned on it.

Fenton was the first youth to be signed as a ground-staff boy by West Ham. His strongest memories were the 'flair' with which Syd King seemed to do everything, the army-style inspections of Mr Pierson, the assistant manager, and Charlie Paynter being a ubiquitous presence around the Club. There were the repeated trips to the Boleyn pub to buy cases of beer for King, an errand that carried a ten-shilling tip from the manager. He recalled that there seemed to be the constant cry to 'go and get Fenton' to undertake a whole range of tasks. Everybody ranked over him and they could all find jobs for him to do.

On 5th November 1932, Ted made his debut for West Ham. It was the game against Bradford City at Valley Parade. He took the field as centre-half. Although the immortal Vic Watson scored for West Ham, the East Londoners were thrashed 5-1. Ted was to be on the losing side five times in his first six outings that season. However, in his dozen games during the spring of 1934, Fenton was on the winning side six times and got a hat-trick against Bury at Upton Park.

Ted was to make his mark at wing-half, creating a regular place for himself up to the outbreak of World War Two. Between 1932 and 1939, Fenton made 172 appearances for the first team, scoring 18 goals. In 1940 he won a Football League War Cup winners' medal and played five times for England in wartime internationals, between serving as a PT instructor with the Army in North Africa and Burma. He played 211 wartime games for West Ham, many in defence, in a team which included the likes of Jim Barrett senior and the superb Len Goulden. Fenton netted 43 times during this phase of his career.

Like Ernie Gregory and so many other promising West Ham players, the war robbed Fenton of the chance to fulfil his true potential as a player. If it had not been for the intervention of Hitler, Ted may have established himself as an international, although he was never in the class of other pre-war West Ham and England men like Goulden and Vic Watson. He left Upton Park for the first time in the summer of 1946, to become player-manager of Southern League Colchester United, a club, which at that time had little more than a decade of history. He guided the Essex club to the fifth round of the FA Cup in 1947-48, bringing them national fame.

We were called 'Fenton's Furies'

A number of managerial opportunities were to arise in the light of this success, including the vacant job at West Bromwich Albion following the retirement of Fred Everiss. Some writers have argued that this would have meant Ted moving straight into a 'top' First Division job, and that this is why he didn't take the offer, not wanting the pressure or responsibility of running a club in the top flight. However, these authors appear to forget that West Brom did not win the Second Division championship until 1949, following 11 years in the wilderness. At this point Jack Smith had been manager since Everiss left The Hawthorns in 1948. Smith was with the West Brom up to April 1952, when Jessie Carver took over. During this period the Throstles had never been out of the bottom half of Division One. One has to look a little more closely at Albion's intentions in 1948 to get a clue as to why Ted turned them down. That said, other than his time in the forces, Fenton was very much a southern based man; it is debatable how much he might have wanted to head north beyond his East London/West Essex homeland.

Ted also seemed destined to return to his former club. The story was that his success at Colchester did not create the opening for him, but it accelerated an offer that might otherwise have been a few years in coming. According to Fenton, he immediately contacted Paynter for advice about how to handle the offer from West Brom, Paynter, having been Fenton's manager, the man who had worked to develop Ted from a novice into a veteran player. Ted claimed that Paynter had advised him to decline the offer from the Baggies and come back to West Ham on the understanding that he would take over when Paynter retired. In effect he would start as assistant manager in what had become a rather mediocre Second Division outfit.

Fentons's starting wage at Colchester had been £15. By 1948 this had risen slightly. He would have looked for an increase in his salary at West Brom. His starting salary at West Ham was £15. This, in itself, was peculiar. Malcolm Musgrove laughingly recalled; "Ted still had his first penny." And according to one professional, who played alongside Ted and who was present throughout Fenton's career at Upton Park; "Ted was a very selfish man. He was always looking for ways and means of getting whatever was going in the way of financial things."

This conclusion was confirmed by a story told by Derek Parker; "Ted and I were still living down here in Colchester. At one point we used to meet the rest of the squad down at Chelmsford. We would get on the front of the train together. Ted knew that the ticket collector would always start from the back. Halfway through the journey Ted would get out and go to the back. He was a shrewd one was Ted."

According to Ken Tucker; "Ted was all self...Fenton earned out of everything he did - he had a terrible name. Charlie Paynter used to give waiters on the trains or the coach drivers a fiver, which was a good bit then. When Fenton took over he gave them fifty bob [£2-50]. I think he still booked a fiver though."

Malcolm Allison has similar memories of Ted's 'astuteness'. "Ted Fenton would cheat you out of anything. We played an England amateur side; there were 22,000 at the match. The FA always gave you £5 to play against an FA team. We used to get £2 as a bonus. When we went to get our money we only got the fiver. They said it was £3 for playing and £2 bonus - they tried to do us out of two quid! I went to see Ted Fenton the next day, looking for my two quid. But he'd gone. When the players came in the dressing-room the next day, I told them; 'Don't get stripped, don't get changed. We're not playing unless we get that two quid, the twenty-six quid he owes us.' So, we're all sitting there - we're playing Notts Forest this game. Fenton always used to come down an hour before kick-off; he didn't come down this day. Billy Moore, the trainer, rang up to Ted. Bill said; 'You'd better come down, they're not getting stripped.' He came down and said; 'What's going on?' I said; 'You done us out of twenty-six quid.' He went upstairs, come straight back down and gave us the money."

It seems that Malcolm was too clever for Fenton, but Ken Tucker picked up some more information later. "I'd been selected for the England squad to play Brazil. I went to train at the Bank of England ground, along with the likes of Nat Lofthouse, Billy Wright and Stanley Matthews. Walter Winterbottom wanted to use me in the training - he reckoned I played a bit like the Brazilian winger. The Arsenal players told me that they had got ten guineas for a game with England Amateurs; that was the FA's rate for such matches. When West Ham had played against them Ted only gave us £5. Apparently the cheque had gone to Ted and he paid us in cash. I didn't get in the team, but England won 4-1."

Tommy Southren recalled; "Ted Fenton, when he played golf, would snatch the ball when it was two feet from the hole and say; 'Mine!'" So, while Ted could not be described as an out-and-out cheat, he was clearly a man that was able to make his own advantage. Things didn't change much over time. Vic Keeble told; "The 1958 side did have a get together for Ted Fenton's 70th birthday." Bert Hawkins recalled; "When we got to there we were asked to put in £20 each to buy him a watch!"

Given Fenton's seeming proclivity for matters financial, why did he move to West Ham? It is likely that when he had telephoned Paynter, apparently about the job with West Brom, he would have realised that the West Ham manager might be contemplating retirement. It was reported that when Paynter had announced his intention to retire, his advice about a possible successor was; "Go and get Fenton." The change from Paynter to Fenton thus seemed a fairly smooth process as John Bond confirmed. "Charlie Paynter signed me on. From what I remember it was a pretty smooth transition when Ted took over." However, according to Malcolm Allison; "Paynter didn't want to leave; he was a dominant character." And Eddie Chapman's perspective didn't reinforce the idea that there had been an easy handing on of power. "The harmony wasn't as great as it might have been between Charlie and Ted. Charlie didn't like the manner in which Ted would shout and holler." Eddie had been in the same side as Ted when both played for the Irons. He recalled; "When Ted played for West Ham during the war, Charlie told him to 'cut out that sergeant-major talk!'

"Ted would have probably made a good captain, but he would wave his hands all over the place and really shout like a sergeant-major." So, there is a second question about Fenton's return to Upton Park, following the mystery surrounding the post at West Bromwich Albion. Why did West Ham offer Fenton the job? This latter puzzle seems the most straightforward within the whole conundrum. Fenton suited West Ham. He wasn't an outsider. He was used to the way the club operated its traditions (or foibles). He would not need to be inducted, and if any insurance were needed, his period 'in waiting' would provide this.

West Ham had a habit of recruiting former employees to senior positions. For Malcolm Allison this was the result of lack of ambition and steel within the boardroom. "The directors had no sense of how to achieve anything or to be successful. The club was like the poor who always make excuses for not improving their situation…It's an excuse to call it loyalty because it really means they're afraid of outsiders. They're people who live in a cut off village, almost like an iron cage, all their lives and appoint their own people." For Allison, the appointment of Fenton exemplified the malaise at West Ham, the 'fear' on the part of the club's leadership to appoint anybody they think might be better than they are.

Ron Greenwood, who became manager of West Ham in 1961, could be understood as agreeing with Allison when he said of West Ham; "One of the things wrong with this club is an over-abundance of loyalty…" However, he did, confusingly, go on to ask; "But what's wrong with that?" Greenwood saw loyalty being less damaging than a lack of the same. He went on to reflect, a little in the vein of Alf Garnett unfortunately, that; "This country wouldn't be in the bloody state it's in right now if there was a bit more loyalty like there has been at West Ham."

Loyalty is a central value within East End culture. To 'stick up for yer own' is a tenet developed out of need, from an historical background premised on poverty and being overlooked by a cold, cruel and oppressive state. Noel Cantwell, who was to succeed Allison as club captain, said; "The Club reflected how important it was to have a sense of loyalty to people...They kept people around, but after all, some in-breeding isn't a bad thing. It gave you a sense of roots. There were people around like Paynter who could tell you what West Ham was like."

The distinguished journalist, Bernard Joy, saw West Ham as an anachronism in modern football, a place 'where loyalty is all important'. This may well have been true, but 'loyalty' has benefits on at least two sides. Fenton was a 'West Ham' man, like Paynter before him and Lyall, Bonds, Redknapp and Curbishley after him. Being one of 'us', the knowledge, understanding and tolerance this implies, is a major asset for an employer. The fans have shown great loyalty over the years to 'their manager', 'he', apart from Greenwood, who was always a remote figure, and the brief and embarrassing reign of Lou Macari, had always been 'one of us', and worthy of support just because of that.

As such, despite all the adversity of supporting the Hammers, the supporters, until the departure of Redknapp, could be assured that the West Ham boss would be the only manager in the Premier League to know all the words to *Roll out the Barrel* and *I'm Forever Blowing Bubbles*. Indeed, under the watches of Roeder, Pardew, Zola and Grant, not a few supporters could be heard to yell from the stands 'Bring back 'Arry'" (at least until Redknapp tied his ginger colours to the Spurs mast). This appeared to suggest we preferred predictable mediocrity, massive over-spending and excuses ('we're down to the bare bones!') from the loom of the familiar, to the whiff of progress by way of the different. Much the same culture has manifested itself recently with many Hammers fans feeling aggrieved at the prospect of leaving confines of Upton Park for the Olympic Stadium, a potential move that has, by some, been described as a 'betrayal'. This is of course understandable, and I, as much as anyone I think, want our manager to have 'worn the shirt' - who didn't want Brooking to become a permanent manager in 2003 (apart from Trev himself that is)? And if the Boleyn Ground could be turned into a 60,000 seater, with adequate car parking and other services, for less than the few tens of millions the potential move to Stratford might cost the Club, I'd be up for that. But that is not the way of reality.

Ted Fenton's willingness to become heir apparent at West Ham was not altogether surprising. He had been part of the club for most of his life; he was a local boy made good. Legendary gossip has it that the board had marked out Fenton as the Club's eventual manager long before the end of his playing days, and that he was quite aware of this, having a connection with West Ham from boyhood; Ted was a sort of embodiment of the Club, it's values and conventions.

One of eight children of a Forest Gate policeman, he would be taken by his dad to Upton Park. "West Ham was our club, East London's club," he remarked. "I'm a Cockney, not a proper one, but still a Cockney, and that's what West Ham is." It is difficult to say if Ted was saying that West Ham was not 'proper' Cockney, but it seems clear that he wanted to say that because he was from the East End, and of the Hammers, he would fit into the Upton Park culture. However, going back to West Ham, to stand in the shoes of Charlie Paynter, for Fenton, had many more possibilities than might have been forthcoming at the Hawthorns.

Malcolm Allison was correct in seeing Paynter was a 'dominant force' at Upton Park. In fact he was as close as one person could get to being omnipotent within the context of the Boleyn Ground. The offer to move back to West Ham might be seen as providing Fenton with straightforward security and a move up, but it also offered the opportunity of being the recipient in a power transfer of considerable proportions. On the other hand, the board of West Bromwich Albion had, on the retirement of Everiss, decided to split the coaching and administrative roles. Smith, in all but name, and later Carver, by contract, were chief coaches.

The conclusion that Fenton was swayed in his job choice by the relative influence involved in the posts on offer might seem to be based on a deal of conjecture. This can't be denied, or avoided, given the character of the Club and Ted himself. However, it is not until one studies Fenton's eventual dismissal that the probability that his ambitions lay beyond the field of play is confirmed. Maybe Fenton wasn't so much avoiding responsibility as looking to maximise his influence. In this respect it seems many 'experts' may not have done him justice. But all this retrospective, psychoanalysis could well belie the simplicity of the man. The explanation given for Ted's choice by one of the players who worked with him seems to hold more than a drop of water; "West Brom didn't offer him enough money."

However, Fenton, from the outset, threw himself into the task of changing the profile of the Club. Straight away Ted had made every effort to alter the West Ham's reputation as an 'unfashionable middle-of-the-table' Second Division side, lacking ambition, desiring only security. He and Pratt were faced with a vicious circle; West Ham's inferiority complex, which promoted a lack of ambition within the Club that in turn generated a general belief among the supporters that the Hammers wanted to avoid the perils of success and top-quality football.

Fenton used West Ham's return to the First Division as a means to develop his public persona. In 1960 he published a book, *At Home with the Hammers*, part autobiography, part West Ham folklore. The book was an example of the school of what the great American sportswriter Red Smith called the 'gee-whiz' sports writing. It did not include a single negative word about anyone or anything; in short it would have saved everyone's time if he'd have just written 'Everything is just great!' However, the tome did have prophetic elements. Ted tried to convince his readers that the Hammers were on a par with the big English clubs. This engenders a feeling of the poor boy making good, looking to show that he has always belonged in the upper echelon. Fenton wrote of his admiration for Paynter, and how he owed so much to this, his mentor. For all that he had much more in common with Paynter's predecessor, the showman Syd King.

In his book Fenton wrote that King was; "Personality plus and adored by the players. He was the Herbert Chapman of his time." Chapman, the legendary manager of Arsenal, was in charge of probably the biggest football club in the world in the pre-war period; he revolutionised the game. King, on the other hand, was a moderately successful manager of a relatively small club. He did not claim any special prowess, and certainly was not gifted in the technical aspects of the game (most of which had not been thought of in King's time). What then was Fenton getting at? King had wanted to get West Ham noticed. Chapman had done this for the Highbury club; he had built a tradition that sustained the Gunners even when results were not all they might have been. Fenton, along with many of those who played for him, saw Arsenal as the big London club, and he wanted to emulate them. The North Londoners were the standard to aim for.

Every spring Fenton would approach the board with a list of possible tours in Europe and matches that could be arranged with sides visiting England. He made contacts and organised fixtures. He pushed hard to enlarge and improve the Boleyn Ground, saying that it would both increase attendances and improve the performance of the team. In his book he wrote about 'our plans for Upton Park,' wanting 'to make

West Ham a glamour club and Upton Park London's jewel of the east'. He wanted 'to make us so ritzy that we will get the kind of reputation Arsenal had in the 1930s.'

Ted believed he could change West Ham and the role of manager at Upton Park; he believed that the function of manager at West Ham would enable him to do this. A limited coaching job at The Hawthorns did not offer this kind of potential. And if you wanted a stage with a frisson of glitz, in the 1950s, London was the place to have it rather than a place between Birmingham and Wolverhamton.

West Ham was unable or unwilling to spend appreciable amounts of money on players. As such, Ted had to find talent by creating a scheme to develop young players. To what extent West Ham depended on local players before the mid-Fifties is arguable. For Peter Lorenzo, the sportswriter, who was born about 200 yards from the ground, and who saw his first match in 1936; "It always mattered that the majority of the playing staff was local…It gave you an affinity and you liked to think it wasn't a cheque book club."

Jack Turner, who saw his first match in 1920 and worked at West Ham from 1950 to 1966, was of different opinion; "The tradition of local players never existed…The teams I watched as a young man were made up almost completely of imports. The club had more success finding players in Ireland than it had in West Ham."

Malcolm Allison's analysis is succinct; "The idea that it was built on local talent is bullshit. They never had anything, youth team or anything else, until 1956. Even then they were copying Manchester United and Chelsea." However, Noel Cantwell pointed out; "Ted was clever. He introduced the youth scheme, learning lessons from Chelsea, who would recruit young players by fair or foul means."

It was around the mid-Fiftjes that Allison became youth coach at Upton Park. The comparison with a massive club like Manchester United and the recruitment-minded Chelsea illustrates that Allison, unbeknown to him, might have been on something of the same wavelength as Fenton, as Ted did want to follow the example of the more successful clubs. Fenton was making an effort to imitate the success of other clubs within the West Ham tradition of operating on a shoestring and within the board's strict sense of propriety and control.

As such, starting in the mid-Fifties, West Ham began a concerted effort to find, sign and develop young players, from the vast pool of schoolboy football traditionally found in the East End and West Essex. From that time on, as Brian Moore recalled; "Fenton's strong point was his scouting, he spent most of his time doing this."

Ted, though, also used established players to hunt down and develop talent. The basis of the West Ham development scheme was a scouting network that covered the whole of their region of influence, and Fenton's aptitude to persuade young prospects to believe that Upton Park would be the best place for them. The watchfulness and character of the scouts provided the Irons with an edge in the race to sign local players. Wally St Pier was the exemplification of this art. Wally had more friends in the East End than any member of the West Ham organisation. These were men like Reg Revins, many of whom like the latter came from families who had for generations been steeped in the football culture of the area.

However, according to Mike Newman, this did not include Ted Fenton. "He had played in the same side as Wally St Pier and they never really got on. They had some run-ins - and Wally would always find himself watching some kid in Newcastle a few days after falling out with Ted. He didn't have much regard for Fenton."

Wally was well known in football circles. His first amateur club was Eagle Park, but he arrived at Upton Park from Ilford in April 1929, following selection for Essex, Isthmian League and FA teams. His debut in the First Division at right-half came against Leicester at the Boleyn Ground, the following October. However, for most his career he was a reserve team centre-half, spending most of his playing days as understudy to Jim Barrett senior. He managed to get 24 games in his four years as a professional. His good friend Paynter kept him on as a scout and assistant trainer after his playing days in the late Thirties. When West Ham started to scout more assertively, this big, avuncular man appeared to be omnipresent. He got alongside schoolmasters and cultivated a unique attitude and approach. Scouts frequently came across as acting covertly, often without great integrity. Terry Venables remembered; "Wally was an honest sort of guy...he gave you the full message. He was a gentleman...he became part of the family."

Wally had the knack of being able to feel at home with people and give them that impression., unlike his lieutenant Revins who struck many as a fanatic. John Bond's view was pretty typical; "It was hard not to like Wally but Reg, he was out of his mind; he spent almost every waking hour watching football. Although he found some wonderful players, his whole life was given over to it; he couldn't talk or even think about anything else. That was unhealthy." While Revins wanted to almost literally capture players, St Pier didn't see it as his job to 'sell' West Ham; Wally looked to show the player and his parents that the club wanted him. He went on to serve the Hammers for 47 years as chief scout and became the greatest star-finder in West Ham's, and maybe any club's, history. Among his many discoveries, with the help of Revins and his huge scouting network, were Moore, Hurst and Peters.

When West Ham made it into the First Division, Wally was able to tell the boys who he saw as having potential, of how the club's star players had come through the youth ranks, and point to the Club's success and the skill of its professional staff. However, Jimmy Greaves and Terry Venables, both great East End schoolboy players, did slip through the net. Rumours about the inducements offered by Chelsea were blamed. Noel Cantwell had it that; "Terry Venables started with Chelsea, but he had initially trained at West Ham." Venables remembered; "Wally was like a smashing grandad… When I signed for Chelsea the only thing that bothered me was that Wally was upset."

St Pier's powerful handshake and his honesty caused teachers and parents to trust what he was telling them. He was unable to make promises - that was for the chairman and the manager, although Wally might have left the Club if they had failed to back him up.

When the scouts identified skilful youngsters, they got in touch with the lad's teacher and then went to see his mum and dad. Fenton was called into the process when the scout believed he had a definite prospect. At that point it would not be unusual for Ted to see the player and his parents himself. This would act as an indication of how much West Ham wanted the boy. When Fenton visited a player, in one case spending days parked up the street from his home, it meant that he wanted him badly. Failures in cases like Venables and Greaves, might have led Fenton to adopt other tactics, but that would have destroyed the straight dealing ethos that St Pier had worked hard to create within the footballing community surrounding Upton Park.

Following Ted's sanction, if the player and his parents consented, the lad would come to training at Upton Park. There he would be introduced to the likes of Malcolm Allison and Noel Cantwell. Allison and Cantwell earned an extra 30 shillings (£1.50) a week for running the training on Tuesday and Thursday nights. This might be followed by an invitation to a game at the Boleyn Ground. The parents would be given a seat in the directors' box, and, following the match, be invited for drinks with Reg Pratt and Fenton. Ken Brown was probably the first of the dozens of fine players to emerge from the youth operation that many fed into and worked within, but it was Ted Fenton who initiated and breathed life into it. The culmination of the first wave youth development was the 1959 FA Youth Cup Final, that West Ham were unlucky to lose by the odd goal of three over two legs, plus extra time at Ewood Park. Mick Beesley, a member of that side (along with Andy Smillie, Bobby Moore and Derek Woodley among others) recalled; "I got on well with Ted Fenton. He had faith in me. He treated the youngsters well. We were called 'Fenton's Furies.'" The next milestone was winning the Youth Cup in 1963, with John Charles skippering the side. Nine of the 1964 FA Cup and the 1965 Cup-winners' Cup winning sides came through the youth system.

Trying to move away from the disciplined approach fostered by Paynter, Fenton seemed to want, at times, to be 'one of the boys'. This changed a little when Jack Turner was given responsibility for financial dealings with the players, but as Derek Parker pointed out; "Ted Fenton was more of a hands-on manager than Charlie Paynter. Charlie was always in the background, but was great figurehead, respected by the players, but he wasn't as close to them as Ted."

Fenton may have adopted this attitude in response to Paynter's continuing presence, both before and after Ted's appointment as manager. In a sense, Paynter was 'the boss'. Fenton did try to redress the situation at points, attempting to keep a semblance of the discipline familiar under the Paynter regime, but it did not seem to 'take' in the same way. Albert Foan recalled; "On one occasion we lost to Fulham in a reserve game, the ground was heavy. Harry Hooper senior, the trainer, told us to report for training on Monday. This wasn't normal. We got together and agreed not to go, only John Bond and Ken Brown went in. We were then told to turn up on Wednesday, otherwise we would be fined £5. Ken Tucker said he wouldn't go. He got fined £10."

However, rather than generating respect, this seemed to earn Fenton little more than contempt from his players. The authoritarian approach really wasn't his way; it didn't suit or work for him. There are indications that he understood this, although he may have failed to see it as the weakness that inclined him to play to his managerial strengths.

Ted was not a charismatic leader like Paynter and King before him. Leadership was not something he had a great gift for, unlike Malcolm Allison, to whom heaven granted that favour. However, Paynter, King and Allison were not the best managers. For Mick Newman, Allison 'led by the force of personality really.' Allison was like King and Paynter in this respect - they all relied massively on the power of character to achieve their desired ends. Although Fenton initially tried to lead his men, calling on his Army training, because of Allison's presence as 'the leader', the more ebullient personality, Ted was obliged to *manage* those who played for him. He was concerned with more than just training and how they played on Saturdays. He began to foster a type of 'total quality personnel management' based on the day-to-day life and practical needs of his staff. This was, maybe, his major insight, and certainly his biggest departure from West Ham traditions. As such, he altered the manager's role but did not attempt to change the way in which the board operated the Club.

Ted appeared to grasp a truth about management that few discover; a manager's job is not primarily to manage, but find other managers and allow them to manage. Of course, from a more negative perspective another truth of management emerged from Ted's reign; if you do not manage, you will be managed - there is no such thing as a 'vacuum' in management.

Andy Smillie recalled something of Ted's method. "Fenton was good at the 'chemistry', he could find people who could play together. He created a structure, right down to the 16-year-olds. Ted was like that. He was good at getting others to free wheel."

Fenton even used some comic irony. Andy continued; "I remember coming in at half- time and seeing Ted hanging from a coat hook, pinching the bridge of his nose. We were looking for a lift and he said; 'I don't know what I'm going to do.'" Mick Newman also remembered this habit of Ted's; "He would hang himself on a coat hanger in the dressing-room sometimes for the half-time talks. A couple of times players took the screws out and he would drop off."

For all his eccentricity, Smillie emphasised Fenton's consultative attitude; "He would ask; 'What do you think?'" Ted would argue points with players, and once in a while Allison or Moroney would show him he was wrong. In any case, Fenton tried to convince the players. It is difficult to picture Charlie Paynter involving himself in sessions like that, and even harder to imagine W. J. Cearns encouraging his manager to sit down and talk with the workers.

For Noel Cantwell, there was a 'change in outlook at the Club' following Ted taking on the role of manager; "Pratt becoming chairman might have been what allowed more worker participation."

In any case, players started to give their views at meetings and the manager listened. Eddie Chapman recalled; "When he gave his team talks he let everybody talk, which is as it should be of course, he got 'em going. I've got to give him that due."

Frank O'Farrell was also impressed with this ideological attitude which Ted brought in team talks. In this respect he might be counted amongst one of the first of a new generation of managers. For example Paynter would never have done this. Ted invited opinions. Frank reiterated the novelty of this approach; "Billy Wright told me that he shit himself when he heard Stan Cullis coming...Ted was a forerunner of a new management style. Just like running a business or a factory, you have to get people to agree with what needs to be done; you need to promote a co-operative approach." But for Malcolm Allison, "Fenton didn't so much give us a chance to put our opinion, we made him listen to us. Sometimes he tried to argue but mostly even he could see his logic was nearly always flawed. No matter who'd been the manager at West Ham then they would have had to listen to us. We knew we were what made the Club work, not Ted Fenton or Pratt."

But that such 'debates' took place puts Ted ahead of his time, but as Andy Smillie pointed out, this approach has its weaknesses; "He relied on his people and it was hard to get things done if they didn't go with him."

One of the most creative things Ted did was noted by George Petchey; "Fenton brought Malcolm Allison in and allowed him the run of the club." Fenton's 'forum' style of management created opportunities for players to express themselves. This allowed innovative ideas to be taken forward, but it also created a gap in authority that was soon filled by Malcolm Allison. As a player of the time recalled; "Allison, Brown and Cantwell were known as ABC United. They dictated so much, and Ted went along with it so often, maybe for his own convenience, its one way of managing, but if that sort of thing gets too strong, then the players can take over - everybody thought they had too much influence, only because of their enthusiasm." But what is 'too much influence'? If Ted could have shut the likes of Allison up is it more likely that he would have gained control, or would he have simply helped motivate a sort of guerilla movement led by Allison as a sort of Che figure?

Derek Parker remembered the way Allison started to fill the void left by Fenton. "We always thought Malcolm influenced Ted. These days the players wouldn't get as close to the manager. He started changing styles, the better footwear was coming in and Malcolm had his shorts up here," - Derek cut his leg with his hand, just below the groin - "Malcolm was always one of the first in everything, in lots of respects. Ted was lucky to have people like that about."

Ken Tucker was more direct; "Malcolm Allison was always a good-hearted player. He got the team organised. We used to stand over at Grange Farm [the West Ham training ground] and Fenton would ask Malcolm; 'What do we do now?' and Allison would step in and sort things out."

Eric Parsons indicated that this lack of direction from the manager was something of a tradition at Upton Park. "Charlie Paynter didn't talk tactics. During a game at

Luton, I passed the ball across the goal when I should have shot - Paynter put me right there. But for the most part the players sorted it out."

Bill Lansdowne recalled; "Fenton would give us a chat and on the way out of the dressing-room, Malcolm would say what to do." Eddie Lewis told me; "Ted wasn't the sort of bloke you could talk to about anything. ABC ran the club." George Wright said of Allison; "Fenton got all his ideas from him. He was more in charge of things than Ted was. Malcolm instigated the coaching." According to Mick Newman; "Malcolm Allison more or less ran the playing side of things." Harry Kinsell, who knew Fenton from their days in the forces confirmed the situation as far as Ted's presence on the training ground was concerned; "He was all right, but the trainer did most."

Modern management recognises that those employees who work most efficiently are those who manage, or think they manage themselves. It is debatable if the form of management that was emerging at West Ham in the early Fifties was purposeful, non-directive, delegation on Ted's part or if Allison simply filled a 'leadership vacuum'. In a way it doesn't really matter. Malcolm had knowledge and skill that Ted did not possess and Fenton, by accident or design, tapped it. The 'Allison effect' was to have a lasting and positive influence on the Club. Fenton was the key to what was happening at West Ham in that he could have sabotaged the changes. According to Cantwell; "He was a good manager with a fair knowledge of the game. Won't go down as one of the best managers West Ham had, but he could take credit for the rise. He scouted good young players. We needed him to guide more, but he might have realised that he had keen and dedicated players and let them have their way."

Frank O'Farrell looked back on the situation and concluded; "When Malcolm was critical of Ted, I think it served to make us more self-reliant and turned us into managers...If we'd have had a strong manager, we wouldn't have blossomed the way we did. That's why so many of us succeeded. Maybe Malcolm knew things already, but I learned some of it from Fenton."

Allison's opinion that Fenton "was promoted out of his depth" is in keeping with his feeling that Fenton was, at best, "a necessary annoyance". However, John Cartwright, who is a great admirer of Allison, concluded; "The manager was willing to let people do things."

Ted Fenton's decade as West Ham manager would be successful. He produced a team that represented the standards of the board and won matches. The Club gained promotion in 1958, along with a reputation for playing good football. Fenton's role in the development was both critical and equivocal; it might be seen as passive encouragement. In that it is true, he reflected the most conservative traditions of the board and the Club, but there seemed to be more to it than just that. Noel Cantwell told me; "We were a new generation of players coming along…We had a good relationship with Pratt…He was a very bad loser."

This might account for Fenton's willingness to allow the team to take chances, even when it appeared to slip out of the control of the manager. Many of the players agree that Pratt made a difference; he gave the impression he cared what was happening, both to the Club and the players.

One consistent feature about West Ham has been the way in which the board and chairmen have desisted from taking actions that would give the impression that they knew more about football than the manager or the players. The board's tradition has been to do little, even when supporters have demanded changes. It is not surprising that Fenton, the manager raised within the West Ham system, might have been understood to have acted almost passively in a situation which his players were doing part of his job for him, and probably doing it better than he could have. But the changes at West Ham depended on the unique personalities and talents of its young playing staff. They had a leader who had no interest in coming close either to the manager or to the board, a man who left no doubt that he was concerned only for his fellow players. They had a manager who was secure enough in his job to let the players go their own way. They had a chairman who would not sabotage what was taking place among them. They were playing for a club that could afford to be different because West Ham had very little to lose.

After 1950, West Ham achieved some significant changes on and off the field. The future Championship was the end point of a steady line of development started by Fenton. The process included changes in personnel and tactics, the improvement of players' conditions, and the introduction of skill-oriented training, together with the youth scheme, that fed players into the first team. Ted Fenton was involved in all of these innovations, if only by giving his approval.

1951-52 – Togetherness is what I remember…

The season opened with Ernie Gregory picking up an injury in the first League game at Loftus Road. He then missed the next 14 League fixtures. The new term was only four games old and West Ham had only one win under their collective belt, but this wasn't the end of the world that threatened to come later. By the end of August, the 33 rpm long-playing record was introduced in West Germany and early in September, Maureen Connolly won the US Tennis Championship at the age of just 16.

In response to the rather ignominious start, for the visit to Hull on 1st September, Fenton, dropped Steve Forde, Derek Parker, Bill Robinson and Tommy Southren, bringing in the experienced Tommy Moroney and giving debuts to George Wright, Bert Hawkins and, on the flank, the 22-year-old Doug Bing. The experiment was quite a success, the Hammers gaining a creditable 1-1 draw, with Hawkins scoring. Doug kept his place for the next game back at the Boleyn Ground. Swansea and West Ham shared four goals and Doug got one for the home side.

Doug Bing was a striking man when he played for West Ham; in the contemporary era he would have been a heart-throb without doubt, with his trim figure and wavy blond hair. John Bond recalled; "The only thing Dougy Bing had wrong with him was two dodgy teeth in the front of his head - black as the ace of spades."

Doug, looking back at his early family life, told me; "There were six of us in the family, five boys and a girl. Dad was a labourer on the council. My brother, Tom, was with Spurs. He signed for them the year after I went to West Ham. He was as good a player; if not better than me, but the side they had when he was there gave him little chance of breaking into the first team. They were top dogs. I played against him in the Combination, we got beat 2-1. I went to St Peter's School. I was helped by Bob Taylor there, I think he played Southern League football."

Doug had completed his National Service, having been posted to Singapore and represented the Army in a match against the RAF. Thereafter he continued his involvement in the game;

"I played for a side called St Peter's Old Boys, in Margate. Aimer Hall, a former inside-forward at West Ham and then manager of Margate, came to watch me. He asked me if I'd like to sign for Margate. I had about ten matches for Margate. Aimer Hall recommended me to West Ham and they asked to sign for them," He joined the Hammers on New Year's Day 1951.

Doug remembered; "The training at Upton Park was different. Billy Moore was in charge of that. He told me to go round with Jackie Omanson, he was such a strong man. We used to train behind the old Boleyn Castle. He killed me. Noel Cantwell always seemed to have so much time; he was a good tackler and passer of the ball. He would help you so much. I saw myself as an average player, I was two-footed, I could play left-half or right-half. When I went to half-back I thought I was quite a good player. But looking back, Noel Cantwell, Malcolm Allison and the others made me look better. I came to the professional game a bit late. There were some great players at Upton Park at the time - Noel Cantwell, Ernie Gregory, Bert Hawkins and Dick Walker, who was helpful to me; he would talk to you, help you all the time. I played against the great Welsh international John Charles once, he was at centre-half. He took a penalty and he said to me; 'Just keep going son.' I'll always remember that. In my first season at West Ham I was in the 'A' team and then I got in the reserves, under Harry Hooper senior. I changed to wing-half - I came to the Club as a winger - when someone got injured. It sort of suited me."

Unlike many players, Doug had some good memories of playing in the reserves; "In the Combination Cup Final at Charlton around 11,000 turned up. The crowd was always good to us. There was never any abuse; they'd always cheer you on, even if you were having a bad game

"I went out with Malcolm Allison, John Dick and Noel Cantwell, for a few beers, over the dogs at Hackney Wick. I'd never been to the dogs before, although there was a track in Margate, but that was the life of a footballer then. I lived with John Bond for a time. We got to know each other quite well. In the summer I'd come home, ten solid weeks off!"

Looking back on when the time came for him to leave the club, Doug said; "Ted released me. I did have typhoid in the Army and I think that might have affected me. I don't think I was doing the job properly. Togetherness is what I remember at West Ham and the way we always wanted to play football. All the lot of us would talk about was football. Even though I was something of an outsider, I got involved with the 'Academy' at Cassatarri's. They'd just let you sit there and talk about how football should be played. No one at the club would demean you."

The inclusion of Bert Hawkins meant that Bill Robinson had played his last first-team game for West Ham. He had scored 61 goals for the Irons in 105 outings over four years. He went on to organise the youth team, making it one of the best in the country before moving up to the assistant manager's post in November 1957.

I met up with Bert Hawkins a couple of years before he passed away. He and his wife, Katherine, lived not too far from where Bert was born in Bristol. He has had a succession of hip operations, four heart attacks and five by-pass operations. According to Bert, it's only footballers who come through these by-passes - "You keep missing the bloody ball." He needed to have cortisone injected into his hipbones every six months; this allowed him to walk for about six weeks. This was necessary, as he would have no more than a 25 per cent chance of survival if he were to undergo surgery. To quote Katherine; "He's a walking miracle."

Although he joined West Ham from Bath City, Bert was officially on loan from Bristol City at the time the Hammers came in for him. He gave me the whole picture. "I started off with Rovers and went to City. Ted Fenton and Harry Hooper senior watched a match at Bath, I happened to have a fair game and I scored a couple. Harry told me that I should get away from here."

Katherine was born in East Ham. The couple married in 1953. They met while Bert was with the Hammers. Katherine recalled; "My friend introduced me to him. I was engaged to somebody else. I hate football." Bert chipped in; "Before she knew I was a footballer she complained to me about West Ham games stopping people getting near the shops. I said to Tommy Dixon; 'I'd better not tell her about playing football yet.'" Katherine continued; "Tommy used to borrow money from Bert because he didn't like to touch his own - he put it in the bank. He gave Bert so much a week back." Bert recalled that he and Tommy, were in the same digs for a time.

Bert was the eldest of seven children; "One was still-born. I have two brothers and three sisters. I went to school at St George's, Brandon Hill. I was head boy, head prefect. I was a good scholar, but I couldn't have pursued that as my family didn't have the money. We would put our coats down for goalposts on Brandon Hill. Quite a few of the lads who played in those games went on to professional football. It all started for me up on Brandon Hill. The police used to chase you off; you weren't really allowed to play football there.

"I started playing organised football in the Navy, during the war years. We played in loads of different countries, which did help us in our young days. Some of these foreign players were very good.

"West Ham started me on about £8 a week if you got in the first team. It dropped £3 for the reserves and lower still for the Colts. We used to have a quick drink after our meals at the Denmark, but you didn't tell anyone or you'd get into trouble. I used to like going to church. I was brought up as a choirboy. To go into church and sing the hymns lifted you. The supporters were a bit like that; they were great - and good at letting you know if you did wrong too!" Bert called out his impression of a supporter; 'Pull your socks up Bert!'

"The Cockney accent was wonderful at times. As long as you done your job well they looked after you. They were a good crowd. No two ways about that. They used to sing *I'm Forever Blowing Bubbles*. That was a sort of a choir; they associated with the team." Again, Bert sang out; "...pretty bubbles in the air." He spoke to me as a fan; "You'll never be on your own boy!"

I liked Bert. Like me, he' was romantic. He went on; "Having the name Hawkins, a lot of 'em called me 'Pirate' [taking a cue from the 1950 Disney film *Treasure Island* the featured Robert Louis Stevenson's young hero Jim Hawkins). Lots of 'ooo, arrr, Jim lad' stuff. West Ham was surrounded by spectators that would do anything for them. In our time they couldn't sing enough for you or praise you enough. I played against Stanley Matthews twice and during the war years, after the game, if he had studs missing off his boots, you'd get people looking around on the pitch for them for souvenirs."

According to Bert, the West Ham team was a cavalcade of characters. "Harry Kinsell and Frank O'Farrell were great lads. Dickey Walker was a wonderful captain. He brought it out in you. He wouldn't tell you off. Danny McGowan and Frank O'Farrell paid for me to go over to Ireland with them. Ernie Gregory was a bloody good bloke and goalkeeper. Gerry Gazzard could draw people; they used to rush back shouting; 'Four in the middle!' Harry Hooper came on wonderful. He was in the reserves during my time. He became one of the best players I'd seen with a ball. Tommy Southren was good." Katherine remarked; "Jimmy Andrews and Tommy Dixon were like fire and water."

Pirate Hawkins scored 16 goals for the Hammers, and in his 37 games he averaged nearly one every other game. Then he picked up an injury and lost his place in the first team. "So it was a case of, if I wanted to get on, I had to get away. West Ham had some good young players. I didn't want to go, I wasn't pushed. I didn't like QPR as much as West Ham. There wasn't the family touch. West Ham was very much a team. The manager at Loftus Road didn't like me. He made my life miserable; he wouldn't play me at all, not even in the reserves. They wouldn't even let me train. I regretted that move.

"I was always so proud to be playing professional football, and my family was proud of me. And the most lasting thing about West Ham was that it was where I met my wife..."

As I was leaving, Bert got up to shake my hand. While still not quite straight, he crossed his arms, his fists were clenched; he looked into my eyes and smiled as he said; "Up the Hammers!" As old, frail and ill as he was, the player was still in there. The soul of Bert Hawkins was alive and kicking.

George Wright's displacement of Steve Forde also had long-term effects on the team. It marked the end of Forde's time at West Ham. Forde had been at Upton Park since 1937. He was one of the finest full-backs to appear for the club in the years just after World War Two. I met with George on a blustery day in early February. It was good to be welcomed into his warm bungalow out of the wind that blew in off of the sea. George lived with his East Ham-born wife Marcella, about five minutes' drive from Margate. Like many Hammers couples, they met for the first time at a dance at East Ham Town Hall. Marcella and George were married in 1953, early on in George's career with the Irons. George looked happy and fit, although he had been suffering ill health in the recent past, including an ulcer and a heart attack.

"My parents were in the fish business," George told me. "I started working as an apprentice carpenter, playing for Thanet United. I joined Margate as a semi-pro, finishing my indentures."

He moved on to Ramsgate but returned to Margate when Aimer Hall took over. It was Hall who asked George about West Ham after the young centre-forward converted to full-back. For all this, George said that he wasn't really interested in football in his early years. His ambitions had originally been to finish his apprenticeship and travel around Britain for a time with a couple of friends, who were also, 'finishing their time'. The lads would go for kickabouts together. Two weeks before they were due to finish their apprenticeships, one boy's mother fell ill and the other's father also became debilitated. This put an end to the plans the group had. George recalled; "So I decided to give the football a try after all. I signed on for £8 in the season and £7 out."

Even well into his career, George was 'happy to play and finish'. "I wouldn't go to internationals. In those days most players went to watch the internationals. I argued with Ted about it and would often make an excuse, until one day, when he went round saying to each player; 'You're going, and you're going', he came up to me and said; '...and you're definitely going'. He had to do that. He had to check at half-time that I was still there though." George chuckled at the memory. "Ted really didn't have much in the way of authority, but he could nag."

It seems that at least some things haven't changed that much at Upton Park since George's time. "West Ham always started off well and fell off, or they started badly and pulled up later on." However, George and Marcella recalled that Upton Park was a happy place."There were dinners and dances what seemed like every night. We got fed up with going out! We had a lot of laughs. Ken Tucker was a mad as a March hare and Tommy Southren was a funny little bloke."

According to George; "If the fans didn't like you, you knew it." For all that, there was no doubting the enthusiasm and adulation of the supporters. Marcella remembered how she was caught in the crush when she and George were trying to get into a car to take them to Upton Park Station. "The crowd was so keen just to see George we wouldn't have been able to make the station on foot."

George lived in a clubhouse in Ravenhill Road, Plaistow, fairly near to Andy Malcolm and John Bond, among others. George recalled how young lads used to wait outside the couple's house for George to arrive home. "I had to go out sometimes and asked them to be quiet when the baby was sleeping," recalled Marcella, "they were nice lads though."

George remembered; "They'd sit on the wall reading Charlie Buchan's football book and ask me to sign it when I came along."

George continued to make good use of his carpentry skills while at Upton Park. "Ted Fenton sorted out a little workshop for me under the stand."

This drew the attention of newspapers, no doubt with a bit of help from Ted. The idea of a footballer making his own wardrobe and bed was seen as a novel story. It would be even more unusual today. A bit like Mohamed Diamé being an enthusiastic plumber, installing his own washing machine and toilet. George was inundated with calls from furniture stores following the publicity, making bids for his handiwork.

"The wives got on well," Marcella recollected. "I looked after John Bond's wife when he was away on the coaching courses with Malcolm."

George looked back on the training and preparation at the Boleyn Ground.

"On match days we would have a steak with a poached egg on top. The club used to send the meat round. You had to have that before 11 o'clock. When we played away we stayed in the best hotels and would generally have chicken for lunch with a bit of toast. We trained hard, a lot of running and lapping. After the Hungarians beat England, we saw more of the ball, but we still carried on with the running, alternating with walking a lot. They threw the ball at you at about 12.30, but we used to be worn out by then. You thought; 'You can keep that!' By then we were about ready to get in the bath. We did a lot of work with weights at one time. We did circuits, a doctor used to take our pulses…I looked beautiful! I put on half a stone, but nobody could move. After 20 minutes in matches everyone would be worn out. When we first started with the weights everyone was phoning each other up asking about aches and pains. You couldn't move at times!"

These were the days of the warrior class in football, as George illustrated.

"Ernie Devlin, he had a body like a patchwork quilt, and Andy Malcolm was tough. Dick Walker was a great player too. We would play football with a medicine ball; that would toughen you up."

It seems this was time well spent. As George related; "Freddie Cooper, the reserve-team skipper, got hit in the head by a ball or a body or something; he staggered about all over the place at first, and was dazed for most of the match. There were no substitutes in those days. But he had a blinder of a game. From then on, whenever Freddie was in the team, the lads would be saying; 'Where's the hammer?'"

Marcella reiterated the Spartan nature of the game in the early Fifties.

"The players' wives did all the laundry and were also issued with a first-aid kit. When the players came home after the match they invariably had injuries, for example black toes. This was treated by an implement, which fitted around the toe and was screwed tightly on to the nail, so that a needle would pierce the nail, releasing the blood under the nail. If this wasn't done the player would be in danger of losing the nail and risked being unable to play."

Marcella told me that on one occasion George arrived home with a long gash from his groin to his knee. This done by the old style boot, the studs of which was covered in leather. However this time the coating had come off the assailant's footwear, exposing the boot nails. The wound was already turning septic and took a deal of effort on Marcella's part to clean up.

In the first Inter-Cities Fairs Cup Final in 1958, George was selected for the London team - at that time the competition consisted of select sides from cities which held industrial fairs; London, Birmingham, Barcelona and so on. He played in the second leg in Barcelona.

"Noel Cantwell was called in late, someone had been injured. They played in the same style as us, perhaps a bit quicker."

George earned other representative honours, twice playing for an FA XI against Cambridge University, and he was also was picked for a trial match between England 'B' and a British Olympic XI at Highbury in 1952. George was a good buy for West Ham. Even though he never scored a goal, he played 170 games. Able to defend on either side of the park, he was an excellent full-back.

In September, King George VI underwent surgery at Buckingham Palace. A lung was removed. The King had cancer. Like so many of his generation, he had been a heavy cigarette smoker all his adult life and the connection between this and lung cancer was only just beginning to be suspected.

Goalkeeper George Taylor was an able enough deputy for Ernie Gregory but he had a difficult day at Sheffield United in September. Although Doug Bing got his second goal for the club, the home side won 6-1 with Derek Hawksworth scoring three. At Rotherham, in October, Terry Woodgate put a blemish on the Hammers' fine disciplinary record when he was sent off. The day before West Ham's sixth defeat in 14 matches, 2-1 at St Andrew's, the Irons had gleaned a single point from a possible dozen away from home.

Britain was again involved in conflict abroad. In a speech the previous year, King Farouk had ordered the British to leave Egypt. The British ignored this but made pretence of placating him. The Government said it was willing to withdraw. However, they omitted to make any firm promises. This prevarication sparked off anti-British rioting and, in September, led to Egypt's decision to rescind the 1936 Anglo-Egyptian Alliance. Britain's response was swift. At dawn on 19th October, British troops occupied the key points on the Suez Canal and abruptly stopped the peace talks. Britain also took the wise precaution of removing all civilians from the Canal Zone and in November, 2,000 women and children who had been threatened by the continuous riots, were evacuated. By this time Britain had a new (or old, depending on how you look at it) Prime Minister. Winston Churchill led the Conservative Party to a narrow win over Labour.

At the age of 36, midway through the season, Ernie Gregory was awarded an England 'B' cap against France. Throughout the early and mid-Fifties, Ernie was on the fringe of the England team. However, his progress was halted early in February 1954 when he picked up an injury to the little finger of his right hand. Ernie didn't play again until September 1955. It also needs to be said that being at West Ham, not a particularly fashionable club at the time, didn't help his international chances.

1951-52 – Togetherness is what I remember…

By the end of November, West Ham had won only five games, all at the Boleyn Ground. On their travels they had accumulated just three points. For the home game against Everton, Fenton decided to make some changes. Gerry Gazzard won back the number- ten spot, ending a five-match first-team run for John Gregory. After a three-game comeback, Tommy Southren returned to the reserve side and Terry Woodgate was shifted across to fill the berth vacated by Tom. The left wing was loaded with debutant Jimmy Andrews.

****

It was early afternoon on a beautiful spring day when I crossed the Severn Bridge on my way to see Jimmy and his wife Dot, who lived in a pretty, but busy little town just outside Cardiff. I had seen Bert Hawkins in the morning and, needing to drive through the centre of Bristol, I appreciated the real beauty of the South Wales countryside.

Jim was one of the last of my interviews. He asked me about some of the other players and said, with the dry humour I found to be indicative of the man. "I was the only one who stayed young."

I remarked on the stunning landscape that surrounded his home. He agreed, but remarked; "Wales is nothing like Scotland, but they're doing their best."

Jim came to West Ham from Dundee for £4,750, and he agreed that this, was a reasonable fee.

"I'd been injured, a broken ankle. I'd got over that. I was playing in the reserves. We had a very good reserve team at the time. Dundee, as a club, was very like West Ham, everybody could play. Again, like West Ham, that didn't mean to say you could win, but if you were at Dundee you were a footballer. In this reserve game I was playing inside-forward -I was a left winger really, it was the first time I'd played in that position. Ted watched the game, he took a fancy, thought I had something, so he saw the manager."

At the time, Jim was very much a hometown boy.

"I didn't want to go. I'd never been to England. It was like going into the wilds. I told the manager that I wasn't interested, because I was engaged to Dot at that time. We went dancing. In those days that's where you met everybody…old fashioned waltz and things. We were dancing around and we looked up on the balcony and Ted was there. We ducked; getting ready to run. But he came flying down and he got hold of me just as we were about to leave. He was a very persuasive feller. He was a good man. He said;

'Come on, were very keen to get you.' I said; 'No, I don't fancy it.' I loved Dundee. But he hung on. Then the manager got hold of me on the Monday.

"I then said to Ted that I'd think about it, which is what I had to do to get him out of my hair. My manager told me that I could be the best left-winger in Scotland and I said" 'I don't fancy being the best left-winger in England.'"

However, Fenton was not to be put off. Jim made him an offer he thought Ted would refuse, but the West Ham manager had made his mind up that the young Scot was a good investment.

"So that was me off," Jim reflected. "The fright of me life I got. Before I went to Dundee, a few clubs were interested in me; Wolverhampton, Hull, Aberdeen - I must have been a fair player." He smiled.

Fenton was right about Jim. He played 120 games for the Hammers, making his first appearance almost before the ink on his contract was dry - a six goal thriller, the points were shared against Everton at Upton Park before 22,500.

"Upton Park was a bit of a culture shock, When I went out on the field at Dundee, the pitch was always in good, beautiful condition, like the pitches are now. At West Ham you were about six inches deep in mud. It was like a different game altogether. Everton were a very good team, with a few internationals in their side. West Ham had some cracking players too. There was a pride about it. If you played for West Ham, you were thought of' as a footballer."

Jim spoke abut the quality of his colleagues; "...Tom Maloney, he wouldn't head a ball; he used to bring his foot up there and bring it down. Billy Dare, what a strong man he was. Tommy Dixon had a good spell but he wasn't a great player."

At that point Jim began to look back at the way football was played in the Fifties. He portrayed the character of the encounters between teams as a kind of combat. Not for the first time I began to understand that these were very much face-to-face physical contests, often brutal, damaging wars of attrition.

"There were some good sides facing West Ham at that time. It was a hard school. There were some tough games up north; up at places like Barnsley they gave you some stick. They didn't just used to roll their sleeves up, they rolled them up to the shoulders, to show they meant business. The full-backs up north, a lot them were miners, they'd put the 'eye' on you. They would go; 'Okay my son, here we go!' I was a small, wee feller and they'd have huge muscles and hairy arms, like apes. You used to get whacked. On the pitches we were playing on it was a question of strength as much as anything else.

1951-52 – Togetherness is what I remember...

I wasn't very big when I went out there and I shrank about four inches in the mud. At Swansea they used to soak the ball, in a bucket, put a couple of bricks on top of it when they played London sides. There were a lot of very strong players, the Tom Docherty, Jimmy Scholar type, hard men, they loved it. The heavier it was, the better they liked it."

Jim came near to becoming a permanent casualty.

"I had a bad injury at one point. I thought I was finished at the time. I got studs shoved into my thigh. I was out for a long time. It put me back a bit; I lost a wee bit of pace and became an inside-forward, on the wing." However, the man from Invergordon was and is a survivor.

"Ken Tucker and I had a great spell then. We just seemed to suit. We were two outright left-footers. We used to come outside, with the right shoulder forward, left foot behind." So, there was some grace to be found.

"A game that lingers in the memory is when we played Blackpool, when they had their great international side, Stanley Matthews and so on. They had eight internationals out. I scored in that game. Frank O'Farrell was playing left-half and I was playing outside-left and we decided that we'd work hard on Stanley. I would go for him first, then Frank would step in, not if he beat me, but when he beat me," Jim chuckled.

Nearly 39,000 watched that FA Cup game against First Division Blackpool at Upton Park in January 1951. The Seasiders, were indeed a star-studded squad of entertainers in those days, boasting not only names like Matthews, but also Stan Mortensen, Harry Johnston, Eddie Shinwell, Ernie Taylor and George Farm. But it was the underdogs who prevailed. Jimmy Andrews scored his first goal, and Frank O'Farrell netted his second for the Hammers as the previous season's losing Cup Finalists were beaten.

The early life story of Jimmy Andrews is truly fascinating - a boy living in the Scottish Highlands between world wars. His hometown was a remote place yet, oddly, a location where the world seemed to meet. I found myself being taken to a different culture, framed within a historical moment when the Royal Navy, a gargantuan organisation at the time, the basis of British industry and endeavour, actually did rule the waves and linked an empire.

"My father was a foreman at Ford's. He had his own business before that. He never saw me play. My mother only saw me play once. When I went to Dundee it was so far away from the Highlands - if you go up there, put your woollies on! My brother played non-League for an Inverness team; he was an outside-right, he played for

Cluchnacullen. I never saw him play. I went to a local school. The teachers never knew I played.

"Invergordon was a naval base, on the Cromarty Firth, and the whole fleet would come in, every ship in the Navy would line up right along. It was a really wonderful sight. The sailors used to come ashore, thousands of them. There were a lot of good players among them. I learnt quite a lot from them. There were troops coming from all over the place, they were shipped from Invergordon to wherever they had to go in Britain; Poles, Canadians, Australians, every nationality. There were some international players among them. I never saw professional footballers, but I saw and awful lot of good, good players, and played against a lot of them."

How can that be imagined? A little boy, in the middle of nowhere, at the centre of everything, playing kickabout with some of the finest footballers of earth at the time. Not just that, but they rated wee Jimmy.

"I seemed to catch their eye because several of them told me to write to their clubs. I knew about all the good Scottish sides, but very little about anything in England. That was a foreign country.

"When I came to West Ham there were a few Irish boys. They looked after me. If you're Scottish, you're Irish. I was under their wing. I didn't smoke or drink at that time, so it was a tough school, but they were great fellers. There's warmth about the Irish. I was put into digs with a Mrs Carroll, in Forest Gate. As I moved in, John Dick was moving out. I got married while I was with West Ham, back up home of course. Dot loved it. They're warm people, too, in the East End. The crowd, it was always, *I'm Forever Blowing Bubbles*. They were there at Christmas time and Dick Walker used to conduct the supporters, standing in the middle. You always got that great warmth. That's where you got the love for the place. It's more than playing football; it's to do with the crowd. It was a great experience West Ham. I loved it I must say. I was proud to be there too."

Jim remembered the more intimate side of the Club; "We all got on well, families mixed. Dot and I really enjoyed that. They were good friends as well as fellow players. Dave Sexton lived just a few doors from us. Shirley and Billy Dare lived next door."

Dot remarked; "The wives were all together. Janet Bond, John's wife, was absolutely lost. I took her under my wing. They were round our house every night of the week... We knew everyone at the Club, you knew everyone on the gate."

Jim continued; "I was pretty close to Frank and Noel and John Bond. In the close season I'd go home. Dot's family were from Dundee."

Jim went to Orient in 1956. It didn't work.

"I think I was comparing it to West Ham all the time. I just couldn't fit in. I didn't want to leave West Ham. It was this bad injury and I lost a couple of yards. I went up to see the specialist at Charring Cross, I'd been having treatment for about a month. The surgeon came to see me. He asked me if I could do anything else apart from football. My heart stopped beating. Of course, I knew nothing else. He told me that I should seriously consider looking outside the game. I was 27! That frightened me to death. I approached it in my normal way and just worked harder. I'm gonna prove 'em wrong. I played until I was 35.

"Malcolm Musgrove came into the side and started scoring goals. He was a two-footer and he could come in [this was an indication of Musgrove's physicality]. He was a great player with a marvellous shot; a strong, straightforward player. There were Tuck and Musgrove and Tommy Southren, about six wingers, so it was time to go."

Jim Andrews was quick, a fast winger, but according to him; "I wasn't a good dribbler, I was a controller of the ball. It was usage of the ball that was my strength. If I had been better at the dribbling it would have made a huge difference. I could cross the ball, that's an art. Beckham is showing it now. It's not just a question of slinging the ball into the box. There's a great variation in the crossing of the ball. I worked very hard on crosses. A lot of left-footers are exceptional. I like to see any team that's got left-footed players on the left and right footers on the right- like Leeds had when they had their great side. The balance is beautiful."

Jim was a man who could see beauty. His intelligence and appreciation of the game's aesthetics and the way he was able to articulate the same in his gentle Caledonian brogue impressed me deeply.

At the start of December, Sheffield Wednesday won 6-0 at Upton Park. Derek Dooley netted three of those goals and went on to score an amazing 46 League goals that season. A week after a six-goal mauling at the hands of the eventual Second Division champions, it was Upton Park's turn to celebrate as Bert Hawkins got his hat-trick against Queen's Park Rangers at the Boleyn Ground. Bert still had the match ball in the 21st Century. It was autographed by both teams. The names were very faded, Bert's children and grandchildren having played with ball over many years. However, when I met him I could still make out the score, West Ham 4 QPR 2, and the names Jim Barrett and Billy Moore (the latter was the Hammers trainer at the time) could also be seen like ghosts haunting the grizzled leather of the weighty, hard, old sphere.

In a League match before the fourth round of the FA Cup, the Irons got some revenge for the tonking at Bramall Lane; Sheffield United were beaten 5-1. Ken Tucker got a hat-trick and Gerry Gazzard made it a five. Thirty-five thousand fans were at Upton Park, hoping for a repeat performance when the Blades returned for the Cup encounter. However, a highly entertaining game, on a bog of a pitch, ended goalless. Back up north in the replay, a white ball was used in an FA Cup game for the first time. United won the tie 4-2. That made a total of 19 goals scored in the matches between the two clubs in 1951-52.

Three days later West Ham ran out at Highfield Road. Fenton, who had developed some consistency in his team selection since the Blackpool result, changed the side around. In attack Andrews and Gazzard were out, while Tucker and Barrett were in. The defence lost Parker and gained McGowan. Kinsell was injured so the 19-year-old John Bond was given his first start in the Football League. This was a tough-looking side and they secured only the second and West Ham's last away win of the season. Barrett and Hawkins did the damage, giving West Ham a 2-1 victory, and doing the double over Coventry, who were bound for relegation. John Bond looked back at that match;

"I played at left-back against a feller called Warner, a winger. One half of the pitch, straight down the length, was frozen over, so you couldn't stand up. The other half was soft. They had a big stand at Coventry that overshadowed one half of the pitch. We had to stand along the side of the pitch in great big roll-neck sweaters, for a minute's silence, because the King had died.

****

On 6th February, a brief bulletin on the railings of Buckingham Palace announced that King George VI had died peacefully in his sleep. Britain now had a Queen. George VI had been a good and conscientious ruler. He had accepted his fate with good grace when his elder brother, Edward VIII, abandoned his throne in 1936 for the love of Wallis Simpson, an American divorcee. George had performed all his public functions admirably, and had been ably supported by a loving wife who had grown with him in popularity and public esteem.

Shortly after his reign began, George found himself monarch of a nation at war and he threw himself into an even more arduous round of public duties. When it was suggested that he and his family should live in Canada for the duration of the war, he turned down the suggestion contemptuously, preferring to share the dangers of London with his people. His house (Buckingham Palace) was hit and badly damaged just like theirs. His family's rations were the same as theirs and he and his family scrupulously observed all the rules and regulations imposed by a wartime government, sharing all the privations and hardships that were visited on his subjects.

The young Princess Elizabeth and her husband, the Duke of Edinburgh, were in Kenya when her father died. They cut short their Commonwealth tour immediately and returned to Britain. She was 25 and had inherited one of the most demanding jobs in the world.

Following the game at Coventry, Fenton wrote to John Bond.

"I got the letter to this day from Ted Fenton saying; 'You must be absolutely delighted with the way you played. Harry Kinsell is fit and I'm bringing him back."

John joined West Ham from Colchester Casuals as an amateur in 1950. He was the first of the successful side of the 1960s to arrive at Upton Park. He greeted me with a very firm handshake at his comfortable home in a beautiful spot between Liverpool and Manchester. John explained how his 15-year association with the Hammers began. "Ted was an army bloke. He was interested in the cadet force. I didn't want to get into uniform, but you used to have to attend once a week to allow you to play for the Army cadet force. Ted was involved and he saw me play while he was at Colchester. He asked me to sign up for them. When he went to West Ham he asked me to come and sign up there. I wasn't approached by anyone else; he was the only one who saw anything in me."

John came from a poor rural background, in the days when mid-Essex was still a long way from London. He carried an Essex country accent that is all but extinct. He went on; "My parents never had a penny. I had to borrow my brother's overcoat to go and sign on. It was a big black thing with one of them tie-up belts. West Ham started me on £6 a week. On the Saturday my sister was getting married. I played in a five-a-side and got injured, I hurt my ankle. I asked Ted Fenton if I could go home for my sister's wedding. He said; 'I hope you don't make that bloody ankle an excuse. You can't play so you can go home to your sister's wedding."

That was tantamount to accusing John of lying, something few people would do today. John Bond could be accused of many things, but, as you will see, honesty and frankness are tangible qualities in the man. He continued; "I never thought about it till years afterwards. How naive I looked.

"Before I signed for West Ham, Ted came round to my parents' house in a little place called Stanway, just outside of Colchester. He told my mother and father what it would be like - we'll teach him to live in hotels, and all this business. Years after I understood all that. I'd never been in a hotel or lived away from home. My mother, in the summer, used to go apple picking, just down the end of our road. I went back on the Monday morning and she used to give me a bag of apples to take to Ted Fenton. I used to go into the ground and walk straight up into his office and give him this bag of apples. When I think back to that it makes me cringe."

He rubbed his hands over his eyes, smiling, almost embarrassed; "Can you imagine that happening today?"

I began to get a picture of John's life before going to West Ham; it is something which is hard to envisage today. England has become a very small place, and the counties that surround London have been transformed into extensions of the capital, their towns are commuter satellites.

"There were few cars, everybody had bikes. It was all very sparse. The first car I ever got was a 1937 Vauxhall, with a running board on it and everything. You thought you were the King of England in that. My dad worked in the sandpit; shovelling sand. He was as strong as an ox. He used to do that all day, then come home and dig the garden. We had a massive big garden. Bless his heart; he died just before he was 90."

John reminisced about his school days; "I went to Stanway School. I'd go down the garden, pop under the hedge and I was in the school. I played for the school. I played my first game for the school and, of course, my mother couldn't afford a pair of football boots. I had to wear the boots I went to school in. It was raining and slippery as could be, I had no studs! Mr Gibbons was our teacher. He said; 'Bond would have been all right if he could have stood up, he kept sliding and slipping all over.'

"My brother, Roland, was a big influence on me. He was brilliant. All the boys round where I lived didn't have thruppence to their name and I was the only one who had a football. He bought that and my boots."

When John first joined the Hammers, Jimmy Andrews gave him a bit of a helping hand. Later, in 1953 when John married Janet, Dot and Jimmy Andrews provided a lot of support to the young couple. John recalled; "When we first got married we used to spend most of our time round Jimmy Andrews' place. I don't know why we didn't pay them housekeeping, we seemed to be there all the time. If I met Jimmy Andrews it would be like I never left him…Jimmy Andrews once said to me; 'Look before you get the ball,' and that always stuck with me. That was the best football advice I've ever got; if you think about it, its not bad advice for life in general!"

At first, West Ham didn't seem to be breaking many barriers when it came to preparing for games.

"There was only two or three footballs in the entire Club. You got out for training about quarter past ten and ran round and round the pitch, run a lap and walk a lap. I used to run with a little feller called Terry Woodgate. You'd be doing this for about three-quarters-of-an-hour and then you'd shout to Billy Moore to get the balls out. Billy would be standing at the entrance to die ground watching, with a fag in his mouth, that he never ever took out. He'd used to say; 'just do another one', then all of a sudden he'd come out and throw two balls out, and there'd be 30 or 40 people there."

Later on, John did his bit in terms of bringing new ideas to West Ham and football in general. For example, the attacking full-back that became the overlapping defender, and eventually metamorphosed into the wing-back, was not a continental import, according to John.

"We started the idea of raiding full-backs, Noel and myself."

However, it wasn't all driven by innate genius alone;

"I didn't want to defend. I hated it. I was always keen to get forward. The hard point about the game from my point of view was running. I didn't like running really. If I could have stood still to play the game I'd have been a happy soul. It was always an effort. The ball wasn't a problem. If the ball came to me in the penalty area, it didn't matter if there were 20 people in there, I'd pull it down, and, without being big-headed, invariably I'd be able to do it. Sometimes you'd make a ricket. Ted Fenton, bless his heart, would accept all of that. I think, to an extent, he used to live off of it. He used to like it really. He liked seeing it. We were his boys. He brought Noel over from Ireland, me down from Colchester."

One person who, at times, didn't enjoy this type of play at all was the man who so often stood behind Cantwell and Bond, Ernie Gregory. Anyone standing close enough to the West Ham goal might have heard some colourful language directed at the two full-backs as they skipped and danced around in his area. Gregory probably appreciated their skill but nevertheless never lost his goalkeeper's instinct to encourage his backs to get the ball away.

John and Noel would always be ready to test their skills in the forward line.

"When he got into trouble, Ted used to put me up front. I scored a hat-trick against Chelsea. We were 2-0 down and ended up winning 4-2. A free-kick, a penalty and a header - and I got two against Bolton. Ted was going to pull me back again at Leicester and all of a sudden I blasted one into the top corner of the net."

There was relish in his voice as he described these moments. It was obvious that John liked to score goals. A lot of fans thought that John Bond should have played for England. He must have been one of the best uncapped full-backs of his era. He was a quality defender with a devastating shot. However, John provided some insights into the situation.

"The press put other people forward, the likes of Jimmy Armfield and Don Howe and people like that played for England and I didn't. I went on an FA tour of South Africa in '55-56. The following year I went up to Manchester with the England squad, trained with Tom Finney, to do with the '58 World Cup. I played for a Football League team at Windsor Park, this included Ron Flowers and Johnny Haynes and all them. Bernard Joy wrote in the *Evening Standard;* 'John Bond secures his World Cup place.'

"I played well. After the game we went back to this hotel in Bangor. It was a time in English football when Joe Richards was in charge [President of the Football League] - there used to be a committee of people going with the England set-up. We were having a drink and all of a sudden the bartender told us that we couldn't have any more drinks. That was only my first or second representative game remember. I said; 'Can't we take some up to our room? Can't you get a crate of beer so we can have a few drinks in our room?' I was one of the newcomers in the side and all the committee people were sitting around there. The barman said; 'You can't do that.' I never played another representative game."

He went on; "Ron Greenwood was involved with the FA, with Walter Winterbottom, who was in charge of the team at that time. When Ron Greenwood came to West Ham he told me that story. He knew exactly what happened and exactly why I didn't play anymore. But I suppose it's like if people do things today, people step out of line, but perhaps they're a bit more lenient today.

"I knew I was good enough to play. I was every bit as good as Jimmy Armfield and Don Howe. I knew what I could and couldn't do. There was no point in me complaining or condemning anybody else. The only person to blame for all of that was me - 100 per cent me."

John may well have been right, but this lack of understanding of the character of youth on the part of the England selectors was inexcusable.

John was a popular player at Upton Park, he knew the people well, living in the area and working in a local school.

"I used to do a bit of coaching at Stepney Green. Ron Greenwood said when he first came to the club that I was, what was the word? Something like an idol at West Ham. It's in his book. That was because I got on famous with the supporters. I used to do things, like I'd dribble in my own area. I'd chip balls back over people's head into Ernie's arms in a crowded goalmouth. I'd go rampaging up, having shots at goal. I think that they liked that. They liked someone being free and easy and adventurous. I was naive enough to think; 'Oh sod it. I'll keep doing it.' I got on well with the Chicken Run. I remember one day that they were moaning and groaning; we weren't doing very well, and I just shouted to them; 'The lot of yer go home. Nobody asked you to come here. Why don't you go home if you don't like it? Piss off home!' They didn't give me any stick for saying that, they didn't say, 'Eff-off Bondy' or anything like that. They just laughed. That was them and us together again. That's how things used to be with us.

"It wasn't all football though. We used to have the odd session at the Central [a local pub]. The social life was pretty good. I was always good friends with Noel. Nothing got on my nerves. The club wasn't quite as big as Manchester United, Newcastle or Arsenal, but given the opportunity, given my time again, I'd still play for West Ham United Football Club. It was a good homely sort of club. I don't like using the word, because I wasn't interested in going to West Ham because it was homely, I was interested because I wanted to play football at the top level, but it was a homely, nice club. The people were good.

"I was one of the foursome. I was one really who played with Ted Fenton all that time ago, with Malcolm Allison, with Noel and Jackie Dick, at the start of the Bobby Moore era. When they all went, I still remained at the Club. Then I spent quite a few years with Mooro and Hursty and Peters. Martin Peters was the best player I played with. He was a different class. Hursty was good. He started out as a run of the mill wing-half, but he was a handful and a half of a striker to play against."

John went to Torquay in 1966.

"I was gone at that level. Compared to Upton Park the atmosphere and training was crap. I went down with Janet and watched them play against Darlington, they were losing 4-0 at home; the game was nonsense. We had to catch the train back to London at twenty to five, I said let's get out of here. I couldn't see myself playing that rubbish. But I was told I could live in London and train at West Ham, and to come down every Saturday and play. I got my testimonial at West Ham, 10,000 people turned up and I got £2,000. I then signed for Torquay and they gave me £2,000. I also got the princely sum of £45 a week. I thought I'd never have to work again. " John laughed at the memory.

"I played there for three years. In its way it was every bit has enjoyable as West Ham. Frank O'Farrell was there. I played, I wanted to play, and I put myself about. We had two magnificent years - we put a good little side together and we should have got promotion.

"I've played football all my life. I suppose. From being a youngster that's all I ever did. I never did anything else but play with footballs, so it was just a natural thing for me. That's how I became a professional footballer. I was as good a kicker of the ball as you could find in English football, and they are not just my words. They used to call me Muffin because of the way I kicked the ball, like a mule."

This was certainly true. Bill Lansdowne noted the technique - "Bond would kick through the ball" - and Malcolm Musgrove confirmed; "John Bond was the best kicker of the ball I've seen."

John, 'Muffin the Mule', Bond looked like the solid old-style full back but he didn't play like one. The gift to bang the ball didn't mean that John lacked accuracy, as Malcolm Musgrove pointed out; "He could plant it on a sixpence."

John said; "I could also drop 'em where I wanted to drop 'em. But I didn't take hints. I didn't take things seriously enough at times and I didn't know what life was really all about. Therein lies my weakness. I was an old country boy."

****

The Korean War went on, with each side taking the advantage if a favourable situation arose. Early in March, the Chinese accused the US of germ warfare. Some savage air and ground battles were fought, while world statesmen attempted to find a solution.

Among the most popular films of the time was the adaptation of Nicholas Montsarrat's famous novel. *The Cruel Sea,* which starred Jack Hawkins as the captain of the *Compass Rose* that was sunk in a torpedo attack in one of the most dramatic scenes of the film. John Huston's film *The African Queen* also pulled in the punters, while

1951-52 – Togetherness is what I remember...

Strangers on the Train by Alfred Hitchcock attracted an audience. Igor Stravinsky's, *The Rake's Progress* probably escaped the notice of some Chicken Run regulars, but the opera was to have a lasting impact and the production was very much of its time. *Catcher in the Rye was* making the name of J. D. Salinger well known in literary circles

Another 19-year-old West Ham debutant in 1951-52 was Silvertown-born Roy Stroud. He was an England amateur international from Hendon FC. He came into the team for the match at Notts County on Easter Monday, replacing Bert Hawkins who had been crocked in the 2-0 defeat at Goodison Park. This was the injury to finish Bert's career at Upton Park, not being able to reclaim a place in the side when he returned to fitness.

West Ham finished in the lower half of the Second Division, in 12th place, an improvement on the previous season's 13th, but they scored one less and leaked in eight more goals. The side achieved a total of 41 points, one fewer than 1950-51. Only three teams had won at Upton Park, but in contrast West Ham had won only twice on their travels.

The Hammers were the Essex Professional Cup holders, having won the trophy in 1951, beating Southend 2-1 in the Final. Malcolm Allison bagged the first and Jimmy Andrews got the winner. In 1952 the Irons again reached the Final, but this time there was only a Jim Barrett consolation in reply to Colchester's triple. Derek Parker recalled; "When we lost the Essex Professional Cup in the 1952 Final Ted was a bit upset, even though it was a relatively minor game. He had come from Colchester of course."

1952-53 — Be amazed... this was Dick Walker

Despite what many supporters believe, between the end of one season and the start of another, the world continues to turn. At the end of July 1952 the enormously popular Eva Peron, wife of Argentinean president Juan Peron, died of cancer. She was 33 years of age. The one-time film and radio actress had married Juan at the age of 16, he was 40 years of age at the time. She became a powerful, tough unofficial political leader. At the height of her popularity she had promised to stand as vice-president. She organised women workers, secured the vote for women, pushed for government spending on welfare, and introduced compulsory religious education in schools. In May 1953, while on tour of South America with England, Billy Wright helped carry a wreath at a service for Eva. I've looked for this event every time I've seen the film *Evita* but I always fall asleep before I come across it.

In Egypt, King Farouk had abdicated shortly after the seizure of power by General Neguib.

The promise of the first game of the season, a 1-0 home win against Southampton, was not carried through the early games of 1952-53. Four points were picked up in the first four games, although the Hammers' record of a win, two draws and only one defeat doesn't look all that bad at a distance. At this point George Petchey was brought into the side in place of Gerry Gazzard.

When my visit to Eric Parsons was over, I made the short journey to the home of George Petchey. George was a big, fit man, looking nowhere near his near his years. He spoke with a Cockney accent, demonstrating his roots in the East End of the 1930s. He was watching Manchester United on television as they continued their march to the FA Cup Final. I feared that I was interrupting things, but he wanted me to start our talk as the whistle went for half-time. First he told me something about his background and how his career in football started.

"All my family lived in Whitechapel. We left there when I was five, and then we moved out to Hornchurch. My dad worked for Manor Crossman in Commercial Road. I have one brother; he played for Millwall and then went to Watford. He's got his own business now; he's the owner of 'K Lifts'. He's done all right…He's done very well…He's very rich actually. I went to Aloft School in Elm Park. I was born in Whitechapel Hospital and lived in Watney Street. I had two cartilages out there. The teacher who worked with me died; he was a Spitfire pilot.

"I was playing for the school and Essex and could have gone to quite a few clubs, most of the London clubs, but I'd always been interested in West Ham, but they were a bit reluctant really. I played for their junior team at Canvey Island. I scored a lot of goals. The bloke in charge of the youths was a horrible man. They always had people that hadn't been in the game looking after the youths. I made sure, when I was on the other side of the game, to look after the kids and get good pro coaches.

"When I first went to Upton Park there were some great players. Len Goulden was there and Stan Foxall. Charlie Paynter signed me. He wanted me to go full-time but I went part-time. At 18 I was about to go in the Army. I was in the Stock Exchange, earning a lot of money. I didn't want to leave the Stock Exchange for that reason. West Ham could only give me a fiver a week - which was still good money, twice as much as my father was earning.

"I went to West Ham when I was 14. I got on well with Charlie Paynter, he would always talk to me, tell me what he was thinking. He told you how he wanted you to play. I signed as a pro on my 17th birthday. I was quite young to get in because there was Ron Cater, Derek Parker, millions of midfield players. To get in the first team was impossible for anyone like me.

"I went in the Army for two years. When I came out Ted Fenton was the manager, and I didn't get on with him very well. He didn't even know I was with the Club. When I came out of the Army he hadn't seen me play. Nobody contacted me while I was in the Army. I went all over with the Army. I was due to spend the last three months in Whitehall, as I got picked to play for the Army. It was in that time that Britain got involved in Korea, so I was in another six months, which sickened me. I was in Whitehall for nine months in all in the end. I used to try to nip off to get to training on Tuesday and Thursday nights, but I could never get down there.

"It was just after I got picked for the Army that I started to play for the reserves quite a bit. Ted must have seen in the paper that I'd played for the Army and that I was from West Ham, I used to play in the 'A' team on a Wednesday, the reserves on Saturdays. If we had a full squad, I wouldn't get a game on Saturday. It wasn't a morale boosting time." He chuckled at the understatement. George had a dry, satirical, almost black sense of humour, and an infectious laugh.

1952-53 – Be amazed... this was Dick Walker

"It was a waste of time, I was getting on, I was getting to 20. If I wasn't good enough I'd have rather have packed it in and got a job. The first year I came out of the Army, it was difficult to become a member of the Club. Derek Parker looked after me when I was demobbed. He was a hell of a good player; smashing bloke. I was all right with the young ones, Kenny Brown, Bondy and Andy Malcolm; I grew up with them and the likes of Derek Parker, Frank O'Farrell, Dickey Walker, Ernie Gregory and Tommy Southren; we played well together Tommy and I, in the reserves. We played about a thousand games together. I think…I always found that if they wanted a player at that time, the young ones got pushed to the side. Being one of the young ones, it was difficult to get involved, because they had over 60 pros, some of them part-time; tremendously big staff.

"I was very competitive. A bit hard I suppose. I could play and I enjoyed beating people. I could do that as well. That was the satisfaction I got out of the game. I scored from midfield. I was an old-fashioned inside-forward. Gerry Gazzard got injured once, and I thought I would go in because I was in the reserves. They bought George Dick, so I went back another three paces. I used to look at George Dick; he was a big fat lump who wouldn't work. He didn't want to know. The fee they paid for him was a record for the club at the time. I couldn't understand how he was keeping his place. I used to kick lumps out of him in practice matches. I used to hate him. I should have been in the team! I got in once, but there was never going to be any future there. It was very unusual for a young player to get a chance in the team in those days. You were 21 and they said you had plenty of time, just stick at it."

George remembered the training regime at Upton Park; "West Ham was all football. They used to have a practice match on a Tuesday morning, and they'd be 40 of us sitting in the stand watching, waiting for a chance to get in the game. It was quite hard because all the players I'd seen play as a kid - Dickey Walker and Ernie Gregory and them - were there. When we had practice matches I always did well. Ernie always talks about the time we spent trying to finish things off; him and George Taylor used to go in goal and make us keep kicking 'em straight at them. 'You're supposed to get them in the net!'" George said this as if he were Gregory referring to the young Petchey. George chortled at the thought of the two Hammers goalies shutting all efforts out.

He went on; "George Taylor had a lot of trouble towards the end". I wanted to explore this statement, there were all sorts of rumours about Taylor and I'd been told things about him that I was asked not to record, but George was on a roll that I didn't want to interrupt;

"Billy Moore used to make me work hard, he was a big help to me. He used to bring me back every afternoon. When I was in the Army I put on over two stone. I went in at 11 stone and came out at 13 stone 6lb. I spent a year trying to get fit. If you lost the day-to-day habit of training you struggled. But I still enjoyed it at West Ham; it was great! The young ones were coming through at that time - Dave Sexton, we grew up together. We had a good time together Dave and me - Bondy and Cantwell too...We all knew each other. It was a great atmosphere because we were all local lads… We were all fans.

"There were no really outstanding players. Ronnie Cater got picked for England B. There was no one compared to the previous generation, who were there when I came through, towards the end of the war; Archie McCauley, the Corbett brothers and Len Goulden. I was sorry to see Goulden go. He had quite an influence. I used to hold on to it a lot. John Dick was a good player. I never wanted to play the way he played, but he scored a few goals". Looking back some of what George told me seems fairly cryptic, but as with all good coaches and teachers, sometimes it's not so much what is said as how it said; it's a bigger picture that gets painted. George had a voice that was easy to listen to, but he also had a type of slightly intimidating authority that sort of said 'shut up and listen and you might learn something'. At the same time the less I interjected the more he elaborated; 'you let me talk and I'll talk' was the message I was picking up.

"I had two first-team games, both at Upton Park, successive matches in September 1952. The first was a 0-0 draw against Hull and the second was a 2-1 defeat by Birmingham. Against Birmingham I was marking an international, it was a battle rather than a game. West Ham were having a bad run at the time, a lot of injuries, that's why I got in. I then got an injury, I chipped a bone in my ankle…It still bloody hurts!" George gave a slight smile. I got the impression it was more than his ankle that was smarting.

"That put me out for a hell of a long time. When I came back from that there were so many players, especially young ones, I had no chance. Malcolm Allison was a good bloke. He had lots of good ideas. He really wanted me in the side; he was trying hard to get me in the team all the time. But it was never going to happen as there was so many people in front.

1952-53 – Be amazed… this was Dick Walker

"The crowd and area were great. We used to get looked after well; the people were always with you. There were no groups who were against you. I got the train from Hornchurch, where I lived, to Upton Park, see the same people every morning. If you won everybody would chat to you…if you lost no one used to talk to you.

"There were people like Ken Tucker at the club, so the social side of things was pretty lively. You couldn't afford to go out drinking. Now they order two bottles of champagne - we couldn't afford a bottle of beer! I was quite close to Andy Malcolm, he used to live near me. But you used to get benefits in those days, three to five hundred quid. At 24 I was due a benefit, but I had to wait another year before I got anywhere near getting it paid. You used to be entitled to expenses, but when I first played for the juniors I didn't ask for it. I was just proud to play for the Club. But when I signed part-time, I got £2 less than everyone else when I played. I thought that was paltry. Anything to do with money, you had to see Frank Cearns. He said you'd get it next week and it wouldn't be there next week. You never got it! You got fed up with going in. It annoyed me, because I used to knock about with a couple of Tottenham lads, and they got their money on time."

This difficulty with money meant George was obliged to find a job outside the game. "I worked part-time in Manor Crossman, putting the yeast in the vats, cleaning the vats. It kept you fit; lot of lifting to do. It was the first hard work I'd ever done in my life; done me a lot of good when I became a manager."

In July 1953, George moved to Loftus Road. He recalled; "The best times for me at West Ham were when I first went there from school, there was a great atmosphere. Charlie Paynter was a good character and a good bloke to work for. He understood the game. I didn't have the same relationship with Ted Fenton. I never really spent any time with him. It took us a year to get to know each other and when we did we still weren't sure of each other. He was a bit strange."

In the FA Cup, the Hammers had only the one game. West Brom, who had the best away record in the First Division, kept up their reputation and their record by winning 4-1 at Upton Park. The special training camp, set up at Letchworth in the snow, by Fenton had obviously not done the job. However, in Egypt General Neguib had. He dissolved all political parties and took dictatorial powers.

A week earlier, the Hammers snatched victory from defeat in recovering from 2-0 down to beat Bury, 3-2. Kearns scored all West Ham's goals against the Shakers, as well as the one against West Brom. This was 25th League game of the season and only the ninth win for the Irons.

The day after Britain tested its first atomic bomb, Rotherham had blown West Ham away, 4-2 at Upton Park. Between this and a 3-0 defeat at Ewood Park, a horrifying train disaster at Harrow put things into perspective. Two trains crashed on 8th October and a third, travelling at high speed, hit the wreckage seconds later. An early morning commuter train just leaving Harrow Station was struck on the rear by an express from Scotland, which had somehow got on the wrong line. An express from Euston then ploughed into the other two trains and brought an overhead bridge down. A total of 112 people died, over 200 were injured and it took days to clear the tracks.

Later that month, just after the announcement of the Mau Mau emergency in Kenya, the Hammers had an emergency of their own, losing 2-0 at Goodison Park. The struggle for freedom in British colonial Africa took many forms but in most cases the transition was peaceful. Only in Kenya did a particular freedom movement, the Mau Mau, led by Jomo Kenyatta, an eventual president of Kenya, use violence, killing white settlers. The British, predictably at this tail-end of colonialism, used counter-violence, historically making matters worse.

Malcolm Allison was now firmly installed at centre-half, and the home defeat by Plymouth Argyle in February marked the final first-team outing for the loyal Dick Walker. Dick's name has been etched into the history of the Hammers by a love affair between the player and the Upton Park crowd, which spanned three decades and almost 600 matches in all competitions, 311 in the first team. Walker scored only two goals for the Club, one a season over the 1947-49 period. Despite first seeing the light of day in view of the sacred football marshes of Hackney, Dick took up the game at a relatively mature age for a future Upton Park icon. It was when he and his family relocated to Dagenham that Dick began to develop his play, on Sunday mornings, as an inside-forward with the local Becontree Athletic side.

It was not too long before he caught the eye of Paynter scout Revins and was asked to turn out for a few games in the London Midweek League, in 1932-33. Following this flirtation, he joined the West London club, Park Royal. And after playing for the Royals against West Ham at Upton Park, the Hammers brought him home to begin a relationship which was to encompass more than 20 years. Dick made his first-team debut at right-half, against Burnley at the Boleyn Ground in August 1934. He performed a range of defensive roles before finally taking over from the formidable Jim Barrett at centre-half in 1936, at a point when the nature of this position was changing dramatically. Had the war not interrupted Dick's progress, it is highly likely that he would have played for his country and maybe threatened Jimmy Ruffell's appearances record for the Irons.

Dick Walker was known for his humour and love of a practical joke. His leave from the Parachute Regiment during wartime to play for West Ham was premised by speculation about his current rank which seemed to be on a sliding scale between private and sergeant and back to private again. He represented the Army in the Middle East and played for West Ham just 24 times in the war years up to 1945, although that figure included every game in the Hammers' triumphant War Cup season of 1939-40.

In 1945-46, in the League South, he turned out on 44 occasions. After World War Two, Dick was elected captain of the side following the retirement of Charlie Bicknall. It must have been a melancholy end to his first-team career when he made his final appearance in the Second Division. The lowest crowd ever for a League match at Upton Park watched Dick and the rest of the Irons lose 1-0, but the centre-half turned in his normal impeccable performance, earning the respect of each of the 8,000 Upton Park stalwarts who had turned up to cheer Dick Walker into the sunset of his career.

On 14 November 1952, the comparatively new popular music newspaper the *New Musical Express* became the first to publish a chart of the best-selling records in the country. Sheet music charts had been around in Britain off and on since 1936, while *Billboard* magazine in the US had been listing the best-selling records in America since July 1940. However, it was not until well after the end of World War Two that the idea of charts started to be thought of as important in the music industry on the east side of the Atlantic. By the beginning of the Fifties, it wasn't so much the song, rather than a certain recording of that song, that was to motivate people to go to the shops and buy a disc. As such, it was inevitable that a record chart should be produced. For all this, the *NME* chart did not eliminate the sheet music chart; that remained at least as important for around three more years, being put together with a greater degree of accuracly.

The *NME* chart of 14 November 1952 was a Top 12 that was in reality a Top 15 because two records were placed in equal seventh, eighth and eleventh places. The sheet music Number One since 25 October that year, *Here in My Heart,* by Al Martino, also turned out to be the Number One record. The two previous sheet music Number Ones, *Homing Waltz* and *Auf Wiedersehen,* both by East Ham girl and West Ham supporter, Vera Lynn, were on the record list. She also had another hit, *Forget Me Not,* in that very first chart, so making the 'Forces Sweetheart' the most successful chart artist of the year, despite Martino staying at Number One for each of the seven charts that year.

With the demise of Dick Walker, the only real competition for Allison's place was teenager Ken Brown, who came into the side for the next game. Ken might be seen to be typical of the home-grown East End player. Bobby Moore once said of him; "Ken Brown was far from being everyone's ideal at centre-half, but he was right for us. He was powerful in the air and his priority was always to get the ball the hell out of the danger area. Sometimes he would whack it away when I thought we should capitalise on a situation and I'd say; 'Brownie, what are you doing?' He'd say; 'Don't worry, it's no trouble up there.' But he was always positive and it took a long while to replace him. He had a good understanding with John Bond." On one occasion Bobby told me, "Ken is one of the nicest guys in football. It's hard to find fault with him." I must say, after meeting Ken, I couldn't agree more.

Brown had been brought up in the style of play developed in the first few years of the Academy, but in other ways Brown was in the tradition of West Ham professionals. He was a favourite of the crowd from the beginning. His smile and ability to accept a mistake caused the fans and his team-mates to warm to him. This was not unlike Dick Walker's style, although Brown probably had greater all-round ability than the former captain. He was a non-nonsense player practically, but he also understood the way aspects of the game (defence and attack) were part of the same system, something that could not be said of the majority of players in the Fifties, certainly beyond Upton Park.

"In those days," Ken remembered, "they didn't have squads, they had three teams. If someone wasn't playing well or they were injured, the reserve came straight in. I was in the 'A' team when both Malcolm Allison and Dick Walker were injured and I got three games on the trot, all draws."

Ken's debut took place in mid-February, at Rotherham's Millmoor Ground.

"In the first match Ernie Gregory was a bit hindered by the sun shining straight in his face from one side. He told me to cover all balls coming into the box from that direction. I've never headed the ball so many times. Anyway, I gave away a penalty, I felt terrible. The penalty was struck well and I knew that it was going in the top corner. Ernie literally flew and he tipped it over. I was so pleased. I was jumping up and down and tried to grab him to congratulate him, but he pushed me and told me to, 'go away' every time I got near him. 'I should have caught it,' is all he said."

I met with Ken at the Lakenham Leisure Centre in Norwich where he was the sports coordinator. I recognised him as soon as he walked through the door, as usual smiling. I thanked 'Mr Brown' for taking the time to see me. "Ken's the name," he said, shaking my hand firmly. He immediately ordered us coffee. He had retained his Cockney accent, although it was tinged with a soft, East Anglian lilt. Snow had fallen the night before and was hard on the ground that frosty morning, so he was looking forward to a winter break in Dubai. He was also looking forward to his second marriage in the coming June.

From the future to the past. Although born not too far from the Boleyn Ground, Ken's family moved to Dagenham, where he became a pupil at Lymington Secondary Modern School. Growing up in Dagenham, he had not paid much attention to any professional club. He had no favourite and knew no more about West Ham than about any other side. He started playing football at 12 and was chosen for Dagenham Boys as 15 year old.

Ken took up the story; "I was playing for Neville United [Ken met his first wife at a Neville United dance in Dagenham]. The team was run by Bobby Flanders, we used to use his bathroom to clean up after games. We had a match against the West Ham 'B' team and after the game I was approached by Wally St Pier. I told him; 'No thanks'. We'd beaten West Ham and I didn't want to play for a team we could beat. I was training to be a wood machinist at the time. Well anyway, I played for West Ham in the London Midweek League, at the Spotted Dog, this is Clapton's ground, an amateur club not far from Upton Park. I liked playing a lot; I looked forward to the games. The firm I was working for, Greves, was based between Bow and Stratford. They told me that I was having too much time off and that, it was either football or work. By then I was a qualified cutter."

Having completed an apprenticeship as a machinist, and not yet 18, Ken had a good job with a solid future. West Ham was paying him for broken time.

"I was training with West Ham on Tuesday and Thursday evenings and decided that I would ask the Pratts [Reg Pratt had become chairman after the death of W. J. Cearns. ; F. R. Pratt, father of Reg, was also on the West Ham board] for a job. I saw Ted Fenton and piled it on a bit. He told me that he would sign me as a professional. 'What, football, not work?" I said. I hadn't expected that. I literally ran home to Dagenham, I was that pleased. I must have looked a bit nuts; I could have been locked up! I told my mum, but she didn't really understand. She said something like; 'That's good.'"

The 17-year-old had to make the choice. He recalled; When I had a chance to get paid to play for West Ham, I told my employer, politely, what he could do with his work." Brown took a cut in wages from £12 to £9 a week for the chance to play football as a full-timer.

Brown's real education in the game came from Dick Walker, who was an important senior player; "Everybody knew him. He was smart, somebody to look up to."

There were not many technical skills that Walker could pass on to Brown, but he did teach him 'never to let anybody down, to work and play hard'.

"Dick Walker was a wonderful man. I lived in the same street as him. The kids would watch him walk the length of the road to where his mum lived and we would look out of the window and be amazed that this was DICK WALKER! When I started at the Club he told me to be at his house at nine o'clock. I got there at five to and he sent me away, telling me to come back at the time he had told me. I did, and as we made our way to the bus stop, he told me that we would take it in turns to pay the bus fares and the tea at Cassatarri's. This seemed fair so I agreed. We got on the bus, he always insisted on sitting on the long seats, and I paid our fares. When we got to the ground, we went into the cafe and I got the teas.

"The next day came and I got to Dick's house dead on nine. We got to the bus stop and the bus came along, but Dick said that he didn't fancy that one, so we waited for the next. This bus had a woman conductress. Dick chatted and laughed with her, but she didn't ask him for any fares. When we got to the cafe, Phil Cassatarri gave him the teas but wouldn't accept any payment. The next day I got to Dick's house about a minute after nine. 'Back to your old habits,' he said. We got on the bus and he told me to pay the fares. I said; 'But it's your turn.' He told me; 'It was my turn yesterday.' 'But you didn't pay," I said. Dick replied; 'We agreed that you would get the fares on alternate days and today it's your turn.' So I had to pay. I had to pay for our teas as well, of course. But he was a good man Dick, as long as you stayed on his good side." Ken smiled at the story that gave me a strong impression about the character of the Club and the relationship between the veteran and the novice player.

Ken had come into the West Ham first team while still in the forces.

"I was stationed at Aldershot when I was called up. When they issued jobs I was the last one left, but Ted Fenton had phoned and I was made runner to the RSM (Regimental Sergeant Major); RSM Bridger. I was in the office doing little jobs. I worked around the sergeant's mess and got a room to myself."

1952-53 – Be amazed... this was Dick Walker

When Ken came out of the Army in 1954, there had been quite a few changes at West Ham, but these were not surprises as he had played for the Club most of the time he was in the forces. A new group of players had joined the Hammers and up to 1957 most of his time was spent in the 'A' side. But Ken was philosophical; "In those days you knew where you stood. Every player had his place. I knew my time would come. I would make that spot mine. I had to be more patient than most people since Malcolm Allison, who, at the time, held the centre-half berth, was more or less running things

"The social side of the Club got better as time went by. I was close to Malcolm Musgrove and to Andy Malcolm, even when I was in the reserves; he was in the first team. I was a bit of skinny lad and Dick Walker thought I should put on weight otherwise, according to Dick, I would never last. Andy had a car and Dick would take the two of us up to Soho every Friday for a glass of stout and a big steak and kidney pie, full of meat and gravy. He never paid, though. 'You'll have a blinder,' he told us."

Ken Brown's first home game was against Blackburn.

"My mum and dad came to the second game. The opposing centre-forward that day was Tony Briggs and at one point he smashed the ball straight into my face and I was knocked cold. My mum was in tears - 'my boy!' That was the last game she came to."

Ken played his last game of the 1952-53 season at the City Ground, Nottingham. He didn't turn out again in the Football League until August 1954, but he was far from idle.

"Dad got a back injury, so for a while I worked for Whitbread's in the summer."

West Ham were always alive to the perils of the demon drink, especially for the working class Cockney boys who suffered from all the stereotypes applied to East Enders. At the same time, when it came to the younger player, the Club was keen to take every opportunity to act in a paternalistic manner. As such, it may not have been a surprise for Ken when Fenton objected. "Ted insisted that I couldn't work in the brewery, so I went on the lorries. I enjoyed that a lot."

Ken Brown got a run of 23 matches at the start of 1954-55 before Malcolm Allison returned to the centre-half position. Ken played in only two games in 1955-56 and just five the following term, but he was almost ever-present in the championship year and the following three seasons.

Often described as 'cool or calm', Ken was a consistent and commanding centre-half. "I could always head a ball. I never got ruffled. People say that I'm never miserable, but when you've worked in a factory, you realise how lucky you are to play football for a living."

This may have also helped Ken appreciate those who came to watch him, those who had no other choice but to work in the factories, shops and offices. "Before a match I would always come out last and run as fast as I could across the pitch, towards the Chicken Run, just to relieve the tension. Every time, I saw this black bloke in the crowd and I had to acknowledge him. He'd always wait until the crowd went quiet and then shout out; 'I'm here again Browney boy,' and he'd give me the thumbs up. Everyone would laugh. One day he shouted out; 'I'm not on your side today.' I looked at him in surprise. 'Blackburn!' he said. That day we were playing Rovers. There were three own goals that day [5 November 1955] - not my fault!" Ken chuckled.

Brown played 455 games for West Ham and scored four goals. "My first goal for the club was a header, from a Peter Brabrook corner." This came in the 5-0 walloping of Birmingham City at Upton Park in October 1962. "In those days it was practically unheard of for a centre-half to go up."

For Ken, playing professional football, in the first year of his full-time career, was the highlight of his Fifties playing days. However, the 1964 FA Cup Final and the sight of the crowds from Petticoat Lane to Barking that welcomed the team back were his most abiding memories. He recalled the home coming from Wembley. "We kept on seeing one bloke in different venues - he had a sports car, but how he got through the crowds was a mystery."

The Korean War was not to end with a bang or a final heroic gesture but was beginning to fizzle out as both sides tired of the sporadic, one-off operations which took place over the early months of the year.

A draw and couple of wins following Malcolm Allison's return to the Second Division side were followed by three defeats for the Hammers, in the process conceding of 11 goals, the attack clawing back just three,

Dave Sexton, who was to become one of the greatest coaches England ever produced, came into the West Ham first team for the next game, Fulham's visit to Upton Park in April 1953. It was not the best of days for the Hammers, who lost 2-1 in front of their home supporters.

"I was born in Islington, which is Arsenal territory." Dave said. "But I grew up in Chingford and went to St Ignatias College, Stamford Hill, which was a rugby playing school. Our pitch was right behind the Spurs ground and we got to know the grounds-man, whose father was a former Scottish professional footballer. He ran a youth team that I got involved with - and that meant I played rugby on Saturday mornings and soccer in the afternoons."

St Ignatias was a Jesuit institution and maybe did much to provide Dave with the discipline he would need to make it to the top of his profession. The Hammers had to ask Dave to join them twice before he took up the opportunity to come to the Boleyn Ground. He was eventually signed from Luton, but as a 16-year-old had been offered a trial at West Ham. "I turned it down because it would have meant travelling to Canvey Island to play the matches. That was a long way from Chingford then and the fact I was happy where I was swung it for me. After completing my National Service I joined Chelmsford City in the Southern League, before being signed by Luton. West Ham signed me from there.

"I was with West Ham when we were a Second Division side who hardly set the game alight, but I've never been with a group of players so hungry for knowledge and so determined to improve themselves. The real big turning point in our careers came in 1953, when the Hungarians came to Wembley and caused a shock by beating England 6-3 with the sort of football none of us had ever seen before. No foreign team had ever done that to England and the way that Hungary played that day opened our eyes and stimulated us. It was an awesome performance, one that lived in the memory forever." In October that year Dave gained the only representative honour of his playing career when he was selected to play for an FA XI against the RAF.

"Upton Park was full of characters in those days, Dick Walker and Ernie Gregory among them. The fact that they had been around a long time didn't give them any fancy ideas and they were always ready to give advice and help to the youngsters. I'm still grateful to this day for everything they did for me and it was people like those two who made West Ham the kind of club it is. It was the best grounding you could wish for, as the way the players work things out meant you were totally involved in how the team worked. We'd meet in the café and work out different ways of doing things, talk about different things we had found out about the game and wanted to try or adapt. That's the best way to learn; having ideas, putting them together with other people's theories, trying them out and then looking at how they worked and how you could build on them. It was very rewarding; exciting in fact."

Dave made 77 appearances in the claret and blue and scored 29 goals. He grabbed two hat-tricks, both at Upton Park. He got all the goals against Rotherham in September 1953, West Ham winning 3-0. His second triple was part of a 6-1 defeat of Plymouth in February 1955. In his final match for West Ham, the last game of 1955-56, Dave got a pair in the 3-0 Boleyn Ground defeat of Bristol City. This made him the only West Ham player to score two goals in their last game for the club. Dave's first goal helped the Hammers to a good 3-2 win at Craven Cottage. Tommy Dixon put West Ham's other two notches on the Fulham posts.

Tommy Dixon looked good when I met with him at the Red Lion pub in Bushey, a town locked fast between the M1 and the M25. Tom was still a tall, muscular man, looking about 20 years short of his age. He put his condition down to not smoking and to playing golf. He started his working life as a cinema projectionist. Although he has lived in the south-east for most of his life, Tom told me about his background and football connections with a definite Geordie twang. "My mum was a cleaner and my dad worked in the shipyards. He would tell me to go and pull the draw out of the sideboard and take a medal out. He said; 'I got this medal for football.' He did, but all he did was carry the goalposts out and play if they were short of a goalkeeper. My family had no football history. My brother was in the Navy. He was a goalkeeper.

"I went to Stevenson Memorial School in Howden. I was 12 when the war started and it was 'dig for victory'. There was 60 of us, 30 used to dig and 30 used to play football and turn around. I was 17 when I went in the forces. I was stationed in Singapore, played a lot of football there. I played left wing for one team, full-back for another team and centre-forward for another team, so I had plenty of football. I was in the RAF." He pointed to his fine head of slicked-back hair that had no hint of grey. "Brylcream boys, can't yer see? Keeps the grey away," he smiled."

It is almost a story book tale, how the young Tommy came into the professional game. "I was in the youth club. I got one night off a week to play. This night we got beat 6-1, but I got the only goal. A feller asked; 'Where's Tom Dixon?' And he was told that I was sitting in the corner. Well that was George Martin, manager of Newcastle United. He says; 'Would you like a trial for Newcastle United?' And I says; 'Well, I wouldn't mind'. I was told to meet him at the Station Hotel to play for the reserves. Well, I told my dad and he couldn't believe it. I went up there and played against Wolverhampton Wanderers, we got beat 2-1 and there was a bloke there who told me that if I laid on the goal-line I might score a goal. So, that was the start of the football.

"I heard nothing more after that, then I got a call from Tot Smith, who used to run the 'A' team and 'B' team at St James. He asked me to come and play for them. I played with them, but I was getting nowhere. My ex-wife's uncle knew Billy Moore, a trainer at West Ham. He phoned Billy up and said; 'This lad's playing in good company and he's worth a look at. So, low and behold, Saturday morning the doorbell went and there was a guy with big horn rimmed glasses and he says; 'My name's Jack Harper and I'm the scout for West Ham. When he came in my dad showed him the programmes and he said; 'He's playing in good company.' And Jack said; 'Would you like to come a speak to Ted Fenton?' I said that I was, going to Butlin's with my girl-friend. Jack Harper told me; 'Don't do anything. I'll speak to Ted and come back Monday.'

"Ted met me at the Station Hotel and we had tea and coffee. He got the contracts out and I signed 'em. He gave me two white fivers. He gave me a little lapel badge and said; 'Welcome to West Ham! Go and enjoy your holidays and I'll see you when you come back.'

"You got £14 in the first team at West Ham and £9 in the reserves, just seven if you didn't make the team. We didn't get paid for goals in those days."

It seems Tom settled down to life at West Ham pretty swiftly.

"When I lived in digs in Macaulay Road, with Bert Hawkins, we used to dread Thursday nights - boiled sausages; that was a strange dish [a Cockney favourite – saveloys]. When I got married we got a clubhouse down Wigstone Road. Sixpence [2 ½ p] on the trolley bus and you jumped off at the corner. I had my wedding reception at Cassatarri's; £5 was the bill. They used to make a fuss of me. I used to go in and pay a pound for my food and they'd give me a couple of ten-shilling notes change. They wouldn't take money for the food. I said to Ted Fenton; 'I'm getting married, am I playing?' It was the start of the season. He says; 'Yeah, I think you're playing.' So I says; 'Well, I got a lot a guests. Is there any chance of some tickets?' He said; 'Yeah, I'll get you some tickets.' He got me 20 odd, but I didn't play. I was sitting up in the stand. That's when Roy Stroud was there.

"I didn't model myself on anybody. At West Ham, Dick Walker used to look after us. I stripped next to Dickey. For a joke Dick would always look at the sheet and ask; 'Nothing for me?' Of course he was rarely out of the side when he was fit. I used to go back in the afternoons and train with Dick.

"Training was very easy going. Billy Moore would have his fag on while he was massaging you. Sometimes a bit of ash would drop on your leg and he'd just keep massaging. We had a practice match every Tuesday morning; the first team would get the home dressing-room. It was red against blues. If you had a red shirt you were in the first team, if you had a blue shirt you played in the reserves. I would sometimes go out in a blue shirt and go up against Malcolm [Allison] and I gave him a runaround. At half-time Ted would say; 'Tom, put on a red shirt.' We'd have Scottish versus the English, singles against marrieds in heading tennis. Sometimes we went up to Hainault on Wednesdays and train there.

"I played at the Spotted Dog [Clapton's ground]. In the dressing-room, above the fireplace, was a sign that said; 'It is better to have ten shots and score once than to have no shots and score no goals.' Not a bad piece of advice generally in life I thought. After training at the ground we'd go to the Denmark. I used to go by the wood factory, Austin's. I always used to have a chat with one of the guys there. The players would go down the old Granada and see the turns in the afternoon at the matinees." The Granada was a cinema, it was the place in Newham where I saw Beatles perform at the height of their fame. My mum took my brother and me; a very odd outing looking back. I say 'saw' because you couldn't hear a thing with all the girls screaming. The Granada is now, guess what, a bingo hall!

Tom spoke about the competition for places during his time at Upton Park.

"You had to fight for your place. You took a drop in pay if you fell out of the first team and you had to have a fitness test. You had to be in the side. Freddie Kearns was centre-forward, Billy Dare came in. Very quiet spoken he was. I saw him at a match at Hillingdon before he died."

The pace and sheer ignorance of training techniques in the Fifties has taken its toll on most of the players I saw while writing this book. Tommy Dixon look very fit for his age, but he told me; "I've got arthritis in me ankle now and a bit in my knees"

It was 4 April 1953 when Tom made his first appearance in the Second Division, but West Ham were well beaten at Vetch Field, losing 4-1. Tom looked back at this game. "In my first game, against Swansea, I admired Ivor Allchurch. He was brilliant. They swamped us they did. We had to report back Sunday morning and I thought; 'Will I get a game?' The sheet went up and the team hadn't changed; Dave Sexton was still inside-forward. We came in on Easter Monday and we beat Fulham 3-2 after being 2-0 down at half-time. I got two. Then, on the Saturday, we lost at Upton Park against Huddersfield, 1-0."

On 16 April Upton Park staged a friendly against Tottenham Hotspur. This made Upton Park only the second floodlit ground after Highbury, so the Irons became one of the pioneers of floodlit friendly games. It was a big event at the Boleyn Ground and a keenly fought match. Goals by Barrett and Dixon gave West Ham a 2-1 win. The

Irons played in fluorescent shirts. One match report stated; 'The lights seem to make the game look faster. It was like watching a fantastic ballet in glorious Technicolour.' Tom recalled; "For some exhibition and friendly games in the early Fifties, West Ham would play in a silk strip. The silky strip came in for the first time at the five-a-sides at Olympia. I don't know why, but I played in goal. Charlton won that night, just because they had Sam Bartram in goal.

"For the Spurs match I got £10 cash in hand. It was all hush-hush. There was a knock at the door, it was Mr Cearns, the Club secretary, and Ted stuffed the money in a draw. After that we got vouchers for the Army and Navy Stores."

A week after West Ham faced Tottenham, a strong, stylish St Mirren side played out an exciting 3-3 draw under the lights. This meant, with the remaining League fixtures, that West Ham had played six games in three weeks.

Tom talked about the fans.

"We'd support the Supporters' Club, if they had dances and that, sign autographs. I was friendly with Fred and Doreen Chadwick, they were supporters. When we played away I got the tickets for them. They went to Butlins with us. They lived in the same street as Jimmy Andrews and Jim Barrett.

"As you ran out at West Ham, a little feller used to play a post horn, the *Post Horn Gallop*. You'd stand in the tunnel and the band would strike up, it was great. Terry Woodgate used to stand and talk to them in the old Chicken Run. He used to ask; 'How much time is there left?' We appreciated the crowd. West Ham was brilliant to play for, great camaraderie with the supporters."

On 14th September, 1953, West Ham and Tom got some revenge at Upton Park. "After I got a hat-trick against Swansea, I read that I had got into Walter Winterbottom's book. 'That's as far as I'll go', I thought. There were too many good players around, Jackie Milburn, Nat Lofthouse, Roy Bentley, and I was in the Second Division. I'd promised that if ever I got a hat-trick I'd give the ball to the local Boys Brigade - they appreciated that. I used to be in 'em myself.

"The big game was Blackpool at home." This was the 1954 fourth-round FA Cup tie. Tom scored West Ham's goal in the first match at Upton Park.

"Up at Blackpool, for the replay, there was three inches of snow on the ground. I didn't think it would be on and I had to have a fitness test. I passed the fitness test and it was my great honour to foul Stanley Matthews." He chuckled, and recalled the ironic response of the Blackpool wing genius; 'Good tackle Tom!'

Tom went on; "Harry Johnstone, the manager of Reading when I was there, told me that Stanley Matthews was a nervous wreck. He was sick in the dressing-room, a mass of nerves. He worried about his vitamins and diet. He was a hypochondriac!"

Tom recalled when the time came for him to leave Upton Park. "Ted Fenton called me in the office and told me that Reading were very interested in me. They were in the Third Division South at the time. He told me if I went down there I'd do all right, with my benefit and all that. I said; 'If that's what you want.' I was 26 and I couldn't see myself getting any further. I was in and out."

Although he admits that in his first season with the Club he hardly set the Boleyn Ground on fire - "I did nothing in my first season" - he did score 23 goals in 42 matches, a pretty good average, given that his longest run in the first team was 13 games. Tom remembered his West Ham colleagues with admiration.

"Nobody could get past Derek Parker. He could run. Harry Hooper was an outstanding player. It was always difficult to say with Tommy Southren who'd go in the side. But on his day Tommy was a great player. Albert Foan was a good player too. Then there were Ernie Devlin, Gerry Gazzard. The Club used to take Dick Walker down to Brighton for Cup tie training because he was such a great character."

Tom also had some good words for the non-playing staff. "Charlie Paynter was a nice bloke, as was Wally St Pier. He was always so softly spoken, always asked how you were. Mr Pratt was a nice man too."

He reiterated what he saw as the main strength running through the West Ham team; "Camaraderie! No animosity. No one wanted to know what the other was earning. We didn't know! The meals at the Denmark kept us together. We had characters at the Club."

Tom's views on the evolving science of football at Upton Park in the Fifties is typically pragmatic;".. .4-4-2? How can two fellers make their way through five defenders? I was brought up on five players up front, wingers coming down the line, crosses coming in...I was 13 years a professional footballer. I'd do it all again."

That Upton Park defeat by Swansea in the spring of 1953, together with the impending visit of London rivals Fulham, caused Ted Fenton to look hard at his defence. George Wright, Harry Kinsell and Derek Parker made way for Doug Bing, Danny McGowan and Noel Cantwell.

I went to the New Inn in Peterborough to meet with the former captain of West Ham, Manchester United and the Republic of Ireland. Harry Hooper, who I had seen earlier the same day on my way north from London, had told me that he thought that Noel Cantwell's place was a wine bar. Instead I found Noel and his wife Maggie running the most traditional of local hostelries. Maggie Cantwell was a good singer. On one occasion she sang in the Yankee Stadium.

Manchester United were on the television in the public bar, playing out yet another cup tie, and I had to wait until this was over before Noel was able to meet me. I understood completely. What is the point in interviewing someone whose mind is elsewhere?

Noel, an affable man, with a warm smile, looked back to how his professional career in England began. "It was soon after playing in a testimonial in Cork - Frank O'Farrell and Tony Mahony were playing - that I was recommended to Fenton. I was signed for a fee of £750. I got £150, which was in August 1952. All contracts at that time were one year. Ted thought I was a centre-forward, quite why I don't know.

"I moved into digs with Tony Moroney in Loxford Avenue, Mrs Turner was the landlady. She treated me like a son." Noel enjoyed his football, and the friendliness of his lodgings made up for there not being much of an Irish community in that part of the East End at the time. People were friendly not because he was a footballer but because the landlady made him part of the street and community. This was much the way of things in the districts surrounding Upton Park. The blitz was a recent memory and unless folk helped each other they were on their own, and with bombs falling nightly that wasn't a good place to be. This is the way of what we have come to call community; such connective collectiveness can't be implanted in some way, it happens when people have both a push and a pull incentive to come together. Sadly this rarely happens in modern Britain, for all the State's wishes to create 'community cohesion' which seems to start and end with 'Neigbourhood Watch' schemes.

The natives did a good deal to make Noel feel wanted, and he wasn't slow in coming forward. A young supporter at the time, who used to turn up with his friends to watch the team train, recalled; "The players would have to park at the top of a grassy slope and make their way to the changing rooms down the hill. Noel Cantwell would always borrow my bike for the trip."

Noel told me; "Although an attack-minded defender, I was played in several positions by Fenton. I wasn't comfortable as a centre-forward. I saw Ted and it was decided that I would move to left-back. I went into the 'A' team and then the first team, replacing Harry Kinsell."

As a boy, life became quite challenging for Noel early on. "My mum died when I was ten. I was the youngest of eight brothers and a sister. Dad was a tailor. He had a tough time, although he married again. His business suffered. Sport was a high priority when I was a boy. We lived near a cricket ground. After school we'd play sport. We had some top sportsmen coming from my area, for example Tom Kiernan, the international ruby player. I went to monastery school. Jack Lynch, a Prime Minister of the Republic, went there. I worked on the railway for a time and at Dunlop's, making Wellington boots.

"At Upton Park you just knew where people were. We were, at times, seen as big-headed bastards and I suppose we must have seemed that way at times. Even if you're not confident it pays to looks as if you are, but we did have confidence in each other and that might look like collective arrogance at a distance."

There is little doubt that Cantwell and John Bond were one of the best full-back partnerships the club has known, as Bill Lansdowne confirmed; "Noel Cantwell and John Bond were as good as any pair of full-backs around, they were quite a pair of characters."

This echoes what Noel told me about his on-field relationship with Bond; "We complimented each other and were not often surprised by what each other did, but I think there was also a sense of competition between us; who would be the most daring walking the ball out of the penalty area for example, giving poor old Ernie a heart attack."

The pairing was a major contribution to the side eventually winning the championship. According to Noel; "John Bond and I were controllers of the ball. Bondy was worse for holding on to it than me. At least I had some sense of responsibility, but John rarely lost it. He was an excellent striker of the dead ball. We developed an understanding where he would send the ball to a particular place and it was my job to get there, to find it. John didn't aim for the person, but the spot. Bondy was a bit of a coward the other way round, but I just went charging in."

Although Cantwell saw Bond's ability with the ball, he noted; "He couldn't tackle a fish supper." Cantwell was the complete opposite of Bond. The man from Cork was a natural athlete, he moved with a powerful grace and intelligence. From schoolboy level he had played for his nation, roving around the field from game to game, mastering a number of positions.

Noel moved from the 'A' team to the League side in his first year at Upton Park, but this meteoric rise did not make him complacent. He applied himself to the game mentally as well as physically. Bobby Moore told me that he was 'a great football teacher but a great student." This is confirmed by Cantwell's attitude to Fenton brining a number of first-class continental teams to play friendly matches under the floodlights of Upton Park. Noel said; "It was good to play the foreign teams under the floodlights; we met our match in Inter Milan, but what we learnt from playing then was invaluable."

Sharing responsibilities in the Hammers defence brought people closer together. "John Bond and Malcolm Allison became close friends. Malcolm took me to my first night club. Tommy Moroney was like a father to me. He wouldn't let me go to the working men's club."

The friendship with Allison was to spark off the birth of the modern game at Upton Park. However, Cantwell had the boldness that would one day see him captaining Manchester United to FA Cup glory, as Bill Lansdowne recalled; "Noel would go through a brick wall." This was confirmed by Malcolm Pyke, who Noel looked after when the young wing-half joined the Hammers. "Noel Cantwell was a born leader, the outstanding player when I was at the club. He was hard as nails, and a great inspiration to practically everyone around him. He's a lovely, lovely man. He was the main man."

Noel went on; "I remember the Chicken Run. Occasionally, when someone got clattered, they'd end up with the supporters. The crowd singing *Bubbles* sticks in my mind. West Ham was a friendly club and an excellent place in many ways. We used to train at the back of the Boleyn Castle, just running sometimes. But Grange Farm [West Ham's Essex training ground at that time] improved things."

The view that West Ham's team-spirit was their greatest asset was reiterated by Noel; "Bobby Moore was a great player, but he still needed to mature when I was at Upton Park. Phil Woosnam was intelligent; he had good understanding with John Dick. Malcolm Musgrove was good on his day. I wouldn't say that any West Ham players at the time had outstanding ability, but they could play well as a team. They had all the ingredients for the First Division, passing the ball, not giving it away. The club reflected how important it was to have a sense of loyalty to people. It's something football has lost. It's always been a business at the bottom line, West Ham was a business first and foremost, but like all businesses if you can motivate a loyal workforce you have got that something extra. You can't really buy that or fit it into a contract."

Noel played 17 of his 36 games for the Republic of Ireland while he was with the Irons. "At times I'd finish playing on Saturday and be ready to play in Dublin on Sunday. The Irish did have get-togethers, but not very often."

By the early part of 1960, when the Club was still recovering from the Munich disaster, with so many Manchester United stars wiped from the skies, United's Jimmy Murphy, deputising for the recovering Matt Busby, made his bid to take Noel Cantwell to Old Trafford. And Noel was about ready to go. "I was wanting to leave West Ham. I was losing things after eight years and it was every Irish guy's dream to play for Manchester United. I got £600 of the £29,500 transfer."

This was a record for a full-back at that time. Noel was one of a new breed of defenders, who could influence what was happening all over the park, a kind of prototype of the 'Bobby Moore effect'.

West Ham was again destined for mid-table obscurity, and this was thanks mainly to the good work of ever-present 'keeper Ernie Gregory, although they finished well above relegated Southampton. Top Hammers goalscorer was Irishman Freddie Kearns, who netted ten goals. Sheffield United won the Second Division title by two points from Huddersfield.

The Hammers had a centre-forward problem during 1952-53. Five men were tried, but less than 33 per cent of scoring shots came from the number-nine shirt. However, on the positive side, the Irons won the London Challenge Cup for a record sixth time. Thhe Hammers defeated Brentford 2-1 at Stamford Bridge, Malcolm Allison scoring a goal for each side.

I played cricket for Ireland

It was Eddie Chapman who told me; "I played cricket at schoolboy level for Essex, at Lord's." Probably from Eddie's first days at the Boleyn Ground, up to the mid-Seventies, there were always a number of fine cricketers at Upton Park. For example, Geoff Hurst played against for Essex against Lancashire in 1962, Joe Kirkup went for county trials, and, a little later, Eddie Presland, who played 30 first-class games for Essex, he continued in the Sunday League for another two seasons. Bobby Moore and Alan Sealey were also a fine players, Bob being selected for the Essex youth side, while Jim Standen had an admirable record for Minor Counties and Worcestershire as a lower middle order batsman and a right-arm seamer. However, Eddie could look back on a tradition of leather on willow within the ranks of the Irons.

"We had a good cricketing side at West Ham, with Jackie Wood, Norman Corbett and Dickey Walker. Dickey was a fantastic chap. With Harry Hooper senior up the other end, you had a good pair there. Albert Foan, he was a good cricketer. Harry Hooper junior and Dougy Bing played for my team, Astra. I'm still involved with them."

For Doug Bing, Eddie Chapman was a nice man, a good cricketer; "I played for his side. Cricket was my first love. I was quite good. I could have played for a living. I played for Margate. If I had my life again, I'd have played cricket. I enjoyed my time at West Ham, but to me cricket was everything. I would have sooner have been a cricketer than a footballer. The worse thing when I had to pack up football was that I couldn't play cricket again either."

Derek Parker confirmed Eddie's and Doug's prowess; "Doug Bing and Eddie Chapman were good cricketers." He also admitted to his own interest; "I was quite a useful player - that was good fun."

"I also played cricket," said Bert Hawkins. "Football and cricket…they're both about having an eye for the ball." Bert's passion for the game was similar to Doug Bing's; "I'd have rather have played cricket than football." This probably had to do with the promotion of both football and cricket in schools at the same time, as George Petchey indicated.

"I was encouraged to play cricket at Sutton School. We had a good cricket team at West Ham." Indeed, this cricketing prowess has been, almost uniquely, in the context of professional football clubs, a West Ham phenomenon. While other clubs might have had a few good players in their ranks, the Hammers produced whole teams, able to take on good amateur sides and County 2nd XIs. Andy Smillie confirmed this.

"Ted Fenton played for Clayhall Cricket Club and I turned out for the first and second teams. The West Ham players gave many a good side a game. We beat an Upminster 1st XI and played a number of charity matches. London-based football players were pretty close then. I played with Eddie Bailey and so on." Andy came across a number of Essex cricketers. Valentine's Park, one of the county's home venues, was near to his childhood home. Some of the Essex professionals would use the restaurant where his mother worked, including Brian Taylor and Doug Insole. Andy soon developed his skill at the game.

West Ham even had their own cricketing international, who had been skipper of a side that met the mighty West Indies in a one-day game. Noel Cantwell told me; "I played cricket for Ireland - we once played the West Indies in a one-day match - and my three brothers played for Munster. One brother played for Cork. In the summer I went to home to play cricket for Ireland - so I was one of the last double internationals. I once went for a trial with Essex and I played with Eddie Chapman's team once or twice."

Eddie remembered Noel's talent; "Noel Cantwell was a great bowler...fast." Bobby Moore was a better cricketer than footballer for a while. As a young batsman with a quick eye and readiness to stand in the line of fire, he captained South of England Schoolboys against the North. Essex wanted Moore to join them and they were also interested in several other West Ham boys, Geoff Hurst and Martin Peters among them. However, football offered greater financial possibilities.

Ken Tucker also enjoyed some success with the bat."I played cricket for Essex as a schoolboy, I was a good left-handed batsman."

Gerry Gazzard recalled; "I enjoyed some cricket during the summer periods." Not every player at West Ham had this level of skill. Eddie Chapman identified Tony Cottee as

"...the worst cricketer I have known as a footballer. He didn't have the faintest idea...but it wasn't his fault."

Derek Woodley didn't quite make The Oval either, although during his part-time work as a gravedigger, he and his colleagues would do their best to improve their strokes; "We'd play cricket between the gravestones. One lad would read a book and keep an eye out. If he saw anyone coming he'd blow a whistle and we'd stash the stumps away."

Today, probably the most popular sport among the players I met while writing this book is golf, and for many players this started at West Ham. I arrived at Brian Moore's home in Cambridge to be invited in by his wife, Christine. She made me a cup of tea while we waited for Brian to get home from his 18 holes. Brian, who had worked as a caddy when as a schoolboy in Ireland, played two or three times a week. Christine and Brian had met at the golf club. Tommy Dixon met his second wife at the golf course; "Joyce worked at the pro-shop…she doesn't understand football," he told me.

Eddie Lewis remembered that Ted Fenton got the players involved with golf and squash. Tommy Dixon confirmed; "Ted Fenton introduced me to golf. One day I was going round with Fenton and Ken Tucker. We got on the tee and Ted says; 'Come on Ken, you've got to address the ball.' Ken got on his hands and knees and I said; 'Good morning ball.'"

Mick Beesley said; 'I was pretty friendly with Geoff Hurst and Brian Dear. We played a bit of golf." And Ron Cater is a devotee of the greens in Spain. Andy Smillie, characteristically identified a philosophical side to the sport;

"The other great sporting love of my life is golf. You can learn a lot in golf. Ben Hogan wrote; 'If you out-practise the best, you become the best.' Natural ability is not the be all and end all."

Ken Bainbridge told me that after retirement he was lost for something to do, so he took up golf. "After moving to Prestatyn I joined Prestatyn Golf Club where I'm still a member with a handicap of 15." David Dunmore has a handicap of 12, but he told me that he has been down as low as five.

In terms of national success, at least two West Ham players were still, in the late 1900s, winning sporting honours. Andy Nelson was a member of the team which won the Spanish fours bowls championship and he became a district champion, while Eric Parsons, told me; "I've taken up bowls. I got to the last eight of the All-England singles championships. I played for the county. I got into the Final of the county and won the singles and pairs, with Jock Munroe. I got six medals for being in the EBA Finals."

Joe Kirkup won honours with a ball of another shape before he gained any success with a football. He played rugby for his district XV and captained his county at both rugby and soccer. Bert Hawkins was a bit of a rugger star at the other end of the country; "I captained the school team at rugby. I played for Bristol Youth and Gloucester Boys. I was initially picked to play for England youth against Ireland, but I came from a poor family and that went against you in those days. The rugby helped your speed and getting knocked about a bit. The rugby gave me stamina and a lot of movement with my body. I loved rugby."

Malcolm Musgrove was also involved in the 15-a-side game. "I was a county rugby player, under-15s for Northumberland. I played rugby on a Saturday morning for the school, and played football for the village in the afternoon. We used to take a misshapen rugby ball to school so we could play football. Most of us wanted to play soccer but we couldn't take a football. We all used to play at lunchtimes. Most of the team that played rugby also played football."

During the Fifties, the sport to vie with cricket for the most popular among the players was greyhound racing. Ken Brown remembered; "Malcolm Allison was a bit of a gambler and we used to go to the dogs together." This was a time when the dockland area had its own track down not far from the River in Custom House at West Ham Stadium. Other regulars included John Dick, Ken Tucker and Noel Cantwell. Many others, including Harry Kinsell, John Bond and Bobby Moore, would go along less regularly. Tommy Dixon remembered; "One occasion at Hackney Wick afternoon racing, Ken Tucker got a big tip in the fifth race, the favourite. Malcolm and Harry Kinsell were there as well. On the last bend the hare came off when the dog was about six lengths in front. They re-ran the race after the last race. It got beat and I think Malcolm lost a lot of money."

Albert Foan recalled; "A few of the players liked a bet. I remember one day a group of them won about £60 each at Plymouth dogs. The next day they were broke again. Malcolm Allison even knew the tick-tack,[the bookies hand signals to communicate odds] he would use it sometimes in the dressing-room."

The dogs were always a favourite of the Hammers, but the horses were also well supported. Malcolm Pike, in his role as a publican and landlord, organised more than a few days out at the races for his regulars. He told me; "I used to take a coach of customers to the Derby and I'd see Ken Tucker there."

Malcolm Musgrove was interested in a more physically demanding form of racing. "In the summer I would go back home and run in foot handicaps, sprint races, for money. My dad had been a sprinter. We used to go to meetings around the county, like horse racing it was. I can remember winning one handicap and the prize was £30. At the time I was getting £12 10s a week at West Ham." Muzzy wasn't the only exponent of track and field at Upton Park. Eric Parsons told of his schoolboy athletic exploits.

"I was the 220-yards champion of Sussex and the 100-yards champion of the school. I was good at the high jump. I was a big boy at school - I haven't grown since," he laughed.

Derek Parker recalled; "I was into local sports and always did well, running and jumping and so on."

Eddie Chapman remembered; "I ran for Essex as a sprinter, so, as far as football is concerned, what I lacked in skill I made up for with speed." If time-travel ever becomes a possibility, West Ham could have a pretty good sprint competition. John Cartwright was London sprint champion and Harry Hooper held the Durham youth sprint championship.

A number of players pursued a more non-specialist fitness regime. In the Army, Ken Brown got involved in the corps sports and did a lot of running. "The RSM got me doing a lot of stomach exercises."

Derek Parker, well into his 60s, was still keeping and looking fit. "I do two three-hour sessions a week at the sports centre."

Like Benny and Ted Fenton before him, Dave Sexton was a useful boxer. Dave's dad, Archie, was a professional boxer. He had 230 fights in ten years, taking the Southern Area championship and, in 1933, he took on Jock McEvoy for the British middleweight title. Dave boxed for the Army, but it was not his destiny to follow his dad into the professional ranks. "I had two uncles - Jim and Billy - who were both pro-fighters as well, and my brother Terry fancied having a go, but he kept getting cut around the eyes so a pro career was out of the question for him. As my dad had lost the sight of one eye because of boxing, my mum would have gone potty if I'd wanted to do it as well. So she was quite happy when I decided football was the game for me.

Doug Wragg boxed for Hyson Green and at battalion level when he joined the Army, but his pugilistic talents never tempted him away from his involvement in football. "Everyone wanted to be a professional," he smiled.

However, some would always save their talents for the beautiful game. John Lyall confessed; My son's quite a good swimmer and my older grandson is, but when I get in they all stand at the edge and laugh. I swallow the water. We go to Centre Parcs at Christmas, and it's coming out my ears - shocking!

Days of Iron – The story of West Ham United in the Fifties

1953-54 – Andy Malcolm, he was never really beaten

The guns of the Korean War were scarcely silent when the rumbles of a new conflict began. The North Vietnamese, under their charismatic leader Ho Chi Minh, were making life difficult for the French with a series of brilliant guerrilla forays. The French Legionnaires and paratroopers were accustomed to winning pitched battles where firepower and weapon superiority could be brought to bear. Now, the shadowy hit-and-run tactics adopted by their opponents puzzled and irritated them.

Football in England had less threatening irritations. In order to create a Saturday clear of League fixtures for the 1954 FA Cup Final, the scheduled programme of games for 1st May was brought forward to August 1953. The Hammers' rearranged match was against Lincoln City on Wednesday, 19th August and was the first time since 1914, apart from the special circumstances of 1934-35, that the Hammers had opened a season on any day other than a Saturday. They beat Lincoln 5-0, the best start to a season the Club had ever made.

John Dick came into the first team for that first game. Six players had worn the number-ten shirt the previous season and it was a problem position. John seemed to be the answer as he became a provider of West Harn goals for the next decade. John had played for Maryhill in Scotland, where he was spotted by West Ham's scouting network and signed, at the age of 23, in July 1953. The Hammers, aware of John's growing reputation as a goalscorer, snatched him from under the noses of Spurs, who were slow to spot the potential in him.

"Several clubs were showing an interest in me while I was doing my National Service in Colchester. I actually played 13 games for the Spurs' Midweek League team," John recalled.

He scored the only goal for Crittalls in a friendly with Spurs, who won 7-1, but by the time Tottenham made their move it was too late."Arthur Rowe and Bill Nicholson drove to my mother's house in Glasgow to offer me a professional contract, but I had already agreed to join the Hammers."

Fenton had been determined, having made the journey up to Glasgow on two occasions specifically to sign Dick. John went on; "The Spurs people were not too happy about that after such a long journey...but I didn't fancy Spurs. Ted Fenton had got in first, so I became a West Ham player - something I never had any cause to regret."

John, who won a Scottish Junior cap while at Maryhill, was to become the first West Ham player to be capped for Scotland, against England in 1959, at Wembley. According to him he didn't play well in that game - "I'd trained the night before we played" - and didn't shine alongside the likes of Dave Mackay and Tommy Docherty because of that.

John Dick is one of five players to score over a hundred goals for the Irons. Ted Fenton remembered; "He often set off from inside his own half with the ball apparently glued to his left boot and, as he put the ball in the net, there behind him was a trail of defenders sitting on their backsides...he was never really happy until he was among the goals."

Two names that had a big influence on John as he was making his way in the game were Vic Keeble and Malcolm Allison. Keeble was the first to make an impression, while John was doing his National Service in the Royal Electrical and Mechanical Engineers (REME) at Colchester.

"Vic was playing for Colchester at the time and making such a reputation for himself that you could not pick up a paper without seeing his name all over it. I was playing for Essex Crittalls Athletic [now Braintree], while on National Service in Colchester. At the time I thought I'd love to be in the same team as Vic. Little did I know my dream would come true when we both joined West Ham and were strike partners in the team that won promotion from the Second Division in 1958...he suited me; I played off him - moving when the ball was played to me. He was a bit like Johnny Byrne; he could lay balls off, spin and go."

In his first season in the Football League, John Dick scored 13 goals in 39 League games. The first was West Ham's goal in their 2-1 defeat at Derby County, in his 13th game. He netted the first of six hat-tricks in a 5-0 home win over Bury. In his second term with the Hammers he equalled Bill Robinson's post-war record of 26 League goals in a season. This gave rise to a deal of speculation about him adding to the Scotland 'B' cap he had gained in March 1954.

John saw the beating of Manchester United on West Ham's return to Division One as a high point in his career, but the biggest disappointment was being put out of the FA Cup by Spurs in 1956. "We were 3-1 up in the first game," he recalled. But of course, Tottenham managed to draw level and the final score was 3-3, John getting all West Ham's goals. Spurs won the replay at Upton Park to go through to the last eight.

For John Dick, the men he played alongside at Upton Park "were a great bunch of lads, who were a joy to be with". He said; "The Club was full of characters, with big Malcolm Allison the daddy of them all."

In nine seasons as a Hammer, John Dick made 351 appearances and scored 166 goals, which places him joint third in the club's all-time scoring list alongside Jimmy Ruffell. In the League, with 153 goals, he is behind only Vic Watson (306), Geoff Hurst (180) and Ruffell (164). He scored four of the Hammers' eight against Rotherham in 1958. His best goalscoring return in one season came in 1958-59, when he netted on 27 occasions - all in the First Division. His £17,500 transfer to Brentford in 1962 was a parting gift to West Ham. He said; "Confidence was half the battle in football, Bondy and Cantwell would ask; 'Which goal will you score in today?' The crowd were close, so this pushed you on, but they could also give out the abuse."

Eyebrows were raised when West Ham beat Leicester City 4-1, three days after their good start. Rotherham, however, put a damper on things by winning 5-0 at Millmoor in the Hammers' third game. By mid-September, after ten games, West Ham had lost only once and were second in the table. Three players had scored hat-tricks at Upton Park; Fred Kearns against Leicester; Dave Sexton, when Rotherham came to Upton Park, and Tommy Dixon in Swansea's visit to the East End. Five goals were scored against Bury when John Dick netted yet another Hammers hat-trick at the start of November.

This month saw the most serious outbreak of anti-French violence in Algeria since the end of World War Two. The Nationalist Movement killed many people in terrorist attacks for the Triumph of Democratic Liberties (MTLD) before the security forces were able to restore order in Algiers and Oran areas. There were hundreds of arrests and arms seizures. The unrest followed one of the most powerful earthquakes of the century, which had devastated the Algerian city of Orleansville on 9th September. Some 1,500 people died and thousands were left homeless.

Notts County came to Upton Park on 5th December 1953 and despite John Dick's fifth goal of the season, the Hammers lost to the side that would, at the end of the season, finish in 14th position in Division Two, a place below the Irons. Andy Malcolm played his first game for West Ham that day. He was 20 years old but had already been with the club for three years, having played 82 reserve-team games. Andy told me; "I don't remember a great deal about the actual game itself. I do remember, however, that I got very nervous before the game and Ted Fenton telling me to relax."

It was the start of a 306-match career, stretching over eight seasons. He had to wait until September 1957 for his first goal, which came at Swansea. Andy scored only twice more for the Hammers - in the February of the championship season and in November 1960 - but that was not his strong point. He was certainly one of the best wing-halves to don the claret and blue -strong, tough, even ruthless at times, but with a skill level rarely bestowed on the Ninja class of his type. As colleague and friend Mick Newman recalled; "I always admired players like Andy Malcolm, he was never really beaten. He couldn't be intimidated, physically or verbally"

Andy is a modest man. His first response to me was; "Thanks very much for the interest shown in my playing days at West Ham." He went on; "I live very much for today, I don't really like dwelling on the past, plus the fact that my memory isn't that good. However, I do appreciate that there are West Ham fans who like to know about days gone by."

He told me something about his background. He was, like so many of West Ham's fine players, a local boy. "I was born at 59 Barking Road in a flat on top of a grocer's shop, just around the corner from the ground. My parents moved to Hornchurch when I was six months old. I was blessed with the best parents a person could possibly have. My father worked on the railway as an electric train-driver. He was an ardent West Ham supporter all his life. My mother, who concentrated on bringing the family up, always told the story of the day he came back from the 1923 Cup Final with his shirt all torn. I had an elder brother Bobby who died in 1939.

"I attended North Street Junior School and later Dury Falls Senior School. My schooling was, of course, interrupted by the war. I had lots of help at school, especially from a teacher called Mr Owen. And Mr Thomas, in particular, was to become a great friend." Andy joined West Ham in 1948 when he left school in Hornchurch. "I started work in the Green Street offices, which at the time were in the old Castle Buildings, with Mr Frank Cearns, the Club Secretary, and Eddie Chapman, he was Mr Cearns' assistant. If I remember right, I got £2 a week.

"I was fortunate enough to be a Schoolboy international and it came as no surprise when I got several offers from clubs to join then, including one from Wolves, who at that time were a very fashionable club. But when I left school I was no stranger to Upton Park. I had, earlier in the year, played there for Essex against Kent and injured an ankle. After the game West Ham offered to give me treatment to enable me to play in the internationals, so I attended the ground several times a week up until the time I joined the office staff. My father was a big influence on my joining West Ham. I signed for the Club in 1950. I was 17.

"Right from the first day I joined the club, there was always a great atmosphere, always plenty of noise in the dressing-room, people laughing and taking the mickey. I can't never remember there being any difficulties in playing at West Ham."

Andy captained England Schoolboys and was West Ham's first youth international. He also played for the Football League in 1959. "I probably brought back a little bit more experience to the side for all this, but I don't remember being too disappointed not being fully capped. I'm probably more disappointed today that I didn't, having grandchildren!"

Described as a 'feared wing-half with the ability to close-mark and block out opponents', Andy was able to snuff out the likes of Johnny Haynes, Jimmy Greaves and Denis Law. Mike Grice said that Andy was 'the hardest player I've ever seen'. For Mick Beesely, Andy Malcolm was tough. "I heard him talking to Noel Cantwell once, they were talking about Jimmy Greaves. He said; 'If he gets past me, just chip him back.'"

Skipper of the FA Youth Cup winning side of 1959, John Charles, told me; "I used to love Andy Malcolm. He never said a word, but he was a real laugh. I liked to watch him mark the likes of Johnny Haynes - he was a hard player."

"I'm not sure how I would describe myself as a player," Andy said. "Alec Stock at QPR once described me as a 'thoroughbred professional with a pedigree'. Johnny Haynes, on the other hand, once told me that I should have been a butcher, so perhaps I might have been somewhere in between!

"I was influenced by the senior players at West Ham. They were always helpful to me. If I had to pick out one particular person I would say Dick Walker - he was a good communicator and had a great attitude towards the game."

For a time, Andy's career had to work in tandem with the national interest. "I did my initial National Service training at Aldershot in Hampshire and got posted to 12 Company RAMC [Royal Army Medical Corps] at Shooters Hill, Woolwich, together with Harry Hooper. Harry and I were together in the Army and became very good friends. We had an excellent station commandant in Captain Webb, who was a great sports enthusiast. He helped Harry and myself whenever he could."

Apart from his time in the forces, Andy always commuted to the club from the Essex-East London border. "I didn't live near the ground, I lived in Hornchurch."

Of course, a player, no matter how good, never came close to earning the kind of wage commanded by players later on. Andy recalled; "In my day, from the end of May until August you only got what they used to call a retainer wage. I had one or two temporary jobs during the close season; that was if we didn't have a tour."

Being at the club for 11 years, Andy would have been used to the supporters as the background and foundation of the Club. He would have recognised how this affected players, and so West Ham's overall performance. As such, it is hard to separate the attitude of the players and their supporters. "In the days of the Chicken Run there was always a lot of chirping going on, although I can't remember anything that struck me in particular. The feeling among the players was good. In my early days at the club Harry Hooper was my mate. When Harry left, Ken Brown and I were mates. During my playing career at West Ham there were a lot of first-class players, to pick out one in particular would be a bit unfair."

Unfortunately Ron Greenwood would never have been able to utilise the type of uncompromising style which was Andy's. Some have argued that Eddie Bovington was a similar type of player, but anyone who was around to compare the two would see that Bovington, while a strong tackier, was much more in tune with the movement and flux football so important to Greenwood. He did not have the demolition instincts possessed by Andy, the innate, primal quality needed by any side wishing to make an impression in the Sixties and Seventies. This was perhaps the most glaring weakness in the make-up of the England manager to be, and maybe the reason why West Ham never really developed the consistency to make an impact on the League until John Lyall took over. Greenwood had no Hunter, Giles, Bremner, or Stiles. He could not call on a Tommy Smith, Maurice Setters or Jack Charlton. The potential that lay in Andy Malcolm and later Harry Cripps, was never honed, simply because it was not in Greenwood's personality to do this.

However, this might have been of little comfort to Andy. He would not be part of West Ham's golden, mid-Sixties period. "I missed out on West Ham's Cup success in the Sixties, but even had I been at West Ham I might not have been in the side with Ron Greenwood in charge. So I'm not too disappointed about that. I can say my memories of West Ham were mainly good, probably the best in my playing career."

1953-54 – Andy Malcolm, he was never really beaten

Andy moved to Chelsea in 1962, in exchange for centre-forward Ron Tindall plus £10,000. Tindall was later sold to Reading for £12,000. Not a bad return for the £10 West Ham had forked out as a signing on fee for Andy in 1950. Being just short of qualifying for a testimonial, this would have cost Andy a pretty penny. "I moved to Chelsea because it was quite obvious to me I wasn't to become part of Ron Greenwood's plans at Upton Park. Ron Greenwood told me during training that he had given Tommy Docherty permission to have a chat with me and that he would be at the ground that afternoon. Unfortunately, it was to turn out to be one of those mistakes people make in life. Amongst other things, I had a contract dispute with Tommy Doc. I all but packed up my career. However, as they say, it doesn't do to hold hate in your heart all your life, so to say I dislike the man would probably be a better way of describing my feelings! I just hope he can sleep at night! My stay at Chelsea was a black spot in my life, but there again, Alec Stock wouldn't have taken me to QPR had it not happened. He came as a saviour to me. If I hadn't have met him and gone to QPR I wouldn't have met the chairman of Port Elizabeth FC who made it possible for me to move to South Africa."

For Andy, like us all, memories are the mixture of bitter and sweet that gives life its tone and contour. "I remember the joy we all got in the dressing-room at Middlesbrough when we won the championship. I remember the anguish felt when I signed for Chelsea after 13 years with West Ham."

However, despite having a relatively successful career, Andy's most abiding memories go back to his earliest days at the club. "I remember, as a young boy, working in the office and running errands for Mr Paynter, including getting his jug of tea and sandwich everyday at 11am in the cafe opposite the ground. I remember the joy I got when Ted Fenton finally signed me on professional forms. How nervous I was playing my first senior game and how excited my father got about it."

Following Andy's first game, the Hammers continued what was becoming a season of mixed fortunes. A run of four games without a win was halted at Lincoln, when John Dick was again on target to give the Irons only their second away victory of the season. However, by January the team had slumped to 14th place. West Ham was robbed of a point early on in the year. They were leading Stoke City 4-1 with only seven minutes remaining when fog descended and the game was abandoned. In the re-arranged fixture later in the season, the teams drew 2-2.

With the beginning of 1954, the war in Indo-China entered its seventh year. It was to mark the final climax of a long and bitter conflict between the French and Vietnamese forces commanded by General Navarre and the Viet Minh guerrillas under General Vo Nguyen Giap. The fighting was waged in a landscape that was to become all too familiar to television viewers throughout the world in the Sixties and Seventies. As the French dug themselves into their stronghold at Dien Bien Phu, which was a corner-stone of their Indo-Chinese defences, and the focus of the fiercest fighting of the entire war during the early months of the year, there was intense diplomatic activity by the international powers.

****

John Dick kept on scoring, getting two when West Ham got their third success away from home, a helter-skelter of a match at Craven Cottage. Trailing 3-0 to a Fulham side including the man who led the end to the maximum wage in football and television pundit to be Jimmy Hill, Johnny Haynes and Charlie Mitten, the Hammers looked set for a thrashing. From this seemingly hopeless position however, the Irons fought back to win 4-3 an all-action game. Dave Sexton and Tommy Dixon grabbed West Ham's other goals following Dick's double. In one eight-minute spell bridging the interval, five goals were scored.

The FA Cup brought a 4-0 win over Huddersfield, but in the fourth-round Blackpool knocked West Ham out by winning 3-1 at Bloomfield Road in a replay after the 1-1 draw at Upton Park. This was not a good game for the Hammers, for not only were they out of the Cup early, again, Ernie Gregory sustained a hand injury that was to keep him out for the rest of the season.

A satisfying double was achieved when Leeds visited the Boleyn Ground in February. With Peter Chiswick deputising for Gregory in goal, a 5-2 win for the Irons translated to a 7-3 home and away aggregate over West Ham's most traditional of northern rivals.

However, this gave the East Londoners only a dozen wins in 28 matches. As such, it looked probable that the Club were not going to be among the contenders for promotion to the First Division. This was confirmed by the next few games; the excursion to Brum ended in a disappointing 2-0 defeat at the hands of the midland Blues; the subsequent 1-1 draw with Nottingham Forest at Upton Park didn't bring much joy. The visit to Brentford resulted in a 3-1 beating, a game that saw the Football League debut of a man who was to become part of the bedrock of modern football and whose career would span almost the entire second half of the 20th century. Malcolm Musgrove recalled the day.

"My dad came down to watch my debut. He also was down to watch the village colliery band. They were playing in a big competition at the Albert Hall. We both went to see that in the morning. I think I had two kicks and a header and I missed that. I didn't have a very good first game. It seemed to pass me by."

When I spoke to him Malcolm is a living chronicle of the development of soccer in England, having seen the game from as wide a perspective as any individual in the history of the sport. He was house hunting around Plymouth when I met with him and Jean. (at the time of Malcolm's passing in 2007 they had been married for half a century). It was Jean, an East Ender from Romford Road, Forest Gate, who told me this. Malcolm responded; "Shhh...," chuckling as he put his finger to his lips. Jean took up the tale.

"We met at the supporters dance at the Harmonic Hall in East Ham. I was engaged to someone else, but I asked him to dance." Malcolm chipped in, smiling; "Shameless hussy she was!"

Jean went on" "I didn't like the one I was engaged to much. Malcolm and I got married 11 months later - didn't waste time did we?"

Malcolm joked; "Well, I was getting older."

Jean and Malcolm have built a big and happy family. "We've got three children, David, Martin and Allison. David's got two boys, Matthew is 13 and Nicholas is eight. Martin has got two girls, Eloise is four and Lucile is two. Allison has got one girl, nine months old and her name is Hannah." [I met Jean and Malcolm for the first time in July 1999]

'Muzzy', as he is known to his former playing colleagues and West Ham fans, spoke in something of a hybrid accent, a cross between Geordie, West Country and just a little bit of Cockney. He began to tell me about the days before he joined West Ham. "My dad, he was a miner, a deputy [tantamount to a foreman in he mining industry of the time]. He could never lie to my mum about how much money he got, because I knew. I was a wages clerk for the Coal Board; it was all of eight quid a week. Mum didn't work - ladies didn't then. My dad played for Millwall. Same position, outside-left. I've got a sister, Iris, who still lives in the village where I was born; she married a miner, a chap called Billy Foster.

"I went to Morpeth Grammar School. It was really a rugby school, but it was always football out of school. In the village where I was born, it was obvious that I would play football. The village had a junior side and a senior side. It was a natural progression."

West Ham was not the most obvious team that a young lad from a mining village would sign for, however. "Newcastle was my closest team. People like Charlie Wayman, the centre-forward that went to Preston, Jackie Milburn, Bob Stokoe, who I worked for later in life, was there. Bob Stokoe was my manager at Charlton.

"In the village there was a big washery being built - that was the place where they washed the coal. The chap that was in charge of the washery came from London, he was a West Ham supporter. He was the one who got me to go down. I played for the colliery junior side at the time, Lynemouth Colliery Welfare. He told me that he could get me a trial and I said; 'Oh yeah?' but it was true."

West Ham was not the first professional club to notice the young Musgrove. "I was approached by Sunderland. I played in a trial game and never heard any more." So Malcolm signed for West Ham following his demob from the RAF."I went down and was met by Wally St Pier at the station, and he took me along to Mrs Pierce's, where I stayed all my time at West Ham. Jean and I got married from Mrs Pierce's, she was a lovely lady. That was at Thorn Road, just round the corner to Johnny Bond, he was next door with Jan. John lived in a flat first of all, in the Barking Road."

Malcolm recalled the team spirit of those days in the mid-Fifties. "Players were all together in those days, most of the Club houses were together in the same area. Eddie Bovington was in our area. Eddie Lewis and Mike Grice were down the road. Jackie Dick wasn't too far off in Hainault. I would come out of Aintree Crescent, Barkingside, where I lived, walk down Craven Gardens and that's where Ken Brown lived. I would knock on his door, when we were travelling to an away game. Joan would go and stay with Jean. There were no cars; we had to take our bags on the bus. Then we'd get another bus and the tube to Kings Cross."

Malcolm was quite candid about his relationship with the supporters; "The fans weren't very good to me at times, when I was going through a bad period. We had a feller, in the Chicken Run, he used to get at me something terrible. I wasn't afraid of going out, but I preferred to play on the stand side for a time. He used to shout; 'I'm here again Muzzy,' and he'd just keep going. The only way you could beat him was to score or win the game. Eventually I won him over. I never met him. He called me Geronimo..." Malcolm laughed as he pointed at his distinctive nose.

Quite a number of former players described Malcolm Musgrove as their best friend at the Club. A typical response was given by John Dick; "I had a lot of time for Malcolm Musgrove, one of the unsung heroes of a very good West Ham team. He didn't have

1953-54 – Andy Malcolm, he was never really beaten

the charisma of some of the others, but he was a smashing down-to-earth guy. He was a very special person for me and I still have a great affection for him."

Malcolm was enthusiastic about the social side of being a player at Upton Park. "The social life at the Club was brilliant. We had a lot of good times. We were all on the same wages and we did a lot on them. We were all together. We saved up £100 with John Bond and Janet once and we went away. We had two kids each then. We went to Margate. We stayed in a guesthouse for a fortnight. - It was run by two men."

Jean interjected, "I was so naive."

"But it was so nice," Malcolm added appreciatively. "They were really brilliant, the food and the weather were beautiful. John went down in his old Vauxhall, it nearly caught fire...We followed him to Margate.

"I was also close to Michael Grice and Eddie Lewis. I got on with everybody, but I didn't go out with everybody. I wasn't a drinker. We had a few drinkers. I like the odd beer on certain occasions where everybody would have a drink. In those days you wouldn't have a drink after Wednesday - that was an unwritten law."

Like many other players of the time, Malcolm did his share of work outside football. "I did some grave digging - I did it with Frank O'Farrell before I met Jean - and later I did a bit of window cleaning with a friend from East Ham. He said; 'I'll pay you to clean windows.' 'Well', I thought, 'I do that at home for nothing!'. But I didn't like going up those ladders. He was an industrial window cleaner, in the factories and that."

Malcolm began to develop his skills in coaching early on. "I coached in the schools in the East End. A few of us helped the education people out and we got paid for it."

The players of the time began to go through Malcolm's mind. "Ernie Gregory was a great goalkeeper, John Dick was an international, Malcolm Allison had played in an FA XI, Michael Grice and myself played for the London Combination. We had seven or eight really good players. I used to like to get up and go to work; there's not many people that at the end of their working life that can say they enjoyed going to work."

Malcolm was a direct, attacking winger. "I was a fitness fanatic, I scored goals, I could run. I was quick and worked 110 per cent. Malcolm Allison was a double fitness fanatic. You finished your day and think that you had earned your money." He laughed; "I only got a couple of quid, but you'd earned it. I don't envy the players today; I can't believe the money they earn."

He went on; "It was never my intention to leave the Club. Orient came in, and I could have gone to Fulham, Johnny Haynes was inside-left there. Trevor Chamberlain was outside-left; I thought, 'why are they looking for another left winger?' I thought I'd be stuck in the reserves. I could walk into the Orient side, Eddie Lewis was there and I didn't have to move house. I thought, 'I'm not going over west.'"

Musgrove played 301 games for West Ham, scoring 89 goals, including a hat-trick against Preston in 1960 in front of the Upton Park fans. He had nearly the same scoring average as Jimmy Ruffell at that time. His first goal, one of two in a 3-3 draw, helped West Ham to salvage a point against Bury at the Boleyn Ground, late in 1954. Looking back he confessed; "I remember my first goal, but I don't recall much about the game other than that."

The Hammers didn't win another game in February. March opened with the nuclear arms race entering a more terrifying phase, with the testing of America's first true hydrogen bomb on Bikini Atoll in the Pacific. Both the Soviet Union and the United States had been working on thermo-nuclear devices for some years. The US Atomic Energy Commission had already tested precursors of the new device in the Pacific in 1952 and in the Nevada desert in 1953. However, whereas 'Mike', the 1952 bomb, used liquid deuterium, the new H-bomb used the solid lithium deuteride, making it much more practicable as a military weapon. The bomb was some 500 times more powerful than the one that destroyed Hiroshima in 1945.

The final away win of the 1953-54 was a surprise 2-1 victory at League leaders Everton before a crowd of nearly 41,000.

Ted Fenton's youth policy began to pay off in 1954 when the young Hammers reached the FA Youth Cup semi-final. During the season the floodlit friendlies proved popular with the fans. Hearts were beaten 7-0, and St Mirren, lost 3-1. The Swiss of Servette were thumped 5-1, but Olaria, from Brazil, held the Irons to a goalless draw.

Everton, who finished well below West Ham the previous season, were promoted, finishing second to Leicester. Both sides had 56 points. Merseyside continued to have a representative in the Second Division however, when Liverpool were relegated with Middlesbrough. West Bromwich Albion won the FA Cup, beating Preston 3-2 at Wembley and also finished runners-up to Wolves in the First Division.

By the time the Geneva conference on Indo-China and Korea began in April, the French garrison at Dien Bien Phu was already under heavy siege. Despite some defensive successes, such as the capture of a number of Viet Minh prisoners, the stronghold fell to the Communist forces on 7th May. The defeat was a bitter blow to French morale and proved to be the final nail in the coffin of her Indo-Chinese interests and the beginning of the end of French colonial ambitions generally.

A West Ham fan was in the news at this time. Anna Neagle, from Forest Gate, filmed *Lilacs in the Spring* with Errol Flynn, who it was rumored Anna introduced to the Cockney Irons, and who thus became a life-long follower of the enigmatic Hammers.

The year 1954 saw another World Cup. In 1950 England had left for Brazil knowing that no foreign side had even drawn a game with England in England. Since that time Yugoslavia, France and Austria had drawn and then there had been the Hungarians. However, before the finals, on 6 May 1954, British sport gained a massive psychological advantage during an athletics match at Oxford between the AAA and the University of Oxford. A medical student, a former President of Oxford University Athletics Club and British one-mile record holder, Roger Bannister, become the first man in athletics history to run the mile in under four minutes - it took him three minutes 59.4 seconds to be accurate.

Both England and Scotland qualified for the 1954 World Cup finals via the Home International Championship. Not one London-based player was taken to Switzerland, although West Ham's Harry Hooper was among the stay-at-home reserves. A draw with Belgium and a win against Switzerland put England through to the last eight, but Scotland went out in the first round, failing to score a goal in their two games and conceding eight.

In the quarter-finals, Uruguay, the 7-0 hammer of the Scots, sent England home, not quite in record time, winning 4-2. However, it seemed that English football didn't actually need this confirmation that it was way behind the times. A few days before the quarter-finals, British domestic football had rejected the merits of the white plastic-coated football. It was thought that the all-leather ball should be retained as a ball that failed to absorb water would change the whole character of the British game. What better reason to get rid of it was there?

Germany and Hungary got to the World Cup Final. Despite goals by Puskas and Czibor for the Hungarians, and the remarkable Grosics in goal, Germany won 3-2, Rahn getting two.

1954-55 – Harry Hooper told me to get a bicycle'

The Hammers made a dreadful start to the 1954-55 season. In the space of nine days at the start of the term, the Boleyn men suffered three 5-2 defeats in their first four games. Blackburn meted two of these out. Rovers went on to score 114 goals that year, but could finish no higher than sixth. After conceding 15 goals, Hammers' 'keeper Peter Chiswick was replaced by George Taylor and a 2-1 win at Anfield stopped the rot. The visit to Hull City resulted in another victory, improving the Irons' League placing. The team was undefeated in September and moved up to ninth place in the table. There were plenty of goals for the Upton Park patrons in December, when home games with Bury and Swansea were both drawn 3-3.

Winifred Atwell topped the Christmas charts with a piano medley called, *Let's Have a Party,* and nearly 24,000 Irons fans did, with a 1-0 Christmas Day win against Derby at Upton Park. Ted Fenton fielded a new signing in this game, the 36-year-old former Tottenham inside-forward, Les Bennett. Les was to turn out 28 times for the Club over the next year. The ageing star, who was a great influence in Tottenham's triumphs of 1949-52, contributed only four goals to the claret and blue cause, but he brought other qualities to Upton Park, skippering the side for most of these games. I was due to meet with Les at his home in Tottenham early in 1999; sadly, he was taken into hospital and died around the same time as Sir Alf Ramsey, another former Tottenham man.

It was at about this period that a young fan attended his first match at Upton Park. He remembered some of the ethos of a visit to the Boleyn Ground. "The road behind the Chicken Run was all two-up-two-down houses, they would charge you 3d to put your bike in the front garden. For 6d they'd put it in the passage for greater safety. Some people would make a living out of that.

"There were not many women at matches, that didn't really start until the Sixties. It was very much a time of the 'cloth cap'. I'd run errands to earn the money to see the first team one week and the reserves the next week. It cost 3d for boys to get into the reserves and 6d for League games." (12d, a shilling, was equivalent to 5p today).

Even when it wasn't a match day, many young lads in those days would still find a means of seeing the players. "I'd go with my friends to watch West Ham train at Grange Farm. After training the likes of Geoff Hurst would join in the football games they found us playing. We would either go to see West Ham train or go back and forth on the Woolwich Ferry all day, watching the big engines."

Many young fans of that time have distinctive memories of being part of the Upton Park crowd; "There was more of the snappy one-line humour then. There was respect for kids, though, men watched their language because of the kids. They didn't eff and blind and there was hardly ever a hint of violence.

"I remember 'Monty' [a character who was still around when I was a young supporter in the Sixties and early Seventies - I suppose I should have known the likes of him would have been around forever, but he may have chilled a bit later in life]. He'd wear army boots, football socks, a grass skirt and a Montgomery type beret. He went round blowing a trumpet. He'd get on the field before the start, pick up an imaginary ball in the middle of the park and carry it to the penalty spot. He'd place the 'ball' and step back about a dozen paces and then run at the spot, swiping his foot at fresh air. The crowd would roar and Monty would raise his arms in triumph. He always scored.

"One evening Monty was crossing the road, blowing his' trumpet after a game, when he was nearly run over by a big American car. He hurled a torrent of abuse at the vehicle. The driver got out and it was Ken Tucker. Monty prostrated himself and begged forgiveness!"

'Paddy' was another character and a tradition; "Paddy would always come out the tunnel to signal when the team were coming out - to get a roar from the crowd. No one seemed to know who this bloke was or if 'Paddy' was his real name… He was just always there! Maybe he got paid for his efforts - a kind of primal/minimalist cheer leader."

Former Barnardo's boy Alan Blackburn joined the first team on the day after Boxing Day. His debut was the second of successive matches against Derby. A draw at the Baseball Ground meant that the Hammers had taken three points out of four from the Rams. Promising fullback Geoff Hallas got the first of his three games at the beginning of March. In the same match, at home to Leeds, Billy Dare, a £5,000 signing from Brentford, made the first of his 119 appearances. Dare maintained his place for the rest of the season, ousting Dave Sexton from the number-nine shirt.

Three points were taken from Port Vale in League games, but the Potteries club eliminated West Ham from the FA Cup, 3-1 in a replay following a 2-2 draw at Upton Park, yet another early set back in this competition. West Ham had not been beyond the fourth round in 16 years.

If you attend an evening match in mid-winter at Upton Park today, you will, floodlight failure notwithstanding, be able to see the game clearly, the colours of the pitch and the players' strips made brilliant by the powerful beams of modern illumination. In the mid-Fifties, a similar spectacle could not be assured. Air pollution meant that fog became, smog, often blotting out the far end of the field in a cloudy soup of greeny-grey gas. This was a serious cause for concern, exacerbating lung disease in adults and aggravating children's skin ailments. Following a run of severe bouts of smog in the early Fifties, an investigative committee was set up under Hugh Beaver (great name for a cartoon character!). The Beaver Committee came up with a Clean Air Scheme, recommending that the emission of industrial smoke should become an offence, that industries themselves should be responsible for removing it, and that smokeless fuel should be used in the home. On 4th February, Duncan Sandys, Minister of Housing and Local Government, proposed a comprehensive Bill for the Prevention of Air Pollution, along the lines of the Beaver Report.

The attendance of 4,500 for the home League game against Doncaster in February was probably the smallest ever attendance at a League game at Upton Park. It took place on a Thursday afternoon in appalling, blizzard conditions. The result did not give much in the way of compensation for the die-hard fans. The Irons lost 1 -0.

An excellent run during March saw West Ham assume third place in the table by Good Friday. In a memorable game at Upton Park at the start of the month, the Hammers beat Leeds 2-1, Albert Foan beating the Welsh giant, John Charles, to score the winning goal.

After torrential rain in the north of New South Wales, several tributaries of the River Darling burst their banks simultaneously. This caused serious flood damage in February and March, and inundated tens of thousands of square miles. It was the worst natural disaster in Australian history. Nearly 100 people died, over 50,000 lost their homes and there were extensive losses of livestock. A massive airlift operation saved many stranded people and a flood relief fund was set up, with substantial contributions from Britain and other Commonwealth countries.

The victory against the Peacocks set up a chain of six wins that took the Irons into mid-April. Malcolm Musgrove had scored in five of those games. It had been rumoured for some time that, although at this time a US citizen, Albert Einstein was a West Ham enthusiast. There were several claims of sightings in the North Bank and in the Boleyn pub both before and after games. His most reported tipple was a half bottle of stout. It was said that he was enamoured by the Irons propensity to defy gravity and stay in the Second Division. If this story had any truth in it, sadly, the Hammers lost a supporter on 18th April when the man who formulated the theory of relativity (inspired, it was said by Syd Puddefoot's right peg) died.

The Hammers couldn't win a single game in their last seven League outings, managing only two draws to finish eighth. This was their best League placing since 1949; significantly, it was achieved with eight of the squad that would win the title three years later. Six away games were won during 1954-55, the Hammers' best record for four years; and their 28 away goals was their highest total since 1939. Leading the Hammers scorers were Johnny Dick and Dave Sexton. Dick score three at Bristol Rovers, while the following week Sexton got his hat-trick in the 6-1 win over Plymouth at home in February.

In March, a friendly with the Dutch side, Holland Sports, had become the first televised match at Upton Park. The 0-0 draw, however, was a poor advertisement. The camera should have been there in February when SC Simmering from Austria seemed to be off the boil when they were beaten 8-2. Reserve centre-forward Billy Dare scored four for the Irons. There were two more floodlit friendlies in October. VFB Stuttgart were beaten 4-0, while the Austrians, SR Wacker, were also defeated, 3-1. At this time Malcolm Allison was injured and missed 16 League games, his place being taken by Ken Brown. On 14th December, a crowd of 35,000 assembled to see the Hammers take on mighty AC Milan. The Italians fielded a side packed with internationals including the giant Swede Gunnar Nordahl and the Argentinean Schiaffino. West Ham were outclassed and lost 6-0.

The Hammers speedy wingman, Harry Hooper, won well-earned honours for the second season running when he was selected for a number of representative games. At Highbury in 1954, Hooper took part in the very first England v Young England fixture.

The year 1955 was one of industrial disputes and strike action in Britain. In March production of national newspapers was halted when members of the Electrical Trades Union and the Amalgamated Engineering Union took strike action over a pay claim. In May, 65,000 railwaymen went on strike and in June, striking dockers from Merseyside came to London to persuade their London colleagues to continue their industrial action. The dock strike was held in support of an attempt by the Stevedores' Union to gain representation on provincial port joint committees. It was finally called off after 40 days.

For most of 1954-55, Ted Fenton stuck with tried and trusted players or those he had blooded the previous term. However, the final match of the season, that took place at the City Ground, Nottingham, was to be the stage on which 21 year-old, Belfast boy Brian Moore was to make his first appearance in the Football League in front of only 5,675 spectators. Brian's memories of that 1-1 draw were really overtaken by the need to focus on the job in hand. "You didn't really notice the crowd. You were so busy concentrating on your game. I worked hard as an inside-forward, back and forth all the time." Although very much a ball player, as Brian recalled, "I was fast."

I made an appointment to see Brian but when I arrived he wasn't around. I feared my journey to Cambridge might have been pointless, but he finally arrived home. In a light-hearted but apologetic manner he admitted that he had forgotten all about me. Brian and his wife, Christine, had been together for 15 years when we met in 1999. She worked in pharmaceuticals with controlled drugs and told me she had heard all the Viagra jokes, and would not take any of rny bribes.

Brian told me about his time at Cambridge United. "Malcolm Allison got me to come to Cambridge. When I told my landlady she said she was pleased that I was getting myself an education! I didn't know where Cambridge was, but I got the job as player-manager of Cambridge United and got to play with former England and Middlesbrough legend Wilf Mannion."

Brian, who has one son and two grandchildren, had quite a career in Northern Ireland before joining the Hammers. Apart from Glentoran, he played for Distillery and Coleraine. Ted Fenton spotted him. The West Ham manager was watching another Coleraine player, but halfway through the season took the young inside-forward to Upton Park for £4,000. "We got £15 for a first-team appearance, £4 for a win and £2 for a draw," Brian recalled. "You got £12 in the reserves. But I never really thought about money."

He showed me two photographs, one recording the Irish Schools team that was beaten 3-0 by Wales at Barry on 3rd April 1948 and the other showing the Irish Schools side that was defeated 4-1 by Scotland at Cliftonville on 22nd May the same year. Brian was in both line-ups and went on to play as a youth international. He was about to be chosen for the senior side when he sustained the eye injury that was to finish his career, although he did play for the Irish League against the Football League, who included West Ham winger Harry Hooper. The Irish lost 4-2.

Brian told me that his father had a bread van, delivering to farmers in the hills around Belfast. "I used to go with him. We would get out of the van and sit on the side of the hill. Dad would blow a whistle and after a while ladies would appear over the brow of the hill carrying baskets."

He remembered, as a 13 year-old boy, being impressed by Tom Finney who scored one of England's seven goals in the defeat of Northern Ireland at Windsor Park just after the war. Brian also recalled; "I was friendly with Malcolm Musgrove at West Ham and we had one or two good nights out at the Supporters' Club in East Ham. But the social life wasn't fantastic, we thought about nothing but football. Even on our day off we played football. Malcolm Musgrove once asked me; 'How do you go by people?' I said; 'I just run up the wing.'" Brian chuckled and shook his head. "I lived for the weekend. On Friday I just spent my money."

Throughout our conversation Brian was cheerful and looked back at his life with enthusiasm, but every now and then I understood that this story did have a tragic undercurrent; a skilful player robbed of a potential career in his prime. This was only detectable at moments, as when Brian reflected; "I was too young. It was a big experience. We played our hardest, other teams didn't matter."

Brian's injury was devastating - he lost the sight of an eye. It happened in the 1955 Boxing Day match at Middlesbrough, when he was hit in the eye by the ball. He was dazed, but Fenton sent him back on - there were no substitutes at that time."I went to Moorfields, but my girlfriend was over from Ireland and I refused to stay in. There was bleeding behind the eye. I ended up passing out. I went back to the hospital and the nurse told me that it 'had healed up nicely' - but I couldn't see out of it.

"Eventually, I told West Ham that it had cleared up, but they wouldn't take a chance that I might lose the other eye - they had us all insured so they didn't lose out."

Brian remembered constantly bumping into people at first, and a few insensitive East Londoners giving him a bad time. This is very much the other side of football. Everybody wants the dashing star of the pitch, to shake his hand, just to pat him on the back as he walks on to or leaves the field of play, but the wounded player, forced out of his environment, does well even to be tolerated.

Brian went on; "I got five goals in the peserves after my injury. Ted told me that I'd be in the team, but I wasn't on the sheet when the team was named. He said I needed a bit more experience. 'How can I get experience', I asked, 'if you won't play me?' He told me to go home for a bit and that he would pay for my flight. But it turned out that we couldn't land at Belfast and had to go to Prestwick in Scotland. I ended up with only two hours in Belfast."

Geoff Hallas suffered a similar injury to Brian's and West Ham decided to arrange a shared testimonial for the players. Brian told me of his treatment with philosophical amusement. However, I couldn't help but be angry at the blatant injustice and abuse involved. "Geoff and I got £980 each for our joint testimonial, but the club only gave us £500. They told us that the rest had gone to the Supporters' Club. Nearly a year later the union came after me for £500 they had given me. They took me to court to get it back. But I had gone home and bought my parents a TV - that had cost £380 - and I had given my brother a bit. I had no money to give back! I won the first case, but they won the appeal."

Because of legal costs, Brian had been obliged to represent himself. He had come away with nothing. At that point, as a football supporter and a lifelong West Ham fan, I felt ashamed and embarrassed for the game and my Club. Brian had played nine games for the Irons. Over 10,000 paying customers had seen him score at the Millmoor Ground not ten days before his injury. In total over 150,000 people had watched Brian play in the first team. Tens of thousands had been present at non-League games that included him. Surely he was entitled to something better than what he got at the end of his career at the top level? Brian's response was typical, totally lacking bitterness; "I enjoyed the case, though. It caught the public attention for a time."

After finishing his involvement with West Ham, Brian took a year off, then spent five years at Cambridge United and five at Cambridge City, with whom he won the Southern League. Brian remembered; "Harry Hooper told me to get a bicycle and fishing rod when I went to Cambridge." He smiled. "I got a rod but never did any fishing."

During the season, William Gelding's novel *Lord of the Flies* was turning people off of kids and pigs. *On the Waterfront* did wonders for Marion Brando - some people actually understood some of the lines he delivered in Elia Kazan's film.

J. R. R.Tolkien gave the world *The Lord of the Rings* (and a seemingly never-ending saga of Bilbo, Frodo and bleedin' Sméagol – what a midfield trio! Thanks a bunch John

Ronald Reuel). There was no substance in the claims that after reading this insane tale, Ted Fenton had made a bid to bring Bilbo Baggins to Upton Park, although later in history West Ham were to sign their share of Hobbits, Wombles and Clangers under the Redknapp (Ori?) watch.

Allison was a god in his own right

The end of Dick Walker's career with West Ham marked a transition at the club. As the old West Ham captain left the field for the final time, he closed an era. The man who came in to take his position and leadership role ushered in a new dawn. Exactly what happened and why has never been fully analysed. Even the role that was played by management is uncertain. Fenton and the board may not have had the insight or the aptitude to generate constructive changes, but they certainly had the power to bring to a halt any attempts to alter things.

Alongside Ted Fenton, Malcolm Allison was the greatest enigma at West Ham in the Fifties. It is strange how two men, seemingly with completely different perspectives on football and life in general, neither seemingly having much time for the other, became so intimately bound together in a mutual project, to make West Ham United into something bigger than what it was.

Allison, a rebel for applause, as a young player looked like a hybrid between Jimmy Dean and Superman. One former player, a young professional at the time Allison arrived at Upton Park, said of Allison; "He had an impact on a few players. He had his pets. I didn't have a lot of time for him. A lot of people got on with Malcolm, a lot didn't. ABC - Allison, Brown and Cantwell - they more or less ran it. Eddie Lewis confirmed; "ABC ran the club."

In essence, this is true, but, as we have found looking at Ted Fenton, it was a tad more involved than this. Ken Brown said; "Malcolm Allison was a big influence on Ted, but they didn't always agree. Malcolm wanted to knock the ball about. In defence this put a lot of pressure on the 'keeper. When he left, the likes of Noel and John Bond stepped in."

George Petchey recalled; "Fenton brought Malcolm Allison in and allowed him the run of it. Allison was a student of the game. Not everyone's favourite of course."

Vic Keeble said; "Malcolm Allison was a terrific coach. I lived with him for a while. He was a bit of a playboy, but he would give you his last ha'penny. He was brilliant in his own way, but he did want his own way. He was unable to bend."

The contrasting views of Allison's role at West Ham are typical of the contradictory way that his position was understood by his fellow players, but it is likely that they reflect the nature and complexity of his personality. However, few denied him credit for his leadership abilities. Albert Foan, for example, said; "Malcolm was a good skipper, he took over the club. He was a strong player and a leader. He had a fair old frame, some would give him the fruit [be insolent/rude], but it was water off a duck's back. Malcolm was confident in his own ability."

The other members of the trinity, Bond and Cantwell, probably knew Allison as a man and a player better than most. John Bond recalled; "At West Ham, Malcolm Allison took me from being a naive little kid to some sort of manhood, really. He taught me about life; him and Noel. After the usual morning training we used to go up to the Denmark Arms, buy our lunch, walk back, go on to the billiard hall or pictures. Then, in the afternoon, we'd go back to the ground till about four or five in the afternoon and train. We'd be knackered at the end of it. I got fit. But Malcolm was terrific, even with the little things like not drinking tea before a game.

"Whatever he said I did. I went from being a country bumpkin to being a man in no time at all. Malcolm took over - he was the one who started the coaching off, and got people interested. Around 1956 I had been to South Africa and when I got back I couldn't get back into the team. Malcolm went up to see Ted Fenton and asked; 'Why is he not in?' He rated me better than he rated George Wright. Your whole life was in Malcolm's hands. He virtually ran the Club. Probably Ted needed someone like Malcolm."

Noel Cantwell said; "Malcolm Allison was a big influence on me. He always looked stylish. He took me under his wing and made me work when I didn't want to. He would listen and push. He was a huge influence on West Ham at that time. When Malcolm joined there was little in the way of coaching at the Club. They were a contented, mediocre, Second Division club, which couldn't play away. Ted gave Malcolm his head and that was clever. We once went to Old Trafford and played with a sweeper. Ted didn't know we were going to do this. Malcolm, together with Bill Watson, a weight training coach, convinced Fenton to use weights and doubled the players' training rate."

Cantwell continued; "Allison didn't like people who didn't like football. Malcolm couldn't handle people. I was good with people. Malcolm got the other guys interested, pulled a group around him and he came back from Lilleshall [the National Sports Centre] with a lot of ideas."

Malcolm himself confessed; "I wanted to change, modernise the training." He did this, to the consternation of more than a few, including Tommy Dixon;

"I used to train with him. We began running backwards. We'd hang a ball up under the stand and both jump for it...no one interfered. Those, who were included in what became known as the Academy, just got on with it. I never saw Ted with a tracksuit on."

Eddie Chapman remembered; "Malcolm, with his flamboyant attitude, is the sort of feller that can take over everything. He used to get the players together round at Cassatarri's, and talk football, football, football. I'm not so sure Ted Fenton was included."

Fenton certainly wasn't part of Malcolm's inner circle. The Academy is a central myth at Upton Park. It was one of those things that was and wasn't; a bit like the 'West Ham way'. It was not an organised seminar, it was a phenomenon that emerged informally around Allison. Malcolm Musgrove recalled something of its nature. "The Press gave the Academy the name. Malcolm deserves all the credit, not just part of the credit. In the afternoons he'd get all the blokes who were really interested in being better players. The ones who didn't come back are the people he didn't get on with. 'We can do without them,' he said. I said; 'On Saturday we'll need them.' We needed people like George Wright and Derek Parker."

As Musgrove pointed out, the effect was to be long lasting. "Noel Cantwell, myself, Kenny, Phil Woosnam, so many of us who were involved, went into management or coaching."

The Academy was a meeting of minds, but at the centre was the ego and football intellect of one man. John Cartwright remembered; "Malcolm Allison generated ideas. He was like a father to me. West Ham would never have got Moore and Hurst without Malcolm Allison. The coaching was originated by Malcolm, he started the Academy."

The nerve centre of the Academy was based at Cassatarri's cafe, round the corner from the Boleyn Ground. It was here that the players went each day. Their conversation centred on football. This was an ongoing football dialogue. According to Allison; "We were like any revolutionary group. We got excited and built up a good feeling... didn't think it was anything special, it was just right for us." Allison used the word 'revolutionary', a label which turned out to be very apt.

No one was obliged to attend this think tank. The participants were all voluntary. Frank O'Farrell recognised the novelty of such a band, coming together through a want to discuss the game. The gatherings produced a definite group identity among the younger players. Football, and their place in it, was a serious business for them. Personalities were diverse. The journalist Peter Lorenzo pointed out that the collective included Dave Sexton, Jesuit-educated, who used to compile quizzes for everybody, to John Dick, who would bet on anything. The cement of their association was their passion for football and common interest, West Ham United.

The Academy was not a chance event. Allison might have felt that West Ham was nothing more than a name, but the Academy's identity evolved out of wanting to experiment to achieve success. It wasn't a club, but at the same time it wasn't a random conglomeration, drawn and connected at some abstract or nondescript place; the gathering was not formalised or convened in any bureaucratic way, such as the coaching clinics organised by the FA at Lilleshall. However, these young men came together in a workers' cafe in the East End because they were Hammers and Ted Fenton had brought them to Upton Park. Frank O'Farrell said; "It mattered to us that we were part of West Ham. We had a sense of loyalty."

Allison and O'Farrell believed they were undertaking different tasks. O'Farrell saw himself as part of an organisation consisting of players, management and supporters. Allison wanted success; he wanted to win, and he wanted to be famous. He looked 'to be good at what I'm doing'. What he wanted was concisely identified by Andy Smillie. "Malcolm Allison went to see the Hungarians play England and that was it for him." For all this, the only way Allison could achieve his ambitions was in the context of a club that appeared to mean little to him, but which allowed and encouraged the kind of innovation he required.

The product of the Academy had to be demonstrated on the pitch - successful, as well as novel and so entertaining football. For a time the new style was not received with a great deal of enthusiasm by the Upton Park crowd. It looked strange. The manner the team played with the ball, especially in defence, made it look like they were attempting to goad the opposition and annoy the supporters. The East End had grown used to solid, hard-working footballers. This group of players looked to play with finesse and attempted something akin to art.

The changes were brought about and developed by the players, but the continued perseverance with innovation was due to management style adopted within the Club. West Ham didn't change its style and win the championship in spite of Fenton. It would not have been hard for the manager to end the experimentation that was taking place at training and on the field. It would have been straightforward to go back to basic football, so escaping any possibility of having the worst of both worlds - being unsuccessful and different at the same time. Indeed, Fenton did, when need dictated as far as he was concerned, revert to 'route one' football.

Allison remarked; "I could take over because they were so confused that any strong personality could." But this fails explain why the players, including Allison, were given the latitude to succeed and often the room to fail. One journalist, a close observer of West Ham, contended; "The players ran the club. Fenton probably never knew what they were doing, but he also knew he shouldn't interfere with what was happening. Fenton had the good sense not to interfere."

That might be an accurate analysis of what the West Ham management was doing during the period of what came to be seen as player power - not getting in the way. However, there were signs that the whole thing was seen as a bit dangerous. Brian Moore told me; "I started to get close to Malcolm Allison and Noel Cantwell but Ted told me to keep away from them."

For all this, anything was possible, according to John Cartwright. "I'm not sure why, but the board let us run things. Maybe it did have something to do with the changes, although most of the players had little or nothing to do with the board. Players were players, the board was the board."

Former players are split about Allison's contribution to the Club's development, his relationship with Fenton and Ted's part in it all. However, few deny that Allison was the focus of innovation. His enthusiasm, excellent knowledge of the game and an insatiable desire for knowledge, to innovate and to bring success to West Ham has never been in doubt.

Allison's perception of what went on is forthright, illustrating the confidence he was known for during nearly half a century in the game. "Paynter was there as a consultant, Fenton was the manager. Both of them had no idea of what a professional football club was." However, one sentence of encouragement from Charlie Paynter, given to the young Allison when he first arrived at Upton Park, has stayed with Malcolm. "I took a penalty and Paynter told me that was the way to do it - whack 'em in!" Malcolm seemed to be proud that he had caught the old man's eye. There was some respect there. However, in most of his comments he derided the management of the Club; "Paynter and Fenton cared about winning, but didn't know anything."

Allison achieved an unexpressed consensus with Fenton that allowed Malcolm to handle the coaching. Looking back to the start of his training activities at Upton Park, he recalled; "I took charge of the coaching at West Ham. I built the attitude. We used to get together and I used to make them come back for training in the afternoons. The groundsman hated me. We used to train on the ground. He'd groan; 'Oh no, you're not training out here again?'"

Allison had more bad news for the groundstaff. Tommy Dixon recalled; "He talked to Ted Fenton about the pitch being bumpy. He told him to order a council roller. The groundsman reckoned that you'd lose the grass in three months."

It was not long before Allison was also having a big say in team tactics and, according to Tommy Dixon; "He used to pick the team towards the end. Mike Grice confirmed this claim.

"Three team sheets would go up for match days. Malcolm would look at them all, take them down and go and see Ted. When they went up again they had invariably changed. Malcolm was a good leader, but he never liked me."

By the second year of his tenure at the Club, Malcolm was, in his own words, 'already running a good share of it'. Bill Lansdowne recalled; "Fenton would give us a chat and on the way out of the dressing-room Malcolm would say what to do."

Mick Newman remembered; "Malcolm Allison was a great influence on the Club. He introduced all-day training, doing weights in the afternoons. That wasn't very popular with most players, who were used to having their afternoons off. But Malcolm Allison more or less ran the playing side of things. He led by the force of personality really."

For Malcolm it seemed a bit more straightforward. "I just told them what to do. It was my determination and aggression that made other players fall into line and realise there was more to the game than they thought."

Malcolm wanted to control important details. He realised the game was more than the sum of its parts, but the parts contributed to the sum. Noel Cantwell remembered; "He once bought a pair of cycling shoes, put studs on them and played in them." Allison recalled how his attention was drawn to West Ham's boots.

"You had to be forward looking. A pal of mine went to play in Brazil, for Arsenal. He sent me a pair of these lightweight boots. Our boots then had hard toes. When I got these lightweight boots they had soft toes, and were cut down like shoes. I thought they were great, very light." The footwear innovations were not to everyone's taste however. Tommy Dixon said;

"We went for the Arthur Rowe boots, but they went like cardboard after three months in the wet weather."

Other aspects of the kit also captured Allison's imagination. "I hated the heavy shirts, I cut the sleeves off."

Noel Cantwell recalled this innovation. "Once, it was 80 degrees and we had long sleeved shirts - he just cut all the sleeves off. He didn't ask anyone if the could, he just did it."

Tommy Dixon thought he knew when Malcolm's scissor fetish started. "Jimmy Andrews found his strip was too long for him, so Malcolm just cut the shirt and shorts down."

Yes, the shorts were next. Allison claimed; "I was the first one to have short shorts. Noel Cantwell recalled; "We got my landlady to cut down the shorts. It was her idea to cut a 'V in the legs."

Sometimes it wasn't as organised as this, though, as Albert Foan testified, "Malcolm would say; 'Give us those shorts,' and he'd just cut the legs right down. He didn't care less what anyone thought about it. Those shorts were made for six footers, not for the likes of me!"

Nothing was now sacred. Allison confessed; "I even played without shin guards a couple of times, but I got done. A feller put his studs right down my leg once, at Birmingham." Malcolm smiled, "So I thought I'd better wear shin-guards."

Tommy Dixon remembered this with some discomfort; "Yes, we started to play without shin-pads! Looking back that was mad. They'd be out to stop you by any means in those days."

Malcolm justified his actions; "I realised that the equipment was all wrong. It wasn't modern, it was too heavy, so I just changed it all." The attacks on kit were certainly as much symbolic as pragmatic. A lot of West Ham players had powerful characters and some were more skilled than Allison. More mature players were not ready to be pushed around or persuaded by a relative newcomer, particularly a brash and aggressive young man, eulogising foreign strategies, with ambitions to dress the Hammers in ludicrously tiny boots and skimpy strips that he had come across on the continent.

Allison's chance to have an impact arose with the new generation of players that emerged in the late Fifties, young men who were willing to take note of practically anything that offered the opportunity of success or simple added interest. He was able to convince these individuals of his ambition for them, himself, and the team. His conviction and ebullience were infectious. His contempt for what went on at West Ham seemed to have no boundaries. He rejected the kit, derided the atmosphere, ignored the chairman and criticised the manager. However, he never expressed his repugnance for Club outside Upton Park. Allison said; "I was going to make the Club a success in spite of itself. I blanked out the board, the manager, everybody who might get in the way. I wasn't sure what Fenton was doing, I think he kept out of the way."

Few feel more strongly about Allison's creative influence than John Cartwright. Allison trained him as a young player at the Tuesday and Thursday night session. He was flattered by the opportunity to learn with the senior professionals. "Malcolm Allison should be revered. They should have a statue to him at West Ham...he laid the foundation for the success of the club, not by what he did on the field, but what he gave to other people."

****

It was a long drive from East London to the home of Malcolm Allison, who was living in Cleveland. I was nervous. I have always identified with Allison; a rebel, a revolutionary in the Che Guerava mould and, for me, the founder of modern English football. Malcolm was still a big man, with a solid handshake. I spoke to him about how, in February 1951, he came to join West Ham. "I told the trainer at Charlton Athletic that the training there was rubbish. The next day I was transferred to West Ham. Benny Fenton was at Charlton, he'd been at West Ham, he recommended me to his brother to replace Dick Walker

"They weren't coaches in those days. Jimmy Seed was the manager when I was at Charlton. I was seven years at The Valley, from when I was 14 till I was 21, and he spoke to me three times. One day I was training by myself. He came with a feller from South Africa, they had bought three or four South African players. He came down with this guy and he was watching on the side of the track. He shouted; 'Lengthen your stride, Malcolm.' I thought, 'You cheeky bastard. I've been here five years and it was the first time you've ever spoken to me.'" Malcolm laughed.

Both grounds had poor facilities and at West Ham the training was again not good. I took a lot of the training and things began to look up. I was 22 when I went there. It was quite a good side. Ernie Gregory was the 'keeper, he was older. Harry Kinsell was also more experienced. Derek Parker and Frank O'Farrell were about my age. Andy Malcolm was a very good player, a very, very good defender. John Dick was a very, very good inside-left. The side that got promotion was made up of the up-and-coming players. We had a good young side. They were mostly very young. Noel Cantwell was excellent - when he joined he was two or three years younger than me.

John Bond was younger. He was a good steady player. Bobby [Moore] was a brilliant young player."

Malcolm told me of his boyhood; "I was brought up in Bexley Heath and went to Central School. When I was ten my school report said; 'Good at sport, but uses his mouth too much.'" He chuckled.

"I played in the school first team when I was 11, alongside 14-year-olds. I had a feller who was about five or six years older than me, called Alf Rosier, he played for Fulham. He was the only professional footballer I knew. He used to train with me. We used to practise things together. He was a big influence on me. I deliberately failed my exams at the grammar school because they didn't play football. Me dad went mad.

"All I wanted for Christmas as a kid was football gear, boots and so on. I just loved the game. My mother's family was very football oriented. Her two brothers both played good amateur football; they used to give me a lift on the handlebars of their bikes to go with them to different matches. The football probably comes from my mother's side. My dad was an electrical engineer, he travelled a lot; did a lot of contracting work all over the place. I went and did that for a little while, but I didn't fancy it. Someone from Charlton saw me as a boy and I had a trial. They signed me as an amateur. I signed professional at 17. That's when I went in the Army.

"I was on National Service in Austria. I played with a First Division team out there called Wacker. The inside-forward and captain of Austria were in that team. The Austrians came to England in the early Fifties and drew 2-2 at Wembley." This was the team inspired by one of Europe's most gifted footballers, Ernst Ocwirk, nicknamed 'Clockwork' by English journalists after the Wembley result. Austria performed a variation of the old' metodo' style, pivoting the whole team around Ocwirk, an attacking centre-half. As such, is not hard to believe Allison when he said; "I learnt some things about training there...but I learnt most of the things from Lillishall. Alan Brown was really my mentor, and Walter Winterbottom. They were very influential in my learning."

Allison became a regular in the West Ham side and was ever present in 1953-54. Despite taking the place of a very popular player in Dick Walker, Malcolm quickly gained the respect of the supporters. "I thought the fans were amazing. We were playing Blackburn; the ground was frosty, coming near the end of the game and they started singing *Bubbles*. They always sensed when we weren't going to get beat. When they sang, we weren't going to lose.

We were going up to Blackburn once and we stayed in Manchester overnight. It was a lovely day the next day. We went to Blackburn that afternoon, there was around 30,000 there and about 100 West Ham supporters. It was a good game, but it went on, and on, and on - nil-nil. The ball came over the top and I kicked it up, it was picked up and we scored. There was absolute silence in the ground. Then all of a sudden this big docker stood up." Malcolm broke into song. He has a good voice, deep and powerful - "'Bye-bye, Blackburn...' I thought that was brilliant." And of course, I was about 11 again and I thought Malcolm was brilliant.

Most players recall that Malcolm nearly always had some ready cash. There was a rumour around the East End that the handsome young man was something of a gigolo, but he told me; "In the close season I used to sell cars and clean 'em. I worked in Warren Street. I earned more money doing that than I did playing football. We were only on about £8 to £10 a week. It went up to £14 I think. I used to argue for everything."

A significant event that changed the secure and straightforward nature of West Ham contracts was provoked by Allison in 1958. Following tuberculosis, that had hit him just eight games into the championship-winning season, Malcolm was working hard on his comeback. He had been taken ill after the Sheffield United game on 16th September 1957. He had made a marvellous recovery, particularly so, having had a lung removed. West Ham offered him £17 per week the next year, the maximum was £20. Allison didn't want to refuse terms or ask for more, so he put together a proposal of his own. He asked for £20 per week in the playing season if he gained a first-team place, backdated to the start of the season. The board rejected the latter provision and agreed to offer him £20 after he had appeared ten times in the first-team. The board felt so strongly about this that the chairman was instructed to let Allison know that if he failed to, accept the terms, they were prepared to grant his request for a free transfer.

There was more involved here than the size of Allison's wage packet, however. It was a confrontation of personalities, philosophies and perceptions about the status of a player. West Ham's initial reaction was a willingness to let Allison go before it would accept his terms. Allison was insisting that he was capable of playing again; the Club wanted proof. Fenton and

Allison were never the best of mates. At the same time, Reg Pratt did not enjoy having any player write a unique set of provisions for himself.

'Johnnie the One' - the first black player to wear an England shirt

In April 1961 some of the heroes of the previous decade returned to Hammers' colours for a fund-raising match. Back row (left to right): Vick Keeble (referee that day) Jim Barrett, George Taylor, Albert Walker, Ernie Gregory, Harry Kinsell (linesman) Albert Foan, Danny McGowan. Front row; Stan Foxall, Ken Tucker, Len Goulden, Terry Woodgate

West Ham players enjoy ten-pin bowling (At 'Dagenham Bowl') - very much in vogue then - Phil Woosnam watched in awe at the performance of Mike Grice

West Ham players, champions of the Second Division, pictured at Kings Cross in April 1958 after returning from Ayresome Park where they had beaten Middlesbrough 1-3

Preparing for training at Chigwell in 1957 are Malcolm Musgrove and Mike Grice

Danny McGowan, Bert Hawkins and Frank O'Farrell pictured in the Upton Park gym

Ted Fenton talks over tactics. Players include Malcolm Allison, George Wright, Derek Parker, Ernie Gregory, Terry Woodgate, Harry Kinsell (back row) and Frank O'Farrell (extreme right, front row)

West Ham United, 1955-56. Back row (left to right) A.Malcolm, G.Wright, G.Taylor, L.Bennett, N.Cantwell, F.O'Farrell. Front: R.Stroud, B.Moore, W.Dare, J.Dick, M.Musgrove, M.Allison

Hammers centre-forward Bert Hawkins rushes in as Sheffield United 'keeper Ted Burgin punches clear at Upton Park in January 1952 - West Ham won the game 5-2 with a hat-trick from Ken Tucker - Gerry Gazzard grabbed a brace

Leonard "Len" Crittenden Cearns - "Mr. Len" or "The father of West Ham"

John Bond (the manager)

Jimmy Andrews (the manager)

Gerry Gazzard

Derek Parker

West Ham United beat Leicester City 3-0 in the first match of the season at Upton Park (22 August, 1959). Ken Leek, Leicester's inside-left, beats Andy Malcolm (West Ham's right-half) to the header, just behind is Noel Cantwell, (Hammers' left-back)

A week after the board's abrupt reply to Allison, the issue was reconsidered and a decision was made to rescind the previous minutes and grant him the maximum wage, if he played in ten first-team matches. They offered to backdate this to 1st August. Until then, his wage would be the £17 per week that had been originally offered to him. Allison had negotiated new terms with the board, the only case in which a player had acted virtually as a free agent and obtained what he wanted for his services.

Allison received a 'Golden Handshake' testimonial match. "West Ham played England for my testimonial", he recalled. However, this should not obscure the novelty or the importance of his last contractual struggle with West Ham. Allison had made a tradition of not accepting terms, but this time he challenged the board and set terms, rather than just the amount. His situation was unique and had no effect either on the board or on his fellow players. Subsequently, West Ham continued to set terms for players as it had since 1900. Throughout the Fifties and into the 1960s the number of players who refused terms remained constant, most of them accepting the offers unchanged within a few weeks. The board made occasional adjustments, always in the case of an established player who was approaching the maximum wage. There was no instance of a player getting the maximum after rejecting terms for less. If that had happened, the directors would have been admitting that they and the manager could not see when a player had reached the pinnacle of his skills.

It is a puzzle why the board put up with Allison. A constant thorn in their sides, a good player, but by no means the best or unexpendable, why didn't they just get him out of the Club? It can only be that his attitude and knowledge was appreciated and seen to be of benefit to West Ham United.

Malcolm talked about his part in the championship season. "I only played five games that year they went up. I was pleased they went up, but I was disappointed. Being fairly young then, it affects you more. I'd been in hospital. I went to the races and saw Jeff Lewis, the jockey, and he loves football. He said; 'How are yer? Come and see me on Monday, I might have a winner.' He told me quite a few winners, so I got a few quid like that. It was another way of life for a little while. Then I went to Cambridge University, coaching, which I enjoyed."

Malcolm played 255 first team games for West Ham. His debut was 2-0 win at Upton Park against Chesterfield in March 1951. He scored ten goals, the first came in a 3-2 home win over Nottingham Forest in October 1952. He told me; "I think the centre-forward butted me and I got slight concussion. I don't remember much about that day."

Malcolm did have a bit of a reputation as a playboy, but he claimed; "I never drank or smoked when I played. I was still living in Barkingside when I finished playing and I took some of the lads out a few times. I won quite a lot of money at gambling, I used to take 'em and treat em."

However, Mick Newman seemed to see things differently. "He had the bearing and the looks and he lived a life that impressed most of us. He was having breakfast at the Ritz while most of us were turning over in bed. I don't know where he got the money, but he managed it somehow."

Malcolm enjoyed playing against the continental sides who West Ham invited to Upton Park. "We played against these foreign teams to get use out of the floodlights. You played against AC Milan. Gunnar Nordahl, he was massive, bigger than John Charles, a Swede. He was their centre-forward. He dragged you along, passing defenders before scoring. They beat us 6-1. I went to the bus stop ashamed. I didn't like losing. Harry Hooper recalled this match; "Nordahl slated Allison."

For all this, Allison was a better than average player. Tommy Dixon told me; "The first man I played against when I got to West Ham was Malcolm Allison. Dick Walker said that he would treat you fairly but play you hard, and he hit me and kicked me and I vowed that he would never do it again. Allison was certainly uncompromising. When I asked Malcolm about his own playing strengths he told me;

"I was a good defensive player. If I had been quicker, I'd have probably got a cap. I was a good positional player and I was strong, but I was always more interested in the coaching. I liked working with the young players at West Ham. I got so much pleasure working with the likes of Bobby, John Cartwright, Noel. I really enjoyed it." It was coaching that made Malcolm's name in football. Andy Smillie told me;

"He was a big influence. He always thought I'd do more than I did. Malcolm Allison was a great motivator. He loved flair, but he was a strong defender. He liked to see good players in midfield. He had a continental view, like 'total football.'"

Joe Kirkup said; "Malcolm brought in some good ideas. I remember the ball on a string under the stands, outfield players had to head it."

Malcolm Pyke said; "Malcolm took a lot of interest in the players who went to the afternoon training, and I think if I'd have gone I'd have become a better player. He was a great coach."

Malcolm looked back at the state of the club after he left; "There wasn't a good feeling in the camp at West Ham after 1959. Bobby was never happy. I remember him saying to me that he was never really happy with the team at West Ham; they never really got it together. He didn't get on with Ron Greenwood. He felt that it was a split camp."

Bobby Moore once said that Allison had taught him to 'be in control of yourself'. Malcolm also told Moore to 'stand big'. This made running harder and slower, but it made him look bigger. Bobby and Malcolm, along with Noel Cantwell, grew to be strong friends, Malcolm told me; "Noel, Bobby and I were very close. Pals." However, Moore, certainly in the first instance, was somewhat in awe of both Allison and Cantwell;

"They were somewhere between teachers and big brothers. Funny and kind but they could be tough and blunt, and take the piss. But I never had anything less than great respect for them both. Totally dedicate to what they were doing. You have to admire that in any walk of life."

Others saw the relationship grow. Malcolm Musgrove confirmed; "Malcolm was Bobby's idol and Bobby was Malcolm's pet player."

John Dick said; "Young up-and-coming players like Bobby Moore were in awe of him and when Bobby got Malcolm's place in the first team, the big man still went out of his way to help him. That's the kind of person he was."

Eddie Lewis said; "The man deserves a great deal of credit for bringing on the likes of Bobby Moore. As a kid, Bobby was slow, he couldn't head a ball and he couldn't tackle, but such was Malcolm's' dedication he was able to help Bobby to become the player he was."

When it came to Malcolm Allison, few people felt as neutral as Eddie Bovington who, when I asked him about Allison, replied; "I trained with Malcolm Allison on Tuesdays and Thursdays, he was alright I suppose."

There were some who preferred to keep their opinion to themselves. When I mentioned Malcolm Allison to Tommy Southren, he smiled and said; "My mind has gone blank." Although, there is practically unanimous agreement that Allison had a great knowledge of the game, views of him as a person differ widely and, not surprisingly, given we are looking at the response of professional footballers, are often influenced and related to his coaching ability. Vic Keeble summed up Allison by saying;

"He was easy going and good for other players, although when I joined he was on the way out. He wasn't in the first team when I was at Upton Park."

John Dick said; "Malcolm, was larger than life and I will never forget him as long as I live -Malcolm was the man who started it all. He was an absolute football nut and used to eat, sleep and drink the game. It was his religion and everyone at the club looked up to him. He influenced everybody. I've heard people say that Ron Greenwood transformed West Ham with his revolutionary coaching methods. But for me, Mal was king and there will never be another one like him."

Doug Wragg told me; "Malcolm was a good chap, the life and soul and was a tremendous influence on us all. He was all the club and a good coach."

Eddie Lewis expressed a complex mixture of feelings about Allison. His admiration and respect were obvious, but he also seemed disappointed with him; "Malcolm Allison was without fault as a professional but in his private life he was an arsehole. He was the kind of bloke who, when I was doing bench press, you'd look to impress - he was charismatic. When he had TB he was given the choice of two operations - one where he had a 70 per cent chance of survival, but wouldn't be able to play anymore or one where he had only a 30 per cent chance of survival, but it may have been possible to play again. He chose the chance to play again. He came back with a scar from the back of his neck to his backside. But he got himself back to match fitness. He would flog himself in training."

Eddie went on; "He was down at Midhurst recovering from his treatment during most of the championship season. I don't think we would have gone up if he'd been around. He needed controlling, that's what Joe Mercer did for him at Manchester City. Malcolm was not good at man management, but he was innovative, probably born 20 or 30 years too soon. He had a big chip on his shoulder about Derek Ufton, the man who replaced him at Charlton, who played for England. Malcolm thought he was a better player than Derek.

"I admired Malcolm Allison for his advanced thinking. Noel Cantwell had a similar sort of passion for the game. But Malcolm always had a different bird on his arm…and he had a lovely wife. He brought a team over to South Africa, Rodney Marsh etc, and it was a right abortion. I was critical of the organisation. When the papers quoted me to him he said; 'Eddie who?' He knew very well who I was. Certainly well enough to know how to wind me up"

Malcolm Musgrove also seemed to have ambiguous feelings when it came to Allison. "Malcolm was up-to-date with things that were going on in football, the technical side. I liked him because of his ability to get the best out of people, I didn't like him for what he could do to people he didn't like. Malcolm Allison was very helpful to me at West Ham. I was a young kid from the North East, green as grass, the first thing I had to do was get a suit. Malcolm helped a lot of lads. He was very influential.

"Allison was a good skipper. He wanted to win, wanted to play football, and this was at the time when there weren't many passing sides about. Most teams used to get it, kick it to the other end and chase it, but we, through Malcolm's influence, always wanted to play from the back. We wanted to pass the ball around. He was a centre-half that didn't just belt it away; he got it down and passed it. He was a character."

Looking back, Musgrove remembered; "Malcolm didn't like Michael Grice - 'don't do this, don't do that.' I told him; 'If you don't want him in the side, why pick him? You've got the influence with Ted, so he must be in your side, then when you play him you crucify him.'"

I asked one player, who shared his career at Upton Park with Malcolm, what Allison was like. The old ex-pro laughed and said; "He was a womaniser. He had a beautiful wife, beautiful kids, but he still fancied the birds. That was his biggest downfall along with liking a bet. He used to like Hackney Wick. He lived on the edge; what we used to call a 'chancer'. But he helped a lot of people, he also helped destroy a few. But as they say 'casualties of war!'"

"I wasn't a gambler," Malcolm Musgrove confessed, "I didn't go to the dogs, half a dozen of the lads would float across to Hackney on racing days. Jackie Dick and Noel, Kenny Tucker, they were senior players compared to myself. I'd never been brought up to bet. I wasn't getting very much money, I was getting a tenner a week at the time. Malcolm was full of life and was great on the field. If he liked you as a person and as a footballer, he'd go through a brick wall for you. But he would crucify those he didn't get on with. He had it in for Tommy Southren, both he and Harry Hooper were outside-rights. Malcolm wanted Harry in the side and Tommy out. Tommy was a good attacking player, hard working. Harry was a good player, but he got away with his skill. He could stand still for 89 minutes and then win you the match. If Malcolm liked you then you were in, if he didn't you were out and he'd see to it that Ted wouldn't pick you. He really loved the game. He loved the training, he was a fitness fanatic."

Harry Hooper confirmed Allison's professional devotion to his own physical development. "Malcolm Allison was dedicated - a fitness fanatic, the rest of us just enjoyed the game."

George Petchey said; "Malcolm was a good friend. He studied the game. He was always enthusiastic about it. He loved new ideas, new ways of doing things. He was a force of nature and for the most part, most people knew where they stood with him. No one felt neutral about the man."

Bill Lansdowne told me; "I remember, during my debut game, Malcolm Allison had a bad cut on his head and insisted on carrying on. A real fighter! Malcolm was fantastic. At a clinic in Brighton, we were training for a Cup game, I remember he was amazing. He slogged himself to death. He had unbelievable determination - he was very directed - he thought in a different way. He had massive imagination and drive."

Malcolm Musgrove told me something of this different way. "Malcolm used to say; 'If you're having a bad game, keep working and you'll get a better one. It will come, but if you sulk, don't do anything about it, and stand about, its no good.' That was it really; it was all about taking action, doing something about a situation; almost anything was better than nothing."

Derek Parker saw that Malcolm Allison was great influence on everybody; "He was dedicated to football, as he proved when his playing days was over. In endeavour! He was so keen and encouraged everybody. He was an inspirational skipper. He wasn't near international class but he made up for it. He showed that people could do a lot to make themselves what they wanted to be; effort trumped any natural gifts. With him people felt they could take control of their destiny. That was the bedrock of his outlook and so people felt he freed them from themselves to a certain extent. And it's true, we often are our own worse enemy, saying 'oh I can't do that' when if you try and work at it you often find that you can do that."

Ernie Gregory said of Malcolm Allison; "He was one of the best trainers I've seen. He would be white when he finished. He was dedicated, although, sometimes on the field I could have kicked him up the arse. I know a lot of the time he was experimenting, but there's a line between that and just messing about with it. He cared about winning, but he seemed to care more about doing stuff differently. He had a rebellious streak, sometimes playing up for it's own sake. But he was a thinker!"

Frank O'Farrell argued that Allison made the Club aware that the game was developing. "But he didn't want to listen. He made enemies. He should have worked alongside Ted, but he was good for the Club. I pointed out that Ted was doing things. Malcolm was a bit harsh or arrogant. He had some good ideas from his time in the forces in Europe. He called most of what Ted said 'bullshit' but I told him that Ted was discussing things."

According to Jim Barrett; "Malcolm Allison tried to change a lot. A lot of what's going on now isn't that new, the likes of him started years ago. He changed things at West Ham but he had an effect on football generally."

Malcolm consistently tried to promote and develop these ideas through his disciples. He told me; "I recommended John Cartwright to Greenwood, and Terry Venables, to look after the youth team and the Under 21s. Walter Winterbottom was the one who really started to turn English football around; him and Arthur Rowe. They looked at the bigger picture, worldwide. Bill Nicholson, Ron Greenwood, Alf [Ramsey] and me, all followed their lead"

Harry Kinsell confessed; "I didn't get on too badly with Malcolm Allison - he would tell me what to do and I'd tell him to mind his own business. He was slow to turn. That was on the field and in his head. If he had an idea he had to try it out, no matter what anyone else thought."

For Dave Dunford; "Malcolm Allison was a top notch. If we'd been away we'd used to go back to his club - he had The Artists and Repertoire. He was a pretty good manager. He seemed to get on where ever he went."

Malcolm Musgrove remembered the day Allison learnt of his illness; "When he got TB it was the first time I saw a grown man cry, really cry, when he found out that his career was virtually finished. He went into the London Hospital first and then Midhurst. We'd take a carload of the lads down to see him at Midhurst and he was always laughing and joking, but it killed him when he realised it. He came back. 'I'm gonna play. I'll play again, don't worry about that.' And he did! Talke about 'mind over matter – that's what he was all about."

Prior to the Second World War and for sometime after, the diagnosis of TB was a death sentence for many. Allison's battle against the disease confirmed what many people always knew, but others were won over by his fight. Andy Malcolm looked back; "I wasn't really one of Malcolm's fan club, but I will say watching him struggle to regain fitness after his operation I have a lot of admiration for the man."

Malcolm Musgrove continued; "I think he got one first-team game and a couple of reserve games, but he couldn't get his breath. I remember an evening game at Sheffield United, it was very balmy; it was one of those summer evenings when it was very warm. You could hear Malcolm breathing all over the ground - he just couldn't do it. That was a really sad day for the Club. But then he picked himself up and became a manager and became more famous than he had been as a player. As a player not many people outside of London knew him, as a manager the whole country knew him. Very flamboyant."

Most players expected that Allison was heading for quite a future. Tommy Dixon, for instance, said; "Malcolm was destined to do well. Allison was a leader. You could see that he was destined to get on. Someone like him was never going to just disappear."

John Lyall said; "Malcolm was a strong man. He wanted to know about football, wanted to learn. He battled for what he wanted. I wasn't surprised he became a very, very good coach. He took responsibility, dealt with consequences. He accepted criticism, he would try anything. He had an open mindedness to try things. He had the same enthusiasm as Johnny Bond and Noel Cantwell; they were people who were progressive about their football. They made training and preparing exciting."

For Doug Bing; "Malcolm Allison stood out at West Ham. It was his stature, the way he used to talk to you. He was a first-class player and a great coach."

Malcolm's alleged lifestyle caused a deal of disagreement between players who admired him as a coach and/or a man, and their wives whose opinions were based on other considerations. George Wright said; "Malcolm Allison was fanatical. He lived, ate and drank football." His wife Marcella added, "I was always friendly with Beth, Allison's first wife, she was nice."

"He wanted everything perfect," George recalled. "Fenton got all his ideas from him. He was more in charge than Ted was. Malcolm instigated the coaching."

Jimmy Andrews told me; "Malcolm Allison was a great friend of mine. I loved the whole game, it wasn't just a game of football to me - it was a way of life. I loved the training, I loved the hard work; I loved the graft of it. I loved to argue and have opinions about the game, as Malcolm did and Noel, Danny, Frank, and Musgrove a little later on.

"The arguments we used to have," - Jim shook his head - "We all had opinions. Malcolm had the strongest opinion, or he had the most to say. We used to battle with him. Nobody wanted to give in. If you didn't agree you told him so. That was a great learning experience, for coaching and managing. You learnt that it was easy to say something, but to back it up was a different thing altogether. We had to back up everything we said. You learn by arguing and by doing what you argue for. You can make a statement without too much thought, but if you know someone is listening, and they're judging, then things change all together. Then you've got to think before you speak. And you've got to know what you're talking about.

"Of course, Malcolm was always over the top. He was an over the top merchant, he was marvellous in terms of his attitude. Nothing was good enough. Everything could be far, far better if you did it his way. But a great feller as well. We were real good friends."

Dot, Jim's wife, quite tellingly interjected; "Malcolm Allison treated Beth like dirt." Jim smiled gently, raised his eyebrows a little and nodded slightly, seemingly resigned to something about the errant character of genius.

Bert Hawkins remembered; "Malcolm was very strict on the field. I got on well with him, but he still told me off like anybody else. He was a good player but a hard task master." He paused a second looking down as if trying to remember something. He looked up suddenly and said, "He had insight!"

Katherine, Bert's wife, responded by saying; "He was an awful man. He didn't get his wife a bit of clothing. He was out with all these women and she didn't have two-ha'pennies to bless herself with!"

However, Bert reiterated; "With the game he was the business. He had this way with him that caused you to want to play his way; he made you think you could do it the best way. It made us a bit big-headed perhaps. We'd see other sides, particularly when they came to West Ham, as being a bit thick." He chucked as Katherine shook her head.

This part of the book was the hardest for me to write. I have tried to let Allison and his peers paint the picture of him and his place at West Ham. However, it is near impossible to encapsulate someone like Malcolm Allison in a few words, a chapter of a book or a whole volume. In Allison, the frail and brave, the weak and strong man, we see so much of ourselves. None of us is perfect, we do some things well; other times, well, we feel we could have done better. The best we can do is be gentle with ourselves. Tolerance and acceptance are the most healing and rare of sentiments, although anyone can tolerate up to the point when they become intolerant; acceptance feels like the bigger ask. Allison's experience at West Ham was made up of these two types of responses; the likes of Bobby Moore fully accepted and embraced his character and intellect, others more or less tolerated him. I suppose it's arguable who got the most from these alternatives. In the end, it is probably true that it is difficult, perhaps impossible, to be truly creative without being destructive. In this sense, as Derek Woodley had it; "Malcolm Allison was god in his own right." Perhaps a bit like the Hindu deity, Shiva, who creates and destroys at the same moment.

There is little doubt that Malcolm, like a lot of brilliant people, was deeply flawed, but maybe you can't have one without the other. Creativity gives rise to excitement, at the same time people are often creative in search of stimulation. This is what made Malcolm's life seem chaotic, exotic and exuberant. This was attractive to many, but frightened or appalled others. Perhaps the person you are will dictate how you respond to people like him.

Malcolm Allison was mad, bad and dangerous to know, but he was wonderful; gunslinger, a lovable rogue, a satanic presence of genius. He was the edge personified; the swashbuckling adventurer, but also an intelligent man. He was that rare entity, a leader who could manage. If it is not true that women fell for him in droves, it should be, because men certainly did, probably mostly in a different way.

He was a man that made others look ordinary. I wonder if it is useful to ask; 'Who would I rather be, Allison or [for example] Fenton'. I know my answer to that, but of course, any choice would be imply theoretical drawbacks and it's rare that we get a choice of disadvantages. But could Ted have achieved what he did at West Ham without Malcolm? I doubt it. Would Allison's life been much disadvantaged had he not had a relationship and run ins with Fenton; wound his accomplishments have been any less? Probably not? Fenton wisely or inadvertently made space for Allison; Malcolm apparently had no room for Ted. Although as the imaginative and half intelligent historian eventually learns, a good deal about people or history was not in actuality as it seems in the dim light of retrospection.

Maybe those of us who are ordinary find in him someone to fear and resent, admire and respect. As such, it may be as well to have summarised his development at Upton Park with a type of eulogy to contradiction. This might not have explained Malcolm, but it could help us understand him and maybe ourselves, just a bit better.

1955-56 – West Ham is a way of life

In August 1955, the lad who would be the man to manage West Ham for much of the Seventies and most of the Eighties, John Lyall, joined the Hammers as an office boy. In many ways he epitomised the feelings of many people who got involved with the Club in the Fifties when he said; "West Ham is a way of life…it was my good fortune to arrive at the club as a young man. My aim was to achieve status in my career as a footballer; little did I realise that the Club would 'mould' my life. The fact that I had relative talent as a sportsman was important, but West Ham's greatest influence on me was the way it taught me to set standards for the Club and myself both on and off the field. There was no one accepted formula, it was simply done and agreed by all involved. During my injury-troubled career, the character of the Club and its people became clearly apparent to me. Having briefly met Charlie Paynter in my early days at the Club, I was acutely aware of the understanding offered by the management and staff in difficult times, and yet equally full of respect for their forthrightness in criticism and praise. Perhaps it is best put by saying that they did their work very well, but offered the individual a little more." Lyall went on to recall; "The early days were not easy, but gradually I was educated… according to the tradition."

One tradition West Ham kept up early in the season was getting off to a mediocre start. The Hammers' first win came on 3rd September when Notts County were beaten 6-1 at Upton Park. Billy Dare, who was now the first-choice centre-forward, scored two while Harry Hooper, who was putting on some dazzling performances on the right-wing, bagged another pair. Frank O'Farrell and Jackie Dick made up the half dozen. The England selectors were aware of Hooper's form; he was capped twice that season at Under-23 level, playing against Italy and Scotland.

October was a good month for the West Ham patrons as 14 goals were scored in three home games. Barnsley were beaten 4-0, Billy Dare grabbed two and Hooper got his fifth of the season. There were ten more goals in the League that term for Harry. Plymouth went down 4-0, crippled by a Ken Tucker hat-trick. Ken hadn't got three in one game since his debut, almost eight years before. Another triple went to Harry Hooper in the 6-1 win over Doncaster Rovers.

Ernie Gregory was now back in goal following his long-term injury. The regular fullback pairing was John Bond and Noel Cantwell. The duo got more daring with every game they played, weaving their way out of Gregory's penalty box, and transforming a potential threat into ammunition for the West Ham attack.

Another amazing goal feast took place in October when the Irish club Distillery were beaten 7-5 at Upton Park. Billy Dare scored four of the West Ham goals. One of the Distillery goals was scored by an eventual Molineux favourite, Derek Dougan. An Irish international to be, Dougan would be the steel alongside the silk of George Best in a formidable Northern Ireland attack.

After victory over Doncaster on 22nd October, the Hammers went another eight games without a win, crashing to 19th position in the League table. However, Swansea were thumped 5-1 at the Boleyn Ground on Christmas Eve and this brought some optimism for forthcoming FA Cup match with First Division Preston North End.

Serious rioting broke out in Nicosia, on the Mediterranean island of Cyprus, when the traditional parades to celebrate OXI Day (the day when Greece entered World War Two) were banned by the newly appointed British Governor, Sir John Harding. Cyprus police were assisted by British troops in bringing the situation under control, and there were many casualties on both sides.

The unrest marked another stage in the deepening crisis in Cyprus. Inter-communal fighting between the majority Greek population and the Turkish minority worsened when Prime Minister Anthony Eden attempted to strengthen the British position on the island. The situation was fuelled by the terrorism of the Greek Cypriot insurrectionary movement EOKA, and the increasingly draconian counter-insurgency methods employed by the authorities. During 1955, EOKA, led by Colonel Grivas, stepped up its campaign of bombings, murder and civil disobedience in the cause of *Enosis* - union with Greece - while Harding pursued negotiations with the leader of the Greek Cypriot community, Archbishop Makarios.

At half-time in the third round of the FA Cup, the Hammers were trailing Preston 2-1, the legendary Tom Finney having scored from the spot. The match report in the *Stratford Express* read;

What a magnificent sparkling transformation in the second half. Man of the Match was inside-right Albert Foan who gave the most dazzling performance from an inside-forward seen in years. He gave a demonstration of slide-rule passing, quick fire shooting that had the Preston defenders running around in circles.

Preston weren't the best team in the top flight but they weren't far off, finishing third, joint second on points with Spurs, in Division One the following season, and runners-up to Wolves in 1957-58.

In the second half Albert scored a splendid hat-trick on a mud bath of a pitch. Billy Dare's contribution gave West Ham a 5-2 win. That season Albert got only a handful of games in the League, but played in all half-dozen encounters that made up West Ham's fine Cup performance. I asked him how it felt when he scored his hat-trick against Preston. He looked at me and asked; "What's it like to score three goals at any time?"

In the next round, another side from the top flight, Cardiff City, provided the opposition. As was his wont, Ted Fenton had taken his team to Brighton for Cup preparation. The players would work out at Hove dog track. Goals by Billy Dare and John Dick generated a 2-1 win for the Hammers and reinforced the mystique that was to grow around Ted's coastal jaunts. However, the win, which was a good one, probably had more to do with the Bluebirds being a not-very-useful First Division side. They finished only four points clear of relegation at the end of the season. West Ham's home advantage, incorporating nearly 36,000 Irons fans willing their side into the next round, was also helpful.

The Hammers were drawn at home again in the fifth round. This time the tale of the balls resulted in a visit by Blackburn Rovers. After a hard fought 0-0 draw the teams met again at Ewood Park. John Dick's couple and one from Hooper gave West Ham a 3-2 win. The Irons were in the last eight for the first time since 1933.

Luck deserted West Ham in the sixth-round draw in a big way, sending them to White Hart Lane. As the first stirrings of spring were reaching North London, a huge crowd of 69,111 turned up to see the two London rivals slug it out. Although Tottenham's League form was not all it might have been, they demonstrated their class in 1956-57, being prevented only by an exceptional Manchester United team from taking the First Division championship.

The first half was dynamic. Dick scored a hat-trick as the Hammers raced into a 3-1 lead before a Harmer goal pegged the visitors back. The second half was a test of skill and concentration, which Spurs won near to the end when Guernsey man Len Duquemin flicked in the equaliser. The 3-3 draw was remembered by most of the West Ham players involved and stayed in the collective fan mind for many years.

In retrospect it was clear that the replay at Upton Park was not going to live up to the first game. West Ham lost 2-1; John Dick saw this result as the biggest disappointment of his career. All memory is relative; events evoke different feelings from the people involved. One person's disappointment for someone else connects into a pattern of a highpoint in their life. For Albert Foan; "The thing that sticks in my mind most from my West Ham days is the 1955 Cup run."

The next day Britain deported Archbishop Makarios to the Seychelles on the orders of Prime Minister Eden, on the grounds that he was encouraging the anti-British campaign in Cyprus. This caused a significant rise in terrorist and counter-terrorist activities on the island. British troops sought to eradicate the EOKA and its sympathisers, but arms searches in Cypriot streets and villages, internment and restrictions on freedom of movement served only to alienate public opinion still further against the authorities.

Eden drew up plans for phased self-determination and for constitutional reforms involving partition of the island, but the proposals became bogged down in disputes between Greek and Turkish governments. While the politicians talked and failed to talk, the bloodshed and unrest continued.

Before March was out, Upton Park said a sad goodbye to Harry Hooper, who joined Wolves for £25,000. This caused huge discontent among the supporters, who loved Hooper for his speed and skill. His departure was also signalled the end of the Hammers' promotion hopes.

In April, Mike Grice, a signing from Colchester United a month earlier, had the formidable job of replacing Hooper, coming in against Stoke City at the Victoria Ground. It wasn't a good day for the Irons who went away from the Potteries well beaten

A blizzard was blowing off the Norfolk coast as I parked outside Mike's home, by a 'For Sale' sign. Mike's daughter was away on a year-long, round-the-world trip with her partner. Mike told me he would be pleased to see them when they got back. As he made me a cup of tea, he showed me his photo collection; some fantastic shots from his time at West Ham and Colchester. There he was with the young Noel Cantwell and John Bond doing squat jumps between two, chest-high, walls, created from benches banked three high. The moment in time captured the three just landing astride the valley made by the benches, each foot about to land atop the stacks on left and right. Another snap showed Mike in 1958, signing autographs under signs indicating stadium entry to Upton Park costing 7s 6d, 6s and 4s 6d - best seats under 38p!

Looking back on the time before he came to Upton Park, Mike told me; "I followed Arsenal as a boy and was a great fan of Dennis Compton. Dad was a driver and I played part-time for Colchester at first, as I was taking an apprenticeship as a draughtsman for a coach building firm." Mike has one brother. "He was picked one day because he was my bother" chuckled Mike.

"I was sitting in a tea-room used by the Colchester players," Mike recalled, "when Benny Fenton told me that he was selling me to West Ham. We went down to Ilford [about a 15 minute drive from Upton Park on a good day] and saw Mr Pratt and Ted Fenton. That was it! Spurs and West Brom had also shown interest, but that came to nothing." The fee Fenton paid to brother Benny was £10,000.

"The most I ever earned was £25, but that wasn't bad money. I did some part-time work when I first joined the Club. About half-a-dozen of us got jobs at a tile factory in Dagenham, the owner was a big West Ham supporter. This upset the permanent staff; there was practically a strike at one point. Now, looking back, I have some sympathy for their feelings."

When Mike got to West Ham he lived in Barkingside, quite near to Ken Brown, John Dick and Malcolm Allison, developing good friendships, particularly with John Lyall and Malcolm Musgrove. He also remembered some other Upton Park characters with affection; "Wally St Pier was a lovely man as was the little bloke, Horace, who helped the groundsman. I had a great deal of help from and admired Frank O'Farrell."

While he was at Upton Park, Mike probably never got over the problem of being the replacement for one of the most popular players to appear at the Boleyn Ground in the Fifties; "When I came to Upton Park I replaced a hero - Harry Hooper. I dreaded playing at home - things didn't go well. I was 12th man at Bristol Rovers, Doug Wragg was supposed to play. When it was announced over the loudspeakers; 'Grice replaces Wragg,' everyone groaned. But I knew the Bristol player I'd have to face; I'd played against him at Colchester and knew I would run him ragged. At half-time I got a standing ovation. You could imagine the last thing I wanted to do was take a bow. Things were better for a while after that."

However, the crowd was never really to take to the blond, good looking young flankman. "I was a winger, so I often took my place up at home games next to the Chicken Run. I'd always hear a voice call out; 'I'm here again, Gricey.' I'd look around and everyone was laughing, there was no way of finding out who was shouting. I'd wish I could just pick him out." However, Mike was philosophical; "Overall West Ham were a friendly club. I don't think I was a good player, but I was playing in a good side. I could run, put the ball there, and I could get it. I often think if I could turn the clock back and play in another period, I wouldn't get in the 'A' team." Here Mike was maybe a little hard on himself. He was a flying winger who was to make a big contribution to the championship side. He made many more goals than he scored and complemented Malcolm Musgrove usefully. He played 150 games for West Ham over almost five years, scoring 19 goals, the first in the opening game of the 1956-57 season in the 4-1 win at Craven Cottage.

Mike looked back on his departure from Upton Park during the 1961-62 season. "I was eventually put on the list and Coventry came in for me." There was some resignation in Mike's voice. Maybe he would have wanted a career at West Ham closer to that of his fellow debutant late in the 1955-56 season.

Bill Lansdowne was a 20-year-old and recently demobbed from the RAF. He played in the last two games of the term, both at the Boleyn Ground. His first match in the Football League ended in a 4-2 defeat at the hands of Lincoln; the second was a 3-0 win against Bristol City. Bill continued to be connected with the Club well into the Seventies, when his son, Billy junior, joined the Boleyn Boys.

The Lansdownes were a big family. "I was the second youngest of seven children [he had five sisters]. Dad had a fruit and veg round in Debden [in Essex], he established it round the new estates. Mum sometimes worked with him." Bill told me that at Shoreditch Secondary School, playtime was football time, and that seemed to be Bill's training for future life. "I used to admire Les Compton when he was with Arsenal. He was so cool and calm, but also a big man - I loved to watch him play. I used to go to Arsenal one week and Spurs the next." However, his future was taking shape in the East, although he didn't choose to go to Upton Park. "West Ham chose me - I was playing for Loughton Town boys when Wally St Pier invited me to play for the juniors. I went on to play in the Eastern Counties League."

For Bill, "West Ham was a family club, you were made welcome and I was quickly made to feel I was one of the boys. Ernie Gregory looked after me when I joined; he was like a dad. We shared rooms, and he took me to get my wedding suit. Clubs had large playing staffs in those days, this, and National Service, made careers slow to get going. I did some part-time summer work. I used to cut the grass at the golf club with Ken Brown to get some extra money. John Lyall and me got a job in a plaster factory. From the Club we got £8 a week in the season and £5 in the summer."

So, by the time Bill got out of the forces, his life was pretty much mapped out for him. "I was going to take an apprenticeship as a motor mechanic before I went in the RAF but it never materialised. When I went in the RAF, I was stationed at Oxford. Pat [Bill's wife] and me were both telephonists, that's how we met." They were married in 1958. He recalled; "All the boys came to the wedding. They were a great bunch of fellers."

After the war, right up to the likes of Frank McAvennie in the early Nineties, there was a tradition of some dedicated drinking at Upton Park, but Bill made the point; "I was never a drinker - it wasn't important to me. One or two of the players liked a bet, but I lived out at Loughton [not far from Debden, in Essex]." This, of course, kept him clear of most of the vices indulged in by some of the senior players, but it didn't stop him having good friendships with his fellow professionals. "I was close to Ken Brown, Malcolm Musgrove and Malcolm Allison. When I got married I moved to a club house in Barkingside, I was one of the first to buy."

Bill, who played 60 games for West Ham, scoring five goals, over six seasons, recollected; "I got my first goal for the club at Upton Park in 1957, we beat Orient home and away that season." But what remained most vivid in Bill's memory were the games he took part in, particularly those played out under the floodlights at the Boleyn Ground. "The night home games were memorable. I remember playing against Aston Villa; I think it was the first time Upton Park had been televised in a League game."

Bill was to be central in helping to build the side that were so successful in the mid-Sixties and played a major role in developing some of the players who were to come through into the first team in the early Seventies. He told me; "There was a change when Greenwood arrived. We trained and thought about the game more. He sent us to Lilleshall to train as coaches." After his playing days were done, Bill was appointed junior team coach in 1965.

On Thursday, 19th April, the American-Irish actress Grace Kelly, star of such films as *Dial M for Murder* and *Rear Window,* married Prince Rainier III of Monaco in the cliff-top cathedral of St Nicholas, Monaco, before a congregation, which included such luminaries as the Aga Khan, Ava Gardner and Aristotle Onassis. The wedding was an international media event with an estimated 1,800 journalists staying in the tiny Principality for the occasion. After the televised ceremony, at which the bride wore a dress presented to her by MGM studios, the couple drove to the royal palace in a cream and black open-topped Rolls-Royce for the wedding lunch. Prince Rainier and

Princess Grace then left for their honeymoon on his yacht the *Deo Juvante* ['With God's Help'].

Perhaps with a bit of 'Deo Juvante' Billy Dare topped the scoring charts for West Ham with 18 goals, plus four in Cup-ties. Two players were sent off during the season, Noel Cantwell at Bristol Rovers and Ken Tucker at Fulham. West Ham had finished a very unimpressive 16th, despite being able to call on a solid group of players, who were developing their style and talent. All four of West Ham's matches against the Second Division's top two sides, Sheffield Wednesday and Leeds United, were drawn; but another Yorkshire team, Hull City, who finished bottom, took three points from their encounters with the erratic and eccentric Irons. Three clubs, Port Vale, Leicester City and Blackburn Rovers, achieved doubles at expense of the Hammers. For Rovers, West Ham had proved to be nourishing prey in successive seasons.

The board turned down two requests that would have changed the character of the Club. In May 1956, Malcolm Allison asked to become a part-time player. The board refused because they thought that there was a greater need for him on the field than working with the younger prospects. Noel Cantwell asked for a transfer shortly afterwards, a request that was curtly and firmly denied.

The European Champion Clubs Cup, or European Cup, was the first European-wide club competition. Early in 1955, Gabriel Hanot, then editor of *L'Equipe,* a French daily sports paper, invited representatives to a meeting in Paris to sound out the idea of creating a championship for the major clubs of Europe. Fifteen clubs responded to his invitation by attending the meeting and it was agreed to organise a tournament for the 1955-56 season.

FIFA were willing to support the idea and so UEFA gave the tournament its blessing, and has organised it ever since. The first tournament was curious in that only half the clubs that took part were the champions of their respective nations (not so strange these day, though). Not until the following season did UEFA manage to restrict participation to national champions.

Chelsea, with former Hammer Eric Parsons in their ranks, were drawn against Djurgaarden of Stockholm, but, to their eternal regret they declined to take part, after being asked by the Football League to reconsider their entry. Although nowhere near being Scottish champions the previous season, Hibernian, who finished behind Aberdeen, Celtic, Rangers and Hearts, got to the semi-finals, but were beaten 3-0 over two legs by Stade de Reims, who lost 4-3 in the first-ever European Cup Final to Di Stefano and Real Madrid.

In June, Colonel Nasser was elected President of Egypt. On 26th July, he responded to the Anglo-American withdrawal of funding for his Aswan Dam project by seizing all revenues from the Suez Canal, the West's commercial lifeline to the Middle and Far East. The move effectively nationalised the Anglo-French Universal Maritime Suez Canal and closed it altogether to shipping from Israel. Britain's Prime Minister, Sir Anthony Eden, favoured a military response but the US was less enthusiastic and the crisis was referred to the United Nations.

Stanley Matthews became the first European Footballer of the Year, beating Alfredo Di Stefano of Real Madrid by three votes. No British player was to win the title again until 1964 when Dennis Law, then of Manchester United, came top of the ballot. The next English player to top the poll was Bobby Charlton in 1966. Bobby Moore was fourth that year. He was runner-up to Gerd Muller in 1970 and tenth in 1971. Bob had moved up to seventh the following year. This made Moore the only Englishman to be included four times in the top ten European footballers.

Days of Iron – The story of West Ham United in the Fifties

1956-57 – It went from one end to the other

In May West Ham started their preparations for the coming season by travelling to Eastern Europe, a trip which took in a match against a combined Prague team that included Macek, then a Czechoslovakian international.

Come August, the Irons' trip behind the Iron Curtain seemed to have done some good because they won 4-1 at Craven Cottage, Billy Dare starting where he left off by scoring two goals. But two successive home defeats, against Swansea and Blackburn, with West Ham leaking five goals and scoring only two, meant that Fenton had to make some changes. The short two-match experiment with Fred Cooper ended with the return of Noel Cantwell in defence. Malcolm Allison was back at centre-half, displacing the young Ken Brown, and Ron Stroud was brought in to the spot vacated by the omission of Albert Foan. The biggest surprise was Malcolm Musgrove's call up in favour of Ken Tucker, who had scored in the three games that had been played. Doug Wragg being preferred to Billy Dare, and Mike Grice to partner Musgrove on the wings completed the shake up.

West Ham spotted Wragg when he was playing in the National Association of Boys' Clubs Final at Wembley in May 1953. It was the Bernard Joy Trophy, the 'Star' Final - the competition was sponsored by the *Evening Star*. A Nottingham scout told Reg Revins about the 18-year-old Nottingham and England Schoolboy international. Ted Fenton was briefed and on 4th June of Coronation year, Doug was signed in Nottingham. He recalled; "I started on £7 a week, £10 when I got in the first team. After I'd signed, Ted said it was too late for me to go back to London. My dad was a good local darts player. We were living down in Bilborough at the time. Ted Fenton offered to go down to his club with my dad and present the trophies. Everyone was over the moon at that. Nothing was arranged, it was all off the cuff."

Doug, one of two Nottingham-born brothers, came from solid Northern working class stock. His dad was a lorry driver and his mum worked in the Players cigarette factory. She passed away on St Valentine's Day 1997, aged 93.

As a boy at school, along with most other Nottinghamshire kids, Doug was encouraged to work at his football. On leaving school he spent a year with the Raleigh Cycle factory, then Coxes, before entering pit work at Wollaton Colliery. He was a miner for just a year before joining West Ham.

I went to see Doug and his nine-year-old cross-Labrador Sam, who Doug had nurtured since he was a pup of just six weeks, in his hillside home overlooking the eastern suburbs of Nottingham. As he gave me a West Ham mug full of good hot tea, he told me that he had been retired from the Raleigh company - he made seats - for a year. He took his pension 12 months early. Doug has two adult daughters, one of whom, although a Nottingham girl, is an ardent West Ham fan, who has often taken the long trip south to lend her voice to the Upton Park chorus. Doug looked at least a decade short of his actual years. He gave Sam credit for this; he needed to take the lad for regular walks. However, Doug had also maintained a thirst for the amateur game, and had played for local sides until the age of 45. Keeping in good shape had become a discipline for Doug - "I always say, we were paid to be fit."

Doug had played in a couple of reserve games for Notts County, but Fenton persuaded the young winger that it was a good idea to get away from his home town, like many other players who had made a success of the game. Doug had never been to London before, but his move to the capital was well organised. He was met at the station and taken to the ground. Doug emphasised the warmth and team ethos that existed at Upton Park. "Everyone was so friendly, the officials, players and the fans - no one ever wanted to shift from West Ham. There was the Cearns family, Eddie Chapman, who was a nice chap, always helpful - if you wanted anything doing he'd get it done - and Dr Thomas, they treated all of us the same, no matter if you were one of the first-team squad or a ground boy. The club was not just a squad of 16, all the players were treated the same."

For his first couple of years with West Ham, Doug was doing his National Service in the RAOC (Royal Army Ordnance Corps), initially at Portsmouth and then in Bramley (sount of Guildford). However, he got away on most Saturdays to turn out for the Hammers' reserve side. As a professional he was retained on £1 per week. This meant he could only play for West Ham. Doug got out of the forces in 1955. He recalled; "I was put in digs with John Bond and Doug Bing in Boundary Road, East Ham. The Club made sure you were all right, checking up from time to time."

Doug naturally became pals with his housemates, but was also friendly with Frank O'Farrell whom, according to Doug, "everybody knew as a really nice bloke". Doug told me that Bill Lansdowne and, in particular, Eddie Lewis were also good friends. "The Club encouraged us to be sociable. Upstairs at Cassatarri's Cafe was always full of West Ham players. Every Wednesday they took us down to Southend for the day. We'd walk to the end of the pier and then have a meal. Some players went off to play squash or golf, to relax, and the Club encouraged this. We were treated well. We got tokens for a steak meal at the Denmark Arms on Fridays. When I got married, the Club sorted me out a flat in the Barking Road."

Doug played 16 first-team games for West Ham during his seven years at Upton Park. Ten of those came in the 1956-57 season. The team changes initiated on his debut for the first team seemed to do trick. Doug's first two games resulted in a 2-0 away win at Blackburn, the Hammers' first League success at Ewood Park since 1950 - poetically Alan Blackburn got one of West Ham's goals - and a similar margin of victory at Sincil Bank. Looking back Doug recalled; "There were so many emotions before that first game at Ewood Park. We were in the hotel just outside Blackburn and the famous rugby league commentator, Eddie Waring, was staying there at the same time." Doug smiled as he told me, "Malcolm Allison called to Eddie, telling him that there were going to be two Dougys at the game the next day, Brian Douglas, who played for Rovers and me."

Wragg remembered the supporters; "The West Ham fans were always very warm and sociable, even in the street. They nicknamed me 'Oily'," he smiled. "The fans in the Chicken Run were great, but the ground was so compact the supporters were physically close to the players and this created a terrific atmosphere. There wasn't the barracking you get today." At that point Doug began to make an insightful comparison with contemporary football. "I think this was because the game then was not so frustrating to watch. It was more open, less defensive - it went from one end to the other. The problem now, especially outside of the Premiership, is that the clubs all do the same thing; the system never changes - plonking the ball into the middle. There's no time to roll it about...

"I was a full-time player. When I got to the Club we were training morning and afternoons most days. West Ham was innovative in their training. We would go down to Grange Farm and rotate around five-a-side, weight training and running, but the big difference today is the fitness of players. It's like in athletics. Then, in the mid-Fifties, to run a four-minute-mile was a wonderful achievement, now it's fairly ordinary. The footballers are the same."

In his early days as a professional, Doug, like so many other players at the Club, was grateful for the guidance of Dick Walker, and admired him greatly. In this respect Doug was a human link between one era at Upton Park and another. "I saw Moore and Hurst come through and I remember Ronnie Boyce coming in for his first game in the Southern Floodlit Cup, I think it was against Millwall. He was really impressive."

In 1955-56, Doug played in the semi-final of this competition. West Ham won 3-1, with goals from Billy Dare, Mike Grice and John Dick. The Irons went on to win the trophy, beating Aldershot 2-1 in the Final, Ken Tucker and Billy Dare doing the damage. Games like this had a definite prestige, and were important enough for clubs to field strong sides. Over 10,000 watched Doug and the rest of the West Ham side beat Leyton Orient in the first round of the 1957-58 tournament, John Dick got the only goal of that game. Some 8,000 of the Upton Park faithful cheered Doug's two goals in West Ham's 3-1 first-round victory over Millwall in 1959 (Malcolm Musgrove got the other). Dick and John Bond played in that game.

Another well-supported competition was the Essex Professional Cup. Again, clubs honoured the ties with some strong teams. For example, in the 1959 Final between West Ham and Orient, the Hammers, who won 4-1, included Joe Kirkup, Noel Cantwell, Andy Malcolm, Ken Brown, Phil Woosnam, John Dick, Malcolm Musgrove and Geoff Hurst in their side. Doug was a member of three successful semi-final sides in this competition. In 1954-55 Colchester were beaten with a pair from Tommy Dixon and a Derek Parker goal to put the Irons through to the Final 3-2. After a 3-3 draw with Southend, West Ham shared the trophy that season. In 1957-58 West Ham beat the Shrimpers 2-1 in the last four; Andy Smillie and Mick Newman were on the mark for the Hammers. Doug went on to appear in the Final that year, but, despite the presence of names like Dick, Musgrove and Lansdowne, West Ham were well beaten by Chelmsford City. A lone goal by Eddie Lewis was the only answer the Hammers could come up with to a handful of Chelmsford goals.

Doug remembered the loyalty the West Ham fans showed by supporting these games in relatively huge numbers. "They were fantastic. Over 20,000 turned out for Billy Moore's testimonial" (a game that I remember well).

Doug remembered his departure from the Boleyn Ground. "I left West Ham not too long after the club won the championship. You need a run in the first team and I never really got that. In those days, when you bought someone he had to be played and you had to have that extra yard on anyone to get in the side. Moving up from the reserves there was a big difference in pace. From the terraces things might not have looked like they were moving too quick, but when you were on the pitch that ball was flying about like a bullet and you needed time to adapt to that. Raich Carter - he was manager at Mansfield at the time - came to see me at Upton Park and told me that he wanted me to talk to him rather than the other way round. He offered me top money, the £20 a week maximum." So, Doug returned to his roots in 1960. "Everyone likes to get back to where they come from and Field Mill was only 20 minutes from where my parents lived, so I went."

As I said goodbye to Doug, West Ham were due to kick-off a Premiership game at Old Trafford. But the floodlights failed and they didn't get started until 4.45pm. The Hammers got thumped 4-1.

On 28th September 1956, the day after West Ham's good 2-0 home win against Barnsley, Britain and France went to the United Nations Security Council about Suez.

October opened well enough for the Hammers when they travelled down the road to Leyton Orient and took away the points. Malcolm Musgrove, later to join Orient, scored West Ham's opener in a 2-1 win. At around the same time Prime Minister Eden met French Premier Guy Mollet in Paris, a meeting which was followed by the launching of an Israeli attack against Egypt. A disappointing 2-0 defeat at Upton Park sent the Terriers back to Huddersfield with smiles on their faces, while internationally rumours of collusion between Israel, Britain and France were rife as the Royal Navy was despatched to Suez in Operation Musketeer. The month ended with a 1-0 at home to Grimsby and an Anglo-French attack on Egypt.

Nowhere did the policy of de-Stalinisation, proclaimed by Khrushchev at the Party Congress in Moscow in 1956, have more dramatic effects than in the troubled Communist state of Hungary. In pursuing the Malenkov new course of economic decentralisation and de-collectivisation, the Hungarian Communist Party leadership had released popular forces for change, which were to prove beyond its control.

In October the people of the capital, Budapest, rose against the Soviet regime, which had replaced the reforming Imre Nagy as Premier. Barricades appeared in the streets, the statue of Stalin was torn down in the city centre. The revolution seemed to involve all sections of society, including women industrial workers, and intellectuals of the influential Petofi circle. The recall of Nagy only fanned the flames and in November, Soviet tanks rolled on to the streets of Budapest to put down the rising by force.

At the beginning of November, West Ham went to Belle Vue, Doncaster, and came away pointless. A couple of days later, despite the UN's attempt to impose a cease-fire, British bombers based in Cyprus supported the Anglo-French action against Egypt. The attrition was to be short lived when, embarrassingly for Eden, the Americans failed to support the action. A Ken Tucker goal gave the Irons their first win in five games when Stoke visited Upton Park in mid-November.

****

West Ham found it hard to fill the number-nine shirt which Billy Dare had worn with such distinction the previous season, although Alan Blackburn and Roy Smith had tried. With only half-a-dozen wins in 16 games, Fenton had to be seen to do something and as usual it was unusual. He attempted to convert Doug Wragg to a more central role, with Ken Tucker and Malcolm Musgrove on the wings. Ted chose the away match against Middlesbrough in November for the experiment. It didn't work out well as West Ham came away on the wrong end of a 3-1 result. For the next match, Fenton brought in his new signing, former Manchester United and Preston centre-forward, Eddie Lewis.

When I spoke to Eddie at his home in South Africa, the former Busby Babe enthused; "I learnt most of what I know about football from my time at West Ham. Even Manchester United was disorganised in comparison. At Old Trafford the idea was to just pass the ball to a bloke in red." Eddie, at that time, was coaching with Batha, one of South Africa's leading sides. He has been in South Africa since 1971.

Lewis joined West Ham in the exchange deal that took Frank O'Farrell to Preston in November 1956. Eddie recalled the atmosphere at Deepdale; "It was like an amateur club compared to West Ham with the likes of Ted Fenton and Bill Watson. Preston was a joke, it didn't matter what time you turned up for training, there was always a bloke there sitting around with his cap on. He was the trainer, the father of Gordon Hill [the Millwall and Manchester United winger of the Seventies]. When we got to West Ham we had weight training and group training - two groups playing six-a-side, another doing heading training using balls that Malcolm Allison had hung up under the stand. Another group would be doing sprints, another weights."

Of course, Eddie had moved down a division coming to Upton Park. "I did find the going very physical in the Second Division. I had never played outside of the First

1956-57 – It went from one end to the other

Division." But he had a good average in his relatively short time at Upton Park, scoring 15 goals in 36 games. He recalled; "Frank O'Farrell told me that West Ham wanted a goalscorer and, if I got a chance, to shoot. So I did and got one in my first game. I was pleased to score." That first goal was scored at the Boleyn Ground against Leicester. The Hammers won 2-1. Ken Tucker was also on target that day. Bob Wylie, a Scottish 'keeper from Blackpool, was drafted into the team for the same game, as cover for the injured Ernie Gregory. Wylie had 13 mid-season games and was on the winning side in ten of them.

Eddie was to get eight more goals that season. "I had a good understanding with John Dick," he recalled. He scored his first Cup goal for West Ham in January, in the third-round defeat of Grimsby Town. This match saw the young John Smith score twice. However, the Hammers went out in the next round, beaten 2-1 by Everton at Goodison Park.

A narrow 1-0 win over Stoke in November changed the home form as West Ham proceeded to win a further eight successive games at Upton Park, seven of which had a 2-1 scoreline. As such, coming in on a run of success, the Boleyn Ground supporters warmed to Eddie from the start. He remembered; "The crowd were always good, especially in the Chicken Run. When they were all swaying and singing *Bubbles* it was quite something."

When I spoke to Eddie he told me, still in a clear Mancunian accent, "My dad was on the railways and my mum was a tailoress; she worked from home. My dad was a big influence on me. He was from Salford. I went to Burgess Street Primary and North Manchester High School. One of my teachers, Mr Norman Entwhistle, was another big influence. I came across him some years ago, he was coaching in Jersey."

Eddie started his footballing life at Old Trafford. He remembered; "They would open the gates 50 minutes from the end of the game to let people out, that's when my dad would come in and see me."

The people who had the biggest impact on Eddie's early development were of course of the United stars. "I admired Jack Rowley, he scored five on his debut for England, against Switzerland. He also played in the 1948 Cup Final." Eddie showed his devotion by naming all the side that won the FA Cup in 1909; "Monger; Stacey, Hayes, Duckworth, Roberts, Bell, Meredith, Halse, Jimmy Turnbull, Sandy Turnbull, Wall." I replied with the Hammers 1923 team; "Hufton; Henderson, Young, Bishop, Kay, Tresadern, Richards, Brown, Watson, Moore, Ruffell." There was something of a pregnant pause, then Eddie responded; "Yeah. But we won!" I was forced to concede. He continued; "Jimmy Murphy, the Manchester United coach, was also a great influence on me. I learnt the value of thorough preparation at West Ham, and I still call on that attitude today."

The move Lewis made from Manchester to Preston was a disappointment; "Going to Preston was the biggest mistake of my life. Tom Finney was a brilliant player, but he was a miserable sod, and Tommy Docherty was uncouth. It's part of my life I'd like to delete. It was a disaster. Even down to the digs. I used to have a landlady who would blow smoke down the spout of the teapot before she'd pour it! You got no help, at Preston."

For all this, Eddie was philosophical. "But if I'd have stayed at Old Trafford, if I'd have been that bit faster, I'd have been dead. The air-crash in Munich see; I lost my best man in that. So, however horrible it was a Preston, it wasn't a fate worse than death."

West Ham in 1957 would always be linked to disaster in Munich in Eddie's mind, when the flower of the Manchester United side was crushed in the snow of that foreign runway. "The game that sticks in my mind was a home match against Doncaster. I took a penalty and scored, but I remember that match because it was my first game following the Munich air crash. Eddie Chapman broke the news to me. Eddie did his job well, he and Pauline Moss in the office."

When the opportunity came to move to West Ham, Eddie had mixed feelings; "I didn't really want to move south, but I hated Preston. I was really a home loving guy and I did get a bit lonely when I first came south. But I made friends easily; I've never had this thing about sticking with Northerners. Ron Greenwood was always a bit like that. Whenever he saw me he would make a bee-line for me, it was out of proportion, Northerners in the land of the Southerners sort of thing.

"I was going to stay at Bobby Moore's parents' house when I first came to West Ham, but that, being in Barking, was a bit too far from the ground for me. I went into digs in Kingsland Road in E13; my landlady was Doreen Scott. When I got married I moved into the club house that had formerly been occupied by Derek Parker."

Like so many West Ham players, Eddie took up coaching at, what was during that era, an early stage in his career. "I did a little part-time work with John Dick at the Saltwell Centre in Chigwell. Even after we stopped playing we used to kick each other about. We were still competitive. We would fall about and almost cry with laughter sometimes. I also got into selling insurance through Jack Turner, who helped a lot of people at the Club with his financial advice. I carried on with that when I went to Orient. Jackie Dick used to gamble a lot, so when he got his benefit Jack made sure he bought his house with it. Jack Turner lived to the age of 89!"

Eddie continued; "The Supporters' Club had a social about once a month. I was fairly close to Malcolm Musgrove, we still write to each other pretty regularly. Mike Grice and Bill Lansdowne were also good friends."

Having done well in his opening spell with the Club, Eddie played in all 24 of West Ham's remaining games in 1956-57. It was surprising that he didn't go on to better things at Upton Park. He was, after all, only 21 when he came into the team, but as Eddie explained; "John Lyall ended my first-team career at Upton Park. He was in goal during a practice match. We were mucking about a bit and John was saying that I'd never score against him. I was going past him and he kneed me in the thigh. I was out for six weeks, that's when Ted signed Vic Keeble. I can still feel the lump in my thigh! But I always got on well with John; he was one hard player. I once saw him dragging Ron Greenwood around by the scruff of the neck - I thought he was going to give him a smack. Of course, later on they were close pals."

Although Eddie made the point that there was a lot of internal bickering and back biting at Upton Park; "There was a deal needless criticism at times. A lot of that was about who was in or out of favour with a handful of players who had a lot of influence." However, like most former Upton Park professionals, he enjoyed his time at the Boleyn Ground and was sad when the time came for him to move on to Leyton Orient. "I was sorry to leave West Ham. I had been sad to leave United, but not Preston. But I stayed in the area and saw the same people, the lads I knew from West Ham, so it wasn't so bad and Orient were really a friendly, family club. When I was at Orient we were going to come in for a fat, overweight boy, who sweated so much that you could see his shirt through his shorts. If Ron Greenwood had arrived at West Ham two weeks later, we'd have got him. But Ron wanted to look at the whole squad before he did anything and he chose to hang on to Geoff Hurst."

The year 1956 was to be a seminal one for popular music. Elvis Aaron Presley, the former truck driver from the Deep South, rocketed to fame as the undisputed king of rock 'n roll in the USA. It all began for Elvis at the age of 21, with three massive hits in 1956, *Heartbreak Hotel*, *Hound Dog* and *Love Me Tender*.

Britain continued to be troubled by events overseas. In January, Eden resigned, drowning in the sea of ignominy that was the result of Suez. Harold Macmillan took over as Prime Minister. In Aden, British troops repelled invading Yemeni forces. The border between Northern Ireland and the Republic became the focus of a renewed campaign of Republican violence in the early months of 1957. Operation Harvest, the IRA's third major campaign of bombing and sabotage, had as its targets a number of administrative and industrial installations as well as the buildings and personnel of the Royal Ulster Constabulary.

Although the Hammers had experienced a good mid-season run, the late winter and early spring period was a grim patch. Three straight defeats, letting in ten goals, hit the Irons hard. This, together with poor form of front man Dick, who had managed to be on target in only five out of 33 League outings, gave Fenton some worries. So, for the visit of Doncaster to Upton Park in mid-March, West Ham fielded the last ever amateur to play in the club's first team.

Mick Newman had been around East End football for some time, playing for Dagenham, Romford, Leytonstone and Rainham. "I wasn't ready to turn pro," he recalled in his unusually (for a footballer) cultured voice. "I started with Dagenham, my family are from that way. Wally St Pier was a big influence on me joining West Ham. He was such a very nice man. It was a bit of extra money and they allowed me to work part-time in the family dry cleaning business. It was all a new world to me, though. I couldn't really come to terms with it. I don't think that I was really suited to the job. I suppose playing and working seemed to be getting the best of both worlds, but I don't think other players liked the idea of football not being my full-time profession. When Malcolm Allison introduced all-day training, doing weights in the afternoons, it became difficult. Mind you, that wasn't very popular with most players, who were used to having their afternoons off."

Mick played seven games for the Club, four in 1956-57 and three in the championship season, scoring a couple of goals. He told me; "In those days you could not sign for more than one season; that was the law at the time. Fenton offered me a verbal five-year contract, on the same terms as Roy Stroud as I remember." However, Mick's reticence to turn professional might be better understood by his perception; "There was always that underlying fear that you'd be laid off in your early 30s with no money - that was not uncommon in those days."

Mick, who was born in Canada, recalled some of the relationships at the Club during his time at Upton Park;"Andy Malcolm was a good friend to me. I remember Dick Walker, who was a great influence on the way the team played, a real swashbuckler. I always found Eddie Chapman to be a likeable man, but Andy Malcolm didn't get on with him. They both came in on the same train from Upminster and they would do their best to avoid each other." He went on. "While most players were ambitious at Upton Park, there was no nastiness, no cut and thrust. Upton Park always had a homely atmosphere. It was an intimate place to play, although at times the crowd, made up of dockers and working men, would not be short in telling you what they thought of you, most of it unprintable. But they, especially those in the Chicken Run, and the players, made West Ham one of the nicest clubs around at the time. The supporters really felt part of the club."

After West Ham won the Second Division Championship, Mick decided that he wanted to concentrate on his business and moved on to turn out for Dartford. In 1956-57, if West Ham had won their final two games they would have achieved their best League position since 1936, fifth place. However, the Hammers had conceded 13 goals in five matches. With Andy Malcolm and Bill Lansdowne injured, Fenton was obliged to shuffle his defence for the game against Bristol City at Upton Park. Ted pushed Malcolm Allison into Bill Lansdowne's spot, Ken Brown filled the space left at centre-half. With demand for wing-halves outstripping supply, Fenton called on the 19-year-old Malcolm Pyke to fill the awesome boots of Andy Malcolm. The first of the youngster's 19 games for the club ended in a 3-1 victory, and this meant that Fenton would stick with his selection for the final game at Anfield - a match that Liverpool had to win to have any chance of a promotion place.

I met with Malcolm Pyke at his pub in North Kent. He was a commanding figure with a firm handshake and strong voice. Malcolm signed as a professional while he was still playing for the juniors. He was a gifted youngster but he got some help along the way. "I went to King's Park School in Eltham," Malcolm recalled. "Mr Pendleton, the German teacher, helped me quite a lot with my football. It was due to him that I really got into playing."

Malcolm told me; "I was spotted by Wolverhampton Wanderers. I was an inside-forward then. I signed a form; I didn't realise this had tied me to them. I was only a lad of 16. Arsenal came along and wanted to sign me. Then Ted came in and sorted it all out, this is cutting the story right down. It was a bit of an on-going saga for a long time. It was a harassing thing."

One of Malcolm's biggest disappointments was that his father had not seen him play for West Ham. "I'd just lost my father as well, with cancer. He was a keen West Ham supporter; he would have loved to see me wearing the claret and blue. He missed out from seeing me by about three years. My dad was born about 200 yards from Upton Park. He'd take my brother and me to Charlton one week and West Ham the next. Dad was a leading fireman at Eltham, he was in the Brigade for 25 years, went through the Blitz."

Malcolm cast his mind back to his first game in the Second Division."I was marking John Atyeo, who was an England international [Atyeo would score two goals against the Republic of Ireland at Wembley in a World Cup qualifying game early in May] …he flattened me out, gave me a black eye, a blinding shiner. John Bond, who was captain at the time, he said to me; 'Get up you big poof; it's a man's game.'" Malcolm chuckled at the memory.

"The social life was very good, but I wasn't a drinker. I just had a tea or a coffee after a game and went back home to Eltham. I lived with my mum, as she was by herself. I did a bit of temporary work painting and decorating. I did that for ten years when I left the game. I was close to Brian Rhodes [a West Ham 'keeper] he was my old mucker. He went to Australia, he came home, stayed with me, stayed with Malcolm Musgrove for a while, he remarried, went to New Zealand, where he died. I was very sad. I got on well with John Smith. He went to Ireland and died at a very early age. I was a very good friend of Bobby Moore."

Malcolm reflected; "When Bob took over I was in the reserves. If I'd have had a father I think I'd have tried a little bit harder. If my father had been alive he'd have made me - because he was keen on football, and came to see me as a kid and all the way through. I think he'd have pushed me and made me play. But it was a privilege to play for West Ham. The fans were marvellous. With the Chicken Run it was the greatest ground you could play on. I loved every minute of it. I trained hard and played it as hard as I possibly could. If I'd have gone Tuesday and Thursday afternoons, I might have been at Upton Park a lot longer. But I had to get home to me mother - she wasn't well at the time. She died when I was only 21. It was a trying time."

Malcolm left West Ham after the Championship triumph. "I went to Crystal Palace for a season. I'd wanted to stay in London. Portsmouth and few other teams were interested, but I didn't want to go down there. George Smith came along, he seemed a nice enough man at the time. I got married that year as well, to Beryl. Smith was a bombastic bastard as it turned out, but his assistant, Arthur Rowe, was the nicest man I've known. When George got the sack, just four games before the end of the season,

1956-57 – It went from one end to the other

Arthur put me straight in the first team. George had you running up and down the stands with packs on your back in pre-season training. I've never worked so hard. All of us had bruises on our backs - it didn't work. Arthur had a great footballing mind."

West Ham lost their final game of the season by the only goal of the game at Anfield. However, Liverpool missed out on promotion by just a single point, being pipped at the post by Forest. Leicester went into Division One as Champions. Both promoted sides had been beaten at Upton Park; the Hammers won only 19 games all term. However, this represented something of a recovery. With three months of the season gone, the Irons had only one home victory to their credit - a 2-0 win against Barnsley.

At the end of 1956-57, West Ham had turned a surplus in the goals account (74-69) of 1955-6 into a deficit (59-63) the following year, but the Club improved their position in the final table by eight places. The Hammers and Fulham had provided the only Second Division London derbies for the previous two seasons, but the promotion of Leyton Orient added another to the schedule. Fenton's men won all the points from their Brisbane Road neighbours in their first League meetings since 1922-3, when Leyton were Clapton Orient.

The never-ending story of acorns and oaks began to be played out yet again at Upton Park. John Lyall signed professional forms in 1957, two years after joining the club as a 15-year-old. He said one reason he signed was that the Irons "treated him like something more than a kid – the Club put a lot of trust in younger players."

In Ireland, Eamon de Valera's new government of the Republic reintroduced internment July. Under Part 2 of the Offences Against the State Act, terrorist suspects could be arrested and detained without trial, and by the end of the year there were around 100 people in detention in the South and 200 in the North. July also saw the arrival of parking meters in London's Mayfair; this marked the end of all-day parking for motorists. The Mayor of Westminster officially launched the scheme. So the next time you get a ticket, blame him. With the new meters parking for two hours cost sixpence (just over 2p) and a further two hours set you back ten shillings (50p).

Manchester United became the first English club to compete in an official European club tournament when they beat Anderlecht over two legs in the European Cup. They defeated Borussia Dortmund, and Athletic Bilbao on the way to the semi-Finals, there going out to Real Madrid, who retained the trophy by beating Fiorentina in the Final. As the previous year Di Stefano scored Madrid's first goal.

1957-58 – I remember in the promotion year... the fans chanted; 'We want six!'

Their performance of the previous term caused West Ham to be one of the club's that was being mentioned as promotion candidates at the start of the season. Most supporters' memories of that season align with that of Bill Lansdowne; "I remember in the promotion year, how, on a few occasions, the fans chanted; 'We want six!'"

But by the end of September the Irons had won only three games and found themselves in 17th place in the table. Morale wasn't terribly high among the players and indicative of this was Mike Grice slapping in a transfer request after a relatively unsuccessful first year in the side.

However, a dramatic change came over Upton Park as autumn turned to winter in 1957. The team that had averaged 13th place in the Second Division throughout the Fifties, scoring less than 67 goals a season on average, would, during the 1957-58 campaign, score 111 League and Cup goals and take the Championship. John Dick would be the leading scorer, but it was Vic Keeble who, for most people, made the difference. The pair got 40 League goals between them, as the Hammers romped to the Title. A supporter of the time, who had been attending reserve and first-team games as a boy for four years, recalled; "When we did get promoted there was a feeling of disbelief. All the way along we thought they would mess it up in the last few games."

Malcolm Pyke commented; "Dick was a great goal scorer, but when Vic Keeble came he turned us around - it was his goals that got us up."

According to John Bond; "We got something like nine points in 11 games in 1957-58, and then Ted Fenton bought Vic Keeble from Newcastle because he thought he could be good in the air, which he was. But what he didn't recognise was what a good target man Vic was. We could play balls from defence into Vic Keeble and he would hold them in to himself or knock 'em off. He brought Jackie Dick into the play a lot more, got more out of Jackie Dick, and made more use of the wingers in terms of crosses. And from there we lost three of the next 31 games. That was all basically because of Ted bringing in Vic." Now wasn't that a fantastic analysis of the whole season, made around half a century after the event!? John Bond had a photographic memory when it came to football it seemed.

John Lyall told me; "I remember when we signed Vic. We were struggling and I think it was getting towards November. I think his first game was a friendly floodlight match. West Ham was third from bottom or something. We won the game well and Vic scored a couple of goals. Then the whole thing changed. When Vic arrived he hit it off with Johnny Dick straight away. Brilliant!

"A few years ago we went to a do for Ted in Gloucester. John Bond, Noel, about 40 players were there in all and everyone was telling stories about Ted. Then Vic starts his story. He was on the transfer list at Newcastle. Ted gets on the blower and says; 'I'm coming up Saturday, I fancy you Vic, I could well put in a bid for you. I'll have a look at you, see how you do.'

"Vic thought; 'Marvellous! Get back to London. I can live out at Colchester and travel in.' I'm not sure that his wife had moved up to Newcastle in the first place. Vic plays the game and at half-time Newcastle was winning 2-0 and Vic's scored both. He's in the dressing-room and there's a knock on the window. It's Ted! He says; 'Don't play too well in the second half, they won't let you go.'"

We laughed at the vision this conjured up, Fenton maybe standing on a box with his nose stuck through the dressing-room window. However, Keeble donning the claret and blue wasn't welcomed by everyone. According to Eddie Lewis; "Ted Fenton was obsessed with Vic Keeble, so I just didn't get any games. Ted wasn't the sort of bloke you could talk to about anything. I really had no one to talk to about the situation so I don't know why I didn't get picked more. After I was dropped I scored four goals in a reserve game."

Others, too, had to be convinced. Ken Brown recalled; "Vic Keeble couldn't kick a ball ten yards, but he could head a ball and moved into position well." Mike Grice remembered; "'Feeble Keeble, the legless wonder' - that's what the Newcastle fans used to say. But he was great in the air. Vic Keeble turned things round for us in the promotion season."

For all this, Keeble gave a lot of credit to the whole of the West Ham side; "The team had some good individual players, but West Ham built their game on team spirit. The 1958 side was a good team. Ernie Gregory was brilliant on angles, always consistent, but Ernie was odd; moody is the word I suppose – he was unpredictable in that way sometimes. T

1957-58 – I remember in the promotion year… the fans chanted; 'We want six!'

"he defence was solid. Bond could kick the lace out of a ball and Andy Malcolm would kick his own grandmother and come back at her again. We had quick wingers."

Vic, a former Colchester Grammar School boy, started out with the King George Youth Club in Colchester before being signed for a £10 fee by the then Colchester manager Ted Fenton. His 23 goals in 46 League games helped the newly-elected Football League club establish themselves. He was good in the air and his deft flicks from head and foot added penetration to the Hammers' front line.

The Irons had managed to put together no more than a dozen points in the same number of games before Keeble signed. Soon after Vic arrived, John Bond told a reporter; "It's made all the difference in the world to us." At the end of the season Fenton confessed; "I didn't seriously begin to think in terms of promotion until after I signed Vic Keeble. Then I thought it would be possible."

Fenton had been attempting to bring Keeble to London for some time. Shortly after Ted moved to West Ham he convinced the club that it should make the acquisition of the play a priority and as such an offer that included Derek Jackman was made. However, Jackman was uncertain about his future and Colchester rejected the offer. Instead of going to London, Keeble joined Newcastle in February 1952 for a fee of £15,000. Although he did not play for the Magpies in that season's FA Cup Final, in the six years he was at St James' Park Vic scored 67 goals and led their attack in the 1955 FA Cup Final victory over Manchester City.

At various times during Keeble's career in the North East, Fenton enquired about his availability. Ted renewed negotiations at the start of the 1957-58 season. West Ham had money, including £25,000 from the sale of Harry Hooper, so in October, Vic was finally reunited with his first manager. He told me; "Ted Fenton had been the manager at Colchester when I was there, and I knew people like John Bond and Malcolm Musgrove, so joining West Ham was like coming home."

When Keeble got to Upton Park, the Club was drifting in its normal place in the Second Division. He was a very capable but not a great player, however he joined West Ham at the right time. He was an instant celebrity, being that rare commodity at Upton Park - an expensive purchase. His first appearance was in Dick Walker's testimonial on 11 October 1957 against Sparta Rotterdam. West Ham won 5-0; Walker completed his final hat-trick in claret and blue and Keeble made a scoring debut. Vic almost upstaged the star of the evening as newspapers reported that the crowd reached 20,000 because so many wanted to see the Hammers' new striker. A few months later, when it was reported that he had been killed in a car accident, the switchboard at the Boleyn Ground was flooded with calls.

He was to maintain his lustre; when local newspapers ran lengthy articles applauding promotion, Keeble's arrival figured prominently, but he was originally important because West Ham had been willing to spend a lot of money and competent enough to buy the right player.

Keeble had a relatively short career at Upton Park. He played his last first-team match at Leeds in January 1960. Injuries forced him out of football the next year. The board took the rare step of trying to arrange a testimonial match for a player who had played only 80 matches for the Club. It was more than the 49 goals he scored during that time that gave him a special place in the hearts of the board, as well as the supporters. Keeble symbolised the year when everything finally went right for the Hammers. However, according to Derek Parker; "Vic was promised a match after he was injured. Ted was there at the time and he never did get his game."

To be a goalscorer you need, above all, supreme confidence. Vic Keeble was still a confident person when he told me; "I was always going to score goals. I scored the fastest 50 at Newcastle. Andy Cole took that record, but a lot of those were scored in the Second Division; all mine came in the First."

Another factor in the West Ham transformation occurred in November 1957. Shortly after the eighth match, a 2-1 defeat at Sheffield United, Malcolm Allison was diagnosed as having tuberculosis. After surgery, losing a lung, and a lengthy recovery, he returned in March as a spectator to see West Ham's record 8-0 win over Rotherham. His influence was still felt throughout the season, through the tactics that had evolved at Cassatarri's Cafe and the personal impact he had on players, as is evident from Ken Tucker testimony; "It was him, Malcolm Allison, who got them promoted. Ted didn't have a clue. Then he barred Malcolm for a time after the promotion."

However, the absence of the West Ham skipper left a void in terms of the team leadership. Noel Cantwell stepped into the breach and took on the mantle of club captain. Players looked up to Cantwell and admired his determination and guidance, as Malcolm Pyke recalled; "At one stage during the season I'd been injured and I was playing in the reserves. Noel was injured too. He watched me, he called me over and told me; 'You'll be in the first team on Saturday', and I was." It had been Cantwell who had persuaded his good friend Allison to see a doctor. This advice almost certainly saved Allison's life.

1957-58 – I remember in the promotion year... the fans chanted; 'We want six!'

Cantwell's style of leadership was very different from that of his predecessor. The team had been together long enough to know what they could do. As a group they respected each other's ability. It was probably no longer necessary to push players in the way Allison had, even if that had been Cantwell's way. Men like Ken Brown responded to the new situation and made a surprising contribution to the championship side. The promotion season was Brown's first as a regular first-team player.

The side that won the title was one of those rare successful combinations of men at different stages in their lives. Winning a championship was the high point of Ernie Gregory's long career, a fitting tribute to years of solid performances. Cantwell was of the new generation and the success was the start of more and greater triumphs for him. John Bond showed that players should not be judged on first impressions, as well as proving Ted Fenton's ability to judge talent and show patience. For all this, the promotion season is often associated with one player who almost did not come to West Ham - Vic Keeble.

The season opened with the Irons acting as hosts to Lincoln. The visitors held the home side to a 2-2 draw. West Ham were able to pull no more than six points together from their first eight games, which included three successive defeats. A minor recovery gave rise to three wins from their next four games, all against fellow Londoners; Fulham, Orient and Charlton.

One of the ugliest confrontations between blacks and whites in the civil rights struggle in the United States took place in the southern state of Arkansas in September. A Federal district court order had decreed that nine black students should be admitted to the previously segregated Central High School in the town of Little Rock. However, the segregationist Governor of Arkansas, Orville Faubus, took every available step to prevent the students being enrolled at the school, including mobilising the National Guard to bar the doors to them.

At President Eisenhower's insistence, the Guard was finally withdrawn, but its place was taken by a white mob that continued to keep the black students out. In an extraordinary move, the President sent in 1,000 Army paratroopers to Little Rock and removed the National Guard from Faubus's control. Only with this military escort could the nine black youngsters enter the school.

So, Vic Keeble arrived during a bit of a run. He scored in his first Division Two game for the Hammers in the 1-1 draw against Doncaster at Upton Park. He quickly formed a successful partnership with John Dick. The Doncaster match was part of a

13-game unbeaten run, which included five-goal victories over both Huddersfield and Stoke. John Dick scored in seven games on the trot. Vic described his relationship with Dick by saying; "I really knocked it off with John. This gave us the confidence needed at the time."

During the last months of the year, the rebel '26 July' movement, operating from its base in the eastern mountains of Cuba, stepped up its campaign of guerrilla attacks on communications centres and sugar plantations throughout the country. The rebel leader, Fidel Castro, declared total war on the dictatorial regime of President Batista in the hope of precipitating economic collapse. On 5th September, the government faced a serious challenge when rebel fighters and Cuban Navy officers tried to seize the naval base of Cienfuegos, but the attempt failed and the ringleaders were executed.

Fenton's long-sighted move for Keeble happened alongside another. The largest radio telescope in the world was unveiled at Jodrell Bank, on 11th October. It was completed ahead of schedule to track the first Soviet satellite, which had been launched the previous week

On 21st December, West Ham travelled to Sincil Bank; they beat the Imps 6-1 and were third in the table, only two points behind the leaders Liverpool. It was just after this game that Noel Cantwell had one of his rare spells out of the side. Fred Cooper covered when Ipswich visited Upton Park and then George Wright took Cantwell's place.

Also during December, Chelsea beat the young Hammers in the FA Youth Cup. Playing in that match were Geoff Hurst and Jimmy Greaves, two players who would make a big impact in England and around the world over the coming years. Bristol Rovers were beaten 6-1 in the same month and West Ham bagged another half dozen when Swansea came to the Boleyn Ground in January. The Hammers were now hitting form and the FA Cup campaign started with a 5-1 win over First Division Blackpool. Keeble scored three and Dick got the other two. For Malcolm Pyke this was a memorable moment in his career. He recalled; "Meeting and playing against Stanley Matthews was wonderful. Ted brought him in the changing room before the game and I asked if I could get his autograph. He shook my hand and signed my programme. That was the highlight of my life. I went to the Football Writers' dinner a few years ago and Sir Stan was talking. I went up to him and said; 'You wouldn't remember me Sir Stanley, but I played against you in 1958.' He said; 'We lost 5-0 didn't we?' I said; 'No, 5-1.' Sir Stan said; 'We scored with a penalty didn't we?' George Wright was marking

1957-58 – I remember in the promotion year… the fans chanted; 'We want six!'

Matthews; George was playing left-back, he usually played on the right. He recalled; "Noel was injured, so I marked Sir Stan and played him out of the game. That was the best game I played for West Ham."

Back in the League, on 18th January, West Ham went to the top of the table as Liverpool lost at home, while the Hammers crushed Swansea 6-2. The fourth round of the FA Cup brought Third Division Stockport County to Upton Park and, in a hard-fought match, the hosts ran out 3-2 winners. The following Saturday, the Hammers drew 2-2 at Fulham; the attendance of 42,259 was the largest post-war gate for a League game at Craven Cottage. Eddie Lewis got one of his rare outings that term and recalled his contribution; "The 'big dipper' goal, as it came to be known, is also something that stays with me. We were playing Fulham and we had to get a draw to keep in the promotion pack. We had just minutes to go and we were 2-1 down. Noel, or it might have been John Bond in a temper tantrum, booted the ball up the field and I got it just inside the centre-circle. I gave it such a whack - it went about 300 feet in the air! Anyway, when it did come down, it beat Tony Macedo in the Fulham goal. We celebrated that for about three minutes as Noel wanted to waste time. At the press conference afterwards Ted claimed that it was something we had worked out before the match, for emergency situations, but that was pure bullshit."

Lewis scored again in the next game, a 1-1 draw at Upton Park against Barnsley, but was promptly dropped on the return of John Smith to the side.

In February a new pressure group was set up, in the words of its founders, '…to demand a British initiative to reduce the nuclear peril and to stop the armaments race, if need be by unilateral action by Great Britain'. The Campaign for Nuclear Disarmament, or CND, was launched under the presidency of the philosopher and veteran peace campaigner Bertrand Russell, with Canon L.J. Collins as the chairman of its executive committee. The Labour politician Michael Foot and the writer J. B. Priestley were also among its founder members.

One of CND's first acts was to organise a protest march from London to the Atomic Weapons Research Establishment at Aldermaston in Berkshire. A crowd of some 4,000 people gathered in London's Trafalgar Square on 4th April to hear speeches by Canon Collins and other CND leaders before setting out to walk the 50 miles to Aldermaston. Many of the marchers carried banners bearing the distinctive CND logo. By the time the demonstration reached the research establishment it was 5,000 strong.

At Doncaster, in March, Fenton blooded local man Andy Nelson, who had followed his older brother Bill to West Ham (Bill moved to QPR in 1955). Andy had been at Upton Park since 1953, having joined the Club as a junior. Andy was typical of many young professional footballers at the time in that his career combined National Service and the game. His memories are mostly of getting to Upton Park from his posting. Players like Andy were, to a certain extent, excluded from the everyday life at the Club, and as such were placed at a distinct disadvantage. For all this, he turned out 15 times for the Hammers and scored the only goal of the game when Burnley visited Upton Park in October 1958. He was spotted by future England manager Alf Ramsey and moved to Ipswich later that season.

When the draw for the fifth round of the Cup was made, West Ham were gifted with a home game against Fulham; it was decided to make this the first ever all-ticket match at Upton Park. Andy Malcolm marked Johnny Haynes really closely, kicking lumps out of him, but Haynes put up a superb show. Each tackle ended with one of them on the ground but Haynes probably just had the edge in the end. He was all over the place urging his team on. West Ham scored after only 90 seconds when Mike Grice seized on a mistake by Jim Langley. Fulham drew level after 12 minutes when, from the inside-left position, Dennis Stevens sent Roy Dwight (Elton John's uncle) down the middle and he lobed the ball over Ernie Gregory. Twenty-four minutes later, the Cottagers took the lead when Jimmy Hill stoked the ball home. Hill had collected the ball from Chamberlain, passed it to Haynes who supplied Dwight. Dwight sent the ball over high to Hill who finished the movement.

Just after the hour, Langley slipped up again, missing a tackle. Grice hit the dirt and a penalty was given. John Bond smacked the ball home in his usual no-nonsense style. With just over 15 minutes left, Langley found Haynes. He passed it to Chamberlain who returned the ball to his skipper; Haynes danced over Bond's attempted tackle to put the Hammers out of the FA Cup.

Johnny Haynes had fantastic energy. Fulham went on as London's remaining hope in the last eight. Besides Haynes they had some quality players, including Roy Bentley, Hill and Macedo. For Vic Keeble, this defeat was a real blow. "My biggest disappointment was losing to Fulham in the Cup." Many former players shared this sentiment. There was a real feeling that the Hammers, in the form they hit that season, could have made it to Wembley. According to Eddie Lewis, who

1957-58 – I remember in the promotion year... the fans chanted; 'We want six!'

played in all West Ham's Cup games that season; "Ernie Gregory cost us the Cup game with Fulham. Roy Dwight got past Noel and John Bond, and Ernie was off his line."

The football clocks of Britain stopped on 6th February 1958. One of the greatest tragedies to strike the world of soccer occurred when eight Manchester United players were among the 21 passengers killed in an air crash in West Germany. The accident happened as the plane that was bringing the United team back to the UK from Yugoslavia, where they had just drawn with Red Star Belgrade to qualify in the semi-final of the European Cup, failed to clear a fence on take-off from Rhiem airport in Munich. Among the dead were the English regulars Roger Byrne, Duncan Edwards and Tommy Taylor. The manager, Matt Busby, was among those seriously injured. The plane, a BEA Ambassador, was reduced to a tangled heap of wreckage. Driving snow hampered rescue workers.

Leyton Orient were beaten 4-1 at Brisbane Road later in February, Dick and Keeble both scoring against the Irons' East End neighbours. On 8th March 1958, the Hammers recorded their biggest-ever win in the Football League, 8-0 over Rotherham United. John Dick scored four. After the match the news came through that Charlton, in second place, and Liverpool, who were in third, had both lost 3-1. Both of these teams were still to visit Upton Park.

In April there was a serious escalation of violence in Cyprus. There were many women among the demonstrators who took to the streets to protest against the detention of political prisoners. Five people were killed when British troops opened fire on rioters in the street of Nicosia

Charlton came to the Boleyn Ground during Easter period and drew 0-0. Two weeks later Liverpool, in the penultimate fixture of the season, managed 1-1 result in East London.

John Bond was very much part of the championship team. He scored eight goals in the campaign and missed only one match in the whole season. He recalled; "It was fabulous. We were losing 1-0 to Liverpool; I scored the equaliser from a free-kick." This left the Hammers on 55 points from 41 games, level with Charlton Athletic in second place and one ahead of Blackburn Rovers. On the last day of the season, Charlton were at home to Blackburn. In an amazing match at The Valley, Blackburn beat Charlton 4-3. West Ham clinched promotion and the championship by winning at Ayresome Park, John Dick scoring their 100th League goal of the season in the process. Bond recalled that game. "We went on to win the last game up at Middlesbrough 3-1. When we asked for the money for winning promotion, Reg Pratt, the chairman at the time, had us all together and he said; 'If you hold a gun to my head, I shall resign.' Eventually we each got a £30 voucher to go and buy something from a shop. We thought we were well looked after."

Ken Brown recalled; "The games against Middlesbrough in the championship year stick in my mind. Cloughy was playing. I sorted him out at Upton Park - he was quick on the near post, but the heavy weather helped us and we beat them; I was able to catch him up in the mud. At Ayresome Park, Noel said he would have a word with their inside-forward, who he had played with in the Eire side, as the game wasn't going to affect them one way or the other. Clough hit the roof, shouting about his teammate wanting the side to take it easy. When we got back there were hundreds of supporters at King's Cross."

That day is one that all those who played in the championship side would relish for the rest of their lives. For instance Ernie Gregory responded by saying; "Of course, my most abiding memory was winning the championship."

Mike Grice noted; "My greatest memory is the Middlesbrough game and all the fans at King's Cross when we won the championship."

Malcolm Musgrove told me; "Middlesbrough away and promotion was the happiest point in my career at West Ham. Coming back on the train was unbelievable. A lot of people had gone up with us to see the game. They were all walking up and down the corridors.

"When we got back to King's Cross, there was a coach waiting for us to take us to the ground, normally we had to get the Tube." Malcolm chuckled, remembering the fans. "They were living it up big style. In the championship season we took each match as it came. We'd win a game and say; 'Well, that's out the way. Now we only have to win so many more to get promotion.' The last game of the season, when we went to Middlesbrough, we had to win to get promotion; I got a goal. After the game, in the dressing-room, it was just pandemonium. We were the longest-serving Second Division club then. Now we were going to play with the big boys."

Doug Wragg recalled; "Of course, everyone enjoyed the promotion. All the staff were taken to the Cafe Royal and the players' wives were given gifts."

Malcolm Pyke told me about the same event. "When they had the presentation, I sat opposite the film actress and West Ham fan Anna Neagle. She asked to look at the

1957-58 – I remember in the promotion year… the fans chanted; 'We want six!'

medal…I've still got my championship medal. Still people come in and ask to see it. I'm so proud of it. Not a lot of people can say they've got a championship medal."

As soon as the result of that final game was known at Upton Park there was festivity. Bill Lansdowne recalled; "The day West Ham won the championship I was playing at Upton Park in the reserves, but we celebrated and had a bit of a sing-song."

Seven doubles were achieved, the last of which was at Middlesbrough. The 101 League goals which West Ham scored in 1957-58 is still their best total for a single season and is likely to remain so, but in terms of results alone, the side did less to get promotion in 1957-58 than to finish third in 1934-35.

Vic Keeble's memories of West Ham, understandably, revolve around the promotion year; "The other big memory for players was the reaction of the West Ham supporters...The fans were always okay. There were thousands at King's Cross when we got back from Middlesbrough, even though it was 11-30 at night."

John Dick agreed; "The players naturally got all the headlines after that promotion triumph in 1958, but for me, the fans deserved just as much credit for standing by a club that had been out of the First Division for so long. They were fantastic, with the Chicken Run providing a unique atmosphere and I'll always be grateful for the support they gave us. The reception we got from them at King's Cross when we returned from our final match at Middlesbrough was fantastic and will live in the memory for ever."

Talking about Brian Clough, who played in the 'Boro side in that game, John said; "I wouldn't have swapped anything he went on to achieve with the way I felt that day." Although his own performance during that dramatic match stuck in John's memory, not least because of his historic goal, he remarked; "Every goal was a good goal." John saw the promotion side as 'a different type of player' when compared to West Ham sides of later eras. For John the team had 'no great stars' of the type of Hurst and Moore, but they were all "good players, especially the likes of Andy Malcolm, Ernie Gregory, Bond and Cantwell in defence".

How good was this side? According to Mick Newman; "It is hard to compare sides of that time with the modern era - players are so much more skilful these days - but I believe that talent will come out, and that 1958 side would have been formidable in the context of the modern game. They were certainly more entertaining than a lot of teams around today."

Vic Keeble provided some insights into the champions as a side; "The team had three groups, its gamblers, drinkers and those who were more home-oriented. John

Dick and me sometimes went to the dogs, but we were more likely to go home after training and games. I didn't have a drink until I was 40, and then it was vodka and lemonade, and you could only really taste the lemonade. I was happy at West Ham. I think we trained a little bit too hard. We left a bit on the training pitch. We also trained hard with the kids."

Of course, winning the championship had a big effect on the East London area. It is hard to describe what it was like now. The Second Division title has become something of an appendage to promotion. However the Wembley Play-off Finals of contemporary times give one a much better idea of what the actual winning of the title once meant. Perhaps a young player of the time, still to get into the first team, summed it up best. Andy Smillie recollected; "Winning the championship was like walking on water, everybody at the club was lifted. In the area, it was like winning the World Cup."

How did it happen? West Ham has traditionally been proud of playing 'entertaining football'. This has become a mantra for the Club which has constantly been reiterated by its officials, supporters and journalists. It is hard to say exactly what this means - maybe it's like Ruud Guillit's saying about 'sexy football'. Whatever, the concept didn't enter the West Ham canon before 1953, and was not totally absorbed until 1958.

Dick Walker said; "During the early Fifties, the idea of West Ham being more interested in playing attractive football than winning is rubbish. Winning is what managers, players and supporters all want. The only difference is that West Ham wouldn't stand for winning by kicking people…it wasn't 'win at all costs' but no one went out to lose; no one liked getting beat and if you could avoid that you would!"

Even this looks at the reality through slightly rose-tinted bins. Upton Park crowds appreciated skill and wanted to see a well-played match, but not at the cost of victory. Indeed, the Irons were traditionally seen as a hard side, and Walker, like Andy Malcolm who followed in his wake, was an uncompromising professional. A team supported by and, to some extent, made up of the close kin of, dockers, stevedores, railwaymen, litermen and bargees, every bit a match for the steel workers, shipbuilders and miners of the North. They played on a mud-patch of a pitch that required physical endurance and power, rather than touch and skill, in a stadium famed for its capacity to induce claustrophobia and intimidate the opposition.

Before the mid-Fifties, West Ham was seen as an unfashionable club, set in the iron pragmatics of the lower, mid-level of professional football. Upton Park was not perceived as a hotbed of innovation nor was the staff known to be the doyens of

1957-58 – I remember in the promotion year... the fans chanted; 'We want six!'

experimentation or the cultivators of the artistic flourish. The Boleyn Ground Tsar was Charlie Paynter and the law was 'character on the field as well as off'. Paynter was not an aesthete, he was a nuts and bolts artisan; much more fish and chips than foie gras. What kudos the Club might have boasted of might have been cited in its demonstration of working class respectability, at the behest of a board made up medium range mercantile achievers and men with upper-middle class pretentions and lower upper-class aspirations, which included knowing one's place and avoiding excess in all things. Modesty and humility were prized rather than creativity and ambition. The culture of West Ham United was a reflection of the historical context within which the Club was founded; the dock strikes of the late 19th century, and the political motivation and social values it was built on; the norms of social hierarchy being passed on from 'betters' to underlings. To that extent West Ham, as an organization, was a mirror of any commercial enterprise of its size at the time; founded on patronage, an ossified hierarchy and an effort to act from the basis of its own traditions.

As such, what happened at the Boleyn Ground in the Fifties can be understood as a kind of revolution, a series of culture changing events, that included worker (player) control. This change in the culture at Upton Park is the only rational way to grasp the transformation that came over the side. The old regime had gone as far as it could and was defunct; what took its place was the vanguard of the future. There was, as John Cartwright described it, a form of communism at the Club; the players really ruled it - in short, the dictatorship of the football proletariat. That is the strongest description of what happened at West Ham in the mid-Fifties, but is not much different from other versions.

However, this situation only went so far. Shareholders and executives only allowed this to happen because it produced (literally) dividends. While the on-field direction of the Club was indeed revolutionized, the basic financial structure of the organization maintained its logic; a capitalist enterprise in tooth and claw, exploiting the labour of its employees, trading on the sentiment (selling it) to its consumers (the supporters) to produce a profit for the shareholders, many of whom never so much as came within a butcher's furlong of Upton Park.

Andy Malcolm's consistency was rewarded when he was chosen as the local newspaper's Player of the Year. At the same time, the *Ilford Recorder* concluded; 'Promotion was a tribute to the long-sighted, imaginative policy adhered to by the men in charge of the club often in the face of fierce criticism...Ted Fenton was fortunate in having the backing of one of the youngest and smallest boards of directors in League football at Upton Park.' A classic piece of journalistic sycophancy if ever there was! Whatever the Club did or has done was and is the result of supporter patience and loyalty for much of West Ham's history in the face of dismissive indifference (at best) from the board. But as far as the media of the day was concerned it seems the players, supporters and the manager didn't have much to do with it.

The season was to be Ted Fenton's greatest achievement, bringing the club back to the First Division after over a quarter of a century in the relative wilderness. Football managers get the blame, and often the sack, when their team fails, so maybe Fenton should get at least a deal of the credit for his side's success. However, ever since 1958, players, the board, writers, pundits, historians, the media and the fans have disputed his precise role in the Club. The lasting question that arises out of the puzzle about Fenton's contribution to the championship side is about the role played by club managers in general. Did Busby or Ferguson win the European Cup for their respective sides? Did Ron Greenwood put together the first and last all-English side to win major trophies?

There is probably no adequate answer to such questions, but what is for sure, no one person won East London's first major football trophy. One can look at the success of the West Ham team in 1957-58 from all sorts of angles, give credit to Fenton or the board or Allison or Cantwell or Andy Malcolm or all of these people. Nevertheless, it is clear, from looking at the way the side played, lived and later spoke and remembered events, that the championship was achieved by the building of a team ethos. A young player at the time, Derek Woodley recalled; "The teamwork of the championship side was impressive."

Maybe this was more or less accidental, but it was very much the West Ham team, including the supporters, that changed the path and culture of the Hammers. Contemporary sides might do well to take note. The Manchester United team that won the treble in 1999, unlike the Arsenal side that finished as runners-up to them in the Premiership, in the main grew up together, coming through the Old Trafford system. They were, in this respect, similar the Watford side that gained promotion from Division One the same year, a team and unlike Newcastle, the club United beat in the FA Cup Final in 1999, and the Blackburn Rovers, who were relegated from the elite that season. The players that made up these two latter sides were more akin to a kind of group, rather than a team; the 11 men on the pitch were individuals who arrived at the same location via different routes, from disparate roots, to form a polyglot football culture with superficially shared aims, tactics, systems or plans. However, they did not have much in common in terms of instinct or innate comprehension of how ends might be achieved.

Maybe the likes of Chelsea in the Twenty-First Century have shown one can put a successful football team together via a sort of 'supermarket sweep' mentality; but any neutral looking at the 2012 European Cup final might be equivocal about this. Di Matteo's mercenaries were not collectively a pretty sight. Yes, they won, but an accomplishment was all it was, and a relatively bland dish for all that; the accusation of 'success' was muted because it was more Bayern Munich's failure. No one but the most love sick Blue could claim that anyone in their right puff would be won over to a lifetime of support by that charade of an event directed by Chelsea's remote owner. 'FC Abramovich' is the souped up Frankenstein of football: a dead thing moving about; a soulless Cyberman of the game, lumbering around the Premiership excreting obscene wonga turds as bait for the avaricious planetary journeymen of the game. It is as far from the West Ham team of the late 1950s as pie and mash is from John Terry's second best Rolex that a slurp of green liquor would likely stop dead! Pass the vinegar.

Noel Cantwell, Malcolm Allison, Frank O'Farrell, Dave Sexton, John Bond, Andy Malcolm, Ken Brown - these men, among many others, were instrumental in developing the style that brought the championship to the Boleyn Ground. They did have different backgrounds, although mainly Cork and East London, but while they were at West Ham they lived with each other or in the same area, they socialised and, at least once a week, at the Denmark Arms and Cassatarri's, ate together. The players were thinking about the game and talking about it among themselves. Most of them are still convinced that they developed a new kind of football.

Proximity fostered the discourse, understanding and the familiarity that allowed for the generation of a novel approach to football. From their collective mind a philosophy of tactics, and more, organisation, arose. In turn this provoked an intellectual attitude that saw the game as a range of conceptual challenges set in the physical context. However, out of this a kind of political consciousness grew; to implement tactics and influence selection, the control of the means of football production, a level of managerial authority was required. ABC - Allison, Bond and Cantwell - facilitated this.

Their type of football was a product of their own ingenuity, professionalism, integrity and the willingness of their manager, or his inability to do anything about it, to let them experiment. Whatever the case, any changes that took place in the training regimen or the style of play would either be made by Fenton or at least would have to gain his approval (maybe at times, whether he liked it or not). This gave rise to what Bernard Joy called 'West Ham's tradition of playing colourful football as a way of getting away from the drabness of life in the East End'. The driving force behind this movement was the spectre of England's demolition at the hands of Hungary at Wembley in 1953, and the massive impact this had on the morale of football throughout the country. From then on the Luddites of football became the dinosaurs of the game. Clubs were obliged to think about new ways of playing; the traditional methods had been exposed as being way past their sell-by date; it was change or die. This was the embryonic stage of the soccer science practised by the elite of the sport today. West Ham was able to lead the way as they had less to lose by experimenting than most clubs. Hence, Eddie Lewis could see the training and match preparation at Old Trafford as primitive in comparison to the regime at Upton Park.

Reg Pratt JP, a local timber merchant with strongly conservative views on politics and social issues, and Ted Fenton, a long-serving player at West Ham, seemed an unlikely pair to preside over this situation. Looking back, John Cartwright remembers that the Club he joined as a boy gave the impression of being "the modern set". There was a 'West Ham run', a kind of arrogant strut started by Noel Cantwell and emulated by other players (although Cantwell put this down to too much weight training – "everyone was so stiff"). Most of all, there was a sense that something was happening.

The tournament that was to become the UEFA Cup completed its first Final at the start of May. The International Industries Fairs International Cities Cup, to be commonly known as the 'Fairs Cup'. The tournament was contested between teams drawn from cities that hosted international trade fairs and was initially organised over two years, but the two-legged Final of 1958 was the culmination of four three- team group games and semi-finals going back to 1955. A London Select met a Birmingham Select (actually Birmingham City) in the semi-finals. London went through to a meet Barcelona in the Final. The first leg at Stamford Bridge in March ended in a 2-2 draw. Jimmy Greaves scored London's first goal. In the second leg, played at the Nou Camp, Hammers' George Wright, Noel Cantwell and Eddie Lewis were brought into the team along with Hammer- to-be Jimmy Bloomfield. Unfortunately London were well beaten, 6-0.

1958-59 – John Dick was an honest playing footballer

England qualified for the World Cup Finals in Sweden in 1958, overcoming the Republic of Ireland and Denmark on the way. In qualifying they dropped only one point in the four games, Noel Cantwell's Republic team having held the English to a 1-1 draw in Dublin. Chelsea's Peter Brabrook - a man with past and future West Ham connections - won a place in the squad. Northern Ireland, Wales and Scotland made it the first and last full British complement.

England didn't lose a game in a tough qualifying group that included Brazil, Austria and the Soviet Union. Unfortunately they didn't win any matches either and finished with the same points total as the Soviets. In the play-off, England lost and so went home with Scotland, who won only a single group point, finishing behind France, Yugoslavia and Paraguay. However, both Wales and Northern Ireland made the quarter-finals. The Irish were well-beaten 4-0 by France, but the Welsh were unlucky against Brazil, the eventual winners of the competition, losing to a second-half Pele goal. England had been the only team to hold Brazil to a draw and Wales had the second-best result against the 'samba boys', who beat the other four teams they played by at least two goals each.

West Ham were welcomed back to the First Division at Portsmouth on 23rd August 1958. Some 7,000 of the 40,000 crowd were Hammers' fans, a very high degree of travelling support in those days. They went into raptures when Keeble and Dick scored to start West Ham off with a win. For so many players at Upton Park this was their first taste of football at the highest level. Bill Lansdowne told me; "Initially there was no difference between divisions - you just went out and enjoyed it - you were not going to waste the experience. You were determined not to be intimidated."

The next day troubles flared after five black men were beaten up by white youths in Notting Hill, North London. The police made more than 150 arrests during three days of serious rioting. On the night of 30th August, some 200 white and black people fought in the streets, property was damaged and one black household was petrol-bombed. The following evening saw some of the worst disturbances, with four hours of continuous running battles involving around 400 people, during which police were attacked and injured. On 1st September, gangs of up to 2,000 youths and children attacked houses where black people lived, breaking windows and causing extensive damage. Police suspected the involvement of extreme political groups.

East London could have been a world away. While all this was going on and within a week of West Ham's opening game, both Wolves, the reigning champions, who would retain their title at the end of that term, and Aston Villa had both been vanquished.

For the first home game in Division One the Upton Park gates were closed long before kick-off, the crowd being in excess of 37,500. A fan of the time recalled; "The kick off was 7-30.T got there at 12-30. I went in the North Bank, from the Priory Road entrance. I got myself behind the goal. I ended up in the corner by the West Stand by the final whistle. The kids used to get passed down, it was a fantastic sight to see all these kids cascading down the crowd."

The Wanderers were beaten in a superb match. Dick and Smith gave the Hammers a 2-0 victory. Ken Brown remembered the encounter; "In the First Division, Wolves whacked the ball, they were like bulls in a china shop. Their 'keeper would bang 'em in high." He went on to look back at the fixture that brought the Brummy Villains to East London; "They were trounced 7-2. Keeble, Dick and Musgrove all scored twice and Bill Lansdowne chipped in with number seven."

The return match with Wolves drew a full house to Molineux and they saw a classic game. Mike Grice remembered; "The game at Wolves was something. At some points in that first season I didn't think anyone could match us – I thought; 'Other teams can't play better than this.'" However, the home side held the Hammers 1-1.

It was Luton Town that put the claret and blue advance to a temporary halt; the Irons were beaten 4-1 at Kenilworth Road. On 8th September, Manchester United, decimated by Munich air crash seven months earlier, came to Upton Park led by Jimmy Murphy, who was holding the fort while Matt Busby was recovering. After leading by three goals, courtesy of Dick, Smith and Musgrove, the hosts only just scraped home (3-2) on an exciting night that saw the debut of 17-year-old Bobby Moore.

Robert Frederick Chelsea Moore, son of Robert and Doris, was brought up in Barking on the fringes of industrial Essex and East London. His young life was spent in Waverley Gardens, a turning off of the busy River Road, not far from the ancestral homes of Dagenham's Alf Ramsey and Jimmy Greaves. He was named Chelsea after a paternal uncle, not the Blues of Stamford Bridge.

1958-59 – John Dick was an honest playing footballer

The story was that Moore was in the side against United because Malcolm Allison was ill. In the following week's match programme one item read; 'The selection of Bobby Moore at left-half proved justified by a display which foreshadows a grand future for a 17-year-old called upon to make his debut against one of Europe's leading sides.' Malcolm Musgrove recalled; "Bobby came into the side against Manchester United. He played in the game as though he'd been in the side for years. I was a lot older than Bobby at the time and I was still a novice, nervous as hell. At the kick-off Bobby stood in the left-half position just looking round. He had an unbelievable temperament. Lots of players have ability, but they haven't got the temperament to make them go even further, as far as they might want to go - Bobby had that temperament. There was no way he was never going to get as far as he got.

"The door was opened for Bobby because Malcolm wasn't fit, but he would have come into the side regardless. Ted thought it was the right time and the right game for him, not without a lot of 'advice' from Noel and John Bond. Everyone knew he was something out of the ordinary and playing against United was part of his education."

Derek Woodley, a team mate of Moore's from the FA Youth Cup Final side, said; "Bobby Moore was the best player I saw at Upton Park. I can't say I liked him as a bloke. He didn't have a football body, but he had a marvellous mind for the game."

For John Bond; "Bobby Moore was simplicity itself. There were loads of people at the time, the likes of Bill McGarry, because they played wing-half all their lives, looked at Bobby Moore and thought he wasn't a good player. They couldn't see what a great player he was. Everything he did he made look so easy, as if it was nothing. He never did anything difficult in his life. Ron Greenwood said that simplicity of that sort was genius. I wanted him in the team as soon as possible; he was extraordinary – a fool could see that!"

All published versions of how Bobby come to get his first match at West Ham centre on him replacing Allison and Malcolm Allison corroborated this when I met him. However Noel Cantwell provided a different interpretation of events; "I remember taking over from Malcolm as skipper and we became Second Division champions. The game against Manchester United was on a Monday night. Fenton called me into the office asking who should play left-half, Allison or Moore. He didn't really want the burden of the decision. Malcolm was not a mobile centre-half, so I went for Bobby. Malcolm found out and we fell out. He resented me for a time, but eventually he told me that I had made the right decision."

As far as Bobby was concerned, he had been obliged to move into his mentor's place, denying Allison a game in the First Division and effectively finishing his career. Bobby always carried a slight sense of guilt about this. Allison had taught Bob so much; he had become a friend, as well as inspirational presence in Moore's young life. The former Hammers skipper and centre-half had helped transform tubby Bobby, apparently least talented of the groundstaff boys, into a classy first-team player. Now Moore was the instrument used to turn Allison away from Upton Park. Others have verified that a place in the West Ham line-up was certainly between Bobby or Malcolm, but they question if it was between Moore and Allison.

Malcolm Pyke, a 20-year-old at the time told me; "There was a lot of paper talk about Malcolm Allison being due to play the night Bobby made his debut against Manchester United. But that's not true; Allison wasn't fit, he wasn't even included. There were three half-backs injured that night - Bill Lansdowne Andy Nelson and myself. Bill and Andy took a fitness test and I was the last one to be tested. If it wasn't for that, I'd have played instead of Bobby Moore - and that's the God's honest truth. And then Bobby didn't look back. Allison was nowhere near fit."

This account was verified by Bill Lansdowne; "Yes, Malcolm Pyke was right, I had an ankle injury." Andy Nelson said of Pyke's understanding of the situation; "Yes, that has to be true."

All this doesn't mean too much at first glance. Bobby got his first game that evening and maybe that's all that counts, unless, of course, you happen to be Malcolm Pyke, who told me; "When we got up, I wasn't included in the first team - that hurt. I did try. I was first reserve at Portsmouth, the opening game of the season. But I didn't get a look in after that." Who knows what it would have meant for Pyke if he had been seen to be fit and had taken the field against Manchester United that evening.

Moore, Allison and Cantwell had become very close over the years. It may have been very simple, as one player said; "I think John Bond was in control at the time - he preferred Bob." However, such situations are always more complicated than this. The scenario, that night so long ago, as so often portrayed, has an almost Hollywood western quality. The inadequate town mayor, Fenton, the young hombre Moore, the sheriff Cantwell, his deputy Bond and the John Wayne figure of Allison, swaggering away into the distance, hurt but with his pride intact, having, done the right thing. This is not saying that anyone has lied. When I put Malcolm Pyke's view of events to Malcolm Allison, the big man said;

1958-59 – John Dick was an honest playing footballer

"I'd just come out of hospital and I'd played three or four games in the reserves. Ted called Noel up to his office. He asked who he should play, Malcolm or Bobby? Noel went for Bobby. I think Malcolm Pyke has got mixed up with another situation. He probably played in place of me in another match." However, there was no sense of that from Malcolm Pyke's attitude. He was certain.

L.P.Hartley wrote in *The Go Between*; 'The past is a foreign country; they do things differently there.' We all need our romance, our lost chances, our moments of courage. As such, our memories shape our experience more than actual events; memory and actuality are related, but they are not the same thing. What I remember often tells more about me than the events I remember. Truth is both contextual and subjective; maybe the best we can hope for is a kind of general understanding of, or feeling about, the lives of others. If I have learnt one thing speaking to the people featured in this book it is, in the end, the world will be, from our own particular perspective, much as we would have it.

West Ham, newcomers to the First Division, beat Manchester United, League runners-up to be that season, 3-2. This was a big result for the West Ham players. Many, like John Dick, would see the beating of Manchester United as a high point in their careers. The next day the newspapers acclaimed Moore's arrival on the scene. Bob was typically modest; "I just hit a couple of balls straight. Nothing really."

The big obstacle to Bobby's continued advance at West Ham was John Smith. When Smith moved to Tottenham to contest for a first-team place with Dave Mackay and Danny Blanchflower, Moore took his chance.

Phil Woosnam came into the side for the 4-2 Upton Park win over Chelsea. Phil was West Ham's biggest-ever signing, but he was a quality buy. According to Mike Grice; "Phil Woosnam was a good player. He was intelligent and seemed to be able to use most positions he found himself in; you never saw him stuck for a move or a pass."

For Doug Wragg; "Phil Woosnam was perhaps the player I most admired at West Ham. He never looked rushed; he seemed to have more time than everybody else - he was always so calm and that spread around the team."

The visit to Old Trafford at the end of September drew a huge attendance of over 53,000. It was not the best of debuts on this northern stage for most West Ham players. Many felt like Bill Lansdowne, who recalled; "I didn't do well at Old Trafford. Ernie Taylor tortured me." A hat-trick from Albert Scanlon went most of the way to giving Manchester United a 4-1 victory. However, in early October, Blackburn Rovers were beaten 6-3 at Upton Park. Vic Keeble scored four goals, and skipper Noel Cantwell got his first of the season.

Cantwell had a good weekend; the day after the Blackburn game he scored both goals in the Republic of Ireland's 2-2 draw with Poland in Dublin. Recognition for two other Hammers came when John Bond and Andy Malcolm played for the Football League against the Scottish League at Ibrox.

In the same month, Malcolm Allison retired and decided to go into coaching. A testimonial match was played at Upton Park in November and a 21,600 crowd were treated to 13 goals (West Ham got seven) and a splendid evening's entertainment by some of the country's greatest talents; Stanley Matthews, Tom Finney, Jimmy Scoular, Ray Barlow, Brian Clough, Don Howe, Peter Brabrook and Bobby Charlton were in the All Star team that played a West Ham XI. An injury to Graham Shaw resulted in young John Lyall being called upon to deputise for the All Stars.

After the Blackburn match, West Ham started to feel the pace of top level competition. In ten games they picked up only six points and two wins; it was to be the worst run of the season. By mid-December, the Hammers' League form had suffered and they were 14th in the table. Fenton moved Cantwell to the number six slot, to replace Andy Nelson, and drafted Joe Kirkup into defence, just four days before his 20th birthday.

It was a bright winter's day, almost like spring, when I met with Joe in the smart yet compact Surrey village that was his home. His wife, Jill, was serving in the newsagent's they both ran. She phoned upstairs to their flat and Joe came down and greeted me. He was just getting over a bad bout of flu. Joe and Jill have two sons, Tony and Nick, who at the time were working in banking and insurance respectively. Joe Kirkup's father had been a chauffeur and his mother worked in service in private houses. As a boy he attended the Queen Elizabeth Grammar School in his hometown of Hexham, Northumberland. It was a rugby school, so his football wasn't a priority.

Joe showed me into the couple's spacious flat and, as he made me a coffee, told me; "Sunderland and Newcastle came in for me at first, but they went for everyone - you had no chance. Burnley also showed some interest." However, Joe chose to join the Hammers; "I spent one season on the groundstaff; there were about six of us at the time. My sister lived in Bromley so I stayed with her." Joe, who had two brothers, signed professional forms at 17.

Joe's elder bother (five years his senior) had a big influence on him, but at West Ham, George Wright took Joe under his wing. Joe recollected, "He lived just around the corner. I often had meals with George. Harry Cripps was a good friend, he lived at the Abbey Arms [on the border of Plaistow/Canning Town, two districts of the old West Ham London Borough] with his mum, Bess."

The team seemed to spend a lot of time together; looking back Joe told me; "We were always round each other's houses. The Club was friendly, no cliques, but two definite groups, not against one another. Geoff, Martin, and Ronnie Boyce were in one, Bob and Eddie Bovington in the other. We were all out on Saturday night, often down the Moby Dick [a pub/restaurant in Barkingside]. We had a good social life. We'd go down the Wake Arms [now the site of a Miller & Carter restaurant] in Epping Forest. Judith, Geoff's wife, used to drink pints; she'd pretend that she was going to dive into them. At West Ham we had all grown up together; we lived near each other. Everyone knew everyone else. Mrs Gregg, she worked in the offices, and George, the groundsman, they were all part of the Club."

Playing for the London FA before winning England youth and three Under-23 caps, Joe was also a member of the Hammers side that lost to Manchester United in the 1956-57 Youth Cup Final. He remembered the West Ham supporters with a great deal of respect; "The fans enjoyed their football. Win, lose or draw, as long as you played half-decent they were on your side. West Ham were a law unto themselves; 11,000 turned up for the Youth Cup Final."

As the Sixties drew nearer, West Ham was still a club of patronage and habit, valuing uniformity. Joe remembered; "We got everything from Arthur Sedgewick's sports shop in Walthamstow." To some extent, during Joe's first years at Upton Park, this mind-set was reflected in the Club's football. Although an adventurous side, the Hammers were not adaptable, as Joe asserted; "West Ham were steady, maybe they lacked steel; they weren't consistent."

A constructive and resourceful defender, looking more like an athlete than a archetypal fullback, his speed allowed Joe to play an overlapping game in support of the attack. In almost six years involvement with the first team he played 187 games. He recalled; "I nearly scored on my debut but Bert Trautmann tipped it over." That was at Maine Road in December 1958. The 3-1 defeat was West Ham's fourth in succession. However, Joe did score six goals in his First Division career with the Irons. He remembered the initial one quite clearly; "My first goal for West Ham, Bond sent me the perfect long pass and I put it past Gordon Banks." Joe looked back on this feat with justifiable pride. After all, Banks is probably one the best 'keepers ever to walk the face of the earth, it was a pity the Hammers lost the game at Filbert Street 5-1.

In March 1966, Joe left the Boleyn Ground. He told me, "Steve Richards in the *Sun* wrote that Docherty had enquired about me. I went to see Ron and he said it was a load of rubbish. But I went." Joe moved to Chelsea for a fee £27,000. Although he played 53 First Division games for the Blues, just as Joe missed out on the 1964 Cup Final at West Ham, he again was not chosen for the Chelsea line-up to play Spurs in the 1967 Final. Stamford Bridge was a very different experience to Upton Park: "The Chelsea players lived all over the place. Tommy Docherty was mad. He would have fights with players. He got himself a new contract and then worked to get himself the sack."

After Portsmouth were beaten 6-0 a week before Christmas, West Ham went on to record six victories in their next seven games, including a double over Tottenham. The 2-1 defeat of Spurs was to be the last time that West Ham played on Christmas Day. It was following this string of results, 11 games after Joe got his debut, that he managed to secure a prolonged run in the first team. Then he played in the last ten games of the season, when Fenton was experimenting with his regular full-backs, playing Bond as a striker for eight games and pushing Cantwell up front for the last couple of games. This was a pretty successful period. The final dozen matches of the season saw West Ham lose on only three occasions, dropping just two points at Upton Park. It was during this stage of the season that Andy Smillie played the last of his four games in the first team that term. He had not been in a losing side in the First Division. His debut was perhaps the most significant of his quartet of outings; a 4-1 win at White Hart Lane on Boxing Day 1958.

I visited Andy late on a February afternoon. His cafe, Smillie's, on the Southend sea front, was unsurprisingly quiet. His wife, Carol, made me a cup of tea while Andy talked about his early playing days. "I was a 13-year-old, playing for Frenford Boys Club, which was based in Cleveland Infants School in Ilford at that time [the Club is now a huge youth provision in one of the greener parts of that part of the East London/Essex border lands]. I was at Loxford Road School at the time. At school Mr Clem Roberts, a Welshman, was very helpful to me. Sports teachers were different then, separate. Their realm was the gym and the swimming pool.

"Ted Fenton had come to Frenford to present some trophies and I was outside kicking a tennis ball painted white. He told me he'd check back on me when I was a bit older. He kept his word. I was signed on the groundstaff when I was 14. That was

1958-59 – John Dick was an honest playing footballer

in 1955; I was playing for Ilford at the time. It was quite a novelty to be signed on so young."

The Smillie family lived at 186 High Road, Ilford when Andy signed for the Hammers. "I was taken on as a pro in 1957. I think I started at something like £7 a week." Andy has a brother. His dad was a builder and his mum worked at a restaurant (now the Conservative club) in Gant's Hill. Andy told me: "My mum lives out at Woodford now." He and Carol have two children, Scan 44, a computer analyst, and Victoria, 42, who is a business travel consultant. "We went to the Palais in Ilford; that was open on Monday, Wednesday, Saturday and Sunday nights. Harry met Carol there," Andy told me, referring to the Redknapps.

Andy thinks and speaks swiftly. He seems full of ideas, perceptions, memories and wise, insightful words, which he fired at me at a lightning pace. His enthusiasm creates an excitement in him and his listener. I felt this reflected the way he played. Andy needed players around him who could complement his skills and intellect. He probably never worked with a manager who understood this. He would have fitted well into a modern England or Manchester United set-up. An observant and intelligent man, Andy spoke articulately about his first days at the Club. "Bobby Moore and Tony Scott were taken on at the same time. In that era there was no coaching to speak of at most clubs. I was brought up playing against the best, Bobby, Jimmy Greaves and so on. Bobby Moore worked with Eddie Chapman in the offices. Eddie was always open; Mrs Rice and John Lyall were also in the office for a time. Bobby Moore was always a slight loner. He was fairly close to Malcolm Allison and Noel Cantwell. I was friendly with Johnny Cartwright, Mike Beesley, Derek Woodley, Harry Cripps, Eddie Bovington and Tony Scott. They were good players and good friends, they were all very amicable." Andy went on; "In 1957, West Ham's youth team went to the World Trade Fair in Brussels. We played on a black ochre pitch, three or four games a day, 20 minutes each way - we looked like coalmen." He showed me a picture, the youthful Bobby Moore still looked whiter than white. "We got beat in the semi-final," he remembered glumly.

"We had some good players, and not too many boundaries were imposed. We were fit. John Smith and me got dropped about a mile from Grange Farm [West Ham's training ground] and we would always catch the others up. We started experimenting with 4-4-2. I was a kind of understudy for John Dick. The likes of Phil Woosnam, Malcolm Allison, Malcolm Musgrove started to bring in a different style of coaching. Everyone was taking badges at the club. Water Winterbottom was in charge of the coaching set-up them. But they brought in people who talked a different language. Instead of making the point that good players look around, they talked about 'peripheral vision' - this kind of thing was foreign to most players. They never got a grip on the basics; they didn't go into the schools. I suppose I became a little disillusioned."

A skilful, ball-player who played for Ilford, London and England Schoolboys, Andy also gained three England Youth caps. "My strong point was my fitness. I had a pulse-rate of 58/59. I could recover quickly, even at the age of eight I scored goals. I could keep making runs. I was a good finisher, and could pass the ball. I had natural energy. I was younger than most and was always practising.

"At 18 I was coaching for the London County Council." He connected the problems of English football in the Fifties with government policy. "I was 15 when the Conservative government got in - things didn't improve for 20 years – no improvements in education, this had bad effect on ordinary kids and sport. The continentals had the better, 'one touch', game. Skill has to be developed at a young age. The Brazilians were using heavier balls with children. The football was all competitive here." Andy was one of generation of footballers who, of necessity, became political. "Jimmy Hill had started the ideas about the maximum wage and we were going to strike." This kind of thing had been unheard of before the Fifties, and would not be heard of again after the Sixties.

Looking back on his departure from Upton Park in 1961, when he refused terms, Andy told me; "If Ted Fenton had stayed then I would have stayed. When you get a new manager, the chemistry is not the same - you upset the apple cart. Ron Greenwood didn't offer fair terms, Arthur Rowe came in for me. The vibes weren't good with Greenwood; I never played a game under him."

Andy moved to Selhurst Park, to link up with his former colleagues George Petchey, Alf Noakes and friend, John Cartwright, but he didn't find happiness south of the river; "Things weren't too different at Palace, but there wasn't the depth of quality. Passing the ball was different, but Rowe let you play. When he left and Dick Graham took over, things changed a bit. He had you running up and down the terraces with sandbags on your back. He was like a sergeant-major. Ronnie Alien would ping the ball 50 yards and you'd run on to the balls, a bit like Watford playd [under Graham Taylor]."

Although he scored 23 goals in 53 games for the Selhurst Park club, Andy confessed; "I got depressed at Palace. I loved West Ham. It took a while to get over leaving. You don't miss things until they're gone. It takes a long time for others to understand how you play - when I went back to Southend it was better. But West Ham had such a potentially good side in the early Sixties. The ability was there before; Keeble and Dick were telepathic. John Dick was an honest playing footballer."

Andy looked back on those who had shaped his early career. "Ted Fenton and Wally St Pier were a big influence on me." But it was clear that his time as a youth player had a great impact on him. Andy reflected; "My greatest disappointment was missing the penalty in the FA Youth Cup Final." Andy had scored in the 1-1 draw at Upton Park. If he had converted that penalty the second leg wouldn't have gone to extra time, during which Blackburn scored the only goal of the game and won the Cup. "The youth team coach, Bill Robinson, encouraged us to be very competitive. We would be presented with trophies at Mario's, in Cranbrook Road, Ilford. You'd get them if you'd played for England." However, the lad's feet weren't allowed to get off the ground for long. "Cleaning out the Chicken Run, you'd swallow a lot of humble pie." He remembered his fellow youth team players. "Peter Reeder was good in goal; we'd played together since we were 15. He had huge hands. Little Caskey - he was only 5ft 7in - was also a courageous 'keeper."

Andy played 23 games for West Ham and scored three goals. The first went in early in the 1959-60 season, during a 3-1 win at Turf Moor. He recalled the event; "My first goal was against a 'keeper called Colin McDonald, he was an England international. He'd also played for the Under-18s in Spain." Can footballers' memories can play tricks? According to the record books, Adam Blacklaw was in goal that day; although the Scottish international was arguably, over his whole career, a better goalie than McDonald. He turned out for Burnley 318 times, in excess of 100 more games than the eight times capped England man.

The former Irons inside-forward has seen and played against some of the best players of his generation. According to Andy, "The best players, week in, week out at Upton Park in the Fifties, were John Smith and Noel Cantwell. Cantwell and Andy Malcolm had tremendous courage, and Malcolm was the hardest player I knew. John Cartwright had natural ability, although maybe his physical ability and stamina might have been better. Bobby Moore was still maturing. He wasn't quick, not very good in the air, but his anticipation, vision and one touch were great. Bobby Charlton was the best all-round player I ever saw. Jimmy Greaves was the best finisher, Georgie Best was the most exciting. I played against the likes of Stanley Matthews and Tom Finney." But this was a philosophical man. He paused and looking into the middle distance, our over the Thames Estuary, told me, "Football is a team game, the striker can't always make his 25." There was an intriguing sense of certainty but at the same time melancholy in this statement and his tone of voice; for me this sentence might have been uttered by any football from any part of the game's history; Andy spoke for 'every player' and his sport. This was both stirring and touching. He is a wise and insightful individual; an intellectual of the game.

For those who play football at the highest level, some memories become like snapshots. They stay with them for no other reason than they symbolise something generic about the experience, Andy demonstrated this trait; "I remember playing in the Cup against Spurs, it was a frozen pitch, we got beat. At Villa, John Bond took a free-kick, Noel Cantwell knocked it in. West Ham were the love of my life - memories of that type have kept me going through the hard times - I was lucky. I don't know of a West Ham player who didn't love it."

Andy's final thoughts were for the supporters. You felt he was expressing what only players and fans can know about the nature of football support. Like all feelings, it doesn't fit well into words, because it is not logical, it is wrought out of sentiment and emotion; "They appreciated you, and I suppose you'd call what they had for you, respect. The away support was unbelievable - the same people, sun or snow. At first I thought that they had to be barmy, the same hard core, but later I understood that without them I wouldn't have been there. It was part of their lives." Spot on I'd say; West Ham is part of my life and my life is part of West Ham.

On 1st January, the beleaguered regime of the dictator Fulgencio Batista finally collapsed and he fled to the Dominican Republic. After six years of revolutionary struggle, the way was clear for the rebel guerrillas of Dr Fidel Castro, who already controlled most of the east of Cuba, to take up the reins of power. Amid general rejoicing at the fall of Batista, Dr Manuel Urrutia was declared President of the new government and named Castro his Commander in Chief. On 8th January, Castro himself, together with 5,000 of his troops, made a triumphant entry into the capital, Havana, along streets lined with thousands of cheering citizens.

The new regime was immediately recognised by the governments of the United States, Great Britain, France, the Soviet Union and most of Cuba's Latin American neighbours. Some doubts were expressed internationally, however, when swift trials and on-the-spot executions followed the round up of Batista officials by firing squad.

It became crystal clear that the FA Cup was destined elsewhere - Nottingham Forest actually - when Spurs defied their League form by beating West Ham 2-0 in the third round. However, the combination of Dick and Keeble was still proving lethal in the League and both scored twice in the 5-3 win over Forest late in January.

After years of escalating unrest in Cyprus, the Greek and Turkish governments met in Zurich in February to discuss the future of the island and agreed that it should become independent. Under the proposed arrangements, the British government would keep its sovereign military bases on the island, but a joint Greco-Turkish administration would be set up to govern the new state. The constitution made provision for a Greek President and a Turkish Vice-President and ruled out union with Greece *(enosis)*.

Even though *enosis* was the goal for which the EOKA movement had been fighting, Archbishop Makarios, along with EOKA's Colonel Grivas, accepted the proposed settlement and on 1st March he returned to Nicosia after three years of exile. Elections were announced and in December, Makarios became the first President of the new Republic of Cyprus.

On 7th March, West Bromwich were beaten 3-1 and Dick scored all three, but injuries to Ernie Gregory and Phil Woosnam forced them to miss the rest of the season. Noel Dwyer, who had been signed from Wolves, took over in goal, and young Harry Obeney came into the forward line. Harry scored in both games against Newcastle over Easter. West Ham came off best, just, winning 3-0 at the Boleyn Ground and losing 3-1 in the North-East.

At the start of April, the Hammers beat Everton 3-2 at Upton Park. In the same month John Dick played for Scotland against England at Wembley to gain his first and only cap. The world of architecture mourned the passing of Frank Lloyd Wright, who died aged 90 on 9 April. He was one of the giants of modern architecture, his work often divided critics. Falling-water, a house built over a waterfall in Bear Run, Pennsylvania, was one of his masterpieces, a living space in perfect harmony with its natural surroundings. The Guggenheim Museum art gallery , which opened to the public in October 1959, was described by the *New York Times* as the most controversial building in New York. The museum's pictures were displayed on the walls of a vast, spiral ramp.

In the final home game of the season West Ham beat Manchester City 5-1. Five players -Bond, Cantwell, Malcolm, Brown and Grice – had played in every match. The first Hammer of the Year award was won by Andy Malcolm. John Dick found goals as easy to come by in the First Division as he had at the lower level, netting 27 times.

Keeble scored 20 and the third man on the sharpshooter list was John Bond. Doubles had also been achieved over Blackburn Rovers (against whom Vic Keeble got five in two games) Bolton, plus the two relegated clubs, Aston Villa and Portsmouth.

By the beginning of 1958-59, the Irons' youth policy was beginning to bring forth fruit. Although a few youngsters like Alan Blackburn, the unfortunate Geoff Hallas, Terry Matthews and Fred Cooper, had preceded him, Bobby Moore's inclusion at senior level opened the floodgates. In Moore's wake came Tony Scott, Eddie Bovington, Martin Peters, Peter Shearing and Geoff Hurst; they were just a few of a seemingly endless stream of Boleyn products. To stiffen this young team, players of some experience were soon to be drafted in. Dwyer and Dunmore were joined by Lawrie Leslie, Johnny Byrne and Peter Brabrook.

West Ham finished in sixth place in the 1958-59 season, only two points behind third-placed Arsenal, who West Ham had beaten at Highbury in March, John Dick, scoring both the Hammers' goals. This was the best League performance by the East Londoners in their 40-year history in the competition. It would remain the best until John Lyall's Irons, with the likes of Phil Parkes, Alan Devonshire and Tony Cottee, took third place in 1986. However, the 1959 West Ham scored more goals (85 to 74). Make no mistake, this was a good side; Gregory, Bond, Cantwell, Malcolm, Brown, Moore, Grice, Smith, Keeble, Dick, Musgrove and latterly Woosnam, Kirkup and Smillie. They had proved themselves a match for any team in the country, having been victorious against all of the teams above them. Indeed, only Birmingham, Preston, Leeds, Leicester and, of course, Luton got away with not being beaten by West Ham. There was much to be optimistic about as football linked the Fifties to the Sixties.

Ben Hur hit the screens in 1959. It is still one of the greatest of the Hollywood epics, famous for the technical splendour of the action scenes, such as the sea battle and the exciting chariot race. This film was to win William Wyler his third directing Oscar. The lavish screen version of George Gershwin's black folk opera *Porgy and Bess* won the Oscar for best scoring of a musical. Set in the slums of Catfish Row in South Carolina, it tells the tragic love story of the crippled beggar Porgy (Sidney Poitier) and the beautiful, reckless Bess (Dorothy Dandridge). The stage version was first launched in New York by the Theatre Guild in 1935.

1959-60 — *You were carried by the majority, you weren't just carried by yourself*

In May 1959, West Ham secured a bank loan of £30,000 and an increase in the Club's overdraft. The money was needed quickly so that the Club could take advantage of a coup by its chairman. After four years of negotiations about the new lease for the Boleyn Ground, the Archdiocese of Westminster, which owned Upton Park, had agreed to sell the freehold to West Ham United. The sale of Harry Hooper had raised most of the finance. So, when you next take your seat at the home of the Hammers, say a little thank you to Harry. Who knows what the site might have been worth by the early 1980s property boom? Whatever, ownership of the ground has meant that over the years shareholders have been able to see profits free of the leasing burdens of many clubs, although there has never been any sign that this would be passed on to supporters. The price of a ticket at Upton Park is still among the highest in the country (the forth most expensive in terms of lower end cost in 2012-13 behind Spurs, Liverpool and Arsenal; Manchester City, with a bevy of dazzling and expensive football talent on display, offer this for less than half the price of a Boleyn Ground seat).

On 18 June there were violent disturbances in the South African city of Durban. Days of serious rioting were sparked off when police destroyed illicit stills during a slum clearance operation designed to resettle some 100,000 black people. Hundreds of black women attacked beer-halls and other property in the black shanty town of Cato Manor on the outskirts of Durban. They were joined by thousands of other rioters who ran through the streets setting fire to offices, clinics, schools, shops and vehicles. Outside Durban a crowd of some 4,000 blacks blocked the main road and stoned cars as they tried to pass.

The rioting continued throughout the month, leaving buildings and vehicles smouldering. Official figures had it that four black people died in the unrest, but the death toll was probably much higher than this, with hundreds injured and maimed. Damage to property was estimated at some £250,000., a massively high sum in Africa at that time. The situation in Durban remained tense for some months afterwards and more deaths occurred in September when police opened fire on protesters.

A decent start was made to the season when Leicester were beaten 3-0 on the opening day. This was followed by victories over Burnley (the champions to be) and Preston. The first defeat came in September, when Leeds won 2-1 at Upton Park. The game was marked by the end of Ernie Gregory's playing career with the Club. He retired to become the Club coach and of course worked closely with the goalkeepers.

There were 58,909 spectators at the London derby with Spurs at White Hart Lane, which finished 2-2. Ten days later, 54,349 turned up at Stamford Bridge where West Ham beat Chelsea 4-2. A good 4-1 win over West Bromwich Albion pleased the Upton Park fans as the season rounded its first quarter and its second month.

In mid-October, Luton trotted down the M1 for their annual visit to the Boleyn Ground, never exactly a red-letter day for the claret and blue hordes, the attendance was almost 10,000 down on the encounter with Preston, just a few weeks previously. This seemed about the right sort of match for Fenton to bring in the 17-year-old Derek Woodley. The youngster hounded, harried and haunted the hapless Hatters, harvesting two goals in a 3-1 humbling of the Kenilworth Road club. Derek recalled; "In my first game I was carried off not long after scoring." Injury at the Boleyn Ground was often as much the fault of the playing surface as the opposition. Derek remembered; "The pitch was terrible." Getting hurt when he did was particularly unfortunate as it kept him out of the competition for selection for the next game and probably cost him the run in the first team he was never to achieve at Upton Park. As it was, he played 13 games and scored just one more goal, in a 3-3 home draw with Blackpool in September 1960.

Derek was good enough to invite me to meet him at his home in Southend. He remembered his early experiences of football. "It took me a long time to get interested. I was more interested in going to Saturday morning pictures! When I did play it was mostly the 35-a-side kind of game. The first time I played in a team with matching shirts was when I played for the school, when they were short - it was a Final. I was told off for not coming to the borough trails."

When the game finally captured young Derek's imagination, getting his kit together became a major project. "My dad worked at Watney's [the Brewers] I talked to him into buying me some boots. In those days you bought them off a line in hardware stores. They took about five seasons to break in and you had to put around two-pound of dubbing on them before each match. I did get a pair of Arthur Rowes after a time. I had to lick boots for them at £7."

1959-60 – You were carried by the majority, you weren't just carried by yourself

Derek has a laid back and slightly self-deprecating sense of humour, but this shows a sharp mind. Often by the time you've got the joke, he's moved on. I could see the personality of his play coming out in our conversation. "I was quick, and had some class, in the same way as Brooking and Devonshire. No crash, bang, wallop." First spotted by Hammers scout Reg Revins, as being a "swift winger and fine young player in general, with a great deal of potential", he won international recognition at schoolboy level and attracted more attention from the Irons' scouting system. "I was approached by a number of clubs, but it was Wally St Pier who persuaded me to sign for West Ham. When I went on the groundstaff I got £7 a week."

This went a long way for Derek. "When I was at Upton Park, I still lived at home and I was able to supplement my earnings out of season; the summer was all bunce. I worked in the City of London Cemetery. There were about a dozen young London-based players working there. When I first went there, this big rhododendron bush caught my attention. The bloke in charge told me to watch as he blew his whistle for tea break. All of a sudden the bush came alive, and a big bunch of lads emerged. The foreman told me that they were supposed to be about two miles away."

It wasn't too long before the young Woodley found himself in the West Ham team contesting the FA Youth Cup Final, playing alongside Bobby Moore amongst others. "We lost the Youth Cup Final 1-0 after extra time. It was probably one of my biggest disappointments. We threw away the first leg; their goal went through Caskey's [the 'keeper] legs. We ran them ragged over the two legs. Fred Pickering, who went on to play for Everton and England, captained the Blackburn side."

The golden time for Derek seems to have been his successful youth career, "We were on an England youth tour, in a massive hotel in Bulgaria I think. We rolled Nobby Stiles up in a great big carpet. We just went off and left him - he'd get out of it one day we thought. He nearly died; the weight of the carpet on his chest almost suffocated him. On the same trip the whole squad of 16 got in a lift that took a maximum of four people. We were stuck in it for four hours. An Arsenal player had a panic; he started having a go at the electrics with his penknife. 'We're gonna die, we're gonna die,' he was shouting. Peter Reader, the West Ham 'keeper, knocked him out. I got my teeth knocked out by a youth international. I got them sorted then it happened again."

An intelligent man, well able to express his thoughts in a cogent and clear way, Derek had a good grasp of the spirit of his heyday as a player. The Fifties was a period of transition. For Woodley, West Ham, more than many other clubs, were moving with the spirit of the time. "Results weren't everything. They wanted to play a flowing game. Woosnam and Greenwood wanted the game played with some style and grace… West Ham was like no other club I've been at. The Club had a kind of different mental attitude. They were entertainers. Maybe this was why they have never had that much success."

Although Derek was as generous about the fans as anybody was, he told me; "The crowd could be hard. They destroyed Malcolm Musgrove and for a time called Vic Keeble,' 'Vic Feeble' they called him sometimes."

For all this, it seems Derek got a lot out of his time with the Hammers. "Geoff Hurst was my room mate. I was good at taking the mick, Geoff wasn't. I was friendly with John Charles and went everywhere with Ronnie Boyce."

Derek left West Ham just before the start of the 1962-63 season, when Ted Fenton, by this time with Southend, made an offer for Woodley and his former youth team-mate, Mick Beesley. Derek told me; "I regret leaving West Ham." His attachment for the Club seemed to have endured, but through the people that were part of it, rather than the organization as a whole. For instance Derek knew that his two old trainers, Bill Robinson and Bill Watson, had died recently. This demonstrated a sentiment about his days at Upton Park and the people who nurtured him as a young talent.

West Ham's next appointment involved a trip to Goodison Park. A Malcolm Musgrove strike gave the Cockney boys a creditable 1-0 win. Fenton's faith in youth continued with this match. Bobby Moore got his first outing of the season, while the 18-year-old Johnny Cartwright was given his debut in place of Phil Woosnam. John recalled; "I made Malcolm Musgrove's goal in my first game. They were top of the League and I was up against Bobby Collins. It was a full house, and the crowd were spitting and shouting. Vic Keeble told me not to worry; 'I'll make you play well'. He said; 'Just get around me and you'll have a good game.'"

I travelled to the Crystal Palace training ground to see John Cartwright, who, at the time, was a member of the Selhurst Park coaching staff. I waited in the players' canteen. The Eagles had just bought two Chinese internationals. I watched them and their interpreter dealing with the very South London menu. John arrived after a few minutes and told me to come and get some lunch with him. As we stood in line with our trays he told me; "Wally St Pier spotted me playing for East London and London Schoolboys. I lived in Bethnal Green. Arsenal and Tottenham came in for me, but I had been training with Malcolm Allison at West Ham. I got £10 signing on fee. I signed on my birthday."

1959-60 – You were carried by the majority, you weren't just carried by yourself

Having obtained our food, we found a table. John exchanged banter with some of the track-suited staff. One asked me to write his life story. Lightheartedly I told him that I only dealt with West Ham subjects, He said; "Oh, I used to play football myself." Before I could think of a polite answer, I decided to concentrate on my reason for being on the turf of a claret and blue crew not of the East London ilk. John continued; "My dad worked at Billingsgate and my mum was a machinist." John has one son who at that time worked in the City.

John Cartwright was an extremely talented inside-forward. He started with West Ham as a junior. "I went to Parmeters School. I played at 16, but wasn't thought to be big enough or strong enough, so I idled for three years. We got no guidance with the weight training; we got stiff and solid. I went from London sprint champion to finding the going hard. Me and George Fenn [another talented junior at Upton Park] were left to it. George was a great player."

John remembered some of his other contemporaries. "At first Bobby Moore and Geoff Hurst were not very good, until Bobby got into the 4-4-2, becoming a holding player alongside the centre-half. Bob got murdered on a trip to Czechoslovakia. Martin Peters was a class player, the best player to play with. Eddie Bovington was a good team player, he'd work hard to get the ball and give it to you. They called me Didi [after the great Brazilian player of the late Fifties and early Sixties]. We played in Liechtenstein, a place called Routie. Brian Dear said that Didi died in Routie!"

John's second game of the three he had in 1959-60 was at Old Trafford. "I remember playing Manchester United on Easter Monday; it was 3-1 at half-time. Bobby Charlton took Joe Kirkup to the pictures. Although West Ham were beaten 5-3, I was man of the match. I lost my way after that. I lost my mobility. At 18 and a half I had found the game easy, but I lost pace with all the weights. That was what the 'West Ham run' was about. Everyone was so stiff."

Like most of his colleagues in West Ham's FA Youth Cup Final team, John recollected the interest taken by the claret and blue army. "They supported us well in the Youth Cup Final. We got on well with the fans. If you weren't doing well you wouldn't get near the Chicken Run.

"I wasn't a great socialiser; I wasn't interested in the dogs. That was fairly much central to the social life of the senior players. I was 18 when I met my wife in 1961, we moved into a prefab in Bethnal Green. The club was a bit cliquey, especially when the wives got involved. But West Ham were a football-thinking club."

John played five times for West Ham in two seasons. If it hadn't have been for the presence of Phil Woosnam and the growing talent of Ron Boyce, he would have undoubtedly have had more of a chance of establishing himself in the First Division side. "I put in for a transfer. I felt I could play, I needed help. I played for a month under Ron Greenwood before me and Andy Smillie went to Palace in exchange for Budgie Byrne. I had wanted to play under Ron and he did tell me that he had wished he could have kept me."xxx

It was now time for John to get back to his charges. As we shook hands he told me; "I remember Fenton shouting from the stands with a megaphone; 'Do things easy' - you couldn't do things easy to be a great player -1 rebelled."

The first three games in November were won; Manchester City were beaten 4-1; there was a 3-1 win against Arsenal at Highbury; and finally a hat-trick by Dick in a 3-2 win over Wolves at Upton Park.

Three days before the Wolves game, and four after the match with the Gunners, Kenny Brown gained what was to be his only England cap, against Northern Ireland at Wembley. He was the first West Ham player to be selected to play for a full England side since Len Goulden in 1939. Walter Winterbottom was on his quest, which never concluded, for a replacement for Billy Wright at centre-half. Ken did well in England's 2-1 win. In goal behind Ken that day was Ron

Springett. The defence also included Don Howe. In the forward line Johnny Haynes had regained the place taken by Jimmy Greaves in the previous two England matches.

It seemed that Ken had been the last to learn that his country wanted him. "Malcolm Allison let me know about being called up for England. Malcolm's first wife, Beth, told Joan, my wife."

The next international was six months later, by which time West Ham were involved in a poor run. Peter Swan took over as the English centre-half for that game against Yugoslavia. He held on to the position for two years and 19 games. Throughout that period Swan was with Sheffield Wednesday, who in 1959 were having a good run in Division One. The Second Division champions of the previous season were to finish in a creditable fifth place in their first season back in the top flight. Swan was in the side that met West Ham at Hillsborough on 28 November 1959. John Bond recalled; "We went to Sheffield Wednesday as League leaders." The Hammers were 4-0 behind at half-time and finally lost 7-0, the elusive Johnny Fantham scoring twice.

1959-60 – You were carried by the majority, you weren't just carried by yourself

Brown wasn't the only West Ham player to pick up honours in 1959. Andy Malcolm was selected, along with John Bond, for the Football League v Scottish League game.

The trip to Blackburn Rovers in mid-December saw a further hatful of goals conceded in a 6-2 defeat. By the end of 1959, the Irons had picked up 29 points. This meant they had dropped 19. At home they were doing well enough, taking all but four points, but they had won only four away games out of a possible 13. With only three draws all season, the Hammers were blowing hot and cold, seemingly unable to maintain any consistency, riding on waves of unpredictability. Organisational behaviour of this type suggests the presence of raw talent, that sustains performance up to a point, but a lack of clear leadership that can generate, maintain and develop coherent or appropriate planning. This can negatively affect individual morale and organisational confidence.

The end of the year also saw the death of the British artist Sir Stanley Spencer, who had been knighted by the Queen in the Birthday Honours list in June. The son of an organist and music teacher, Spencer received little formal education before going to the Slade School of Art in 1908 at the age of 17. There he developed the techniques, which formed the basis of his highly distinctive work.

A true visionary, Spencer created paintings that fused the divine and the commonplace. It is a shame that he never was able to look closely at some of the likes of Haynes, Moore and John Charles. These men, from the commonplace in commonplace surroundings, could produce action and movement close to the divine. Spencer often transfigured the scenes of everyday life he saw around him in the Thames-side village of Cookham, where he was born and spent most of his life. He reached the apex of his creative powers in the 1920s with his murals in Burghclere Chapel in Berkshire and paintings such as *Resurrection Cookham*. His last work, an altarpiece dedicated to his first wife, Hilda, remained unfinished when he died

The Hammers' team was losing all confidence and Burnley got revenge for their early-season defeat at Turf Moor by winning 5-2 at Upton Park on a bitterly cold early January day.

The FA Cup brought further misery. After a 1-1 draw at Huddersfield, the Yorkshire team

inspired by a young Denis Law, won 5-1 in the replay. A recurrence of an old injury kept Vie Keeble out of the side for most of the second half of the season and a number of deputies were tried. In February, full-back John Bond was moved to centre-forward and he did well in scoring six goals in six games, which included a hat-trick in the 4-2 win over Chelsea.

London derbies at the very highest level are not the easiest games to play. They would certainly not be chosen by everyone as the ideal debut matches. However, just a few days short of his 20th birthday, John Lyall was walking out at Upton Park for his initial first-team game, a confrontation with the blue-clad rivals from the capital's westerly regions.

When I had telephoned to make arrangements to see John Lyall, Yvonne, John's wife, had told me he was out mowing one of the meadows! A few days later, after mowing one of my meadows in Canning Town, (well, taking the empty Red Stripe can out of the window box in a vein attempt give the three asthmatic carrots a chance, actually) I drove down to Suffolk. I had arranged to meet with John at his beautiful farm just outside of Ipswich. The late spring landscape was a verdant green and the sky a cloudless azure.

John joined West Ham in June 1955 as an office boy/apprentice, after being watched by Ted Fenton and Wally St Pier, at the recommendation of John Cunningham, John's teacher in Ilford. He signed professional in 1957.

According to John, a new breed of young men were coming into football. "I left school at 15. I watched West Ham and Spurs on alternate Saturdays. It was a dream in those days. Football was so far removed from what ordinary lads did. I was at grammar school and they expected you to go on a complete your education, possibly go to university, and so to be involved in sport was something different. There was a different generation of people coming through who were sports people. Geoff Hurst was at a grammar, as was Bobby Moore, Eddie Presland and Ronnie Boyce. Those who went into football in my early days tended to be the lads who were not scholastic. But that changed a bit in the mid-Fifties, late Fifties and certainly the Sixties. It was looked on not just as a job but as a profession. It was something you felt privileged to do, and I think that every other boy who tried to become a footballer felt the same."

John began to give an idea of what that time was like, the changes in expectations and ambitions. 'Towards the start of the Sixties there were a lot of people who weren't going to be pigeon-holed. They were good people, intelligent, they thought, and they said no. You got four Beatles, you got a Bobby Moore. Ten years before, Bobby would have gone in a bank. He had his five O Levels, but he said; "No, I want to be a footballer".'

1959-60 – You were carried by the majority, you weren't just carried by yourself

John's dad was a policeman in the East End, but his roots are a little further north. "My family were Scottish, but I was in an English environment. When we went up to Scotland as kids there would rib us a little bit, and down here, if Scotland beat England we would say; 'Well, we're half-Scottish anyway.'

John, who laughs and smiles a lot, chuckled. "You could use it as a strength and not just a weakness. It is something I'm proud of. It was so different going north of the border. My mother came from the Outer Hebrides. To see people working looms and making Harris Tweed was far removed from London or Essex. The way the crofters lived gave you another insight into life. As kids, in the summer, we had to help cut the peat and bring it off the moors. One of my uncles had three or four fishing boats. He also had buses and lorries on the island, he was a bit of an entrepreneur. All those things were another part of your life. We looked forward to it, it was so different from the environment we were brought up in. So, it was a nice thing. My elder brother still goes up there, very often each year. I don't go up so much, but we have a great affection for Scotland. People in Scotland, in football, were good to me.

I got very friendly with Jock Stein, without name-dropping, and Jim McClean. I think that little link with Scotland helped."

John was quickly noticed as a football talent. "Mr Carter, at Park Hill Primary, helped me when I was very young, and Mr Pyman, at Ilford County High, he was the PE teacher, and he still comes to see me now. He contacted me through the publishers of *Like My Dreams,* [John's autobiography]. Mr Pyman visits about once a year. He was a fitness fanatic. He was ex-navy, a tough, hard disciplinarian, but a lovely man, with great charisma. He's still the same, does quite a lot of swimming, about half a mile a day. He lives in the Channel Islands."

The district team swiftly recruited John to their ranks. "I played for Ilford Boys with Andy Smillie. We grew up talking about the game. Now, if you're 13 and you're good at something, everyone comes after you. No one came after us, we ran after them. We went looking to be footballers. We weren't expecting you to come and find us, we were going to have to do something if we were going to be any good, to prove to you that we wanted to stay in the game. Once we got in the door, we had to work out how we were going to stay there. So we trained, did extra training, no one told us, we went and did it. We went in the gym and headed the swinging ball. You'd be at it for two hours at a time, but in the end you could head a ball. But if you have West Ham, Tottenham, and Chelsea after you, where's the motivation? We had nothing, we weren't anything. We were ordinary little lads, little snotty toe-rags."

John played for England youth in 1957, against Luxembourg, alongside Jimmy Greaves, Barry Bridges and John Cartwright. This was the same year he played in the FA Youth Cup Final, alongside Joe Kirkup and John Cartwright. Manchester United were West Ham's opponents. The Hammers lost 8-2 over two legs. John recalled; "West Ham didn't have the status of Manchester United, but in the mid to late Fifties, Wally St Pier, who was a wonderful man, along with Ted Fenton, was beginning to develop a youth policy, searching for good young players. Chelsea had a lot in those days, but really West Ham and Chelsea dominated the London scene and then Tottenham started to do it, and then Arsenal."

The young Lyall started off his days at Upton Park working in administration. "The first year I was at Upton Park there was something like 60 to 65 professionals. I used to have to help Frank Cearns - lovely old chap - do the wages on a Friday. We used to go and get the money, and put it all in a case. Dad, being a policeman, told me I should think about this, taking the same route every day. I told Mr Cearns; 'I hope you don't mind but my dad says you ought to be a bit careful.' Mr Cearns told me that once someone had tried to rob him." The old man had informed his youthful assistant; "I stuck this," - John clenched his fist - "right up between his legs." The belligerent, seasoned Hammers servant reassured John; "No one came after that!"

The army of players that clubs used to employ must have seemed like a human wall in a young player's career; "We used to work all the money out, and it would hit you how many players were with the club. There were first team, reserves, 'A' team, 'B' team, youth team and juniors. If you wanted to see how important football was to the individual, you just had to be around when the contracts had to be renewed, they were all one-year contracts then. On a certain day, at the end of the season, the manager would have everyone in. They'd all arrive at ten o'clock and start to queue up. He used to ask for the next one and I'd call them in and some of 'em were saying; 'I'll go in', and others were saying that they would leave it a couple. You could see they were concerned by the thought that they might not get taken on again. It was a great insight. A place in the club was worth working for. The fear factor, although not always a great motivator, was a motivating factor in those days. You thought; 'I've got this, I'm in football and this is where I want to stay forever and ever. I don't care what I have to do to do it, but I'm gonna do it.' People would come out of the first team and play about eight games for the fourth team. You said; 'That's the way the game is, that's the way it has to be.' Gradually it developed. Then the maximum wage came, and players got that much more independence."

Despite the fear factor it seemed players helped each other and worked together. "All the senior players felt they had the responsibility to help the younger ones. Johnny Dick and Noel Cantwell were always very friendly. Dick Walker would have a lot of those lads, the Dagenham-type lads. Dick would look after them. Then they would say to me, and the likes of Joe Kirkup, who arrived at the club about the same time as me; 'Well, you can come out with us.' But you had to follow the rules. You did it right, and if you skylarked at the wrong time they said no. They set great standards for me. Vie Keeble was a super fella as was Mal Musgrove. They all had their own qualities and strengths. You could talk to all of them and say; 'I've got a bit of a problem, what do you think?'

"As a teenager, in the very early part of my career, I was close to people like Kenny Brown, Andy Malcolm, Mike Grice -I knew him very well - were good to me. Mike had been a draughtsman and came into the game late. He had a good knowledge of life. He told me to save and be aware of insurance. It was the same at home. My mum would tell me to ask Mike what to spend when we were out with the lads. I got very friendly with Mike. I'd been in the office so I also had Eddie Chapman. I'd go to him if I had a big problem with money, or if I needed advice about a mortgage or insurance."

This community spirit even facilitated John's courtship of his future life partner. "Albert Walker was marvellous to me, he lived not half a mile from us. Yvonne lived in the middle. Some days Albert would say; 'I'l pick you up,' and I would see Yvonne.

Albert Walker was a strong defender who started his playing career in Lancashire a decade after World War One. Born in Little Lever, Albert grew up in a part of Lancashire with a long history of football and had been at the centre of the controversy of professionalism well before the turn of the century. From the school team he joined Little Lever United in the Bolton and District League. He then took on amateur status at Southport, before moving to Bolton Wanderers in Division One. However, he was in competition with the likes of Haworth and Finney and a year later he was playing for Barrow in the Third Division North. However, they couldn't afford him at Holker Street and things didn't look too promising until Ned Liddell, a West Ham scout, sent him to Upton Park in 1932. Back in the Second Division after nine seasons among the elite, the Irons were fighting for their lives as the 1932-33 season began. They finished in 20th position, barely missing the drop to the Third Division South. Albert reinforced the side with some true northern grit, turning out in claret and blue for the first time in the 5-2 defeat of Oldham at the Boleyn Ground to begin an enduring partnership with Alf Chalkley.

In 1938, Albert went to Doncaster Rovers. He had done six seasons of sterling service at Upton Park, ever-present at left-back in 1934-35 when West Ham finished third in the Second Division, missing out on promotion on goal-average. Ironically for Albert, the Hammers ended with the same points, wins, draws and losses as promoted Bolton. He missed only one match the following term when again West Ham were unlucky not to go up, falling short by just three points.

After spending the war years in the National Fire Service, Albert joined Ted Fenton at Colchester. It was Ted who brought him back to Upton Park in 1952 to act as coach for the Hammers 'B' team in the Metropolitan League. He was soon responsible for the Easter Counties League side and then the Reserves and eventually worked with the first team.

John Lyall is not a man to forget those who looked after him. "Mrs Moss was like a mother to me when I first went to Upton Park and in the end I was manager and she was still the same." John recalled some of her good advice; "Go to bed early - that's what I call caring." My secretary's been gone two years. I still phone her husband, Jack. He's 75. I honestly feel I've got to. I feel responsible."

Care for each other, and the younger players in particular, was evident to John from his earliest times with West Ham. "My first day I was at the club, I was going in the gate, I had to be in the office at ten. It was about quarter to nine, so I was well early. There were a couple of senior lads, Gordon Johnson and Andy Nelson. I said; 'Excuse me, can you tell me where Mr Fenton's office is please?' They said; 'He won't be in for a while, what time do you have to see him?' I said I was joining the club and they said; 'Come and have a cup of tea with us.' They took me in Eddie's cafe, just across the road. We went and had a cup of tea for half an hour. They said; 'Don't do this, do that. Make sure you be careful there...' That was my first day. So it wasn't difficult, they took me in, showed me where to go."

Of course, John's association with the club had begun as a supporter. "I can remember seeing John Bond as a school boy - he could bang a ball, he could kick a long way. But when you came to the club you saw him working on his skills. He developed a way of kicking the ball, how long, where to send it. You'd see how he changed. I would say; 'I used to watch you,' and he'd say; 'Yeah, well, I went out and practised didn't I?'. That's how I learnt. You developed yourself that way."

John's relationship with the supporters fostered an empathy with the fans that lasted throughout his career. "In my early days at West Ham I thought the supporters were great. They used to say that West Ham fans don't like defeat. I thought, you've got to be joking. But they don't lose their head. They'll moan among themselves, but outside the East End they'll still say their side is the best team in the country." He spoke of the fans with affection and a kind of amazed amusement, although he made the proviso; "They're all a bit cute - don't worry, they'll turn you over any time."

He obviously has a special kind of respect for these people. "The little lads used to come in to the ground from the market. [Queen's Road market is just a stone's throw from the Boleyn Ground] They used to have Christmas cards for you, selling them dirt cheap. They'd get you anything. They loved the players and the players loved them. There was a bookies' runner, a little fella called Lou Borne, and all sorts. Lou put on bets for the lads. Lou used to come in with Christmas cards in the middle of summer! Less than five foot tall he was, he had a big homburg hat and a crombie coat, in the hottest weather. He'd sell you anything - 'Do you want any of these?' John mimed the furtive way Lou would pull condoms out of his pocket - It was like *Fools and Horses*. One of the lads got hold of a Donegal check coat. He asked if I wanted one - my dad was a copper!

"The fans were great characters coming out of the East End, and you knew them. The one from the fruit market, he'd say; 'If you want anything let me know.' You'd go up there and get a bag of apples for half price. There was a great comradeship in the whole of the East End. If you had a problem the fans were behind you. Even when they moved away and didn't live in the area, they still retained that comradeship. It really was a great pleasure in my early days to be involved. The fans, with the greatest respect, could be tough, but most of them were decent, and if you were really struggling they'd say; 'Leave him alone, let's help him.' That was the area. For all its rough edges there was a niceness about it. That's why I've always had great respect for the fans. West Ham, in the time I was there, was about players and fans. They were lovely days, but things have to move on. West Ham, on a Cup night, was a bit of an ordeal for the opposition. I used to think the terraces at West Ham were the best thing in the world, the best weapon West Ham had."

It was obvious that John regarded his playing era as a special, even unusual time. "I was lucky. The people I played with were great. Johnny Byrne was a huge influence on people. Bobby Moore was a wonderful player, and a great player to play with. Although people didn't think he was demonstrative in a game, he was always talking to you. When the ball came he would say; 'If you want to give it to me, I'm here.' He talked you through it. I'm sure Jackie Burkett [one of West Ham's star defenders of the Sixties] if you talked to him, would tell you the same. It was done in a sensible, discreet manner. That was the great thing about the club. While there was some marvellous characters, they all had a code of conduct, and standards. They had to help you. You helped the young ones to develop and come through. I think that's how West Ham was built."

John looked back on the Upton Park culture as the Sixties dawned. "They were lucky to have the likes of Allison, Bond and Cantwell - that group of people that got promoted - with a lot of young ones coming on because the young ones were of a good standard. They were all workers at the game. They all loved the game. They talked the game. You went into that environment and you'd sit for hours asking yourself what they were talking about. They'd ask you what you thought, and you'd say what you thought and they'd say; 'No, you can't do that.' They'd then explain why and you'd say; 'Oh, I got yer.' That was the Cassatarri's thing, it was that sort of fanaticism." It struck me that the word fan is a derivative of fanaticism. John was telling me that the players were football fans.

What John had described to me, without using the word, was the Academy. He was a late graduate of this Football University founded on critical discourse. John flashed back to one innovation that came out of this environment; "There was a fella, Redfern, played at Oldham, and people kept saying to me; 'That's a new thing, no ones ever done that before, he keeps running from outside-left in among the strikers and scoring goals.' I'd say; 'There was a fella at West Ham in 1958, Musgrove, they'd cross it from the right and he'd be heading it in at the near post. This was the attacking full-back, the overlapping defender, the wing-back. That ain't new, that's 30 or 40 years old. I saw Muzzy at Kenny Brown's 65th. I said; 'Muz, you kept doing that and all of a sudden they call it the modern game.' He said he used to like making that run. We used to say; 'It ain't half a long way back Muzzy, if you don't get it.'" John smiled. "There's nothing new, they were doing it. But it was all about doing the job right."

Part of doing the job right was the dissemination of the football knowledge generated at Upton Park. "I did around two years playing, then six or seven of us started to work at a school in Stepney. I coached three afternoons a week at Stepney Green School. So I was involved in coaching from an early age. It helps give you an insight into the game.

1959-60 – You were carried by the majority, you weren't just carried by yourself

When you're watching other people you can then relate it to yourself. I could do that, or I could do that next time, or I do that wrong. You could mirror yourself. You need to take responsibility as a player to play and there's nothing better than coaching others to help you learn how to do that, because you've got to work the problems out."

This process bore ample fruit; John gave just one example. "I can remember Alan Curbishley and Paul Brush. We used to go to Pretoria School [a secondary modern, now Eastlea Comprehensive, in Canning Town] on a Thursday night, when I was youth coach. We were in this Bedford van we had. I'd better not tell you how many we had in it! Alan and Paul, only two little 13-year-olds, nine times out of ten, would be in earshot. They'd ask; 'Did you think the team played well on Saturday?' You'd look at them and say; 'What are you talking about? Who are you?' Alan would ask; 'Why did they do that?' When he came to the club he was still the same — 'Why did you play that way John? Why did you do that?' I'm not surprised he became a manager. I told him 'one day you're going to be a manager and have all the problems, so don't start moaning then.'"

John Lyall constantly reiterated the morality generated by the club, but seemingly mostly acted out and developed by the players. It seems that the values of the club's environment seeped into Upton Park. These attitudes shaped the way the game was played at the Boleyn Ground. "If we were going to do it, we were going to do it the right way. I think the area was like that. Someone has a problem in their family, and the next thing everyone in the streets giving 'em three bob or tuppence-'appney, but they were all giving. You were carried by the majority, you weren't just carried by yourself. If someone had a bad time, like if a player got suspended in those days, we'd have a whip round for him — he might end up getting three times what he got for playing. We'd used to say; 'Watch him!'" John chuckled. "Everyone put their hand in their pocket. That was just the done thing, there was nothing special about it, you just did it. If you had a car and the other lads didn't, then you gave them a lift. They were simple, little basic things. It wasn't just about football. They taught you about life and respect."

Ethical management, the importance of the individual, is part of the currency of modern business organisation - it gets the best from people and draws out the best from the manager. However, according to John, contemporary management gurus were preceded by the West Ham creed. He spoke of his mentor, Ron Greenwood. "Ron once told me; 'You don't need to be intelligent, you don't need O Levels, you don't need A Levels, all you need is good manners and respect - you don't need any education for that. Say please and thank you.' You'd go to a ground and Ron would asked the attendant how they were, say hello, how's the wife and so on. If he forgot he'd kick himself and go back. He would say one day there might only be one car parking space, but also that 'it could be me or you, John. Their life is as important to them as ours is to us'. Ted was the same. He'd insist on calling people Mister, just to let you know that there was a spot for all of us, but don't jump out of your's till your day comes. It was nothing to do with being soft - there were some real hard, tough men at West Ham - but they had a niceness about them. That's what I always liked about the club. But if you were young and you misread it, you couldn't get away with it."

It is hard to portray the respect which John demonstrated for those he worked with and among. He impresses you with his dignity, integrity and intelligence. No longer a manager, he has become a philosopher, not only of the game, but also of life, and how it should be lived. Like most of the players he worked with, and I have spoken with do/ens, writing this book, *Bubbles, Hammers and Dreams*, *The First and Last Englishmen*, and a future work on West Ham's black players, when talking to John Lyall I was struck by the feeling that this is a man to learn from.

He told me; "There were so many people that I admired and still do to this day. I must have been asked 20 times to name my best West Ham team and I wouldn't even start. If I offended one of the people I respect that would be wrong. That's not ducking an issue. I used to stand behind the goal with the chap next door, who used to take me to West Ham. We'd watch Ernie Gregory and he say; 'The Cat's at it again.' Everywhere you shot, Ernie would be waiting for it. Then you'd think of Phil Parkes, if you asked me to pick between them two I'd say that I can't pick. What would you say if I said I'd have the likes of Pat Holland and Geoff Pike in the team? They would die for you. When one or two of the others were a bit off they'd be going; 'Come on, come on.' Patsy is an incredible lad, as is Geoff. I still talk to them now. They ring me up, ask how I am. That is good friendship and loyalty. Not many people would have them in their best-ever West Ham side, but if I was going to war, they just may be my men."

John began to cast his mind back over those young men who he had worked so dedicatedly with over the years. "Billy Bonds, Frank Lampard, Alan Devonshire. Now I think Devonshire comes from another world, but I wouldn't like to pick between Devonshire and Brooking. I've got great admiration for Trevor, I think he's a wonderful footballer. I tell David Cross; 'You weren't a bad player David.' Now what would you pay for him now? They've just sold one for seven million. No disrespect to the boy, but can they be compared? Now I'm getting old, so maybe it's me, but I'm sure my eyes don't lie. Geoff, Martin, Bobby, you pick which one you want, I'll take the other two. If you want Billy, I'll have Trevor; if you want Trevor, I'll have Dev. If you want Dev, I'll have Frank. You have Ray Stewart, I'll have Phil Parkes. That's why I liked them, because they were such good men. Frankie McAvennie, Tony Cottee, they weren't bad players either.

"When you were in the club you were influenced. Ted set the rules, the players followed 'em, the young ones followed the older ones, so it was a good school. That tradition has gone on and on with the club. You respected it and you hope it goes on today."

John waited a long tome to get into the first team, injury often preventing his selection, but he played 31 games for the first team. That first game against Chelsea, John was given the job of watching Peter Brabrook. He recalled; "I was useless in the first half. Noel, who was injured, came up to me at half-time and said; 'You're a tough tackier and you've not tackled yet. The first chance you get I want you to tackle him.' From the start the ball went out to Brabrook and I went bang into him. Noel was on the side shouting; 'You'll be all right now.' They used to say, when you're a full-back, make 'em show you the whites of their eyes. That was the saying of the old players. I sat with Mike Grice and Muzzy and Vie at Kenny's do and we were going through all the old sayings, like 'a rolling ball gathers no moss'. We used to say; 'What are they on about?' But they all meant something - 'If you don't do this, that won't happen, if you do this, that'll happen.'"

John understood these brief proverbs and maxims as part of an oral philosophy handed down the generations from player to player. They epitomised wider truths about the game, and some were applicable to life in general. This tradition was in a state of constant development, inspired and provoked by what had gone before. John used the example of Tony Scott, a winger who came into the side about the same time as him, to illustrate this process.

"He was just a little bloke. He said to me; 'They might kick me, John, so when you get the ball, I'll run away and when I say Yeah! I'll come back and get it.' He told you what he wanted. That was a player thinking about the game. He'd say; 'If I cross it with my left foot, they can come across me, but if I go like that with my right, they can't get their leg ready.'"

John stood and mimed the whole process for me. I should have videoed it really. Indeed, John is a very animated speaker. Throughout our conversation he was up and down, almost acting out his experience. This was someone steeped the physical architecture of the body and the poetry of its movement. In front of me, the philosopher artist performed and at the end of it all was the wish to perfect communication. This told me more about John Lyall the man, his attitude to football and the West Ham he had been, and was still part of, than all the words in this book.

"We used to say; 'Cross it with your early foot, so if you do it with that one rather than that one, it's that much earlier.' Tony was 16 and I was 17 and we used to plan out the game. Mooro would say; 'When you get it there, give it to me, I can give it to him.' We used to talk through games. Ernie [(Gregory] used to say; 'If there's anyone in your way, play back, but watch your back.' If you got clattered he'd say; 'I told yer.' But it made you learn. They noticed that when I got it on my right foot I wasn't too sure. 'Just do that with it,' I was told, 'I'll help you out.'

"I was left sided," John explained. "That was a great advantage in football because it looks different. If there are two left-footers in a team, they'll stand out. It's a bit like a blond player in the team of dark-haired players. I was a forward as a schoolboy, so I had reasonable technique. I had power and I could pass. When I got to the club they had a lot of midfielders, but no fullbacks. So Ted asked me if I'd try as a full-back for a few games. He said; 'You'll probably get on better there as there's six left-halves, and there's only one or two full-backs', so I couldn't say no. I just said; 'Yes Mr Fenton. I'll do that.' One or two of the older players told me that I was naturally strong but I didn't use my strength very well. 'So get your foot in and tackle' - Albert Walker used to say that. You couldn't be a full-back without tackling. So, I learnt to tackle and, in the end, that became a better asset than the passing. I got strong. I was certainly an aggressive player. I loved to win."

Reflecting on his playing career, John said; "I wasn't successful enough as a player to appreciate the joys of it. That will affect any feelings I have for the playing side. I loved playing football, but I did have a lot of injuries and the club were great keeping me on for that long. My time with Ron Greenwood I wouldn't have traded for anything to this day. I worked for about a decade with him as youth manager and assistant manager and they were magnificent years for me, they were everything that I believed should go on in football.

"He was an incredible man, who never received nearly enough credit for how good he is -and I don't make outrageous statements. He is so knowledgeable and capable about football. He never ceased to amaze me. I could go now and sit with him for three months and listen to him. He still motivates me to this day. An incredible man. I'm sure players will tell you. He opened people's eyes to situations. Ron was unique. I think he says now that he's done his bit. He got so much out of players. Geoff Hurst is a good example. Geoff is the first to say that Ron made him a player. To make a good wing-half into a world-class striker you've got to know what you're doing. He did it with finesse. The man had class. Everything he did he did with great demeanour and character."

John talked about his departure from, what has always been, 'his' club. "When I left, it is your life, but these things.. .1 think that you've just got to live for today and tomorrow. Yesterday can't be taken away from you, I don't need to talk about it to anyone, they were great times. You just have to say, well, I was just grateful for what I had. I'm not a religious man, but, do unto others...When I left West Ham I had well over a thousand letters, it would have made a marvellous book. I can't believe there's that many good people about. I don't think you'd get that now. The club was good to me and the fans were good to me and the players were good to me. That means a lot to me. They're the people you've come through.

"Football people are always grateful, they don't want anything. I've offered people work scouting and they've said; 'No thanks, I'm all right.' I know they need money, but all they want is for you to give them a ring, to ask if they're all right. I still get people ring me once a month after five years. I think that's terrific. If I was in a position that I could help in any way I would give them anything. That's more important than anything. It's a great game and it should have great people. It needs great people.

"As a young boy, I was a football fan. I loved football. Then when I became a player, the players that I was with helped me. Players helped me when I was a coach and when I was a manager. They're your own people. I've still got a lot of great friends at the club. I can't control what happens, that's part of your job. I, at least, had a chance, because some people go into work, they work 30 years at something they hate. I loved my days at West Ham."

As John walked with me back to my car, he told me; "Football belongs to us all. It doesn't belong to the football people, it belongs to us all. West Ham; its people. Right from the youngest fan to the chairman. That's how it always was for me. It belonged to all of us. I didn't look on it as a religion. But it was people. There were people who stood in the Chicken Run who had made it, were doing well, in more than good jobs, but you wouldn't have known - that's what I liked about it. Like a friend of mine, a buyer at Moss Bros. Seven million pounds a year! Him and his three mates, all with Rolls-Royces, parked in the streets outside the ground - used to get in the Chicken Run.. .We don't forget. The club wouldn't let you change - you had to do it right, you had to be polite. They set a standard."

He continued; "If you're one of those lucky enough to be in it, you're entitled to spend a little bit of time with some of those who support it. You should never be anything other than grateful. People like you got me that lovely view." John looked out over the wonderful scenery which surrounds his home. Still looking he said; "That's what football did for me."

John's conclusion summed up his feelings about being at Upton Park and his life in general, but it also, maybe, had something for us all. "I was just pleased to play. It's a long race. I can remember sitting at West Ham, doing the wages for Bobby, Geoff and Martin. Then, some years later, I'm their manager. Good people will tell you; 'Don't worry about it today - tomorrow's another day.' Be grateful and take it in your stride. If you start living for today, it can be a bad day or a good one, the best thing is to ride right through the middle."

****

On 19 February 1960, the Queen gave birth to Prince Andrew, the first time a child had been born to a reigning British sovereign since the birth of Princess Beatrice, Queen Victoria's youngest child, in 1857. A week later, Princess Margaret took the world by surprise with her engagement to Anthony Armstrong-Jones.

Following the good victory over Chelsea, John Lyall lost his place when Noel Cantwell returned to the side for the visit of Newcastle to Upton Park. That game ended in a 5-3 defeat for the Irons and the dropping of goalkeeper Noel Dwyer. Brian Rhodes took up his place for the remaining 15 games of the season. The walloping by the Magpies was followed by press allegations that the result had been 'fixed', but the rumours proved to be unfounded.

The rot set in over the next few games, in fact, including the controversial match with the Geordies from St James's, before the home game against Blackburn on 19 March, West Ham had achieved only one win and two draws in nine matches.

I made the long journey to York to meet David Dunmore at his home in the suburbs of the

1959-60 – You were carried by the majority, you weren't just carried by yourself

City. It was Cheltenham Gold Cup day. Dave hadn't had a bet, but he told me that if he had, it would have been on the favourite. "I don't bet much now," he told me, smiling. Although he is grey, he is still immediately recognisable as the dangerous striker of the early Sixties. In his soft Yorkshire accent he told me about his move from White Hart Lane.

"It was the night before the deadline day, 16 March. Bill Nick - Bill Nicholson, the then manager of Spurs - had asked me if I fancied going to West Ham. This meant that he was ready to get rid of me. Newcastle had shown some interest, but I said; 'It'll do me.' We used to get a percentage of our provident fund, and £150 benefit a year after five years' service, so it wasn't so bad. I left Tottenham in 1960, they won the Cup in 1961 - then when I left West Ham, they won it." Dave smiled at the irony.

As a boy it was clear that Dave was talented. "I went to Cannon A. R. Lee School and the teachers pushed me. It was good for the school that I played for York City and North Riding Boys. When I left York for Tottenham, the fee was £10,700. It was the record for York at the time. They had got to the semi-final of the Cup and had beaten Spurs on the way."

When he got to West Ham, it didn't appear to be a difficult transition. "Ernie Gregory, lohn Dick and Phil Woosnam were very helpful when I came to West Ham." As he lived between Upton Park and White Hart Lane, there wasn't any domestic upheavals either. "We didn't have to move house," Dave recalled.

He played 39 first-team games, his debut match being a win at Blackburn when he got the ball in the net. But as Dave explained; "It was called offside, somebody else was offside. Today it would have counted. It wasn't interfering with play." He scored 18 goals, including a hat-trick against Arsenal in the 6-0 win at Upton Park on Bonfire Night, 1960.

"That must have been my best game for West Ham," remembered Dave. "Jack Kelsey was in goal for Arsenal; it was nice to put three past 'em. I hit one with my left foot from just outside the box. It was a bit of a Ginola effort.. .well, not quite, nobody can be that good."

Dave, who still makes the trip to White Hart Lane every now and then, went on; "I'd gone from the right side, then along the box and then smacked it in the left.... That was maybe my best goal for West Ham. One in that game was a 30-yarder - bang! From a long way out, instead of running, why waste energy running when you can hit it?" Dave chuckled. "Could have gone anywhere, but went high into the net. I got one at Liverpool the same." Dave got his first goal for West Ham in the 5-3 defeat at Old Trafford in April 1960. "I think we were winning at half-time, but they got on top in the second-half."

The way the Hammers played seemed to suit Dave. "West Ham were a good footballing side - if you like playing football that's what it's about. They had players like Bobby Moore who could play balls into your feet rather than over your head. You don't want that every two minutes and chasing. Malcolm Musgrove was a very good winger, and Andy Malcolm could tackle. He was only young, but Bobby Moore stood out at Upton Park when I was there. Head and shoulders. The game against Brazil, he tackled the bloke with his wrong foot, but he got the ball. Phil Woosnam, he thought about it and played at all levels."

West Ham was a youthful side and Dave brought some useful maturity to the team. "We played at Manchester United, Moore and Hurst were playing. The average age was about 18 or 19. I was about 27. Noel and John Dick were the only other experienced players."

The atmosphere was fairly relaxed at Upton Park at this time. It was clear the players were calling the shots to a certain extent. Dave gave an example.

"There were five of us, we'd been down to Plumpton Races, we were playing Fluminense or someone, we beat them 6-2 or something. They were all little blokes, not one over five foot six.

We were a bit late, but we still went into the cafe around the corner, Cassatarri's. We were supposed to be in about an hour before kick-off and we overshot the mark by about 20 minutes. So Ted fined us £1 each. John Bond said; 'I'm not paying.'

"We'd play a lot of cards, talk about horses. We had a good thing among ourselves. Jackie Dick was all right. We used to go round a Jewish lad's place, a bloke called Lowe, and watch his telly. He'd put a bet on for you. We only had the odd quid, nothing stupid, only don't tell the wife - she'll think I'm a gambler!" Dave laughed. "I had a bet yesterday," he confessed. "Cheltenham. Must be the first bet I've had in three years."

Dave reiterated what so many have told me about the Hammers. "West Ham was a friendly club. The camaraderie among the West Ham players stays with me. The reserves were just the same, a good set of lads. They started me on £20. I don't think it went up until I'd been at Orient a couple of years, then it went up to about £25."

Dave went to Orient in 1961 as part of an exchange for Alan Sealey. He told me; "That was the last day again. It was a carbon copy of the move from Spurs." Dave had done well for the Irons and it was strange that West Ham were prepared to lose a relatively young, proven goalscorer. Looking back Dave agreed; "I got a goal every third game. I didn't get enough games. It does just stick a bit, why they got rid of me. I had a good shot, was fair in the air. I did pretty well by most standards. I was just getting to know people, a year isn't a long time in football. I was just getting into the rhythm. I have to ask, would I have been there for the Cup?" One has to have some sympathy with Dave. He was a good, effective forward, at the time better than Geoff Hurst and certainly a better centre-forward than Alan Sealey who replaced him.

It all seemed a bit sudden. There was no sign that Dave's transfer was imminent. All the indications were that he was going to be with the Hammers for some time. Even a move of house, nearer to Upton Park, had been arranged. "We were due to move into Clayhall Avenue when Lawrie Leslie, a West Ham 'keeper of the early Sixties, moved out, but the move to Orient came through just before we were due to move in. But Orient got us a house in the same avenue. Ted was in charge when I went to West Ham and Benny was at Orient when I went there."

Dave's final reminiscence was of the crowd at Upton Park; "I remember the crowd singing *I'm Forever Blowing Bubbles*. The Chicken Run was always very fair, but if you were having a bad game they'd let you know it. There was some good banter. You only do your best whatever it is. If it's not your day, then it doesn't happen. The fans were all right, you couldn't argue about the fans."

Two days after Dave's debut, what began as a peaceful protest ended in tragedy in the South African township of Sharpeville when police opened fire on a black crowd, killing 67 people and wounding 186.

The shootings happened on a day of mass demonstrations against the white government's hated pass laws. In a campaign organised by the Pan-African Congress - a breakaway group from the African National Congress - black people all over the country left their passes at home and gave themselves up at their nearest police station to be arrested. Thousands took part in the protests, which were peaceful in the majority of places.

However, at Sharpeville, a township five miles north of Vereeniging, police officers confronted the crowd outside the police station and opened fire, apparently without warning. Official statements claimed that the shootings took place in self-defence, when the crowd of 20,000 tried to storm the station. Black witnesses at the subsequent inquiry said that only 5,000 people were involved and that they had gone peacefully to the police station to discuss the pass laws. A medical expert testified that some 70 per cent of the victims had been shot from behind.

Eddie Bovington was the last player to be brought into the West Ham side in the Fifties decade of football. He came in as cover for Andy Malcolm in the defeat at Old Trafford, just three games from the end of the season. It was his first and last game that term. He was kind enough to see me at his business premises in Archway, North London. He told me; "You always remember your first game. With United being at the front again you tend to think of it all the time I suppose. They've always been the biggest club around. It was a capacity crowd and I was playing against people I had only read about, the likes of Charlton, Viollet. That is my first outstanding memory, that's something for every player."

Eddie signed professional in 1959. He recalled; "Ted Fenton took me on at 18, although 17 was usual. I had signed for the juniors in 1957. West Ham were the only team that wanted me. I started on £4 a week."

Born in the heart of London's furniture trade, Eddie told me; "Both my parents were involved in the upholstery trade in Edmonton. I was an only child." Eddie attended Croydon Road Junior School and then Tollington Hill Grammar School, Muswell Hill.

He looked back on his early days at Upton Park. "Bill Robinson - he came from Hartlepool - was a big influence on me. He was the first person to ever tell you what to do as a professional player. He trained you and he picked the team."

Eddie recalled his daily trip to Upton Park; "There was no cars then. I used to travel to the ground from Edmonton by bus. There were four or five of us from that area - Scotty, Mickey Brookes, Bobby Keech, Jackie Burkett - we would meet up at Bridge Road. After I got married I lived in Ilford, in Clayhall."

Although a member of the 1959 FA Youth Cup Final team, Eddie said; "It doesn't really stand out. I gave a penalty away. The Cup Final was the biggest thing." However, he saw winning the Second Division as a milestone for the club. "The championship put West Ham on the map. It was big for the players in the first team, but not so much for the juniors. You got nothing out of it yourself, except that you were a First Division player. I think the reason they never built on their success in the League was that they played too adventurously. We could always score goals but we gave away goals. You've got to get them, but not give them away."

Although the squads got smaller as the club moved into the Sixties, according to Eddie; "There were a lot of good players at Upton Park. They were good players because they knew how to play, they weren't coached as such. They came to the club that way. Johnny Dick and Noel Cantwell were outstanding players. I was an average club player. My strength was tackling." This was perhaps a little modest. Eddie was a dependable wing-half, who gave the side a deal of stability and defensive security, much as Andy Malcolm had done before him.

He said; "West Ham fans were all right, when they were on your side. They were good fans, West Ham have always been well supported. Win, lose or draw, they always come back."

When Eddie left the Boleyn Ground he was ready to move. "It wasn't such a wrench. I felt myself slowing down. I'd had my business part-time for two years. I knew what I was going to do, I'd planned it. A year or so out though, you miss the camaraderie, you're with a load of fellas, you have a laugh every game. There was a good social life at the club. I used to go about with

Bobby, Johnny Byrne, Alan Sealey. I've seen most of the players over time. Work is nine-to-five. West Ham were the best club for any youngster to go to. They were friendly, they played good football and they treated you well."

West Ham lost 16 games after November. There was only one win in the last eight games which gave a final League placing of 14th, only four points clear of relegation. This was a disappointing end after being top of the table in November. Malcolm Musgrove was top scorer with 15 goals. He missed only one game all season and was voted Hammer of the Year.

The French existentialist novelist Albert Camus, author of *La Peste (The Plague)* and *LEtmger (The Outsider)* was killed in a car crash near Villeneuve-la-Guyard on 4 May. The car in which he was travelling as a passenger was written off when it collided with a tree. He was 47.

Princess Margaret married Lord Snowdon to be in Westminster Abbey on 6 May.

Days of Iron – The story of West Ham United in the Fifties

I could never lose my gratitude for Ted

BY THE end of the 1960-61 season, Ted Fenton was history at West Ham, only three years after the high point in his managerial career. It was true" that after 1959 the team seemed to be going backwards, but there had been no serious complaints from within the club or from the press. The media had little to say about the details, a surprising fact given that Ted had been quite publicity oriented and had a relatively affable relationship the press. John Lyall rated him as being, "superb with the media".

The timing of Fenton's resignation and the probable cause are the most dramatic evidence of how West Ham directors ran the club. Questions abound about Fenton's managerial career at West Ham, and none is stronger than that surrounding his departure. Nothing in Ted Fenton's career as a manager of West Ham United is as significant in terms of analysing the nature of the club as the way he left; how and why it happened and its immediate consequences.

On 19 March 1961, the first sign of anything happening came byway of a report in the *Ilford Recorder*. This told of how Fenton had disappeared from Upton Park, and no one at the club was saying anything more than the prepared statement to the Press Association on 16 March 1961, to which the board had given its approval. The statement by the chairman read; 'For some time, Mr Fenton had been working under quite a strain and it was agreed that he should go on sick leave. For the time being, we shall carry on by making certain adjustments in our internal administration.'

The *Recorder* concluded its article by reminding readers; 'The Upton Park club are proud of their tradition of never having sacked a manager. The present position gives a distinct and undeniable impression that a compromise has been attempted to preserve that tradition.'

The sports editor of the *Recorder,* Trevor Smith, was right when he pointed out that West Ham had traditions to look after, but not necessarily those he had highlighted. What was at stake was not the idea that an Upton Park manager had never been dismissed, but that the club being doubtful if Ted was acting in line with other West Ham traditions. The board was working in something of the same way it had in 1932 when Syd King had been replaced. King had been, 'moved on', for reasons that had little connection with how the team were doing. He just didn't behave in a way the board saw as appropriate. His suicide prevented most people from remembering the fact that Syd was sacked. In 1961, sick leave was used, as it had been in 1932, to divert attention until things could be sorted out in a manner that would enable both sides to avoid publicity and give the impression of an amicable, mutual decision. The board was interested in achieving a couple of objectives; it wanted Fenton to go, and it wanted to keep the knowledge of what caused the break 'in the family' to itself.

Ted left football for outside business. Malcolm Musgrove told me; "Ted had a sports shop." Terry Connelly confirmed the family trade. "Fenton's son had a sports shop in Brentwood High Street." It was said that the former manager had preferred the whole issue not to be brought up again. The board and its ex-employee were in agreement on at least thing; what happened would be kept confidential.

If the board gave any protracted consideration to their decision about Fenton, it was kept quiet. There were no published rumours about Fenton's impending departure, nor were there any comments in the board minutes about the subject having been discussed. This may have been a purposeful attempt to keep things off the record, but a more realistic conclusion, premised on what the club actually did, is that the decision was made swiftly and was made by the chairman.

Until the board meeting that sent Fenton on sick leave, the manager had attended such meetings regularly. Five weeks before the fateful day, Ted had submitted the retain and transfer list to the board. In early February he was instructed to make arrangements for a visit to the ground by Inter Milan and for a proposed tour of Israel. When he went on sick leave, everyone outside, and most inside, the club claimed to have been taken completely by surprise. The majority of the board did not know that there were reasons to consider dismissing Fenton until the weekend before the Monday board meeting. The players at the time seemed genuinely shocked by Fenton's dismissal and unaware of the reasons for it. Most now do no more than guess at the possible rationale for the decision. They did not talk about it to the press after it happened. The public were also clueless. Even writers who had established close connections with the club had written nothing about a possible change.

As John Lyall pointed out; "No one, on the playing staff really had much of an idea why Ted left." The gossip was rife. There was some talk about Ted being upset about the sale of John Smith, or the whole affair being a backlash in response to the allegations about the Newcastle game at Upton Park.

Joe Kirkup has similar memories of the situation. "Ted just went off on sick leave and never came back. It may have had something to do with the senior players, but I couldn't say."

Fenton's staff were left to make guesses about what had happened, or draw what conclusions they could from rumours. Malcolm Allison came up with a remarkable story. "Ted got the sack. They were rebuilding the stand and he was pinching some bricks and paint. Putting it in the back of his car. One of the directors caught him." Ken Tucker seemed to think that he had negotiated a reduction in the price of equipment, but was only passing on a percentage of the savings to the club. Ken told me that Ted had been found out and was immediately dismissed.

One of the young players at the time, Derek Woodley, thought; "He had to go or be sacked." For George Wright; "Ted was unfair, he'd often skip off. Fenton was not a popular manager, he didn't get involved, that's why he left."

Andy Smillie conjectured; "I think Ted might have been a casualty of player power, especially the newer ones." Mick Beesley concurred; "Perhaps it was player power that got rid of him." Ken Brown had the same feeling; "Ted's departure was maybe one of the first examples of player-power. There was something of a mini-revolution."

Malcolm Pyke went some way to confirming this. "Ted was a bit soft, he wasn't the hardest. A few people ruled him." Malcolm was one of many players who had some respect and affection for Ted. "He was one lovely man. About 20 ex-players went to his 75th birthday up in Gloucester, just before he died." For all this, it is clear that Ted was, at time, not always valued by the professionals. One former player told me; "It was a first team v reserves game, at the start of a season. Ted was in the stand, he shouted at John Bond. John went marching up, right in front of him; 'If you could play at my level, you could tell me what to do,'John slaughtered him."

About a year before Ted's demise, the *Ilford Recorder* had approached Fenton to write an article about why West Ham had dropped so quickly from first to ninth position in the table. Fenton had told the paper that he 'was too busy to give the matter his attention'. The newspaper was to reiterate a familiar theme; how could West Ham succeed on a shoe-string? The writer asked; "Are West Ham seeking men of established repute, or are they persisting with the 'empty-kitty' policy? Only one man knows the answer AND THE MAN ON THE SPOT JUST NOW IS TED FENTON."

Debate about Fenton evaporated over the following months while the papers concentrated on which players might be coming or going. By January 1961, the club was rooted to the lower reaches of the table, but there was no public talk about Fenton leaving the club. The big rumours were that John Bond might be on his way, and maybe even Phil Woosnam, the Welsh international who had been West Ham's most expensive purchase.

After Fenton left Upton Park, within a week Pratt issued another statement to the press in which he said that the board had no plans to name a manager and that no one was being considered at that time. West Ham would be 'managed by the board' with the help of trainer Albert Walker and Phil Woosnam. This statement was not totally correct. The board was not talking to anyone specific, but Pratt and others had begun to make enquiries about possible replacements for Fenton. It was near the end of the season and West Ham were in no danger of relegation, so there was no immediate urgency. Fenton had produced the transfer-retain list, so the incoming manager would, in the first instance, just need to think about who he wanted to bring to the club, not that the board anticipated splashing out straight away.

When Fenton left, it was under two weeks before the AGM of the shareholders and, as such, no manager was in attendance at the meeting. Fifteen shareholders turned up, which was about normal. Following the financial report the chairman briefly reviewed the season and gave the usual thanks to staff and players. Not a word was uttered about the managerial situation; nothing about Fenton, possible successors or how the board were currently running the club. No questions were raised from the floor. It was almost as if nothing had happened.

The manner in which the board restructured the manager's role following Fenton provides some clues about his departure. On 13 April, Ron Greenwood was named manager. The board told the press that Greenwood's work would be 'concerned solely with the coaching and training'. All administrative jobs would be delegated to Eddie Chapman, the secretary, and his staff. Eddie would also take care of all West Ham's public relations. This split mirrored the division of labour which Ted had seemingly rejected when in negotiation for the job at West Bromwich Albion before he returned to Upton Park. This suggests that the board wanted the club to be run at two distinct levels, without the connections between players and the day-today running of the club developed under Fenton. In effect, throughout most of the Fifties, there was a two-way conduit between the field and the board. This new regime sought, as far as possible, to make the links between the players and the clubs administration a 'one-way street', using Chapman and Greenwood as circuit breakers. This also meant that managers' plans for the club would be restricted to the field of play, rather than the club as a whole. The latter had been Fenton's focus, as he openly admitted in his book. Syd King had ambitions of a similar amplitude.

As soon as Ron Greenwood turned up at Upton Park he became a focus of controversy. He was the first manager with no previous ties to the club. Years later he still described himself as 'the new boy around here'. Over-statement was never a part of Greenwood's make up; his description demonstrates that he understood how he was perceived by people who identified strongly with the club.

The decision to employ Greenwood was made swiftly, but it was not a snap judgement by Pratt. The board was making a statement about how it wanted West Ham to develop. Greenwood's qualities and appointment surprised most of the fans, but it came as less of a shock to the leading players or close observers of the club. The Hammers were in transition. No one already with the club could step into the manager's seat, and none of its former player was a likely candidate. John Cartwright described the situation; "We needed somebody to conduct the orchestra....but unfortunately I didn't stay long enough to be conducted." For John Lyall; "When Ron came he saw things in football that we were aware of, but didn't know the reasoning behind them." Derek Woodley reflected; "You could listen to Ron Greenwood for hours." For Joe Kirkup; "Ted was the last of the old school. Greenwood was knowledgeable." Noel Cantwell saw Greenwood as the hope for a new future at West Ham, and Ken Brown goes even further, claiming that if Greenwood hadn't come 'we would have been relegated'.

Brown was not the only player to feel that Fenton had taken them as far as he could. John Bond recalled; "About 1961, without a shadow of a doubt, the best thing that ever, ever happened was that Ron Greenwood came to the club. He was a different class, from a different world. Ron Greenwood did a lot for the players. He taught you about football, but he also taught you about life. I was very fortunate."

Brown added; "When Ron Greenwood took over he had a bunch of fit fellas, so he gave us the chance to play with the ball. Fitness was Ted's strong point, he had been a PTI in the Army of course."

Malcolm Allison saw Greenwood bringing good ideas and a concept of good football to West Ham."... the drive and fire was already there in the players." Malcolm Musgrove echoed many others when he told me; "When Ron came along that was a breath of fresh air for at least eight of us who were qualified coaches. We all thought we knew a little bit, but we didn't know anything until this fella came. He was able to get the best out of people. Make them feel wanted. I never felt so wanted on a football field as when Ron was there. He used to pick me up and make me feel ten feet tall. He told the side sometimes, 'give it to Muzzy, he knows what to do'. I thought, 'I'm not that good. I can't do that, but he's telling them I can.' He'd work on you during the week. He'd give you the confidence to go out on Saturday and think, 'well, I can do that.' That was the difference between him and Ted"

This was important. West Ham had to get a manager who could coach. This was not an imperative conceived out of the board's collective wisdom, it was an obvious necessity. To quote Eldridge Cleaver, one of the founders of the Black Panthers, the radical Black American organisation of the Sixties; "Too much agreement kills the chat."

What Greenwood had was knowledge. Although the players at West Ham were sharp, they were always going to be impressed by the likes of Greenwood and allow him to take the lead. Allison had created the appetite, now here was a person who appeared to be able to feed the same. Instead of banter, argument and discussion between players, there was now lectures and instructions, led by Greenwood. Many players, hungry for knowledge, listened with baited breath. Others, either disinterested or unable to grasp the ideas, were left behind. For one or two others, however, this formality did not match the more inclusive, informal attitude of the Academy. For them it was bland in comparison, and kept the power very much in the hands of one person, Greenwood, not by charisma, but by a kind of authoritarian pedantry.

So, prior to Greenwood, the structure of influence could be seen as follows;

Fenton —— Players —— Board

This is what is called in management parlance a 'flat organisational structure'. After Greenwood's arrival, the system gained 'height', simple hierarchy, and a level of detachment.

Board —— Greenwood —— Chapman Players

Although it would not have been a conscious intention of the board, this placed the means of production back into the hands of management. Before development of skill, tactics, the generation and knowledge of systems and, to a certain extent, team selection and salary had been disseminated between the players. As a representative of management Greenwood monopolised these 'means of football production'.

Pratt went to Greenwood because of Ron's coaching reputation; as such, the field of play would always be Greenwood's main concern. This would give the directors room to take the club along the path they dictated. Pratt didn't speak to Ron about why Fenton had left. He let his new manager know that West Ham had some very good young players and that he wanted someone to develop them into an aggressive, attractive, winning team.

There has always been a question as to why Greenwood joined West Ham. He was then the assistant manager at Arsenal, and although passed over once for the top job, would have probably have been offered the manager's post at Highbury sooner or later. Perhaps the exclusive emphasis on coaching which the West Ham post offered was telling. For instance, apart from Johnny Byrne, Ron never bought well. Ken Brown recalled; "After the 1966 World Cup, Gordon Banks was supposed to sign for us but Ron thought he was too old." Of course, the 1970 World Cup in Mexico saw Banks at his best, the 'miracle' save from Pele being a lasting testament to the brilliance of the man.

According to Malcolm Allison, Eddie Chapman had been 'as strong as Fenton' while Ted had been at Upton Park, but now the club secretary became the pivotal person in terms of the every day running of the organisational side of West Ham United. He was the voice of the board, the person that stood between them and the rest of the world. For the first years of Ron Greenwood's employment, Eddie handled all transfer negotiations and details. It was he who faced the press and the public in difficult situations. One such occasion was when a bottle was thrown during a match against Leeds. Chapman stated that West Ham would not be judged by the actions of one person in a crowd of 28,000. "By and large the Upton Park patrons are a pretty fair crowd. They appreciate football and are not slow to applaud football, whoever plays it."

He later remembered that during those painful years before the promotion season, the crowds were usually more critical of the home team than they were of the visiting side. Two weeks after the incident, Eddie released a letter to the press signed 'Miserable, Ex-Hammer', allegedly from a 60-year old man who had thrown the bottle. He had contacted the victim and asked if he needed financial help as a result of the injury. The offence had been caused 'by a split second of craziness' when the opposing goalkeeper had kicked a West Ham player. He ended his confession with a poignant note; "Mr Chapman, this is the end of watching football for me at Upton Park, but I wish the club every success. I cannot sign my name. I am not a yellow belly, but I am still scared." This self imposed punishment and general contriteness seemed to satisfy all involved, which was, of course, good for the club, relinquishing the board from any blame or need to improve conditions.

So, by the end of 1961 another revolution had taken place at Upton Park. The board had gained control and 'player power', that Fenton's personality had made room for, had been replaced by a system of board control, with Greenwood and Chapman as its ambassadors on the pitch and within the organisation respectively. The whole episode had been an exercise in covert activity. The 'old guard' of 'player power' was broken up. Allison was gone, Cantwell would soon be out of Upton Park, almost without a murmur. Bond would be threatened with exile in the near future and censured by exclusion from the first team. The new wave of possible militancy, including Phil Woosnam, and maybe the likes of Mick Beesley, were swiftly sold.

It was, without much doubt, a coup for the board, but for Malcolm Allison it was a bit like the bottle throwing incident, just one more example why West Ham was 'just another unsuccessful football club...where everybody hides from the situation and doesn't accept responsibility for anything'.

Maybe the above gives some idea of how the political culture of the club, more than any particular individual, rejected Fenton, but this does not altogether answer the questions surrounding his departure. People can adapt and change according to circumstance and Fenton was a 'ducker and diver' par excellence. In background he was not too far away from Matt Busby, Bill Shankly and Jock Stein. He didn't have their success rate, but apart from Busby, neither did they at the time.

What happens in organisations always has something to do with systems and culture, but what makes them unpredictable is the individual personalities involved and Fenton was indeed an individual. There was no typical response to Fenton. At one extreme Malcolm Allison had it; "Ted Fenton was useless as a manager. I wasn't very well liked at Upton Park. I never got on with Ted Fenton. I don't think that Ted Fenton ever really felt that he was a good manager. Charlie Paynter was there for years and years and Ted was just taking over from him when I arrived at West Ham."

Allison joined West Ham two months after Fenton became manager and while Paynter was still a consultant. Allison's opinion of both of them was straightforward; "They were incompetent, neither had any idea of what a professional football club was... it was a pathetic club, [the board] didn't have any idea what to do."

Towards the other end of the continuum, Ron Cater, for example, insisted; "Ted Fenton was a very nice person... I always got on with him okay." But maybe Albert Foan got as near as anyone when he said; "Fenton didn't react too well at times. Some players were a bit outspoken at times. Ted would rattle on for an hour and they would lose their patience. If you were a regular in the first team, then the manager was okay. He didn't talk to you enough. He was not the best, but he was goodhearted"

Mick Newman summed the situation up perceptively; "Ted Fenton was not a very good manager, but for the time he was a good manager. He would have no verbal abuse, no swearing. He was a bit remote, very much a collar and tie man - always smart. At times he seemed to do no more slap the team sheet on the dressing-room door and run off.

"He once told Billy Dare, when the player had asked him why he had been dropped, that he wasn't tall enough. Bill had been playing well for the club for years at that time and responded by asking Ted if it had taken him six years to work out that he was too small to play for the team. But Fenton could be more direct. When Freddie Cooper questioned why he was being kept out of the side by the likes of Noel Cantwell, Ted told him that 'he wasn't rucking good enough', although he was against swearing he could use bad language with effect at times"

Mick went on; "Ted and his brother, Benny, were fairly hard men, both had been boxers in their time. He had a big nose, Ted. Once one of the players told him to wipe his nose and Ted said; 'You do it, you're nearer'. But he had some good ideas and his 'southern confidence' made him persuasive. Tactically Ted was nowhere, but he might not have got the credit he deserved for what he did at West Ham"

Malcolm Musgrove shared Newman's feelings about Ted's coaching abilities. He told me; "In those days you had a manager, and a fella that helped him, who had more to do with the kids and the reserve team, not coaches or technical advisers. Tactically, and technically Ted wasn't the best. He wasn't a coach. That's why Malcolm was able to take over. We got more done with Malcolm anyway. Ted knew where his strengths were, he knew how to get the best out of people. He let Malcolm do the work and played the part of the front man. I'd have gone through a brick wall for him. But I'd have done the same for Malcolm Allison in a different way. I had respect for Ted, because he brought me into the game. He signed me, so I've always got a soft spot for him. He saw something in me as a player that I never thought was going to happen. I'd come in a bit late, I'd been in the forces, he only saw me play 45 minutes and he saw something, he gave me a contract. He knew the game, and he knew how to get the best out of a player, by talking to them, encouraging them or kicking him up the backside"

Noel Cantwell commented; "Fenton was not a coach, he was a trainer - a good manager but not the best - he was consistent, although Malcolm thought he talked a load of crap." John Bond said of Paynter and Fenton; "Neither of them did too much. Ted was as good as gold, but he never did anything, he never did any training. George Petchey remembered; "I couldn't talk to him without getting annoyed. He was always on about running - I did a lot of running." Dave Dunmore reflected; "I don't know if Ted was a players' man, he was all right. Bill Nick would come out on the training areas. You never saw Ted." John Cartwright saw Ted as 'a figure head' and being 'of the old school'.

However, a number of players gave Fenton much more credit. Ernie Gregory pointed out how innovative Ted Fenton was. Ted certainly promoted modern tactics. "We were the first team to eat steak before meals." Fenton's gift for innovation is exemplified by Ernie's claim; "There's nothing I see today that I haven't seen before. There's nothing new in football. We were told to put a ball between two players and you take two players out. John Bond and Noel Cantwell were the first of the overlapping full-backs [wing-backs] and the best pair of defenders in the country. We used to train at Forest Gate skating rink - it was narrow, so you could practise working in tight situations."

Ernie identified, perhaps, Fenton's main strength when he said; "Ted Fenton allowed people to have their head." Gerry Gazzard concluded; "Charlie Paynter was a very patient manager. Ted Fenton was so enthusiastic, with many ideas for improving the status of the club. Both managers did everything to assist progress by the club and give encouragement to everyone."

For John Lyall; "Ted Fenton had a very good knowledge of the game. He came up with plans, the 'F' plan and so on." These were one-off tactics, often curious and unconventional, designed mostly with Cup games in mind. Occasionally they had a retrospective element to them, Ted claiming the use of a plan that only he, apparently, had known about. Lyall continued; "He'd work things out for Cup-ties, and the other side would be wondering what he had up his sleeve. If they got a shock result he'd say the plan worked. They call it 'mind games' now."

Jimmy Andrews recalled; "Fenton was on to one-touch football, that was very unusual at the time. The heavy pitches didn't help with this, but I think he improved our game, to a degree, but I felt it was a little bit overdone. Due to the state of the pitch you couldn't do it. We used to practise it an awful lot. It certainly got a big place in football, as you can see with Manchester United shoving it about. But the pitches are so much better. Ted was infatuated with it 'come on get it, give it!' If you're a winger, which I was at that time, if you got it and you just gave it away…? It was natural for me to want the ball and go with it, but I'd have to give it to whoever was there. It was a battle with ourselves I think. It was good, up to a point, but it had its failings after that point."

So, Fenton was the man to bring ball play to Upton Park as a whole team tactic, but Ted did have a way with people. Malcolm Musgrove gave one example of this when his wife, Jean, dealt with Fenton. "Jean got on to Ted for a tea room, and we got it. Ted wanted a friendly, good, happy club, he was always looking along those lines, he wanted the players and their families to *be* happy. He believed that if the wife was unhappy, then the player wasn't going to play well, worrying about her. If the wife was happy, the player was happy, the team was happy and Ted was happy."

Ken Brown gave a more lighthearted example of Fenton's 'people management.' "George Wright used to go up to Ted's office just to get a fag. One day Fenton moved his desk and George came down complaining about it, his rhythm and been spoiled." Nevertheless, his skills were not always apparent. George Petchey told me; "I went to West Ham when I was 14. I got on well with Charlie Paynter. He would always talk to me, tell me what he was thinking. Charlie would tell you how he wanted you to play. Charlie Paynter was a good character, a good bloke to work for. He understood the game, I didn't have the same relationship with Ted Fenton. I went in the Army for two years. When I came out, Ted Fenton was the manager and I didn't get on with him very well. He didn't even know I was there. When I came out of the Army he hadn't seen me play. Nobody contacted me while I was in the Army. Once I got picked for the Army, I played in the Reserves quite a bit. Ted must have seen in the paper that I was from West Ham. I used to play in the 'A' team on a Wednesday, the Reserves on Saturdays. If we had a full squad, I wouldn't get a game on Saturday. It wasn't a morale-boosting time." George laughed. "It was a waste of time, I was getting on, I was getting to 20. If I wasn't good enough I'd have rather have packed it in and got a job. I never really spent any time with Ted. It took us a year to get to know each other and when we did we still weren't sure of each other."

Fenton did bring a deal inventiveness to Upton Park. Eddie Lewis recalled; "Ted Fenton was full of bright ideas. We used to put olive oil on our boots and hit the toes with hammers to soften 'em up. Ted brought in people like the athlete Gordon Pirie and John Salisbury [he 400-metres champion] to help us. I've worn Adidas since my days at West Ham, that's where I was introduced to them by Ted Fenton." It is often thought that the introduction of modern footwear was something that had come from Allison, but Ernie Gregory confirmed; "Ted was the first person to bring Adidas boots into the country." John Lyall also remembers kit innovations pioneered by Ted. "I think West Ham were the first to bring Adidas boots into this country. Ted noticed that the German players were all wearing short shorts, and he brought a couple of pairs into the club, next thing Malcolm does is get his missus to cut his shorts down. We were a bit taken aback at first but it was progressive. He was also a very progressive man." Mick Newman said; "Before big games Ted would take us down to Brighton, where there was a bit of a chance of warmer weather in the winter."

However, some might see the publication of *Nineteen Eighty-Four*, just before Ted's arrival at Upton Park, as symbolic. George Orwell's bleak anti-Utopian view of a totalitarian future, given West Ham's results, and how some perceived the new manager, may have seemed quite accurate. According Bill Lansdowne for example; "Fenton was a difficult man. Sometimes he wasn't fair, he'd say different things to different people. Mike Grice confirmed this feeling. "Ted was all right, but I thought he should have called you up and talked to you before he dropped you."

Others were not altogether impressed by Ted's contribution. Ken Tucker was of the opinion; "Charlie Paynter was a good manager, Ted wasn't. He was never straight-forward. He was against the players. Ted always used to ask why I didn't get on with him but was okay with his brother, Ben. I told him that Benny was okay. 'It's you that won't get on with me, not the other way round.' I remember Billy Moore would put up three team-sheets. Nobody ever touched them, if they did he'd go mad. I looked at the names and I wasn't there. So I went up to Ted's office. I went in and started to look round the floor, walking round his desk. 'What are you doing?' he asked. 'I'm looking for my name,' I answered; 'You must have dropped it on the fucking floor when you were pulling it out of the hat.. .the fucking teams you pick are no good'. The players always used to say he just pulled the names out of a hat. Hetold me to get out. Later he phoned down to say that he was sorry I wasn't on the sheets, and that he thought Billy had put me on the injured list. I was told that he was annoyed but I thought; 'Fuck him!' Once I threw my boots into his office and said; 'You wear them.' He told me that I could 'go tomorrow for all I care', but I got on okay with the directors."

However, many players liked and appreciated Fenton. John Dick had a lot of respect for Ted, although he agreed that 'he was not a coach'. He added; "Ted, ooked after players and he was a good manager." John Lyall recollected; "Before I underwent an operation in 1958, Ted Fenton told me; 'If you'd been fit you would have made your debut in the first team.' He had other problems to worry him, but he still had time to help. For Tom Dixon; "Ted was always very helpful, although when I used to ask Ted for more money he'd say no. Benny, Ted's brother, was a better player. Ted was always very helpful"

Derek Woodley said; "Although we had our rows, Ted Fenton was a gentleman." Bert Hawkins said; "Ted was a good manager and person. He was a player before. He never asked me to do anything he couldn't do himself." According to Jim Barrett junior; "Fenton was a good bloke. Him, my dad and Dick Walker played in the same position. When Ted first came back to the club he looked after the 'A team. Both he and Charlie Paynter did their bit on Saturdays." Brian Moore said that Ted was 'a nice man', and Doug Wragg remembered; "Ted was always ready to help. He told me if ever I wanted any advice, 'don't be frightened to ask.' He was a good manager."

"Doug Bing told me; "I got on all right with Ted, he was okay, straight. He was strict, told you where he thought you were going wrong." Harry Hooper said; "Charlie Paynter kept in the background, Ted Fenton was fair, never did his nut on the line."

This kind of response could be put down to diplomacy, dignity and loyalty. These qualities, that were evident in most of the former players, may well, 'guild the lily' a little. For example, a former West Ham professional, who was with the club for much of the time that Ted's was at Upton Park, gave me a glowing list of Ted's human qualities and then told me; "I wasn't very keen on the chap. There's very few people I don't like, but he wasn't a nice fella, in my opinion." He then instructed me not to attribute these remarks.

This was not the only ex-player to react in this way. As John Lyall said; "As a player, you have a loyalty to the people you work with and you're naturally sad when they leave."

It has to be remembered that even in the Fifties, football was a business. Like all financial operations that last over a relatively long period of time, it has become more complex, maybe more itself than part of something else, the community or the East End for example. However, the game was a much more precarious way to make a living then than it is now. I am particularly thinking of the top level. For all the ideas of 'family' and 'community', West Ham provoked anxiety in its employees and as such the 'dog-eat-dog' mentality at times. Tom Dixon recalled; "They didn't treat Dick Walker too well. He died a tramp so they tell me...sad, sad."

The end of Dick Walker's career was indeed sad. When Fenton returned to Upton Park he had to face the problem of all new managers - how to assert his authority over players who had grown accustomed to the previous regime. Dick Walker, the captain and the most popular player, was the first to have problems with Fenton. Walker's description of the situation is simple; "I didn't like him and he didn't like me." It was a clash between very similar men. Walker saw Fenton's actions as; "A matter of taking over from somebody popular and wanting to show you're in charge."

Walker had lost his place to Ken Brown, whom he called 'a lovely lad who I tried to treat differently than I had been by the senior players when I was young'. Dick once remarked; "The club put pressure on players after the war to save money and buy houses, but it had little effect...other players didn't think or talk about the future."

He hadn't got on with Fenton, and by 1957 Ted 'had made it unpleasant for me long enough. It was finally time to go'. West Ham didn't renew Dick's contract at the end of the season. The club offered him a job 'to attend to the players boots' at £4 a week - something less than 25 per cent of his playing wages. As the new season started, the former club skipper was doing the job he had done as a groundstaff boy 25 years previously.

Again, Tommy Dixon recollected; "Dick used to stud my boots for half-a-crown, [about 13p]. He'd ask if I wanted them ordinary or de luxe, so I went for de luxe. That meant he'd paint the tips white!"

Following his testimonial match against Sparta of Rotterdam, Walker became a scout with Spurs. He was popular professional, respected by players and fans alike, a bit like Julian Dicks in another era. As Tommy Dixon remembered; "You would walk round Plaistow and Poplar with Dicky and go in a pub. All the people would say; 'Hi yer Dick!'"

Maybe it was that popularity that made Fenton anxious about Walker. The former captain and centre-half would have been a popular choice as manager. A bit like Julian Dicks in another era.

It may be a bit harsh to judge actions from today's standpoint. What seems like injustice now, may well have appeared to be generous half a century ago. Dick Walker, for instance, saw himself as being well treated - "After all they even gave me three benefits." Former players who fell on hard times were occasionally helped, although rather than being given money they were allowed to sell programmes or chocolates at the ground. For example, Jim Barrett senior had been ill and unemployed for many months when his situation became known to friends and supporters. One of them wrote to West Ham in January 1956, asking the club to hold a collection before a match to raise funds for Barrett. For years, West Ham had allowed charitable organisations to raise money at certain matches, but that had ended in 1951, when the club limited charitable activity to pre-season practice matches. The board's reply to the request reminded the writer of the club's policy about collections and added; "We have helped Barrett on many occasions and were still trying to help him." The admission that the club had been helping Barrett was unusual, as West Ham preferred to keep its charitable acts confidential, looking to avoid the embarrassment to the recipient. At the same time it did not wish to encourage other former players to look to the club for assistance. West Ham continued to help Barrett with clothing and efforts to raise money from other sources. Nevertheless, it is hard to see this kind of patronage in a positive light, given the money the club made from the players.

Ted Fenton was, like us all, not a totally good person but certainly not a bad man. He was a man of his time and context, and it is clear that he wanted to do the best he could for West Ham United. He came to Upton Park about the same time as what came to be known as the 'Colombia rebellion.' The likes of Charlie Mitten were being poached from clubs like Manchester United to play for teams such as Sante Fe in South America. The money that was being offered was astronomical for the time - £5,000 signing on fee, £5,000 a year, £35 for a win, £17 10s for a draw, against a maximum of £15 per week in England. It was a time of change, rebellion and revolution in the game.

On joining Manchester United after the war, Matt Busby had taken the novel step of bringing in Jimmy Murphy as coach. Players like Bobby Charlton said Murphy had 'taught them everything'. Murphy saw the Busby Babes as his 'golden apples'. Fenton may have thought that he could use Allison in the same way, but Malcolm wasn't as passive as Murphy, who returned to the background after taking United to the FA Cup Final after Munich.

Charlie Mitten said he never saw Busby coach. "He never said a word to me about improving my play at outside-left. I always wished I had somebody who would read the game for me, tell me what I was doing wrong." This shows that Ted was of his time. Maybe if Fenton had gone to West Brom instead of West Ham, he might have emulated

Busby more closely. As it was, the smaller club could not sustain the kind of regime established at Old Trafford.

Again, much like Fenton, Busby had an overall vision of how football should be played, but he was not a tactician. Just after he signed for United, Noel Cantwell smilingly remembered asking him; "How do we defend, what system do we use?" Cantwell said; "He just looked at me. He must have thought; 'I've just bought you and you're asking me how are we going to play? You're a left-back, you're a good player, just fit in.'"

In the early Fifties, Busby set up a youth policy, sending scouts out across the country. In 1953 he fielded seven teenagers in a match at Huddersfield, showing a commitment to youth. For him, football was best played naturally. Management of football was about creating an environment for talented players to express themselves. This simple philosophy was to be overtaken by the emergence of 'football science' in the Sixties. Bobby Charlton recalled that Busby made Manchester United into a 'close-knit community, a family'. Busby was a master of the media and local journalists were recruited to this 'family', providing favourable coverage.

This whole approach is similar to what Fenton tried to do at Upton Park. It was more than a straight forward attempt to ape the bigger team. It is worth noting that there was very little in terms of skill, know-how or background between Busby and Fenton. Both Fenton and Busby had been PT instructors in the Army before becoming managers and there they learnt a lot about leadership. Indeed, what they both attempted was to 'lead' rather than 'manage' their clubs. What the two scenarios show is that leadership is relevant to some places and not to others. Fenton was able to reassess his situation, if more by instinct than anything else. In the end he did develop a management strategy that implicated the leadership of Malcolm Allison and this brought the club its success. Who knows what might have been achieved it the relationship could have continued?

Johnny Giles, the former Manchester United, Leeds and Republic of Ireland player, when talking of Busby said; "A great football man - a great manager, is not necessarily a great man." Giles went on; "Clubs didn't look after you. The players had the impression that the club would look after you, but when your usefulness is done, you're done, you're out. "

Bill Foulkes, a survivor of Munich and member of the post- Munich FA Cup-winning side, had to sell his medals. Another survivor from the air-crash, who helped pull Busby out of the wreckage, Harry Gregg said; "Whilst the club was successful and

I was successful, I was wanted. When I wasn't as good as I had been I wasn't required. Sentiment and Munich didn't come into it." This was and is the nature of football the business. We, the supporters, should not do this. To us the game is not about profit, but emotion and sentiment.

In the final analysis, circumstances had moved Fenton on. He had many ideas that were way ahead of his time. He was an iconoclast and entrepreneur, like Syd King. This meant he was a character that aroused a range of emotions and responses. Organisations don't really like that. West Ham, like most organisations, wanted predictability, stability and a logical, scientific approach. They wanted a technician, not a philosopher, to implement that science. We should not reject Ted Fenton but see him as the man he was. And, in his way, he was 'all West Ham', as Jimmy Andrews testified. "Ted Fenton was a very genuine person, he really loved West Ham, he felt he belonged there. That came through."

For Eddie Bovington; "Ted was the governor and that was it." And that is maybe all that matters. He did what he did, laying the seeds for the West Ham of the future. Andy Malcolm placed Ted in his historical context. "I was involved with the club when Charlie Paynter, Ted Fenton and Ron Greenwood were in charge. Mr Paynter was an absolute gentleman. Ted Fenton, when he came, of course, was a much younger person - more go-ahead. Ron Greenwood, when he came, brought his coaching skills with him."

John Lyall, who, although he gained much from Greenwood, and became a accomplished 'scientist' himself, also had a bit of that West Ham tradition in him. He was brought up in the club. Talk to John and you will see that he is also a bit of an entertainer. A nice bloke. He took on the best of the science, blended it with good humour and it matured into a philosophy based on decency. Maybe John summed up Ted Fenton and his contribution to West Ham best when he said; "During my injury-troubled career the character of the club and its people became clearly apparent to me. Ron took on what Ted had built, and developed it. You just hope that Ted would get credit for the players he brought to the club. I could never lose my gratitude to Ted. He gave me a lot of good advice. Being in the office I probably saw more of him than a lot of the players. He would talk to me, tell me he'd watched me play, say; 'You could do this...you've got to learn that...you could do this better.' With Bill Robinson and Wally St Pier, he was a great influence on my life.

Days of Iron – The story of West Ham United in the Fifties

'I think I'll have a bit of that jam pie and custard' — The tale of the Fifties

In retrospect it is clear that, as the Sixties dawned, the face of football and the world had changed dramatically over the previous decade. This was symbolised for many on both sides of the Atlantic in November 1960, when John F. Kennedy was elected President of the USA. This opened a new era for American and international politics, not merely through his youthful approach and good looks, but because of his broad appeal, not least to America's black population. It would not be long before the Right in the US would see the threat posed to their interests by a Kennedy/Luther King and maybe even a post-Mecca Malcolm X partnership.

In 1960, the European Nations Cup got off the ground. No British sides took part, but Noel Cantwell played in the preliminary round in both legs of Eire's defeat by Czechoslovakia. The Soviet Union, with the immortal Lev Yashin in gaol, beat Yugoslavia 2-1 in the Final in Paris.

Wolves reached the quarter-finals of the European Cup but were bundled out by Barcelona, 9-2 on aggregate. Glasgow Rangers went one better, but were to lose to Eintracht Frankfurt 12-4 over the two legs. The Final, at Hampden Park, was considered one of the finest football matches ever played. Real Madrid won 7-3, Di Stefano got a hat-trick and Puskas did the rest for the Spanish giants. That was five consecutive European Cup Final wins for the Spaniards. Real went on the win the inaugural World Club Championship against Penarol. The same two players got three of the five goals which destroyed the Uruguayans at the Bernabeu in 1960. Di Stefano had been European Footballer of the Year in 1959. He finished fourth in the poll in 1960, behind Uwe Seeler in third, team mate Ferenc Puskas was voted runner-up, while Luis Suarez of Barcelona topped the chart. The only English player to make the ten was Bobby Charlton, who tied for seventh place with Welshman John Charles, at the time, playing for Juventus.

Chelsea made the last eight of the Fairs Cup, but were unable to get over the obstacle of a Belgrade Select XI. Birmingham City made the Final, but couldn't make the most of the home leg. They were beaten 4-1 in the Nou Camp. A former Hammer, Harry Hooper, got a late consolation goal for City.

It was clear that Britain was, at the end of the Fifties, light years behind continental football. Generations of snobbish isolation had taken its toll. However, the new English champions and FA Cup winners of 1961 would soon lead the way in turning that around. In 1963 Tottenham won the European Cup-winners' Cup. West Ham, who, of course, became the first all-English team to win a major European trophy in 1965 (throughout the competition fielding only English players) repeated this triumph. By the late Sixties, England was beginning to be a dominant force in European club football.

For all this, the Fifties was one of West Ham's most successful decades, much more so than the Sixties (game for game) that has come to be recognised as the golden years for the Hammers. In League matches they came out winning nine more games than they lost, scoring 28 more goals more than they conceded. If FA Cup games are also included the record is hardly diminished;

The tale of the Fifties pans is as follows;

	P	W	L	D	F	A	+/-	Pts	Pos
Division Two									
1949-50	42	12	18	12	53	61	-8	36	19
1950-51	42	16	16	10	68	69	-1	42	13
1951-52	42	15	16	11	67	77	-10	41	12
1952-53	42	13	16	13	58	60	-2	39	14
1953-54	42	15	18	9	67	69	-2	39	13
1954-55	42	18	14	10	74	70	+4	46	8
1955-56	42	14	17	11	74	69	+5	39	16
1956-57	42	19	15	8	59	63	-4	46	8
1957-58	42	23	8	11	101	54	+47	57	1
Total	378	145	138	95	621	592	+29	42.8*	12*
Division One									
1958-59	42	21	15	6	85	70	+15	48	6
1959-60	42	16	20	6	75	91	-16	38	14
Total	84	37	35	12	160	161	-1	43*	10*
FA Cup	P	W	L	D	F	A	-/+		
	27	10	11	6	54	52	+2		

* Average

'I think I'll have a bit of that jam pie and custard' – The tale of the Fifties

However, in the Fifties it was not just the League and FA Cup games that grabbed the public attention. Reserve games were well supported - indeed some fans attended just reserve matches. The first team took the field for competitions such as the Essex Professional and Southern Floodlight Cups. Nearly 16,000 supporters turned up to watch West Ham lose to Arsenal in the third round of this latter competition in the 1958-59 season, and almost 17,000 saw West Ham lose 2-1 in the Final against Coventry City the following term. Although the Floodlight and Essex Cups were not officially first-team games, the Hammers did enter teams of first-class quality in these tournaments. West Ham's record in the Fifties in these Cup competitions was good;

P	W	L	D	F	A	+/-
36	22	9	5	88	63	+25

So, if these games of the Fifties are also considered, West Ham won 19 more matches than they lost and were 55 goals to the good. The Irons were good value for money too. Home and away you would have seen an average of nearly seven goals in any two matches following the Irons in the Fifties.

Maybe the symbolic ending of the decade came when Billy Moore, the Hammers Cup Final player and Fifties trainer, who joined West Ham from Sunderland in 1922, retired in 1960. At that point no one had been at the Club longer. However, football, like the rest of life, isn't really as 'hygienic' as that. As you may have sensed at the start of this book, the Fifties linked with the Forties, Thirties and even the Twenties. In a similar way, the same decade is linked by people and the events they live through, to the Sixties, Seventies and Eighties; the last Fifties first-team player to take the field for West Ham was Bobby Moore, that was in 1974. This being the case, I wanted to include in this work a couple of players who were with West Ham in the late Fifties, but who made their mark in the Sixties for different reasons.

I met Mick Beesley at his sports shop just outside Southend. His first game in Division One was in September 1960, a 4-1 defeat by Everton. It is true that Lyall, Scott, Hurst, Dunmore, and Bovington had come into the First Division side in the 1960 part of the 59-60 season, but this means that the start of their West Ham careers straddled two decades. Mick was the first Sixties player in the first team, in that he had not, like all his colleagues who had played in the first eight games of the 1960-61 term, played in the football decade of the Fifties. He recalled; "The night before my debut first team game at Goodison Rob Jenkins [the Hammers physio] had to give me sleeping pills. I scored after ten minutes -I headed it in from a Malcolm Musgrove cross. No one could catch me. Dave Dunmore finally grabbed me and said; 'Calm down boy.' That was probably the best moment for me at West Ham."

Mick's dad ran a garage in Plaistow, in Northern Road. He passed on when Mick was just 11. Mick told me; "I missed his influence later on". Mick's mum was a secretary in a furniture company. At the age of 14 his family moved to Harold Hill, in Essex, but Mick stayed at South West Ham Technical School as he wanted to play for West Ham Schoolboys and not Redbridge. He recalled; "At school, Mr Usher was very supportive." It was while Mick was at school that a former England amateur international, Vivian Gibbons, told him; "I'm the most capped England amateur, but you've already got more talent than I ever had. If you don't make it, it will be your own fault." Mick said; "At that time it took Geoff Hurst half-hour to turn round." For Mick, contrary to most people's view, "Geoff would have made it even if Greenwood hadn't converted him into a centre-forward."

In 1958, Mick was playing for the West Ham Schoolboys. At 17 he said no to the opportunity to sign professional for the Hammers as he wanted an England youth cap - in those days you couldn't get a youth cap if you were a pro. Mick, who had already represented London at youth level, recollected; "I had been promised a youth cap from the year before, when West Ham's youngsters had beaten England 7-1 and I scored five. I trained with Malcolm Allison. He told me I was daft, anything could happen in a year. I could have been injured, anything. In my first international youth game I scored four."

Of course, Mick finally signed for the Club. "I started on £9 as an apprentice. This rose to £18 when you signed pro." This doesn't sound much today but, according to Mick; "You could buy a suit for a week's wages." However these were no ordinary suits, "We all got our suits from Phil Seagle." You'd be lucky to get such a suit for under £500 today. Not a bad starting wage for a teenager.

Mick was another of the FA Youth Cup Finalists who made the West Ham first team in the late Fifties and early Sixties. "In the Youth Cup Final I knew Andy Smillie would miss the penalty. We played at Blackburn and there was a divot on the penalty spot. Andy kept moving the ball, but the ref wanted it placed exactly on the spot. Andy struck it great, but it just went high. Mooro nearly strangled the ref that day; he had a right go at him. The biggest disappointment of my career was losing the Youth Cup Final."

'I think I'll have a bit of that jam pie and custard' – The tale of the Fifties

When he got to Upton Park, Mick found it hard to get into the first team. "Ernie Gregory told me that if I could establish myself I'd be the centre-forward for ten years. I got 34 goals in the Combination, but Ron Greenwood wouldn't put me in the first team. I suppose he had paid for Alan Sealey, God rest his soul. I remember a practice match we had out at Goodmayes. I scored two against the first team and Greenwood told me that he wished that

Andy Smillie would play like me. It just didn't make sense."

Mick was a talented player. "I was quick, good in the air and had a good first touch. I think I was thoughtful." This made him popular with the Upton Park crowd. He said; "The Chicken Run either liked you or they didn't - they like me, as did a few girls who followed the team!" He smiled and went on, "I enjoyed playing with top-class players and learning form Phil Woosnam, Malcolm Musgrove, Ken Brown and John Bond. All of them influenced me. We played Aston Villa. John Bond was playing emergency centre-forward. I scored two. John said to me; 'That's how you play centre-forward then?'

"Mooro was the best player I played with. We were playing at Villa in the Youth Cup, Andy scored after 90 seconds and we were under siege from then on. Bob was like a colossus in the six-yard box. At one point he got the ball, strolled out and pinged the it right to my feet.

"West Ham was a friendly place. Harry Cripps was a great bloke. I remember he was told to lose weight and he went into Cassatarri's and ordered a plate full of cabbage. 'I got to follow my diet,' he said. When he finished he said; 'I think I'll have a bit of that jam pie and custard", We both laughed at this well meaning innocence.

"I lived in Romford, near a few of the boys, and the social life was pretty good. One time a few of us, including Brian Dear, Martin Peters, Geoff Hurst, Andy Smillie, Ronnie Boyce, went to a holiday camp in Hopton, Great Yarmouth, together. We put ourselves down for the football trials, to play Gorleston Town; we didn't tell anyone who we were. Gorleston had never lost to the holiday camp…we beat them 9-0. In the second week a few West Ham supporters recognised us and Gorleston refused to play us."

When Ron Greenwood took over the manager's role, things looked promising for Mick. "One of the first things Ron Greenwood did was give me a rise. He told me to keep it up and I'd be in the first team. Then, before the season started, he told me that he wanted me to go. He had brought in Peter Brabrook and he was getting rid of people who spoke up - he told me that my chances would be limited at West Ham. That's when I missed my dad. I should have refused to go, but if I had, I'd have found myself playing sub for the third team. I spoke a bit to Phil Woosnam who reckoned that Greenwood was a nasty piece of work, so I went." Even though Mick had been a prolific scorer in the Combination, he'd been allowed only two first team games to prove himself. In July 1962, he moved to Southend United with Ted Fenton. As I shook his hand and said goodbye, he remarked; "West Ham lacked consistency, it was maybe to do with the way we played." This seemed to sum up a lot of what I have found out about the Hammers' teams of the 1950s.

Record Retailer, now *Music Week,* began its top 40 in March 1960. The first number one demonstrated the change in popular music taste since the early Fifties. It was pouting, moody, Jimmy Dean clone, Adam Faith, with *Poor Me.* This was overtaken a week later by *Running Bear,* rendered by Johnny Preston. However, it seemed music might still need a Malcolm Allison of its own when Lonnie Donegan took over at the end of March with what was to become, alas, an enduring Cockney anthem, *My Old Man's a Dustman.* Soon the North Bank at Upton Park were adding it the growing repertoire, that, apart from *Bubbles* included *The Okey-Cokey,* and the perennial *Knees Up Muwer Brown.* Sadly we were still a few years away from singing Martin Peters' praises to the tune of Elgar's *Pomp and Circumstance.*

Also in March, John Smith requested a transfer. Fenton and the board looked for the best possible deal. The key was Vic Keeble; West Ham needed someone to replace the centre-forward and Tottenham Hotspur's David Dunmore appeared to be the man for the job. An even swap of Dunmore and Smith took place. Dunmore was ready to step into the first team and Bobby Moore was there to take Smith's place. Smith, a man with over 350 League matches under his belt, an Under-23 and youth international, became famous as the man who made way for Bobby Moore. He had been a bright prospect at West Ham, but never really made an enduring mark at White Hart Lane.

For all the innovation that had marked the late Fifties at Upton Park, West Ham seemed bound to carry some more 'traditional' traits into the Sixties. In November 1960, the 'Woosnam-for-transfer' controversy started in the press. West Ham needed money to buy a goalkeeper and other players. The Welsh international had been brought from Orient to West Ham for £30,000. There had been rumours that talks had been going on with Wolves about a possible deal that would bring Malcolm Finlayson, a sound goalkeeper, and Bobby Murray, a fair centre-forward, to Upton

'I think I'll have a bit of that jam pie and custard' – The tale of the Fifties

Park in exchange for Woosnam. Woosnam went to the chairman and asked for an explanation. Reg Pratt advised him to forget about it, and told him that the deal was off. A few days later, Woosnam asked to move. Reg, was shattered.

Woosnam, who had been playing under a microscope since his record move, was now scrutinised with even great rigour. The *Ilford Recorder,* reported a statement from Reg Pratt, which also appeared in the programme the following week. Copies were sent to each of the many fans who had written protesting against the deal. This was unusual for Pratt, who made every effort to avoid involving himself in publicity. The statement was published because what was happening with Woosnam represented much of the past behaviour of the Club. One section of Pratt's statement was printed in capitals, to make clear that; AT NO TIME WERE WE EVER PREPARED TO LET PHIL GO FOR A FEE, JUST LIKE THAT."

The supporters had never really taken to the graduate Welshman. The deals proposed for him seemed to be logical, given the Club's needs - remember they had John Cartwright and Ronnie Boyce waiting for their chance. As such, it appears strange that there seemed to be such coyness in connection with Woosnam's possible departure. The answer to this conundrum was that the West Ham board wanted to be seen to be prepared to spend big money to help the team. Woosnam did this for them, but now they were trying to sell him. The fans had seen their best players sold off too many times, Hooper in the Fifties, for example, and Syd Puddefoot before that. And in November 1960, in retrospect almost predictably, Noel Cantwell was on his way to Manchester United for £30,000. No publicity had surrounded the deal for Cantwell, even though he was a popular player with a successful career at West Ham.

A lot of fans might have shared the sentiments expressed in letters in the local newspapers; "We have bitter memories of the star players the board has sold, Goulden, Macaulay, Hooper, Smith etc. Now Cantwell and how can that be explained?" However, the fuss that had surrounded the possibility of Woosnam leaving wasn't evident. Cantwell's analysis of his own situation reflected the general felling; "It was a good deal for West Ham, they got £30,000 and had John Lyall ready to play in my place." Cantwell almost decided against accepting the transfer; "There were many reasons for wanting to go the Manchester United, but behind it all was the question of did I want to leave West Ham...I had been so happy there... and I don't throw things like that away easily." Cantwell was convinced, had he stayed at Upton Park "that the Club would have respected my opinion and there would not have been any trouble there. They just would have realised that I didn't want to go."

The week the board settled Cantwell's move, it heard from Eddie Chapman that after nine matches, home attendance was down 68,000 from the previous year while receipts had plummeted to the tune of £1,978. Two weeks later "plans for new floodlighting, which will cost between £15,000 and £20,000" were announced. No one labelled the floodlights as 'paid for by Noel Cantwell.'

As was traditional, the board could be understood to have 'pulled a fast one'. Some fans, with many years experience of the board, suspected that the whole situation had been planned well in advance. They alleged that the rumours about Woosnam were a ruse to cover the sale of Cantwell, the cash from which had been long earmarked for expenditure on the floodlights, a'la Harry Hooper. Fenton's youth scheme meant the board did not need to dip into profits to buy a replacement player, while the fruits of the scouting system had been cashed in to pay for ground improvements. The directors and shareholders were, as the local vernacular would have it 'laughing'.

Many see this strategy repeated over and over again at Upton Park. In the spring and summer of 1999, rumours about the imminent sale of young prospects Rio Ferdinand and Frank Lampard junior were rife. Such was the commotion that the sale of Israeli international Eyal Berkovic to Celtic went almost unnoticed. Needless to say both Lampard and Ferdinand signed new contracts.

From the ridiculous to the sublime. I met John Charles and his wife, Carol, at their home in Ilford. "I was one of nine children," John told me. "All different colours. Jessie, Josey, Bern, Len, Bonzo, Clive, Marg and Rita. Dad, who originally came to Britain from Grenada in the West Indies, was a seaman. Mum was always a housewife." It was an early summer evening and John was readying himself for the night shift at Tesco's. "It was Christmas 1959 when I joined the West Ham," he told me; "Me and Reg Le Serf were asked by Ted Fenton to go to trials at Cumberland Road organised by Wally St Pier. After that I joined."

John became the first black player to make the first team at Upton Park and one of the pioneers of multiracial football in London. 'Charlo' (as he was known to fans and fellow players alike) continued; "When I was taken on the groundstaff, Ted told me that I would get called a few names, but to keep kicking 'em. I went to Pretoria Road School. John Roberts, the head, was in charge of West Ham Boys. A lot of good players went to Pretoria - Alan Sealey, Frank Lampard. Another lad, Peter Turner, who was at Faraday School, and me were asked to visit Southampton. We went and had a look, but it was too far. The West Ham Boys team was a good side. We used to win everything. We made the English Schools Cup Final in 1959-60, but were thrashed 6-1 by Manchester. I was picked for Essex and London Boys. I went to England trials too."

John captained West Ham's first Youth Cup winning side in 1963 and won six Youth caps for England. "I will always remember the Youth Cup," he said. "It made history. I recall Greenwood saying to me; 'The next time I see you I want to see you up there holding the Cup.' He was so made up when we won. About 16,000 turned out at Upton Park that night, the Friday before the FA Cup Final. Martin Britt was brilliant, he was in everything. We came back to beat Liverpool."

West Ham had lost the first leg at Anfield 3-1, but Martin Britt had scored a vital goal. Back at Upton Park the young Hammers won 5-2, Britt scoring three. It was a team for the future. Apart from Charlo and Britt, there was FA and Cup-winners' Cup winner Johnny Sissons, and Division One players Dennis Burnett, Bill Kitchener, Trevor Dawkins (who also scored in the Final), Bobby Howe, and Peter Bennett. One lad who seems to have disappeared without trace was Harry Redknapp.

John made his League debut in the 1-0 Upton Park defeat at the hands of Blackburn in May 1963, the same year as the Youth Cup victory. John remembered; "I was playing against Ronnie Clayton that day, the England skipper. Martin Britt and John Sissons were also playing their first game. It was before that match that my brother-in-law asked me to come for a drink, down Grange Road, where my mum lived. I had two pints, and that's the least I've ever had in a pub." John smile the mischievous smile that over the coming years I'd come to know well.

"I got two goals for the first team, the first was against Grimsby in the League Cup and the other against Manchester United, when they won the League in 1967. They beat us 6-1. Martin Peters reckoned he touched it before it went in, but he got plenty, it didn't hurt him to let me have one!" John laughed at the thought.

Throughout his seven seasons at the Boleyn Ground, John played in the same defence as Bobby Moore. He turned out 141 times for the Irons. It was only towards the end of Charlo's career that other black players started to break into the First Division. "I remember one other black lad, Ernie Mackenzie, he played for South London Schoolboys, but he never made it into League football. I never remember any real racism, certainly not from other players at West Ham or our crowd. They would call out; 'Unload him - kick him!' I was always detailed to mark the likes of Greaves and Best. You got the odd 'black bastard', but that never worried me. My mum would go mad if anyone called me a black bastard. She said she was the only one who could call me that!

"I remember Greenwood showed one game on a projector. It had no sound, it might have been the 8-0 against Sunderland in 1968 - I think that was my best game. I remember Peter Brabrook saying; 'Chas, you had it off there!' Ron was a great coach, he knew the game, but he was a bit careful...maybe sly even. For instance, he'd just leave you out and not tell you."

John told me; "I loved playing for West Ham, but I got injured and couldn't get over it, so I turned to drink. I was an alcoholic and in the end had a breakdown. I was so bad, once, in hospital, I dreamt I was eating my sister in a sandwich!" John chucked gently, shaking his head.

It seems that John's problem was part of a whole drinking culture that emerged at West Ham in the early Sixties. John conjectured; "Maybe the team didn't build on their success in the Sixties because we were always on the piss. We went from the club to the pub. I was part of a hard drinking crowd - Brian Dear, Bobby Moore, Eddie Bovington, and Budgie [Johnny Byrne]. I used to live on the Barking Road. John Cushley was a good mate and Dave Bickles. We went to the Retreat after training at Chigwell. Greenwood never seemed to notice. We used to hide our cars round the back. Then we'd go to the Slater's Arms, a right old dive of a pub in Romford, but they did afters. We'd go to and from away matches to places like Newcastle by first-class train. By the end of the journey home the bottles of miniatures were piled up in a big heap and we'd thrown half out of the window!"

John left West Ham in the summer of 1971. He was only 26. Having turned down a chance to join Orient, he told me what happened next; "Carol's dad was a greengrocer. I was earning £65 a week at West Ham. My first week as a barrow boy I got £200. I soon had stalls all over Kent, but then they started to open the supermarkets and we went skint. Three years after the breakdown I was 16 ½ stone." When I first met John he looked slim and fit. "A friend who lives nearby, Gary Levie, said; 'We've got to do something about you,' and I started working with him on the buildings. I was about six months with him, and it got me motivated. I now work nights in Tesco's; Carol works in Sainsbury's. I've been five years without a drink. I remember going to the *West Ham Who's Who* book launch. I was on the orange juice with Budgie and over walks Alan Sealey with his orange and he said; 'You can tell who the F,F,F,F,Fucking drinkers are!' Alan had his illness, of course, he was never a drinker."

John looked back. "There were one or two players I didn't like playing against; nost of all George Best. I used to tell him to 'fuck-off over the other side of the pitch,' and he'd just laugh. I used to always have a kick-up with Jimmy Robinson and Brian Douglas. Terry Paine of Southampton was a hard player. I liked playing alongside John Lyall, hard as nails John. He would tell us; 'No one's gonna pass us down this side today, they might get up the other side, but not this side.'

"I was a good defender, good at winning the ball. I got it and passed it…When Ron brought in the idea of over-lapping, I could do that well, I got in a few good crosses."

Our conversation wandered to possible successors to Harry Redknapp, at the time of our first meeting the West Ham manager. We agreed that Alan Curbishley was a top candidate. John recalled; "They used to call his brother 'Blower'; he used to smoke 150 Capstans a day. He died a while back. He used to draw them right down." John mined the action and remarked; "Lovely fag!"

Before I left he told me that he had visited the West Ham training ground some time ago and introduced himself to Ian Wright as 'Johnny the One.' I didn't understand but he explained; "That's what they called me." Then he took me out to his kitchen and showed me a West Ham team photograph on the wall. John was standing in the back row. "I'm Johnny the One," he said again, pointing at the print. I looked for a few seconds and clicked. His was 'the one' black face. John chuckled.

What happened to "West Ham?

It took 27 years to better the performance of the 1959 League position. Many players, like Andy Malcolm, were left wondering why the club could not have built on the legacy of the Fifties. Andy remarked; "I can't say why West Ham was unable to build on what they did in 1959." Tottenham Hotspur, Leeds United, Liverpool, Newcastle Derby, Manchester United and Chelsea; what do all these sides have in common? Well, in the late 1990s, like West Ham, they had all been Second Division or new First Division Champions since 1950. Former European Cup winners Nottingham Forest had also won it. Aston Villa, another European Cup winning club, could only finish as runners-up in 1975. It is understood that West Ham has never been as 'big' as Spurs or Manchester United for example, but Derby, Leeds, Forest? If anything, these clubs did not have the potential fan base that the Hammers can command.

So why the mediocrity? In 1958, West Ham took with the Second Division Championship with some style and went on to surprise the First Division, punching well above their weight. They won their two trophies in the Sixties. Then, the next quarter of a century, produced just two FA Cup wins. Why didn't this Club done better? A club that in 1999 could fill their stadium for the second leg of the FA Youth Cup Final, which West Ham won handsomely, and then, just a few days later, get a near capacity gate for an Under-19 Final. The stadium might be relatively small, but why wasn't it been made bigger, or the Club seen fit (before the Olympic Stadium) ever seriously contemplated a move?

It may well have been a matter of finance, but finance is generated by will and action. West Ham may have not had the will to take action, but is there is more to it than this? John Bond had some thoughts. "West Ham really didn't build on the success of the late Fifties. It is puzzling that they were unable to do more in terms of their League performance, given the potential for their support, and the level of technical know-how in the Club at the time. It was strange, we had some good players. We needed the final piece of the jigsaw. We had Mike Grice, Malcolm Musgrove and Harry Hooper who were not bad. They were good wingers, they could play a bit. There was Johnny Dick, who could score goals up front. We had little Johnny Smith in midfield, bless his heart, who was a good grafter. Noel and myself at the back, Kenny Brown and Malcolm, Ernie Gregory in goal, it was a good little side."

Eddie Lewis chuckled when I asked him the question. "The Cearns family were interested in money and not much else. They could have made the ground a bit bigger, brought in a few more good players, but negative thinking meant that West Ham were not going to move on much from where they finished in 1959."

It is the supporters' educated guess that these considerations are both partly true.

What will happen to the Hammers?

West Ham is now West Ham. The mercurial East Enders. A whole mystique has grown around the Hammers. While other clubs sought glory and/or glamour, the Irons become the romantic team, steeped in legends about family, loyalty and friendliness, myths which have a deal of truth in them. In a way it would be a shame to lose this ethos, but it has to be said over the last decade this persona has diminished. But West Ham, unlike Manchester United, Arsenal and particularly the chillingly hollow Chelsea, still have the vestiges of a soul. Most supporters, for a long time the manager

'I think I'll have a bit of that jam pie and custard' – The tale of the Fifties

and still some of the players, are local people. It is something of a mystery to most West Ham supporters how, for example, Chelsea fans can situate themselves; apart from concrete nightmare that is Stamford Bridge, nothing about the Club represents a place or signifies locality; they could move to Disney Land or Alton Towers if finance dictated and no one would notice the difference. If this happens to West Ham, if the board were ever ready to sell the Club's identity, the point of being a supporter would cease. This is so much the case that the Board is seen as taking something of a chance by even contemplating a move from the cramped and limiting Boleyn Ground a few miles down the road to Stratford!

One supporter since childhood, recalled; "In the Fifties, a lot of the players lived around Central Park Road. You were aware players were local - that was part of the ethos of the Club. They were part of us." He remembered John Lyall showing him a picture of the club. The fan and the manager had both looked at it and John had said; "We're in there, part of our spirit." He also confirmed what I had found when talking to the dozens of players I have spoken to while writing this book. "Most players say it was the most enjoyable time of their career being with West Ham." If a club can achieve this type of feeling, whereby it can take a whole locality and community with it, to become part of it, then it has harnessed a truly powerful and enduring force. To lose this would be cruel from one perspective and patently stupid from any point of view.

Talking to and remembering the men I interviewed and researched for this book, I glimpsed the spirit of West Ham United: the Hammers: the Irons. It looks out on the world with a little puzzlement, but mainly courage and defiance. In the end, I will go with them; every one of them decent, honest and good men - the salt of the earth. That's said it. If you need more, maybe put this book aside and read it again in ten years time. Perhaps then *Days of Iron* will guide us into the future. The board and the management of West Ham would do well to

recognise that 'we', the supporters, do not want to be like Manchester United or Arsenal or anyone else, certainly not the sad and remote Blues of the West wastelands. We want to be ourselves, as we were, as we are and as we will become. This was epitomised by the fan who told me; "When we won the European Cup-winners' Cup you couldn't hear *Bubbles* because they were aping Liverpool singing, 'E-I-ad-e-o, we won the Cup.' That was a real disappointment." But the fair weather lot swiftly disappear, and the theme of our comfort and consolation is soon to be heard again.

In the meantime, think of those days, when the fight to get out of the Second Division seemed to be unending, but we did it, we went up, won the title, won it in style, the 'West Ham way'. We might, just might, do the same thing in the Premiership. One day…why not? If we don't, then let's at least make it worth trying, not by importing faceless mercenaries who will not have the love I have seen from the men I have met while writing this book. Let's look for the future in 'our kids', the people rainbow that the East End now is. Then, if we don't make it, so be it. I'll tell you what we can do, we can have a beautiful, silly, exciting, funny, frustrating, interesting claret and blue journey together, the thousands and thousands and thousands of us. We can try again, and again, and again. In the words of the bleedin' 'Okey Coley' 'and that's what it all about!' – UP THE IRONS !

Extra time

SHORTLY before finishing this book, I was sitting in Glasgow's St Mungo's Cathedral. One of the stained-glass windows depicted the coats-of-arms of a number of the city's guilds. As I sat contemplating the rainbow which they cast over the interior of the old building, their mottoes began to seep into my consciousness. My mind may have been too full of all the people I had seen and all the miles I had travelled in pulling the Fifties at the Boleyn Ground into the present. However, these words, minute philosophies in their own right, began to seem applicable to the Irons of half a century before. The Weavers asserted; 'Weave Trust with Truth'; this could so easily sum up the character of the Academy, who looked for a truth in the game, all the time understanding that this could only be wrought out of trust in the integrity of each team member. The team spirit generated between all the Hammers might have been encapsulated in the preaching of the Wrights, who proclaimed; 'Join All in One.' However, the Trades House, at the top of the window, cried, equally applicably; 'Union is Strength.' The Gardeners acknowledged; 'Gardening, of the Arts, the First.' Wally St Pier would have approved - he knew something about growing from seed.

In the left-hand side of the window, the Hammer Men of the city particularly caught my eye. These metal workers of the Clyde were the working brothers of the Hammer Men of the Thames who founded, Thames Ironworks, the primal Irons who would become the West Ham of the Fifties and now the 21st century. For these Scottish workers; 'By Hammer in Hand, All Arts do Stand.'

That which is the Hammers - the supporters, the players, the area of East London where West Ham United Football Club is situated - stands on the passion and dedication of people, the basis on which 'All Arts do Stand'.

The Hammer Men who contributed to *Days of Iron* all moved on from West Ham. Some after a short stay, others following many years' service. The words below make up the story of what happened to them after they left the club, but they are also reflections on the character of football over a decade and the years since the Fifties. At the same time they reflect on facets of players' lives outside of the game, although for many, these inevitably intertwine. For them all, their time at Upton Park, their *Days of Iron,* were filled with a panoply of emotions, as various in hue as the riot of colour so eloquently cast by the windows of St Mungo's. This would shape and inform the rest of their lives; in each of these men, their wives and their families, there is some blue mixing with the claret. That blood, collectively, is what keeps the true heart of the Hammers pumping, and the art of life flowing.

Malcolm Allison lives with his wife, Lyn, and their young daughter. Malcolm told me that he had a son in Hong Kong. "He's been there for 28 years. He worked for a brewery, San Miguel, in public relations. He's now in insurance."

Malcolm's personality might be summed up by the advice he told me he gave to Ron Greenwood when the former West Ham manager was England boss - "You're quite a good coach Ron, but never have anybody around you any good."

Allison spoke about the very last stages of his playing career. "The doctor said I was okay. I'd been training and played two or three games in West Ham Reserves. Then I was told I'd have to retire. When I left West Ham, I had a little club in London, but after about six months I started training with the kids, Bobby Moore, John Cartwright. They used to come up to my club. I just wanted to play. I went and saw Jack Chisard at Romford, he was really on the defensive. He was worried about the money I was going to ask for. I said; 'I don't want no money.' I signed a contract for no money."

After playing a few games for Romford in the Southern League, Malcolm became the soccer coach at Cambridge University. "After Cambridge my brother, who was in Toronto, invited me out there, and I met Steve Stavrous, who was a very wealthy guy who owned Toronto City. I took Tony Book and Charlie Fleming, two or three players. We won the League and the Cup that year. Stavrous was a Greek and he hated Italians, who had won the championship four years on a run. He wanted to beat this Italian team. If we won the last game of the season we'd win the League _ we'd already won the Cup. He gave me $6,000 for the players. I said; "That don't make teams win that money." We won the match and I gave them $3,000 and took them out that night."

When he came back from Canada, Malcolm managed Bath City, Plymouth and then entered into a successful partnership with Joe Mercer at Manchester City, winning domestic and European honours. Malcolm Musgrove, who was in Manchester with United when Allison was with City, said; "He didn't like it if Joe was getting the limelight in the *Manchester Evening News* for example. He was doing all the work. But you should only be worrying about the people that are really close to you. They know what your doing and that's all that matters."

It was only natural, for a man like Allison, that he wouldn't want to play second fiddle, even if this was the best thing for him. He went on to Crystal Palace, complete with fedora hat, huge cigars and champagne. Following a second spell at Maine Road, he took Sporting Lisbon to the Portuguese championship. He then had time with Middlesbrough, and with non-League Willington. In March 1986 he returned to Britain after coaching the Kuwaiti national side. He takes up the story; "I was doing some television work and I was asked if I wanted to go back into management. I said that I didn't, but I thought I'd like to be a consultant.. .just work with players. Bristol Rovers invited me to do that. I was only there two games and they lost both of them 5-2!" Malcolm laughed. "The manager walked out, so I finished up manager there." In fact, during his short period with Rovers they got a draw at Aston Villa in the FA Cup and beat local rivals City.

Now nearly 73, Malcolm still can't stay away from the game. While I was with him, he was making arrangements to watch a young player. "I just went on to do what I do now, scout for Arsenal," he said.

Jimmy Andrews confessed his feelings for West Ham were intense. "I loved the club right from the start, when I got used to the pitch. I liked the whole atmosphere. The warmth of the crowd. There was an awful lot that was good about it. Everybody welcomed you. Some places they say, nice to see yer, and they don't mean it, nothing behind it, but the Cockney warmth came through - it was really lovely. I remember the directors, there were two Pratts. I've been called a few Pratts since." Jimmy laughed.

Jim joined Alec Stock's QPR. "That was fine. I was living again. I became player-coach, then I became manager. I had a person called Mr Jim Gregory, the chairman at the time. He and I weren't on the same wavelength. He used to come into my office, have a word with Alec, who had moved upstairs. That never works. Then Gregory would come to me and tell me what I should be doing. I couldn't stand that.

"I had one or two clubs interested in me as a manager at that time. I wanted a player from Tottenham, Alien. He was going great. I told Jim Gregory that the man I want now is Alien. We had a bunch of kids that could have gone like the Leeds boys - they were as good as that. I had brought up and coached all these young lads. That team won the London Combination. I got on the phone to Bill Nick - Gregory was in my office at the time. Bill was coming to our games regularly. He's a very quiet fella, not a mixer at all. Each time he came there he'd hang about a little while, but I always had the habit of staying in there. At the end of a game I had to soak up how we had lost or how we won. Bill asked for £18,000. He said; 'He's a good player, he'll do you well.' And he knew because he'd seen QPR quite a lot. But that's what he wanted. He was the type of man to say what he wanted. He wasn't the type to barter. I said; 'That's a bit Strong,' and Bill said; 'That's the price, if you want him that's the price. I've got five clubs in after him.' Then Gregory came in, when I was still on the phone. He came straight up, put his hand over the phone -I can still go as white as death when I get angry. Gregory said; 'What's he asking?' I said; 'Eighteen thousand.' Jim said; 'Offer him three.'

"Bill was the top manager in Europe. Gregory was a car salesman. All the blood drained from my face. 'What?' I said, 'offer him three?' I called him a cheap bastard and chucked the phone and walked out. That was me finished. I was due a benefit, too, about £10,000.

"It was so sad, they were smashing kids. I'd really grafted on them and they were mine. Then Tommy Doc got in touch with me. We'd thrashed his kids a couple of times, so I went to Chelsea as coach. After that I bumped into Benny Fenton at Highbury. He was very different to Ted, a cracking guy. He asked me to go to Millwall. It wasn't much money...about £45 a week. I accepted, laughing. Little Eamonn Dunphy was there."

Dot, Jim's jovial wife, added; "I went to the toilet and, oh my god!" She laughed, remembering the diabolical state of the ablutions at the old Den.

Jim continued; "Then I went to Coventry. Noel Cantwell was there. I moved on to Luton with Alec Stock. We got promotion, and I worked with Malcolm Macdonald. I then took a job at Spurs - it's such a great club, it was an honour. The pay wasn't good, but Bill was such a genuine, honest man you were proud to be with him.

"Hoddle was one of the youngsters, and Graeme Souness. Jimmy Bloomfield, then the Leicester manager, got in touch. He asked me to be assistant manager. Bill asked me to stay, so I did, but the money never got better, and what you're paid is what you are. I told Bill I had no chance. Even Bill was on low pay, but he wouldn't ask for more money. But if you don't ask for anything in the game you don't get anything.

"I was offered the job as coach at Cardiff by Frank O'Farrell. When he went to the Middle East I took over. I was there for five years, and then did a bit of scouting for Southampton, under Laurie McMenemy, for a while.

"I was in Jimmy Hill's international side. We went all round the world for about ten years. I played in nearly all the games. There was Matthews and Budgie, the Tottenham players, John

Charles and his brother, Jimmy Greaves. Off every weekend I was. I was the grafter. You learn so much about confidence with people like that. So many of those players had super confidence in themselves. They very seldom blamed themselves for anything. They would shake it off. It was gone. If you make a mistake and it stays with you, then you go. Jimmy Hill could go on for 24 hours. He'd take a nap and could go on. He was an incredible man. Tommy Doc was the same. He didn't need sleep - he had tremendous drive."

Jim and Dot have one daughter, Hazel, who works for HTV. Dot laughed; "He was only naughty once!"

Jimmy Andrews was an artist Hammer. He scored 22 goals - 22-carat gold goals - in claret and blue.

Ken Bainbridge was a fast winger who was with West Ham from 1945 to 1950. Ken attended Ripple Road School in Barking and then Eastbury School. "The teacher I remember was Mr Bullen, the sports master. He encouraged me. I represented Barking Boys in the Hospital Cup, the Sun Shield and the Corinthian Shield."

Ken told me; "I have two brothers and two sisters who are all still well. I have a son from my first marriage who runs his own taxi in London."

After leaving West Ham, Ken did well at Reading, scoring 17 goals in his first season, a very good average from the wing. In 1953 he moved to Southend, playing 78 games and scoring 24 goals. "After leaving Southend I was offered a job at the Ford Motor Company looking after the football team, but it didn't work out very well as work came first. I joined Chelmsford City FC and played each Saturday. I stayed at Ford for nearly 30 years and then took early retirement. I now live in Kinmel Bay and am happily married."

Ken has an interesting proposal for contemporary football. "I think the game today is played with a plastic ball, which doesn't get wet like a leather ball. What I would like to see in today's football is a leather ball soaked in water and then put out to play. I liked the game to be played up and down the field. The tip-tap, how it is played today, does get a little boring.

"...I'll always remember the day I signed as a professional footballer. I thoroughly enjoyed the seasons I played for West Ham, Reading and Southend. I sincerely hope I have given you the best of my career as a footballer..."

Jim Barrett has three children, two girls and a boy. "I have six grandchildren," he told me proudly.

He spent a year with Birmingham City before returning to Upton Park as player-manager of the 'A' team until 1968. "I went to Millwall with Benny Fenton and later went to QPR with Les Alien. I was coaching for two years at Loftus Road."

Jim then went into licensed trade. "I got a pub in Halstead, Essex, the Napier Arms, for six years. I managed Cambridge City for three years before doing some work in a local sports centre. I still go to West Ham once or twice a year. Harry Redknapp makes sure I get any tickets I want."

Mick Beesley moved from Southend to Peterborough in 1965, but returned to the Essex coastal club a couple of years later, finishing his football career at Roots Hall. He recalled; "At Southend they tended to play the ball over you rather than to you. In my second spell there, under Arthur Rowley, Lawrie Leslie was the coach-physio. He was an army type. I helped out with the coaching, but did things with the ball. The players liked that. That year I was named as the players' player of the year. I was playing at the back. Andy Smillie told me that I should have played at the back from the start, he reckons this would have kept me at the top. Peter Taylor, the England under-21 manager to be, was keen on me becoming player-coach. But then I was sacked."

Doug Bing's wife, Joy, passed on several years ago. He now lives with one of his two sons, Brad, a printer. Football has left Doug with a legacy of suffering; he has had four new hip joints over the years. He said; "I haven't been to Upton Park for about three years."

Doug was good enough to make time to see me at his home on the South Coast. He played 33 games for West Ham, scoring on three occasions. He recalled; "When I went back to Margate I enjoyed my football. I was local and you didn't have to be so fit - it suited me. Alec Stock, then at Orient, was interested. I think it was Malcolm Allison who suggested I go back to Margate. So I phoned Aimer Hall and he said; 'Sure, we'll have yer back.' I forgot my boots. I left them at West Ham. Ken Tucker passed them on - he was a good player, a good left foot.

"When I came back to Margate I was in my niche - my level. I was sick to pack up. We played Walsall in the FA Cup. We drew 2-2 at home, lost 6-1 away.l got injured and was told I couldn't play again." For all this, Doug was philosophical. "Show me a footballer who doesn't have problems with his knees or hips when he's finished playing."

Doug told of his working days after football. "I worked for Hornby Hobbies as a setter. I was there while I was with Margate, after I came back from West Ham. If you played for Margate, you either worked for Thanet Press, where Brad works, or Hornby. I think a director of Margate was involved with Hornby.

John Bond met his wife, Janet, when he was in the Army in 1951 in Oxford. They have two children, Toni, and Kevin, a former professional and a classy player in his time. Kevin is now coaching at Portsmouth. John and Janet have two grandchildren.

John told me more about his family, starting with his father. "A few weeks before he died, he gave my mum a hundred quid that he'd saved, that's as much as he'd ever saved in his life. It never did him an ounce of good. She used to get the money, gave him about two quid a week. He'd saved a hundred pounds! My mother died the day before her 97th birthday. She looked after herself right up until she died. Her sister died when she was 105. I have two brothers and a sister. My older brother played for Colchester Casuals too."

John joined Torquay United in January 1966. "At the end of 1968-69 I mutually agreed to terminate my contract.. .1 went to Gillingham to coach. At Christmas 1969 we had eight points, but we avoided relegation in the last game of the season. We won 2-1 at Leyton Orient and it relegated Bournemouth. Bournemouth sacked their manager, Freddie Cox. The chairman of Bournemouth was sat in the stands at Orient when we beat them. He said to the person sitting next to him - he told me this afterwards - 'This Gillingham side have done very well,' and he was told that it was all down to the young coach. I applied for the job and got it."

John's spell at Bournemouth was followed by jobs at Norwich, Manchester City, Burnley, Swansea, Birmingham and Shrewsbury.

John recalled the arrival of Ron Greenwood. "Our first game under Ron was a 1-1 draw with Manchester City at Upton Park. Then we went up to Burnley and drew two each. Me and Phil Woosnam were injured and didn't play. We stayed at Porthcawl for a couple of days and then we played at Cardiff on the Saturday, the last but one game of the season. That's where the confrontation started between Greenwood and me. We were training on the Friday morning, prior to the Cardiff game on the Saturday, when he pulled me over and said; 'I'm not playing you tomorrow.' I said; 'What do you mean, you're not playing me?' He said; 'I'm going to leave you out.' I said; 'But I'm fit!' He said; 'I know that, but I'm the manager and I can do what I like. I'm not playing you.' I said; 'You're playing Phil Woosnam.' He said; 'That's right, but I want to bring Phil Woosnam back and I don't want to bring you back.' So I had all sorts of confrontations that year. They then wanted me to leave the football club. I could have gone to QPR. I'll always remember I stood in the roller-rink in Forest Gate on a Monday morning, when we were training there. He pulled me over and said; 'What are you doing? Are you going to QPR?' I said; 'No,' and he said; 'You'll have to take the consequences.' I said; 'I'm prepared to do that.'

So, I then played for over a year in the 'A' team. I was a senior player at the time. I had played more games than anybody else and I was just left out of the side. All the wives and all the players were taken to America that summer. We got to the sixth round of the FA Cup against Liverpool. West Ham took all the wives up there, Janet and I didn't go. I used to play at the Isle of Sheppy and places like that. I'd played 300 odd games for West Ham. That was him saying; 'You're not going to start to get the better of me.'

"One day I walked down the passageway from Thorne Road, where I was living, and it just struck me - it's not Ron Greenwood who's at fault, it's you. Get yourself sorted out. From then my approach to everything changed. I'd play in the 'A' team and I'd try for my life. I'd train, I never spoke to anybody about it, it was just me, and it was me who confronted it, and sorted it out. Some time after that I was in the treatment room at West Ham with Bill Jenkins, and Ron Greenwood came in and asked if I would like to come to Aston Villa in the League Cup. We won that game and I scored a goal. From there I never looked back. From there on in, I idolised the man. I keep wanting to and never do it, go down and see him. There are two people in my life that are real heroes. One is Lester Piggot and the other is Ron Greenwood. I'd love just to go down and talk to him because he stimulated my brain so much in terms of football, more than anybody. More than Malcolm Allison - and Malcolm did a good job.

"When I left West Ham to go off and coach, Ron told me that all I needed was a good memory. He said; 'If you remember all the things we done together, you'll be all right.' From being a 31-year-old when he came to the football club and thinking I knew everything, I found I knew absolutely nothing. He taught me all about the game, about coaching. Ron sorted my life out in terms of my personality and things like that and how to behave and everything. A while ago I got a note from Mickey McGuire. He used to play for me at Norwich. He was writing in the Norwich programme, saying that John Bond was ahead of his time in terms of his coaching, but if I'd never met Ron Greenwood, I wouldn't have known anything about it."

It seems that John's son, Kevin, is a chip off the old block. "If you'd have seen Kevin as a young lad. He didn't start getting hairs where you should have hairs until he was

18. He was always about two years behind everybody else, he was a slow developer. He's bigger than I am now, but if you saw him at 17 you knew he was going to be a big lad, and I based everything on Kevin being a player. He never had toy lorries and cars when he was a little lad, he used to have footballs. He used to love 'em. Kevin had exactly the same skills with the ball as me. Kevin took some stick when he played under me. Nepotism they called it. Kenny Brown called me one day and I said; 'You never had to put up with what Kevin has had to put up with, you'd have gone under. He was one hundred per cent right. The last game of the season, Kevin played for Manchester City. From the time he walked on to the pitch to the time he walked off the pitch, they booed him. Every time he touched the ball, the whole crowd booed him. Afterwards there was a demonstration outside the ground and he had to be smuggled out. Simply because he was taking the place of a boy named Mickey Read, who was an idol. The next year they made Kevin player of the year. If I'd had his qualities, I'd have played for England. But that's life, there's no good crying over it."

John played 428 times for the Hammers' first team, scoring 35 goals. He confessed; "I was a bit fortunate because I was always going to score half-decent goals from where I came from, being able to use the ball quite well. I could score from a distance. We played Sparta Prague at home in the quarter-finals of the Cup-winners' Cup. Ron Greenwood asked me to play as sweeper, behind the defence, to catch people coming through, but Sparta were not that kind of team and no one was coming through So, at half-time, Ron asked me to sweep in front of the defence. We were finding it hard to break them down."

Then, like a machine gun, John rattled off the details of the goal, it was imprinted on his mind; "I hit it from about 30 yards out, as it was cleared from a corner, it was a left-foot volley, it screamed into the back of net.. .that put us 1-0 up."

John continued; "The home match against Blackburn Rovers on Boxing Day 1963, we got beat 8-2. Ron Greenwood made one change, bringing Eddie Bovington in. We won 3-1 at Blackburn. In the FA Cup semi-final against Manchester United, we were told not to bother to turn up. We slaughtered them 3-1. The journey home that night was great. It was better than winning the Final."

Shrewsbury was to be John's final managerial posting, although he is a director of his local side, Witton Albion, in the Unibond League. "There are lads there," he told me, "who won't make Premier League players, but they could be better players. They go to work every day of the week, play on Saturday afternoon and know sod-all about the game, that's sad. There's a big tall lad down there, who scores goals for fun. I said to him; 'I don't think you're all that keen.' He's 20 or 21 and he could make a career." John has done a bit of coaching at Whitton and he carries out a little scouting for Portsmouth.

He recalled; "When I was with Manchester City I was in the three or four top managers in the country. At the time, I was on £50,000 a year. I got offered a job at Benfica, £75,000 a year. Tax-free! I turned it down. I went to Lisbon with my assistant at City. We were on the flight home and agreed; 'No, we don't want that.'"

While John was at City, the job at United became vacant. "If I'd applied for the job at Manchester United, I'd have got it. My fault!" He shrugged, raising his arms slightly.

Eddie Bovington and his wife Pauline were married in 1963. They have two daughters and three grandchildren. Eddie I said; "I took my grandson for the first time at Christmas, that was his first time. It was the game against Chelsea."

Ken Brown recalled; "Geoff Hurst was a bloody cracker of a player, but I must have played with Bobby Moore more than anyone else. I often thought; 'He's gonna miss this,' but he hardly ever did. One time he had ructions with Ron, but this was unusual. He always wanted it on the edge of the box, that didn't always seem to make sense, but as the 'keeper got it to Bobby, he was always in space. After I left West Ham, they could never find a centre-half to complement Bobby."

Ken was the last of the promotion team to leave Upton Park, at the end of the 1966-67 season. His testimonial in May 1967 drew a crowd of nearly 15,000 to watch the current West Ham team, that included Billy Bonds in its ranks for the first time, play a Select XI. Ken looked back at the period immediately after his departure from the Boleyn Ground.

"Frank O'Farrell took me to Torquay, John Bond had been there. For a time Ken was drawing a wage from Torquay and West Ham, as he continued to manage the pools promotion at Upton Park. When Frank left I went on to Hereford, to play alongside John Charles, the legendary former Wales and Juventus player. He would pick me up at Newton Abbot and bring me back after games. By that time John couldn't run, but you weren't able to trick him. I had a year of fabulous football with him. In a particular Cup match he was having lumps kicked out of him by one chap. I wanted him to get his own back, but he told me he would get even in the replay. In the return he again got clogged by the same player, and again he didn't touch him, but he did score three goals.

In the dressing-room I again told him that he should have paid the bloke back, but he said; "Three goals is enough punishment."

Ken moved into coaching with Bournemouth. He went to Norwich City to assist John Bond, and when Bond took on the management of Manchester City in November 1980, Ken became the boss at Carrow Road. Ken led the Canaries to League Cup success and twice into the First Division, sticking closely to the entertaining football he had learnt at Upton Park, but he was sacked at the start of 1987-88. He was very hurt by Norwich. He spent a week at Shrewsbury before taking on the management of Plymouth Argyle, assisted by Malcolm Musgrove. He resigned from the Home Park club in 1991.

Ken told me that when he was offered his current job, the managing director had asked him what he was getting. At the time he wasn't working and he told his prospective employer that he was getting nothing. Ken said that his employer-to-be immediately offered double this! He said that he had been given 30 rises since he started and was still getting 'sod all'. In seriousness, he loves his job and has great affection for his boss. He got a real kick out of assessing players for Terry Venables and Glen Hoddle with the England set up.

Ken has two children - Kenny, who played for West Ham, and Amanda.

Noel **Cantwell** made his final appearance for West Ham at Goodison Park in September 1960. He scored 11 goals in 263 matches, pretty good for a full-back. He wasn't to open his goal account until the visit of Sheffield United to Upton Park in February 1957, it was Noel's 119th game for the Irons. West Ham won 3-2 and Eddie Lewis and John Smith scored either side of Noel's effort. Before September 1960 was out, Noel was wearing the red of Manchester United in their First Division campaign.^He eventually skippered them to a 3-1 FA Cup Final victory over Leicester City in 1963 and the European Cup-winners' Cup win against the holders, Spurs, the following season. However, his chances in United's two successful mid-Sixties Championship campaigns were limited.

He recalled; "At Manchester United there was no coaching. Things were harder at Old Trafford. They had the likes of Maurice Setters. People were in the team on their own merits, there was little in the way of team playing. We played off the cuff. At West Ham you could play blindfolded, we played to systems. I recommended Malcolm Allison to Matt Busby."

He told me; "I met my wife Maggie when she was singing at the Dorchester on Valentine's Day. We've been married for 38 years. We had three children, Robert, who tragically died a few years ago, Elizabeth, who lives in Fort Lauderdale, and Mary. We have two grand-children."

Noel had experience as chairman of the Professional Footballers' Association and as player-manager of the Republic of Ireland, and this readied him for his eventual move into full-time management. However, over time Noel admitted; "I got fed up with football in the end. I was five years at Coventry, taking over from Jimmy Hill. He got them as high as sixth in the top division in 1969-70. I built a youth policy and we had a hostel for the young players. At one point we had five international youth players on the books. I went to Peterborough, and we got promoted into the old Division Three. They called me the Messiah!" Noel smiled. He continued; "Phil Woosnam phoned and I got a job with the New England Tea Men in the NASL. They were sponsored by Lipton's. The club later moved to Jacksonville, but I wanted to come back to England, and Maggie didn't settle either."

John Cartwright moved from Crystal Palace to Bath City and later joined Southern League Wimbledon. John became assistant manager at Highbury in 1985. However, by March 1986 he had moved on. "I left Arsenal backing up Don Howe. They wanted me to stay on as caretaker manager but I didn't want it. It was like West Ham, a pedigree club with the right ideas, looking to play the game the right way." John has also worked with the Charlton youth set up and spent some time in Kuwait. He managed the England youth team for a while, and worked with England managers Terry Venables and Glenn Hoddle.

Ron Cater told me; "I met my wife Joyce when I was in the Army. She was an ATS girl. We have one daughter, one granddaughter and one great granddaughter, who is now two years old and the light of our lives. We all live in Spain where my daughter and her husband have a bar restaurant, Bar Tropico, which is very popular. We have lived here in Spain for the past 13 years and love it here, the climate, the people and plenty of lovely golf courses.

"I loved every minute at West Ham. I still follow them and love watching them on the TV and reading about them. They've got a good manager in Harry Redknapp and I wish them well.

"I was sad to leave West Ham, especially leaving all my good friends. I had such good times there, but I also enjoyed playing for the Orient with my friend Arthur Banner. We miss him so much as he passed away a few years ago, but we still keep in touch with his wife and family.

"When I left the Orient, I went into the Kent League playing for Dover, then to Sittingbourne, where again I met up with Arthur Banner who was manager there. I enjoyed my playing days there as well.

"I have got such wonderful memories of the great Hammers. Thank you for getting in touch and helping me share my memories with you."

I visited **Eddie Chapman** at his home, not too far from Ernie Gregory. Eddie played for West Ham between 1937 and 1956, but he was with the Upton Park club up to 1986. Eddie and his wife, Edith, have two sons and four grandchildren, and wonderful kids they are too. "Both my boys were football and cricket potty. And athletics, but not the top level. They made the district team, but they never said to me that they'd like to go on further, and I didn't encouraged that because they may not have been good enough, they probably wouldn't have been. But they were both very fine cricketers."

Eddie retired two years before he had to. "I saw things were going to change so much." When I saw him he was just getting over a triple by-pass operation. "Sometimes, after the operation, I just I couldn't sleep. I sat in bed watching Scottish football in the small hours."

According to Eddie; "After Ernie I was West Ham's longest-serving employee. Over recent years we've sat together during every home game and pulled the team to pieces. Like a pair of old codgers would…!"

John Charles said;" Me and Carol have four lovely grandchildren; Jessica, who's eight; Sunnie, she's five; Erin, seven months; and Jack, who's six months. I married Carol in 1963 at St Matthias. We met through my sister who worked with Carol."

John Dick was transferred to Brentford in September 1962 for a fee of £17,500. He netted 23 times, helping the Bees to the Fourth Division championship. In 1965 he went to Southern League Gravesend, but in the Seventies was to return to Upton Park for a time, taking charge of the junior side. After professional football he worked for the Inner London Education Authority, at the Oakfield Sports Centre in Barkingside, and Hackney Council, still involved with teaching the game.

In a total of 351 games, John was on target 166 times. Four of this total were put away in West Ham's record 8-0 win over Rotherham in the championship year. Only Vie Watson, with 306, Geoff Hurst, who scored 180 times, and Jimmy Ruffell, with 164, have done better in West Ham's entire history. John's best season was 1958-59, when he hit home on 27 occasions. He has recently undergone a heart by-pass operation.

John still lives only a few miles from the ground, although he never goes anywhere near Upton Park and has not seen a match there for years. He confessed; "The last time

I went I actually paid to get in. I'm not blaming the club for that, because I didn't ring up to ask anyone for a ticket. I went along on my own and queued up at a turnstile with all the other fans." Nowadays the lads of Santos in the Essex Corinthian League, who play on a local park at Fairlop, appear to satisfy John's appetite for football. "They're as honest as the day is long and give it all they've got and I get a kick out of coaching them. I still get a buzz from being involved at that level."

John still sees Vie Keeble from time to time. "He pops in for a cup of tea and it's always nice when he does that." John recalled that the former young Hammer and Millwall full-back Harry Cripps 'was a regular visitor to my house, sadly no longer with us'.

The lofty inside-forward from Glasgow, born within earshot of the Ibrox Park roar, concluded; "I enjoyed my football at every club I was with and gave my best shot to everyone I played for. No one can ask for more than that, can they?"

Tommy Dixon has one son from his first marriage. Tom told me; "He hated football. However, his son from his second marriage is 'nuts on West Ham'.

"He's just gone to Australia on a year's leave from the Post Office. He hates it when the Hammers get beat. If it's on the tele, he says; 'Don't tell us the score.' He loves the old football."

He went on; "The football was different at Elm Park. Bobby Campbell was the coach then and Harry Johnson came. There wasn't so much finesse. I was told; 'When you get a pass here you just can't pose and look around, you've got to make your mind up what you're going to do with the ball.' This proved to be right. In my first game, against Aldershot, I got hit as soon as I got the ball. I played for Reading against West Ham in the Floodlight Cup. They said to welcome one of their old players back. I said to the lads; 'Come on, let's get stuck into this lot. We want a result here.'"

Tom remembered his return to Upton Park a while ago. "When I went up for one of the Supporters' Clubs do's, they said; "Put your hands together for the old West Ham centre-forward Tom Dixon. You could see the faces of the younger fellas saying; 'Who's he?' The older ones said; 'Oh Tom, how you keeping? You're looking good.' The young ones didn't have a clue who I was.

"I lost all my photos. Left them in a cupboard when I moved from Bishop Auckland. Stanley Matthews and everything. I got one photo of me in front of the Boleyn Castle, just when I got into the first team.

"I had a happy 13 years in the game. I was a bit of a worryguts. Waiting for the letter to come through the door to say I'd been retained for the next year, but I was scoring goals all over the place, but that's just the way I was I suppose. I used to love training and all that - looked forward to it."

In some places it has been written that Tom played with Dave Sexton at Brighton, but according to Tom; "I never played with Dave Sexton at Brighton. That was my worst day's work that was. Joe Harvey wanted me for skipper at Workington. I went up there and it was like Dodge City. He wanted to come to Newcastle and sign me, but I said; 'No, I'll come over.' He was playing golf. I didn't want to go. They offered me a three-bedroomed house and I stayed with them just under a year. When I went to Barrow I was given a house on Walney Island. I was about a year there. When they bought the floodlights, they gave all the old 'uns free transfers."

Although out of full-time professional football, Tom wanted to continue playing the game he loved. "I went to train as a pub manager for Scottish and Newcastle Breweries. I played for their Blue Star team. I scored six goals the first time I played. The 'keeper says; 'Ex-professional? I said; 'Yeah. Only finished a fortnight.' He says; 'I never saw any of those goals.' I was made redundant in 1984. I did a bit of painting and decorating with some mates. I hated that. Now I work for a guy building electric golf trolleys. Keeps me ticking over. I play a bit of golf.

"When I was in the pub trade, who should walk in but Lawrie McMenemy. He was going to be coach for Sheffield Wednesday. 'Put in for the team coach job at Bishop Auckland,' he said, 'you'll get it.' 'No,' I says, 'I don't want it.' He said; 'Come on, put in for it.' So I did and I got the job. Everything went well until I had to deal with committees. I couldn't deal with committees. All they wanted to win was the Amateur Cup. We got beat by a little team called Eastwood United, 1-0 on the Saturday. I went to train with the lads and told them that I wouldn't be there on the weekend. We were top of the league. My brother-in-law was in the hotel trade and he spoke to someone down in London and we came south as relief manager and manageress."

Tom got back to London and was soon involved with a future member of the Thatcher cabinet. "My boy from the first marriage wasn't going to school. He went to Highbury Grove in Islington. Rhodes Boyson, the head of the school at the time, phoned me and said; 'Your boy's not going to school.' He was roaming round the West-End looking in shops. I told my ex-wife that we had to get out of the trade. So I got the *Evening Standard* and just stuck a pin in it. The job was in cellar fitting for pubs in the west of London. I got made redundant and bought the house for me and me second wife."

Dave Dunmore told me; "I was in the Army for two years. I got a lot of football in the Army, but it spoilt things a bit. I was an apprentice when I left York. I finished my apprenticeship in panel beating when I was commuting from York to Tottenham. I went back into my old trade when I packed up football, with the same firm I started with. I did that until I retired, just last month. I'll go back to work a couple of days a week, just driving cars about, so my hands will be clean now." Dave smiled.

Dave and his wife, Barbara, met in a cafe in York. "We've been married for 45 years. We have a daughter, Ann, and two sons, Peter and Michael. There's three years between each of them. The two lads have got the same birthday, 9 October. We've got five grandchildren."

Top scorer for the Orient in 1961-62, Dave netted 22 in 39 outings, helping secure the Os promotion to Division One behind champions Liverpool. In his five years at Brisbane Road, Dave played 168 games, notching up 58 goals. "I was happy at the Orient. I still scored goals. I was a bigger fish at Brisbane Road. The training gear was rubbish. Johnny Kelly was all right at the Orient. He was a quiet sort of bloke but he made you think you were a better player than what you were - pull the others down and lift you up. I moved from Orient back to York, then to Wellington Town, which is now Telford United."

Dave scored a total of 132 goals in 369 League games. This shows his class and begs the question why West Ham saw fit to lose him at a crucial time in the club's development. Dave continued; "When I finished at Wellington I played for Scarborough, Harrogate Railways and then Sligo in Ireland. That was the best money I earned. I'd fly from Leeds on Saturday, play on Sunday and come back Monday. My boss at work let me have Monday off. Ken Taylor, who had been at York, was the manager of Sligo.

"I've just had my 65th," Dave told me. "My daughter arranged the party. A cutting was read out. It was written by James Lawton, in a morning paper, sometime in 1995 or 1996. He was talking about Orient in the 'good old days'. He went through some of the players and came to Dave Dunmore." Dave's voice rose... "'a majestic centre-forward,' he'd written. I just had to walk away from this. It went on 'good in the air, sweet on the ground.'"

After leaving Southend, **Ted Fenton** went into the pub trade. After retirement he passed on his sports shop to his son, Alan, who also played for West Ham, in the 'A' team in the Fifties. Ted went to live in Gloucestershire, where he was able to play a good deal of golf. He died in July 1992, aged 77, after a car crash near Peterborough.

Margaret and **Albert Foan** have two sons, Andrew and Patrick. Margaret has worked at the BBC for 25 years. "I got a Ronson lighter as players' player of the year once," Albert said. "I've still got it.' He showed me it.

After moving from Upton Park, a former Hammers inside-forward took interest in Albert. "Aimer Hall took me to Margate. There were two or three ex-West Ham players there at the time. It was a well-run club, but obviously on a much smaller scale than West Ham." After his period in the Kent League, Albert spent four seasons with Lowestoft, where his former Upton Park colleague Mike Grice was on the opposite wing. They both turned out for the East Anglians at Brisbane Road when they met Leyton Orient in the first round of the FA Cup in 1966.

Albert told me; "After I finished with football I became a rent collector, working from City Hall until I retired. I enjoyed the work.

"I was lucky to play for West Ham. The team were a nice bunch of blokes, I enjoyed it. When I was leaving, everyone was talking about Harry Redknapp.

"I don't really regret missing the championship season - the older you get, the more kindly you look on things. Norwich was a bit cliquish. If you thought you should get £1 more, they would talk to you and you'd often get it, but no one would tell you what they earned. The money is good now - and that's good - but the boot was on the other foot then."

When **Gerry Gazzard** retired from the game he returned to Penzance and ran a sub-post office in the town. "I continued to help out the local team with some knowledge from my experience at West Ham. I eventually retired early and have an enjoyable life. I have grandchildren and they all enjoy sport."

Ernie Gregory and his wife, Yvonne, have one daughter.

Ernie brought many good players to the club. "I went down to the Spotted Dog to watch a little centre-half, but it was a little coloured boy that caught my eye - that lad was John Charles."

When he retired, Ernie was asked by the board to continue coaching part-time. Following his record-breaking 51 years of service to West Ham, he worked two mornings a week for eight years. "I do miss it... go to all the home games."

Ernie was an architect of the modern West Ham, helping to build the successful Sixties teams. "I can see them all now - Moore, Peters and the rest.. .when they were on the ground staff. After work it was always over to Sid's cafe over the road."

It is hard to compare goalkeepers from different eras. Conditions, divisions, standards, defences and attacks change. However, when one looks at the Fifties, Ernie played for most of that decade and is by far the best goalkeeper to turn out at Upton Park during that period. Was he better than, say, Phil Parkes, who actually played more games? Parkes has a better average, about 1.1 goals conceded per game, but that was playing in the Eighties, for what was probably the best West Ham team ever. Everyone will have their opinion. Charlie Paynter reckoned Ted Hufton - the West Ham 'keeper of the Thirties - was the best goalie he ever saw, yet Gregory has a better average, conceding 1.48 goals per game compared to Hufton's 1.49.

Supporters who saw Ernie Gregory play will tell you that he was the best goalkeeper they have ever seen, better than Banks even. Consistently faultless, a great team player, with courage that warranted the badge of a hero.

Sadly, burglary has cost Ernie most of the memorabilia collected from his lifetime in football. But he retains a hold on the image as the big man, which had been gained at Upton Park.

If ever you meet Ernie Gregory, you are immediately hit by his tremendous, natural dignity. He is an honest person. Upright in every meaning of the word, he is able to combine strong common sense with an understated, but justifiable, pride in the life-long perfection of his craft. The West Ham United goalkeeper is that man you meet so rarely; he is chivalrous, provoking immediate admiration; he evokes respect from the moment you shake his big, secure hand.

In 38 games **Mike Grice** got six goals for Coventry, but this wasn't good enough for the incoming manager. "I had no real problems with Jimmy Hill when he took over at Highfield Road - he just didn't rate me. I went to Bournemouth when Bill McGarry came in for me." After a short stay with the Cherries, Mike returned to Layer Road for a while. Turning out for Lowestoft in the Eastern Counties League in 1966, he and former Upton Park man Albert Foan raided down opposite wings. Mike told me; "When I finished football I went back to being a draughtsman with the firm I'd done my apprenticeship with. They sold out and I worked for a couple of oil companies. I packed up work in 1991."

With a trace of that smile on his face he said; "When I can't sleep, I try to remember all the grounds I played on!"

Bert Hawkins told me that he and his wife used to go out to the Bahamas every year. "Our daughter lived there. We've got two daughters. We're quite happy, we've got our two grandchildren here."

Bert recalled; "After QPRI was approached by Cheltenham, then Bridgwater on a part-time basis. We wanted to come back to the West Country to start a family,"

He showed me photographs of Bristol Rovers players with the Lend-a-hand-on-the-Land movement. He made the point; "We all kept fit doing that in the summer, picking plums, cutting the corn. It was hard work, but we had some fun."

He went on; "After football I went all over the country as an engineer with the Reed Hoist Crane Company, working on overhead cranes. I liked that, but they went bankrupt. I did a couple of months at Fry's and played for their football club, then I went to the *Bristol Evening Post*, in the stores. I got promotion on the papers, as a printer."

Bert suffered his first heart attack at 61. Gerry Gazzard writes regularly he said, as does Harry Kinsell.

"I've got a black and white TV in the bedroom now," Bert joked, "but I don't know who to shout for!" He reflected on modern football; "The wages today have spoilt the game. You get what you can get, but people can't afford to come and see you. The crowd makes all the difference to the team playing."

Harry Hooper scored 19 goals in 39 games at Wolves. However, before the end of their 1957-58 championship season he moved to Birmingham, where in 105 League matches he found the back of the net on 34 occasions. In September 1960 Harry moved to his childhood love and hometown club, Sunderland. After 65 outings and 16 goals for the Rokermen, he went into non-League football. "I played for Kettering for a couple of years, then had cartilage trouble. As an ex-pro I was always a bit of a target. I went on to be a sales engineer."

Meg and Harry's daughter had played badminton for the county and their son, a sales manager, had played rugby at the same level.

"Harry remembered; "I went to a big dinner a few years ago. I met up with some of the players from my days at the club. I should have never have left West Ham. I can go to matches any time. I loved the life at the club. It had great supporters and atmosphere."

Vie **Keeble** retired from football with a back injury at the age of 29. He worked as a football reporter and became general manager and then club secretary of Chelmsford City in the Southern League. Chelmsford gave him a testimonial in 1985-86. West Ham sent some players to provide the opposition.

Harry **Kinsell** recalled; "I went to Central School. One of my masters had played for Albion as an amateur. I played for Cannock Schoolboys and Birmingham Schoolboys, and had a trial for England at Highbury.

"I had one brother, who played for Hednesford Town. He died about two years ago. He was six years older than me. I had two sisters. I've got three children, two girls and a boy, and five grandchildren."

Harry was given a free transfer in 1956 and went to Bedford Town after West Ham. When he finally went out of football he started to work for himself, taking an off-licence in Gere Road, Stratford, East London.

After losing his first wife, Harry married Vera, who was living in Gere Road when they met in Harry's off-licence. At the time, Harry was still going to Upton Park. "I went to matches when I had the off-licence. Vera used to come in to buy her cigarettes. She had worked for Newham Council and still does accounts work part-time." The couple married at West Ham register office in 1977.

Harry went on to tell me about how he found himself back in his hometown. "I retired in 1983, after a break in. They come at us with iron bars and hammers. We chased after them with bottles, but that was it - we sold up. We moved to a mobile home down in Kent. We liked that for a time — we had three quarters of an acre of ground — but the neighbours changed for the worst. Property prices up here suited us, so I moved back in 1990."

Harry is very much a Baggies man. "From school I had a chance to go to Wolves and Villa, but the Baggies were my club." Albion is still important to him. He enthused; "As a young player I admired Teddy Sandford at West Brom. He played inside-left." He opened a large book on the history of West Bromwich Albion. The page he showed me had a picture at its foot. The caption below the photograph claimed it showed Jack Vernon shaking hands with Dick Walker at West Ham. Harry told me it was wrong and that the picture actually records Sam Small welcoming Vernon to Upton Park.

Before I left him, Harry summed up his passion for football. "When I played football on the Saturday, I was waiting for the next Saturday, for the next game."

The highlight of **Joe Kirkup's** career was playing at Wembley in the 1965 European Cup-winners' Cup Final between West Ham and TSV Munich. However, he told me; "The last time I went to Upton Park, I got lost. But he remembered; "Ronnie Boyce was a good player. Ron Greenwood once said he was always the first name on his team sheet."

Joe left the Hammers in 1967. After Stamford Bridge he moved to The Dell for another big fee. Joe seemed more comfortable with the Saints. "Southampton was a bit like West Ham," he said. He turned out 169 times for Southampton; that made almost 400 First Division outings.

In 1975, Joe emigrated to South Africa, taking on the role of player-manager with Durban City, taking over from his former teammate Budgie Byrne. Things didn't work out for Joe in the Southern Hemisphere. "In the end I got turned off football in South Africa. I couldn't stand it. I wasn't working with good players, although they could run at 100 mph. The chairman was a gangster, someone had shot him on a plane. He used to be a racing driver and he would turn up at training with 15-year-old girl friends and shout at the players." In 1976, Joe left football and joined Byfleet Machine and Tool Co Ltd as a progress manager, working for the former Chelsea managing director, George Thompson. In 1979 Joe was managing the Rose and Crown at Upper Farringdon in Hampshire. He then went back into engineering for a time before running a sports shop near Guildford.

Bill Lansdowne invited me to meet with him at his home not far from John Dick, Ernie Gregory and Eddie Chapman. After his playing days, Bill stayed with the junior Hammers for around a year and then, having qualified for his FA coaching badge, he recalled; "I became the manager of Eastbourne [where Ron Greenwood started his managerial career]." Bill came back to Upton Park in 1967 to work with the youth team and later the reserve squad. "But when John Lyall was in charge *he* changed things. I worked in a garage for a few weeks, but Pat [Bill's wife] is a curtain maker and my brother was a fitter for curtains and tracks, so we started up our own business." In Bill's kitchen you could see the evidence of the family trade. It was good to see that he seemed to be doing well.

Bill continued; "We had four children, three boys and a girl." Bill junior, who was with West Ham between 1978 and 1981, works as a commentator for Swedish TV. Greg, the youngest, has just finished at university and will be joining Bill junior working on statistics.

At Orient, **Eddie Lewis** converted to full-back and played an important role in their promotion to the old First Division in 1962. Following his time with the Os, he moved to non-League football. "I was with Folkestone for around a year, starting in 1966." He also managed Ford Sports in the Greater London League for a time. Eddie takes up the biography; "I left England on 20 March 1970 and arrived in South Africa on 5 April. I was fed up with Britain, the unions seemed to be ruling the country and I had a couple of little girls, one three the other nine, and it seemed they had little chance in Britain.

"When I left football in England I went full-time with Royal London Insurance. It was Leslie Grade [of the entertainment/entrepreneurial family] that got me to work for African Life Insurance and the chance to come out here. But soccer was always my first love, so when I got the chance to work for a side called Jewish Guild, in East London, I jumped at it. We won promotion in my first season. They brought over people like Terry Venables, Bill McGarry, Bobby Moore and Geoff Hurst to help them with their game. It was through Bobby that I got the job. I loved Bobby. I used to give him 2s 6d to clean my boots and he never forgot that. He was always a modest man.

"I moved to Wits University - they're really White Waters University of Johannesburg. We got promotion in 1974 and beat Kaiser Chiefs the same season. I got to be national coach for a while in 1978, but Rhodesia declared UDI and that meant I never got to lead the national team out on to the field of play. I did some work for the South African team in France during the World Cup, team assessment."

Eddie is still developing players. "I've got some kids with Juventus. Gary Bailey and Richard Gough started with me. I started a lad called Demach who cost Benfica $2m recently. South Africa is a great country, but it's getting fucked up with all the crime."

Eddie told me; "I have one sister, she's two years older than me and also lives in South Africa. I have two daughters, again both are in South Africa. Julie is 40 - she's got three kids - and Susan has a six-year-old. He's only six but he looks as if he's going to be a good footballer and cricketer. My wife Shirley died in November 1990 and my mother died just six weeks later, so that was a hard time for me. But I'm with another lady now."

John Lyall was with West Ham for 33 years. He is West Ham's most successful manager. His playing career was brought to an abrupt end in 1963 after a long fight against injury. He was given a testimonial the day before the Cup Final, against Spurs. He took over as team manager from Ron Greenwood in 1974, winning the FA Cup the following year. He led his team to the Final of the Cup-winners' Cup in 1976.

Although West Ham were relegated in 1978, John rebuilt his side and became the only Hammers manager to win the FA Cup twice, in 1980 beating Arsenal in the Final. The very next season West Ham won the Second Division championship and were unlucky not to win the League Cup. The Irons took Liverpool to a replay at Villa Park. Liverpool were on their way to winning the second of their three consecutive League championships and would be European Cup Finalists in both of the next two seasons (winning the trophy in 1983-84). However, one of John's most significant successes was bringing the FA Youth Cup to Upton Park.

In 1985-86, Lyall's side became the most successful League team West Ham has ever produced, finishing third in the old Division One. West Ham reached the sixth round of the FA Cup three more times in the Eighties and although they also made the semi-finals of the League Cup in 1989, John Lyall was sacked as West Ham were relegated.

Looking at West Ham's form over the years, John warned me; "Don't make easy comparisons. If you look at some of the teams West Ham played against, they were magnificent sides. We had a few good players, but West Ham didn't have the resources. They would always find it hard to compete with six, eight, 12 of the top teams. That West Ham gets compared to them, I think is a credit."

Talking of the Fifties John asked; "In those days, who were West Ham? Were they any more important than Wolves? Compare any West Ham team with Arsenal at almost any time, or Tottenham. Teams with a permanent nine or ten internationals in their line-ups. Look at the teams who the Cup-winning West Ham sides of the Sixties beat. To beat Manchester United in the semi-final…you can forget the rest of it. That is a feat in itself. We should hang our hats on that and ask, well what else came out of it? We won the Final, we won in Europe. Few sides in those days, other than the top clubs, could dominate. The Busby Babes, were magnificent players, but West Ham, relatively, did equally as well with their youth policy and went far beyond expectations.

"I came down to Ipswich when I was manager at West Ham and we'd finished fifth or Sixth from bottom. Ipswich had one more game to play. I knew the club well, I came down to watch them in Europe. John Cobbold, the managing director of the club at the time, said to me; 'You've had a great season, John.' I said; 'Well, we didn't do so well.' He said; 'You're no worse off now than when you started playing at the start of the season. That means you haven't done badly. Look at that as good and anything else you get, be grateful.'

"It comes back to standards. When I first started, they'd say; 'All the best John, hope you win, hope you get the points today.' Now they say to me; 'I don't know why they play that team like that.' Or if they don't get the points; 'They're in trouble.' There's a difference there. They used to be up your backside, saying; 'Go on, good luck, we'll be behind you.' Now, if you don't do the business, you're out. You just wish that you could sit in the middle of those two things. There's that desire to get there, but there's also trying to find that niceness about how you're going to get it. I don't know how you do that."

After leaving West Ham, John did some work for England and Spurs before going to Ipswich in 1990. In his first season at Portman Road, the Suffolk side were still not good enough to finish in the top half of Division Two. By 1992, John had taken the Town to the Second Division championship. He told me; "Ipswich supporters were very respectful, like the West Ham fans, but it's a more sedate atmosphere. Ipswich fans are very loyal, they're good to their team, they try to understand the problems. It's more modern probably. This got us on to the subject of all-seat stadiums and the demise of the terrace. I couldn't talk about football without using my hands. Sit in a seat and you can't wave your hands about. We've developed the continental concept of watching football. You go, take your time getting there, you have some food on the way, you watch, you go away, have a drink. You go home, say that was lovely. You used to stand in a queue for about three hours to get into a Cup-tie. That's the modern game, and its finance, and I don't know how you're going to change that. You've got to have money to survive."

Almost five years ago, after becoming general manager and a board member at Portman Road, John retired, but he said; "I like talking to football people. I'm not being condescending, people like yourself, people who like the game. I had to stop playing at 24. I was then working six or seven days, 120 hours a week, for the next 30-odd years. I loved every minute of it, but we then got this place. I was two months away from 55 and I said; 'Well, we'll have some time with the family,' and I retired. We did the barn and the stables, both houses, we put extensions on. My son's a carpenter, so we worked together for three years and it's been brilliant, because really, I've learnt more about him in these three years than I did in the rest of his life, because I'd never see him. Yvonne just ran everything all our lives. Now the last four and half years it's been different."

John married Yvonne in 1961. He has one son and three grandsons, aged ten, three and 18 months. He has two brothers, Jimmy, in cars, and Roddy, who is a builder.

John continued; "Now, when you go, we'll go down there fishing." He pointed to the lake about 300 yards from the lounge window where we sat. "Now she loves fishing. I've got a tractor out in the fields. You need to look at other things in life, because there's a danger you get spoilt. It's not a working farm, although we keep working. There's a lot to do here. You need to see another way of life, you realise it's not too easy doing the jobs other people have to do. I get up on the roof, look down and say; 'Oh dear!' It does you good."

Although living a completely different life now, John told me; "I retain an interest in the game. I so enjoy having the three grandchildren. They're great fun. This place is worth looking after and I like looking after it. Football makes you a little bit insular. Do I really know what troubles you people have in your life? I don't. I get in the car, it's a lovely car, I'm up the motorway and I go and sit in the directors' box. You need to see the other side of life. Much as you see the fans and care for 'em, you still don't know what it's like to live what I call normal. You can't live normal."

John looked serious; "You mustn't forget where you come from. No matter what you achieve or what you get, you've still got to be prepared to look back and say; 'If it hadn't have been for that, that and that...'

"Ron, like Ted, was a great philosopher. You do philosophise as a manager because you see lots of things that you can give advice about. Ron used to say; 'No matter what team he's got, his team is his life.' If you were doing a coaching course, and someone says something, there's a little tendency to say you want to have it at our level. Don't do that, because his little old team that plays on Hackney Marshes, or Wanstead Flats is *his* team. If they get beat 3-0 he'll go home to his missus and say; 'I don't want that bleedin' dinner!' It's the same for the fan, doesn't matter if you sit in the stand, or stand on the terrace, or bunk in through the back door, it is still you and it's your life. You need to remember that, and the game needs to remember that too. We all have to retain that affection for the game and it's done through good memories. If you take those memories away from people, then they are less and the game is nothing."

John's life is indeed much more straightforward, but he still has his management problems. "My middle grandson tells me after a couple hours that he's going home, because I'm boring. I do my best. I've been doing thingj I don't want to do," he chuckled.

Andy Malcolm informed me; "I was married in 1958 to a lady called Allison Nash who came from Thornton Heath in Surrey. We have two boys, Nicholas and Paul. Nicholas is married and I have two lovely grandsons, Joshua and Rowan.

After Chelsea were relegated in 1962, Andy went to QPR in Division Three for a fee of £10,000. At this point, the Super Hoops were playing at the White City Stadium. Although picking up a nasty eye injury, Andy completed over 80 Division Three outings for Rangers. In 1965 he went to South Africa for the first time, to join Greek, Port Elizabeth side, Apollo FC. He told me; "I got divorced and re-married in 1967 to a young lady from Port Elizabeth called Marjorie Brough."

Andy returned to Britain to play for Brentwood in the late Sixties. He takes the history on; "I gave up playing at Brentwood when I took a Truman's pub as a tenant at Maiden in Essex, the Ship and Anchor, in the High Street. That was in 1968. The pub had a Sunday League side called Heybridge Social in the Chelmsford League. I got a permit to play in Sunday football, so I finished my career playing on Sundays with the lads in the pub.

"I left the Ship and Anchor late in 1976 and returned to South Africa. After seven or eight months I returned to the UK and took another Truman's tenancy, this time at the Lion, Latchingdon, about five miles outside Maiden and my previous pub. That was early in 1978. In 1981 my second wife and I got divorced and she got remarried. I stayed on in The Lion until 1986 when I came back to Africa. After a while I decided to live permanently in South Africa. I went back again to the UK, just to sell up. That was in 1988. Since then I have renovated a house and sold it, worked for a very nice chap called Eli Schlom, in a car wash, until he sold the business and returned with his family to Israel. After that I started working for a VW main dealers called Embassy Motors on an occasional day basis and still do today. But I must say I am now almost feeling retired.

"I've had a very chequered life both on and off the field but I wouldn't swap it for anything. I have had a very lucky life indeed and being in South Africa is, in itself, a bonus."

Andy Malcolm was ever-present in the side that won the Second Division championship. His biting play at right-half was a major factor in the team's success. "We knew we were champions in the dressing-room at Middlesbrough after we had won 3-0. The feeling was tremendous. The journey back in the train to London and then the reception the supporters gave us at the station is something I will never forget."

If you know anything of West Ham, English football or even general knowledge, you will already know much about **Bobby Moore**. So much has been written about his life and career after the early Sixties, it is redundant to repeat it here, and I have written elsewhere of how he was ill-used by football when he decided to hang up his boots.

Remember, he was a bit of a footballing enigma, as Vic Keeble, among others, has indicated. "When Moore was on the way in, we thought he was a bit slow, but we knew he was going to be a good player."

Those who did know Bob from an early age, the likes of his fellow apprentice at West Ham and cricketing team mate Eddie Presland, knew that, in essence, Bobby remained very much the East End boy, no matter how much he or others would try to create a persona of something other. His simplicity endeared him to many of his long-term colleagues. His intuitive dislike of pomposity, at points, made his relationships with Ron Greenwood and Alf Ramsey a little difficult.

This native quality could, however, bring its own problems. Each of us, from our backgrounds, bring things into our lives that are more or less hard to take by others, things that seem more appropriate to one person than another might think. As Derek Woodley illustrated, looking back at a moment when working with Bob at Roots Hall. "At Southend, the boys were swearing and the women were in an adjoining room. Bob's attention was brought to this. He went in and told the players; 'Stop effing swearing...the effing women are in the effing next room.'"

Woodley went on; "Things could always be different. If Bob had gone to see a specialist sooner. He would have found out that he didn't have irritable bowl syndrome." It is almost certain that if he had been still playing at the time of his illness, whatever club he had been with would have sought the best possible attention for their investment.

All the England caps, the obvious and magnificent feats of 1964, 1965 and 1966. You, good reader, know of this. You perhaps also know that he was the best footballer that has ever lived and I, and maybe you, saw him play, hundreds of times. Yes, I know about Pele, but Bob tackled Pele plenty of times. After Bobby Moore everything was downhill. Worship Beckham if you must, talk of Shearer, Cole and Yorke, but be sure, be oh so sure, Bob would have ate 'em. Like all the others - Best, Marsh, Bowles whoever - they would find themselves having run five yards without the ball before they knew Mooro had taken it away from them and set up an attack threatening their goal. Bobby Moore was given his football boots by God!

After finishing with Cambridge City, **Brian Moore** worked in the sales office of a pharmaceutical company. Now he spends much of his time on the golf course.

Brian was the eighth child of five brothers and two sisters. Two of his brothers played for League teams. One, Walter, played for the Irish Schoolboys before Brian. He had died playing football at the age of 34. His son, Brian's nephew, was watching at the time. Brian, although looking tremendously fit and spry, had been obliged to take early retirement following a heart attack.

For **Malcolm Musgrove** when he was playing; "The summer couldn't get over quick enough for me, I wanted to get started again." He recalled how after the championship the side stated to break up; "The club made a few bob, thinking maybe that the players coming up were ready to replace us." He began to recall his former colleagues

"Eddie Lewis still corresponds with me, about four times a year. He thought he was the best thing since sliced bread." Malcolm laughed affectionately. "Well, he told everyone he was. His granddaughter is a good swimmer. Shirley, Eddie's first wife, passed away, that was very sad, he and Shirley were very close. He's with another lady now, Stephanie.

"I saw Vie Keeble at Ken Brown's 65 birthday, he's still scruffy," Malcolm chuckled. "Brian Rhodes died [the former West Ham 'keeper] but we still keep in touch with his wife, Sylvie. She still lives in Australia. John Smith died at 42. They didn't come any tougher than Ernie Devlin, he was a right-back from Newcastle before he came to West Ham."

Malcolm mentioned Aimer Hall. I told him his first name was Almeric. "I never knew that.. .1 bet he got some stick for that," he laughed.

"Johnny Arnott was at Gillingham. Roger Cross is in Barking. Gordon Johnson was only with us for a little while and went off to America to be an opera singer. I was in digs with him at Mrs Pierce's. Roy Stroud's at Hillingdon near Heathrow. Peter Shearer's wife was killed in a car crash years ago. Tina Moore is still out in Miami."

Jean, Malcolm's wife, chipped in; "A couple of months before she got married, Bet, her mum, seemed to transform her. When she walked down the aisle I've never seen a bride so beautiful." Malcolm said; "I thought she was a bit stuck up at first, but she wasn't."

Jean told me; "I'll always remember when he went to Czechoslovakia with West Ham, he sent a card to some friends of ours and couldn't remember the address. He wrote on it; 'To Mr and Mrs Groves, next door to cemetery, near Manor Park.'

Malcolm remembered; "When I got to Orient they were bottom of the table. I was supposed to help them out with Bobby Mason, who they bought at the same time from Wolverhampton Wanderers. I scored in my first game, against Newcastle. We won that match. They were good professional footballers at Orient, but they were having a bad time. The further down we went, the more difficult it was to pick ourselves up. We started to look as if we might escape at one point, but we didn't, we got relegated."

Malcolm has had a number of varied jobs in the football world. He coached at Orient (with Dave Sexton), was player-coach at Charlton, chairman of the PFA between 1963 and 1966. He was at Aston Villa with Tommy Cummins, and worked with Leicester as assistant to manager Frank O'Farrell. He was again with O'Farrell at Manchester United, and managed Torquay in the mid-Seventies, taking over at Plainmoor after almost joining Bob Stokoe at Sunderland and so missed being involved with the Wearsiders' 1973 Cup Final win over Leeds. After Torquay he moved to the USA, spending time with Connecticut Bicentennials and Chicago Sting. He came back to England for a spell with Exeter City, but was on his travels again when he went out to the Gulf with Qatar, taking them to the Asian Games and the Under-16 World Cup in China.

"Jean loved the Gulf," Malcolm told me. "Entertained for three hours before a feast!" Back in Britain again, Malcolm worked with Plymouth and Shrewsbury.

He had been retired for just a few months, but told me; "Now I want a job. I've done some coaching at Winchester College, three days a week. I enjoyed that. My son lives in Winchester."

He went on; "I wrote to Harry about getting a signed shirt or something for my testimonial. He didn't even reply. Roger Cross got it for me. Harry was a young player when I was at Upton Park, but I know him, and he knows me - all he had to say is sorry but that they don't do that

After running a dry cleaning business in Dagenham, **Mick Newman** now lives in happy retirement in the English countryside.

Frank O'Farrell spoke to me from his home on the West Country coast, taking a break from French polishing. A classy wing-half, between 1950 and 1956, he played 210 games for West Ham. He scored seven goals, the first in his 42nd game for the club, the Hammers single reply in a 3-1 defeat at Ewood Park. Frank went to Preston in 1956 in exchange for Eddie Lewis. He made 118 First Division games at Deepdale and went on to become player-manager of Southern League Weymouth, before managing Torquay United. He moved to Leicester, taking them to the Second Division championship and the 1969 FA Cup Final. He became the boss at Old Trafford and then Cardiff City before branching out to Iran. Returning to England he worked as a scout for Everton and Bolton before he retired in 1993.

It had been in 1952 that Frank had reminded the board about his benefit. He was to be paid £750. He thus almost became the first player to be granted a benefit at an increased rate. However, Reg Pratt, vice-chairman and head of the finance committee, countermanded the original board decision. Although he didn't receive the benefit he wanted, Frank used this as a bargaining tool when the club wanted to transfer him in 1956. Frank told Ted Fenton that he would only accept the move to Preston if he was given a £600 tax-free benefit. The club did not feel he deserved this, but O'Farrell had learned how to stick up for himself and got £575. He thought the club was a good one to play for, but his handling of the benefit and a later testimonial showed him to be a shrewd, intelligent individual, determined to establish his worth.

I met with **Derek Parker** at his modern, comfortable house in mid-Essex. He looks slim and fit and appears to be a couple of decades younger than his years. Derek told me about his family. "I've got two older brothers. Dad was a manual worker. I lost my wife, Betty, 12 years ago, she was 49."

Derek still has feelings for his old club. "I still go to Upton Park every now and then. They're quite generous to me with the tickets and so on because my name is on the honours list, having played for the FA."

According to Derek; "Very few players played more games than me. And there were very big staffs in those days - people talk about competition." Derek laughed softly. "We must face the fact that if we could see films of when we played, it would be quite embarrassing."

Derek's mood became reflective. "I had wanted to stay on in a coaching capacity. After football it was difficult to settle down in work - awful! When I started work after football it was like being in prison. I was in a building for eight hours, being told what to do by little upstarts. Like all things in life, you don't know what you've got till it's gone. When I left football I worked for social services with handicapped people and in a psychiatric hospital. The money we earned was good, but it wasn't fantastic."

Before I made my way back to London, Derek mused; "I can't believe I'm 73 next birthday! I feel good. When I look back, after finishing with football, it was such a wonderful life playing for West Ham. It was such a lovely place to be around. I will always remember the companionship and comradeship of the players. We were close. It was just nice to among them all."

Eric **Parsons** said; "My mum had three kids that died early on. They were quite young when they died. I had a brother and two sisters, one still living in *Canada*."

Eric met his wife, Joan, at school. They married in 1948 - "29 December, in Worthing," Eric recalled. "We had our honeymoon at the Cumberland Hotel. I was playing on the Saturday. The Cockney boys in the crowd were shouting; 'Get off your knees your knees Parsons!'" (Eric is not a tall man.)

Eric and Joan had a son and a daughter, but their son tragically died at the age of 29, some years ago. They have two grandchildren, a boy and a girl. Joanne is 31 and Andrew is 18.

The couple has always had an interest in running their own businesses. Eric told me; "I went into poster and ticket writing when I was still in football, until I got called up. From Chelsea I went to Brentford. I played for Dover for four years, we won the Kent League. At that time we had a grocery business, we sold that in 1963. We had that for three years. We started up the cigarette vending machine business and covered the whole county. The whole family mucked in. I sold out to Imperial Tobacco."

Before I left him Eric said; "It's nice to be remembered."

Malcolm Pyke told me; "After leaving Crystal Palace I went to Dartford for seven seasons, then I had two years at Tunbridge. There was a young lad at Tunbridge, 17 years of age. I played in front of him, he was Malcolm Macdonald." Supermac was to make his mark as a prolific striker with Luton, Newcastle, Arsenal and England. Malcolm continued; "Then I had a call from Dartford. They asked me go back there for another two seasons. I got a pub in Dartford in 1969, the Plough, and was there 23 years. I was there 21 years to the day when I got a letter from Bass Charrington. I thought they'd be wishing me all the best for all those years' work. It actually said that I'd got two years to get out! - the pub was being taken over. I've been in this pub for just over five years. We've got a lovely restaurant.

"Andy Malcolm had a pub for a time. I walked into the Windmill and he was training there. I couldn't believe it."

Malcolm told me about his family. "My brother John died last year, a sudden heart attack. He was assistant sports editor at the *Daily Star*. I have a sister who has lived in America for 38 years. My other sister died about two years ago in Australia. I was the baby of the family."

Gillian is Malcolm's second wife; they have been married nine years. "I've got a son, Martin, he's 38, a good golfer, and Gillian's got a daughter of 32."

West Ham supporters have never forgotten Malcolm. He told me with a hint of surprised affection; "I still get loads of letters and photos to sign."

I spoke to Andy Nelson at his home in Alicante, Spain, just after the death of his former manager, Sir Alf Ramsey, the man who led Ipswich to the Second and First Division title and England to the 1966 World Cup triumph. Andy remembered how the knight of '66 had an incredible memory for players and would be able to analyse their performance after a single viewing. Andy skippered Ipswich and went on to management success with Gillingham and Charlton. He remains an affable and approachable man.

George Petchey informed me; "I met my wife Molly - she's from Brighton - after I came out of the Army. I was about 24. We got married when I was at QPR in 1955. We met on holiday in Torquay. A lot of the lads went on holiday together. It was a cheap holiday to drive down to Torquay. I've got a boy whose an accountant, he's got three boys, they're all keen on football and play for their school. I've also got a daughter, she's got three boys too, she lives just round the corner. Two of them play for the Brighton youth team."

George recalled; "QPR were very good. They came in for me. The fee was about six grand. There were a lot of pros there too. The training wasn't much different. There was more physical work, but I'd been doing a lot of physical work anyway, I'd had to get two stone off in a year. I was at QPR a year."

From Rangers, George moved to Selhurst Park in 1960. He made 153 appearances for Palace and was ever-present in Division Three promotion year of 1964. "I was at Palace six years as a player."

George was forced to give up playing through injury in 1965, but stayed with the South London club. "I was with Palace for another six years as coach and assistant manager to Bert Head. We got promotion four times. From the Fourth Division to the First while I was with them."

Following his long apprenticeship at Selhurst Park, George took the helm for himself at a number of clubs. "I managed Orient and Millwall and moved on to Brighton in 1986. Liam Brady asked me to come back to Brighton when he took over there. He wanted me to organise the youth; organise the whole thing, which I did. I left there in July 1998, when there was a change in manager. I've always done something in the game. I started analysing teams for Sunderland. I was there for about five years, between my spells at Brighton, and am now doing analysis for Newcastle."

Dave Sexton remembered his departure from Upton Park. "I was sick when it was time for me to leave because I loved it there and didn't want to go. But Ted Fenton had an offer from Leyton Orient. He accepted, so there was nothing I could do about it,"

Extra time

As manager of Chelsea, Dave won the 1970 FA Cup and the European Cup-winners' Cup the following year. In 1972, the Blues were runners-up in the Cup-winners' Cup. Dave took over QPR in 1976 and led them to second place in the old First Division, within a point of the championship. Four years later, by this time with Manchester United, his side finished only two points adrift of champions Liverpool, but United went to Wembley with Dave at the rudder.

Dave has had an active role on the international stage. He has worked with managers like Bobby Robson (assistant manager in July 1983), Terry Venables, Glenn Hoddle and Kevin Keegan. He organised the 'Soccer School' and the Under-21 squad, selecting West Ham's Julian Dicks to play in the Final of the Toulon Tournament in 1988, despite the 'Terminator' being sent off in the quarter-finals. After the 4-2 defeat against the French, Dicks stormed into the dressing-room and smacked a ball against a bucket, sending water everywhere. According to Julian, Dave told him; "Do that again and I'll knock you out!"

Dave puts all the success he has had down to the early years he spent as a player at Upton Park. He was old-fashioned inside-forward, who became one of the founders of the West Ham school of football philosophy, the Academy. According to Dave; "The sessions at Cassatarri's got really deep and intense. So many ideas came out of them that we took with us after we left the club."

That Ron Greenwood was not around at the time Dave was playing at West Ham is something of a disappointment for him. Ron took over five years after Dave left.

However, Greenwood had a strong influence on Dave's management philosophy and coaching technique.

"Ron was absolutely brilliant. By far the best coach this country has ever produced. His knowledge was unrivalled by anyone and the way he got West Ham playing was admired by everyone. I was so deeply influenced by his ideas and methods I had no hesitation introducing them at Chelsea when I went there as number-two to Tommy Docherty. I had become quite friendly with Bobby Moore, who was really making his mark in the game at that time, and I would ring him and ask about the drills and practices Ron put on for the Hammers lads. He was the first manager in my time to put on a tracksuit and go out and demonstrate the way it should be done. The game in this country owes him so much.

"Football has given me a wonderful life, with my time at West Ham the highlight. The club is unique in that once you are there, you want to stay forever. I don't know one player from my generation who wanted to leave. You have to be realistic and accept that you have to go sometime. But it still hurt me when that time came. I'll always have a soft spot for West Ham."

After his time at Orient, Dave went to Brighton, where he won his only honour, a Third Division South championship medal in 1958. This was followed by a spell at Crystal Palace, but injury in January 1962 helped him make the initial move into coaching and then management. As well as Chelsea (with whom he had two spells as manager) and Manchester United, Dave also worked for Fulham, Arsenal, QPR, Coventry City and Aston Villa before going full-time with the FA in 1983.

Dave was involved in a scouting capacity in the World Cup finals of 1986,1990 and 1998. In 1999 he was working with then England Under-21 boss Peter Taylor, making sure he was aware of every talented *player* in the country. His efforts paid off with a good showing by the team in the European Championships. Dave's expertise is still in constant demand.

Andy Smillie moved to Scunthorpe 'just to get Palace out of my system*.

Andy told me; "After a spell with Gillingham I finished up at Folkestone with Mike Beesley and Derek Woodley. I had about 18 months there before I had to pack it in because of a dodgy knee. I had an industrial cleaning business for four years and then went in with Mike Beesley and ran a sports shop in Basildon - I was a director for ten years before I got the cafe"

Tommy Southren remembered; "I lived in digs for two years in Birmingham. Mrs Carl was the landlady. When I married we got a club house. This was rent-free."

He also recalled; "Moving to Dean Court from Villa we travelled down in the back of the pantechnicon, sitting on easy chairs in the back. It was hot, the summer of 1959." Tommy played 64 Third Division games for Bournemouth, scoring 11 goals.

He went on; "When I finished at Bournemouth I started a 29-year stint with Shredded Wheat. I took early retirement."

Tommy and Elsie have two children. Their son, born in 1960, is a scientist; their daughter works in school catering. They have four grandchildren.

Wally St Pier was given a well-deserved testimonial in May 1975. He retired the following year. Wally passed away in 1989

I spoke to **Ken Tucker,** a former pupil of Godwin School, in Florida, his second home. He spends his summers based in Basildon. Ken values his stays in America. He missed the West Ham's centenary dinner because he was there at the time, but he sees former colleagues every now and then. For example he often meets up with Ron Wilson, who lives in Virginia.

Ken said; "When I moved to Margate I was on £20 a week. I was only getting £17 at Upton Park. I got a job as a sales manger with a victuallers company. They found my name could open a few doors for them. I then got a pub, the Bell in Rainham. I was there for nine years. After that I joined my son in the betting-shop business. We ended up with six shops."

Ken's son is an owner of trotting horses in the States.

Albert Walker retired in 1980 after 34 years' combined service at West Ham as a player and a coach. He passed away in 1993, aged 83.

When **Dick Walker's** career neared its end and he was no longer an automatic choice, he switched his attention to helping the younger players with the same enthusiasm as before. After his final first-team appearance in February 1953, it was another four years before he hung up his boots completely, completing over 200 appearances for the Reserves and 'A team. His final game for West Ham was in 1957. Dick was given a well-deserved testimonial match in October 1957 and later became a full time member of the scouting staff at White Hart Lane, a role he carried out for many years. Dick's later life was not happy. He was beset with poor health that required him to spend long spells in hospital. His death, in February 1988 at the age of 75, represented a sad demise for a man whose greatest legacy was the help he gave to young players making their way in the game.

Marcella and **George Wright** have one son, who has taken over the video business they started in the mid-Eighties.

George went to Leyton Orient with Alec Stock just as West Ham started their promotion campaign. He began with an own-goal against Bristol Rovers. He recalled; "There wasn't as many players there and the football wasn't as flowing, but we were well looked after. The president was a good man. He'd take us on outings to Shoeburyness every year at the end of the season. He'd also take us down to his factory to take our pick of shoes and stockings and he put on a dinner-dance. One year we needed a win or a point to avoid relegation. We got the draw and he treated us like royalty, sending us all on a free holiday to Germany."

George made 87 League appearances for the Os. In 1961, he moved on to Gillingham, making just four appearances. He told me that a man who was walking round the country visiting all the ex-Gillingham players recently called on him. He just knocked on the door, unannounced. It was a hot day and he was sweating. He had a little rucksack on his back. It's always nice to know there is someone around a little bit nuttier than yourself!

George finished his football career with Ramsgate in 1963

Derek Woodley's departure from Upton Park was a bit of a surprise. He explained; "I had first wife troubles. I was asked if I wanted a move. Peter Brabrook was on his way to West Ham - I didn't really want to play football. I thought a move away might change things - things had gone sour for me at West Ham. I was very young."

Twenty-four goals and 181 League games later, in 1967, Derek moved to Charlton, but returned to the Shrimpers after only four months at The Valley. In 1970 he made the short trip to Gillingham. "In the end I went to Folkestone and then worked for Prudential Insurance. I never fancied managing, there's got to be something wrong with you if you want to do that.

"I've been 30 years married now. I have five brothers and a sister. Annette and I have four children. I've got two grandchildren in Australia and one on the way and two in Britain."

After Mansfield, **Doug Wragg** moved to Rochdale. He said; "If ever you get told that it's always raining in Manchester, then believe it." He appeared in the first leg of the 1962 League Cup Final (it was then contested on a home and away basis) for the Dale. The Fourth Division side, the only one to make a major Final, came up against Norwich, but during the course of the game Doug broke his ankle and as there were no substitutes at the time, Rochdale's fans had to watch their ten-man side go down 3-0. At Carrow Road they defended well and were unlucky to lose 1-0.

Doug Wragg's next stop was to Chesterfield, with whom he picked up a bad thigh injury at Meadow Lane and was out for some time. As he was recovering, he was involved in a serious car crash in which one of his teammates, the former Norwich and Derby centre-forward Ralph Hunt, was killed. Doug got back for the last 14 games of the Spireites' season, but moved on to spend a year in the Midland League with Grantham Town before giving up the professional game to go back to his first employer, making car seats.

Chronology of West Ham in the Fifties

1950 January July September

- Reg Pratt elected chairman after the death of W. J. Cearns.
- Charlie Paynter retires; Ted Fenton appointed to succeed him as manager.
- Testimonial match for Charlie Paynter, with the elite of the Football Association and the Football League in attendance.

1951 February

1953 April

1955 March – April

1956 March – August

1957 April – September, OctoberNovember

Malcolm Allison is transferred to West Ham from Charlton Athletic for £7,000.

First Floodlit match at Upton Park - a friendly v Spurs (West Ham win 2-1).

First televised match from Upton Park v Holland Sports (0-0). The Boleyn Castle is demolished.

First League game under floodlights v Bury (West Ham win 3-2). Eddie Chapman is named secretary.

Youth Cup Final v Manchester United (West Ham lost 8-2 on aggregate).

Benefit match for Dick Walker.

Vie Keeble is transferred from Newcastle for £10,000.

Malcolm Allison is diagnosed as having tuberculosis and is out of the game for the rest of the season.

1958 April October November

West Ham win the Second Division championship and are promoted to Division One. First League match for Bobby Moore.

An agreement is reached between West Ham United and the Supporters' Club which gains 'official' recognition.

1959 May

1961 March – April

West Ham buy the Boleyn Ground for £30,000.

Ted Fenton leaves West Ham.

Ron Greenwood is appointed the new manager of West Ham United.

Bibliography

Allison, M. *Colours o/My Lr/e* Everest 1975

Belton, B. *Bubbles, Hammers & Dreams* Breedon 1997

Belton, B. *The First and Last Englishmen* Breedon 1998

Fenton, T. *At Home With the Hammers* Nicholas Kaye 1960

Football Association *The Complete Guide to England Players Since 1945* Stanley Paul 1993

Gambaccini, P., Rice.T. *Top 40 Charts* Guinness 1997

Green, G. *Soccer in the Fifites* Ian Allan 1974

Hogg, T. & McDonald, T. *Who's Who of West Ham United* Independent UK Sports 1996

Irving, D. *The West Ham United Football Book* Stanley Paul 1968

Irving, D. *The West Ham United Football Book No.2* Stanley Paul 1969

Korr, C. *West Ham United* Duckworth 1986

Leatherdale, C. *England's Quest for the World Cup* Methuen 1984

Lyall, J. *Just Like My Dreams* Penguin 1989

Moynihan, J. *The West Ham* Story Arthur Barker 1984

Nawrat, C. & Mulchings, S. *The Illustrated History of Football* Ted Smart 1996

Northcutt, J. & Shoesmith, R. *West Ham United. A Complete Record* Breedon 1993

Northcutt, J. & Shoesmith, R. *West Ham United. An Illustrated History* Breedon 1998

Oliver, G. *The Guinness Book of World Soccer (2nd ed)* Guinness 1995

Pallet, J. (ed) *The Virgin Film Guide* Virgin 1996

Powell, J. *Bobby Moore* 1993

Steggles, J. *Vintage Claret* Hammers News November 1998

Venables.T. *Venables* Michael Joseph 1994

Glossary of players

In the process of writing this book I have contacted over 70 former professionals, most of whom played in the West Ham first team in the Fifties. However, over a hundred players turned out for the Hammers in the First and Second Divisions in this period. Around 30 have died, the rest cannot be traced. If you are a former West Ham player, or if you know of the whereabouts of any player(s) from this or any other period in West Ham's history, I would be very grateful if you could let me know, through Breedon Books.

No history of West Ham can be complete without the inclusion of certain individuals; Bobby Moore, Ted Fenton, Wally St Pier and Dick and Albert Walker for example. As most of you will know, these men, sadly, are no longer with us. I have, then, brought them into this history by way of research. They, together with the players I have met and interviewed, are the 50 from the Fifties, the men who will tell the story of the Irons in that era.

The list below includes the players who have been kind enough to have helped me with this book. I am deeply grateful to them for their assistance, without which the project could not have been completed. I have also given details of a few other ex-players who have been often mentioned in the pages to follow.

Player Name	Career span	Position	Place of Birth	Date of Birth
Malcolm Allison	51-57	Centre-half	Dartford, Kent	5/9/27
Jimmy Andrews	51-55	Left-wing	Invergordon, Scotland	1/2/27
Jim W. Barrett	44-54	Forward	West Ham, London	5/11/30
Ken Bainbridge	46-49	Winger	Barking, Essex	5/1/21
Mike Beesley	59-62	Inside-forward	High-Beech, Essex	10/6/42
Doug Bing	51-55	Half-back	Broadstairs, Kent	27/10/28
John Bond	50-65	Full-Back	Colchester, Essex	12/12/34

Glossary of players

Eddie Bovington	59-67	Wing-half	Edmonton, London	23/4/41
Ken Brown	51-67	Centre-half	Forest Gate, London	16/2/31
Noel Cantwell	52-60	Full-back	Cork, Republic of Ireland	28/2/32
Johnny Cartwright	57-61	Inside-forward	Northampton	5/11/40
Ron Cater	37-49	Defender	Fulham, London	2/2/22
Eddie Chapman	36-86	Forward	East Ham, London	3/8/23
John Charles	59-69	Full-back	Canning Town, London	20/9/44
John Dick	53-62	Inside-left	Govan, Scotland	19/3/30
Tommy Dixon	52-55	Forward	Newcastle-Upon-Tyne	8/6/29
David Dunmore	60-61	Centre-forward	Whitehaven, Cumberland	8/2/34
Ted Fenton	33-46	Forward	Forest Gate, London	1914
Albert Foan	50-56	Inside-forward	Rotherhithe, London	30/10/23

Days of Iron – The story of West Ham United in the Fifties

Days of Iron – The story of West Ham United in the Fifties